Zoonie Sails Home

Zoonie Sails Home

*One Couple's Voyage from the
South-West Pacific to the UK*

Barbara White

SELF | PUBLISHING HOUSE

Published in 2025 by Barbara White

Copyright © Barbara White, 2025

barbara_boon@hotmail.com
skipperbarbwhite.com

Publishing services provided by Self Publishing House
Permission to use the chart on pvi–vii provided by UKHO

A CIP catalogue record for this book is available from the
British Library

Paperback ISBN: 978-1-7396874-7-2
eBook ISBN: 978-1-7396874-8-9

To all our keen mariner grandchildren,
Henry, Ruby, Rupert, George, Milo and Clara,
and maybe Mila (one year)

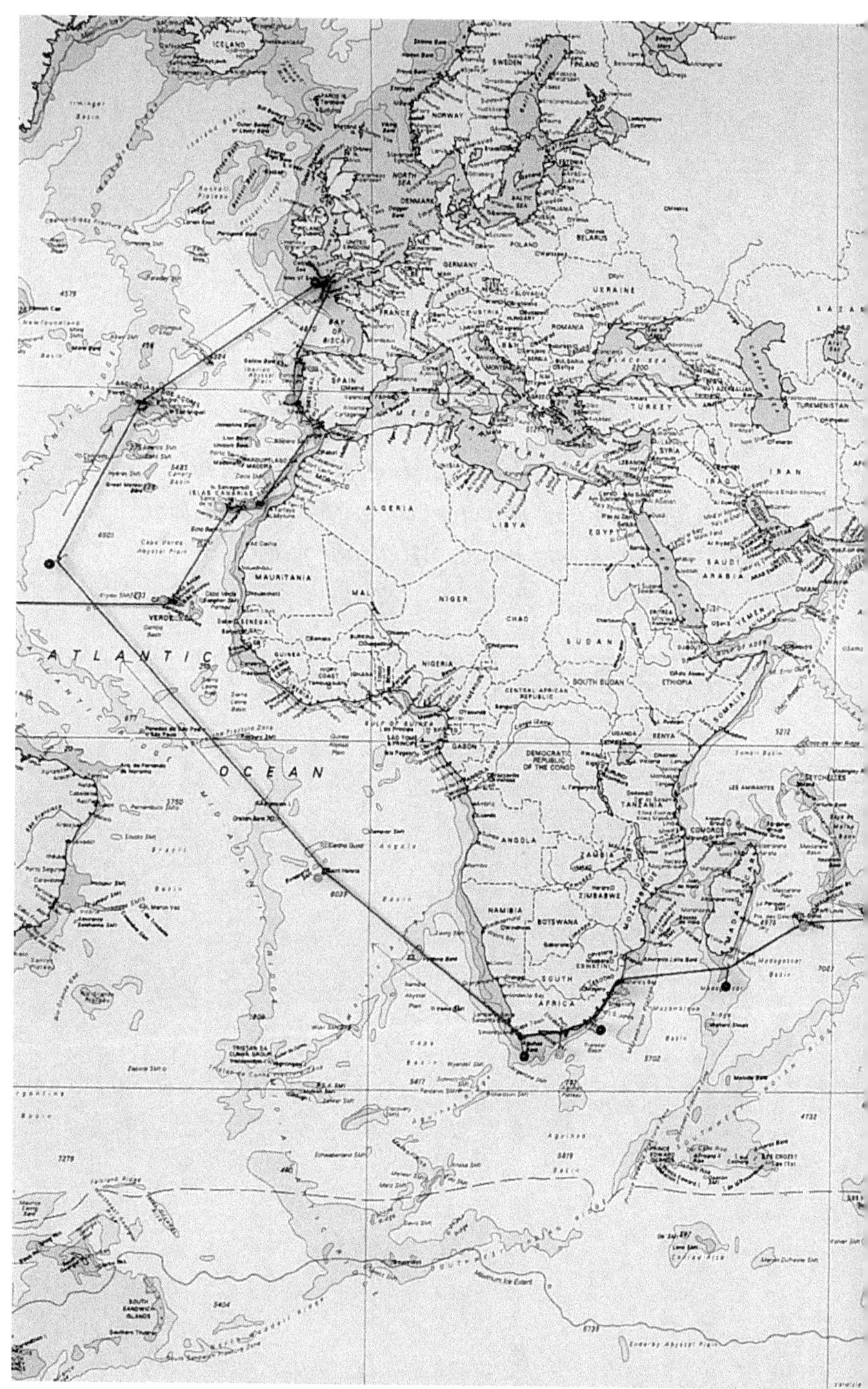

Westwards from New Zealand to the UK on *Zoonie*

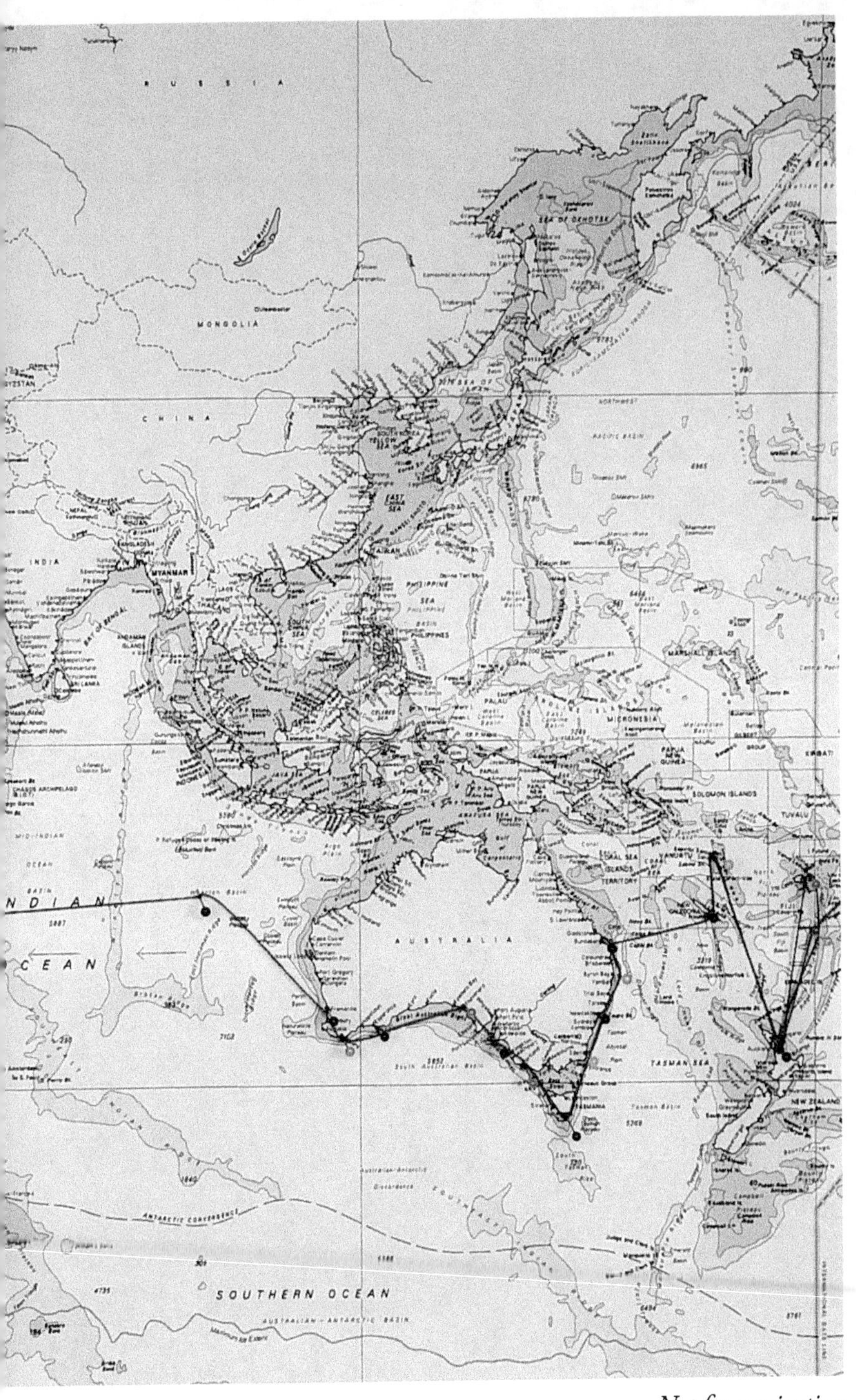

Not for navigation

Contents

Prologue

We were sitting in Vicky the Volvo on the pretty waterfront in Picton, South Island, New Zealand, before our planned return to *Zoonie* after a seven-week camping trip around the lovely lower half of the country, just taking in the view, when Rob's phone started ringing. Rob put it on speaker so I could hear the conversation too. The caller was Jeannie from the yacht *Meridian Passage*, whom we had come across before in Whangarei (north of Auckland and where *Zoonie* was moored) with brief greetings as we came alongside the pontoon near them in our tender to go ashore. Her tone was distracted and very concerned.

"Rob, I am looking across at *Zoonie* and she appears to be very low in the water. Merv and I are making our way to her in the dinghy. I'll call you back once we are on board."

Once Sharron and Brian from the marina office were aboard, one rescuer asked, "Should we break in?"

To which Sharron replied in a fraction of an instant, "Yes," and our gas cylinder was grabbed for the purpose and used to instant effect.

A few moments later Rob's phone rang once more.

"We've broken in and are bailing her with buckets. The water is coming in rapidly. where are the skin fittings?"

Rob explained they were all closed except for the bilge pump outlet and the cockpit drains.

Over the next two hours the drama unfolded with frequent calls from Jeannie to update and ask for more details. *Zoonie* was bows down and sinking fast, river water pouring in from two sources, including over the sink, and was now near the level of the watery surface outside.

People we hardly knew were risking their lives aboard *Zoonie* as she was slipping down into the murky depths. At any moment she could have sucked in her last gulp and dropped to the riverbed with these good people trapped inside. And all we could do was sit and listen in horror.

"Nah," as Merv joked later, "we'd have soon scrambled out!"

During the previous five days the weather had been deteriorating as Cyclone Debbie approached, and for three days before – since 9 March 2017 – the rain had been hard and incessant. *Zoonie*, our beloved elderly Oyster, struggled for three days to resist her fate.

Three overalled and helmeted firemen were brought out to *Zoonie* in a tiny inflatable tender along with their pump (just imagine the sight of that), which took them a few minutes to start, but once in operation it made short work of returning the river water to the place from whence it had come. Merv had located the bilge outlet closure lever in the aft heads cupboard, and once that was closed the water stopped pouring in and *Zoonie*'s flooding was over.

"OK with you if we tow her to the pontoon outside the office, Rob? That way we can keep an eye on her and she is easy to access if necessary."

This activity late on a Sunday afternoon had attracted a fair crowd on the shore and over the canopy pedestrian bridge that spanned the river in front of where *Zoonie* was moored in her pile berth, a stout post at each corner, but not secure enough to stop her going down. Among the onlookers were the good folk who had brought the situation to the attention of a security officer.

Zoonie's dilemma, the sinking yacht in Whangarei Marina, made the national TV news and the newspapers. After the traumatic devastation caused by Cyclone Debbie, of which this incident was a part, the media needed a happy-ending story of human altruism, and *Zoonie* was the subject.

Two savvy young cruisers who could recognise a yacht in trouble at a thousand paces noticed *Zoonie*'s downward slide. They raced back to their mum, Miriam, on *Enough*, and she also raised the alarm. We had previously met this sailing family in Tonga and later on our New Zealand perambulations during the first half of our circumnavigation.

We felt pretty helpless where we were, so we drove to the terminal to see if we could catch an earlier ferry than the one we had booked five days before and that was to leave at 11.00 am the next day, Monday.

"Well, it leaves in 45 minutes and that won't give you enough time to get back to Spring Creek, pack away your tent and return here before it sails," the sympathetic lady reasoned. So, ironically, we would be on the same ferry we had already booked but would head straight back to *Zoonie* rather than spend the planned few days around the Hawke's Bay area.

Since our arrival in New Zealand we had worked hard on the many jobs to be done on *Zoonie*, and when we left on the camping trip she was in a state of near readiness for the new season back in the tropics.

While sitting on the ferry we told our sad story to two German lads. They listened sympathetically then one of them turned his coffee cup around to show an advertisement for the Top 10 Holiday Park Company, the slogan of which read 'Something to float everyone's boat!' That relieved some tension.

I think the adrenalin had started coursing through our systems, because the drive back was easy. It was dark by 6.30 pm and we each did around five hours driving, during which time the roads were almost empty for 860 kilometres, except for the two houses that were on the move. It's a big thing in New Zealand, to visit a house show area, choose the home of one's dreams, all perched up high on wooden stilts ready to be loaded, and have it delivered to the prepared site. A bit like *Zoonie*: raised, moved and re-connected.

The calm after the storm

As we drove back we called our electrician, Scott, in Whangarei and asked him to check *Zoonie*, and while on board he opened the bilge pump outlet valve and heard the pump start once more.

"Ah, did you hear that, the bilge pump just kicked in once, that's good, means that's still working then. Oh sh*t! She's taking in water again, it's bubbling up…" He quickly re-closed the bilge pump fitting once more, just as the rescuers had done, and that gave us our first clue to the problem. Without an air vent to break it, the solid column of water in the pipe was ready to syphon water on board again.

We arrived home just after 1.00 am to a *Zoonie* who looked her usual self with nothing apart from the grubby marks of toil, splinters of the wooden companionway boards and a broken hand bilge pump in the cockpit to show for her ordeal. Down below all was clean and tidy. The windows were slightly damp on the inside but the upholstery was all dry, including the mattresses in the forepeak where the bow had dipped lower than the rest of the hull. They are fixed higher than the settee berths in the saloon, and that was how they had escaped.

With the car unloaded and parked, and relieved with what we had found under the circumstances, we climbed into bed and grabbed a few hours of sleep before the massive task ahead of us began.

An extreme amount of rain and a lot of wind had hit the area as Cyclone Debbie raced up the river, and because *Zoonie* faced the same direction as Debbie was driving and was unable to swing and confront her, the rain, instead of hitting the front of the mast and travelling down to the deck and harmlessly over the sides, formed a constant trickle running down inside the mainsail groove on the back edge of her mast into her bilge, where it triggered the bilge pump.

The pump worked constantly until it ran out of solar electricity in the batteries, when a solid column of water started to flow from the river into *Zoonie*'s bilge. Because the hull outlet was below the waterline she started to backfill, syphoning water from the river into the hull; just like me when I'm bottling my beer. Thank goodness help arrived in time to prevent her sinking completely.

Would we have gone ahead with a total refit had she sunk to the bottom? Yes, we would, even though it would have taken time in the ordering of parts and their installation and all the modifications that would have been needed, along with arranging specialist work projects that we could not have done, to say nothing of the cost.

Also, Rob and I are not quitters; our project was halfway along and we were determined to see it through to the end in a vessel we knew to be absolutely right for the job. *Zoonie* will sail on.

Chapter 1

Cyclone Debbie's Second Blow

It took a while for the enormity of what had happened to sink in. But feelings of guilt at not being aboard to prevent it happening soon passed in the healing level of support we had from friends, some, like Jeannie and Merv, made while the disaster was taking place, and from the arrival of our family for their long-anticipated visit!

The burden of work to be done was a distraction from more emotive thoughts. What could we do and what would require expert help? Would the disaster delay our circumnavigation and cause us to be away from our family for even longer? And how would *Zoonie's* refit and the effect on our psyches change our plans? We would have to wait and see.

Fortunately, the insurance company accepted the claim as caused by extreme weather; they had already seen the national newspaper report showing a picture of *Zoonie's* rescue. So, we could get on with gathering together estimates for the repair work.

After some form filling and a medical examination each, in which the doctor heard a slight heart murmur when listening through Rob's back – "Many people have one without knowing, likely nothing to worry about," he reassured us – we were allowed an extension on our visas to carry out the work.

Rob acted with his usual sense of immediacy, and within a couple of days of being back on board, *Zoonie's* swan necks were all breathing nicely, her pipes could all be shut up and her non-return valves, where they hadn't already been fitted, were ready to block any unwanted ingress.

Three weeks of repairs were completed while we lived aboard, as we looked forward to the arrival of my daughter, Emily, her hubby, Gary, and their children, Henry and Ruby, for a family camping adventure with us around the North Island. On our return the rest of the work would start.

A whistle-stop tour with family

Our tour was a brief one and so should this account be, because if you are anything like me, dear reader, you are keen to get going on our voyage, but that does not lessen the uplifting effect the presence of our family had on us, after nearly losing *Zoonie*.

From splashing in the hot water pools on a Coromandel beach we moved on to the geologically and culturally rich Rotorua area, where, during one evening of great entertainment, Mitai warriors had the children's eyes popping as the men in full fighting costumes paddled towards us in their fabulous Māori canoe (waka) with eyes wide and tongues outstretched.

Mitai Māori warrior

"Granny, how many more countries do you and Grandad have to visit before you come home?" Ruby asked as we wandered through the hot water lakes and steaming craters near Rotorua, hand in hand. A child's honest question deserves an honest answer, so I listed the countries and we counted them together, arriving at eight, but then I softened the answer by a promise to come home as often as we could, including later that year.

What were we doing, spending years away from our quickly growing grandchildren? This is such a painful side to cruising and draws many a voyaging couple back to home shores. It certainly maintained our momentum.

Rob and I watched from an elevated walkway as the blue and white jet boat, with our precious family occupying the back seats, sped and spun around in the white water at the base of the Hukka Falls. We couldn't hear but poor Ruby was crying and screaming at the ferocity of the motion until the imaginative driver pointed the bow of his craft at a small waterfall and convinced her the trickle was named Ruby Falls, just like her.

Family on the rear seats for the thrill

In the dry Spellbound Glowworm Cave Jimmy did not play the "turn torches off...........BOO!" game as he had with us recently in our seven-week camping trip; perhaps he thought it might frighten the children. Instead, he made Henry our leader, the one to hold the handrail and lead the group forward in the darkness as we each held the left shoulder of the person ahead of us.

Much further north, "That is doubtless a bay," Cook said, and the name stuck. We were awaiting the sunset which had the promise of surreal beauty, but before then we paddled, combed the beach, marvelled at the tiny chitons wedged into crevasses on the rocks and chatted to a local who was saving up for his own boat so he could go fishing.

During the night we lay awake listening to the ear-splitting screeching kiwis and the owl-like calls of a pair of moreporks.

More high adventure was called for at Ninety Mile Beach.

Our tourist truck waded up the Te Paki Stream Road, with its patches of quicksand, to the giant sand dunes and a touch of sand tobogganing for the intrepid amongst us. Gary and Henry decided to have a go and clambered up the steep dune, becoming little dots in the distance queueing up for their turn.

Positioned ready to catch them on camera, I remember feeling the surge of pride as they took off downhill, since it must have been more than a little daunting a prospect from 100 feet up there. Big hugs all round for our heroes of the day, Gary and Henry. I wondered if Māori children centuries ago enjoyed such fun here. I bet they did.

Our final trip was local, to the Kiwi North home of the two little kiwis we had seen twice so far.

Henry and Ruby understood the need to be very quiet and still, and their patience was rewarded when the little kiwi started to circuit the front of the enclosure really close to us. Not only had they heard kiwis but they had also seen one.

Alone again – return to the repairs

---

21 April 2017. After five oil changes, crouching in tiny spaces for poor Rob, the engine is back to normal. The watermaker motor and compressor Rob extracted from the tight confines of Zoonie's bow are away for testing, and we have received the go ahead from our insurers to lift Zoonie out and fit a new bow prop. As the electrics and cables lie along either side just above or below the floors, they all had to be removed – screw by screw and jubilee clip by jubilee clip – and replaced, including the batteries which weigh a ton, after Rob thoroughly cleaned the last of the dirty river water out of the bilges. Pilot books are drying in the sunny cockpit and Zoonie is dressed overall with her entire wardrobe of flags, not only to thank everyone for the parts they played in saving her but also to dry them.

It could have seemed like a never-ending task at the start, but then I always think of it as one job done = one less to do. Don't think about the end result, Barbara, I have said many times, just take each day as it comes – time passes quickly enough.

2 June 2017. Just for a change we walked up the hill to the Māori encampment around the Parihaka lookout the other day, a favourite walk we did many times, and a steep climb and descent we felt would be good exercise. The valley through which we ascended was tucked away from habitations and roads, and the only sounds were the birds as we climbed past rimu, tawa and kauri trees growing in healthy abundance. It was easy to imagine groups of Māori hunting amongst the trees centuries before the first Europeans arrived.

Back down again and sitting on the riverside in the sunlight, we reflected on how pleased we were that the family explored this area while they were with us. Clouds of gold dust pollen glistened in the sunlight as it fell from the pōhutukawa trees onto the water surface, having been released by sparrows nibbling the seeds above.

Zoonie's lift-out and refit

Early on a pleasant winter morning in June, because we were in the southern hemisphere, Brian of Whangarei Marina came up to *Zoonie's* stern in his launch and tied it to *Zoonie's* starboard side in readiness to give us an alongside tow, down to the Riverside Marina where she would be lifted out. The prop seal behind the engine had seized, and had we started the engine, river water would start seeping in, and we did not want that; we'd had quite enough water on board, and the bilges were clean now after Rob's efforts.

Within an hour of our arrival Karl operated the hoist and Mo started spraying off the thick, furry coat of weed, barnacles and oysters (appropriate!?). The row of osmosis blisters that had been growing along the waterline over the past three years were revealed, and as the antifoul on the waterline, which we had had raised by six inches when *Zoonie* was in Hamble Point Marina, was cleaned the paint flew off in places revealing the old waterline. The blue boot topping had barely been rubbed down before applying the new Coppercoat.

Re-wiring *Zoonie* required all the floorboards on one side to be lifted, so living aboard would have been a nuisance to Mark, the electrician, and impossible for us, so we carried our small clothes bags onto *Cetacea* upon Gail and Tony's kind invitation and spent a week sharing meals, films, drinks and fine company. We first met Gail and Tony in Tonga on our way to New Zealand.

The day after 'the lift' our New Zealand Visitor Visas arrived; without delay we booked our flights home for 17 July, arriving in the UK the next day.

All going well… then a worse disaster strikes

14 June 2017. The jobs are flying off the list like migrating swallows, but then we hit a black (poo) water tank issue, and it had to be removed as it sat over where we needed to replace the bow propeller motor and prop beneath. Mo helped Rob with the charming job of spray washing the tank, and Rob has now taken off all the pipes on the top and re-installed the tank ready to refix the pipes so they are tight. The loosest one did not have a washer or sealant under it. So, along with the non-self-priming pump that burned out after the first use and no washers under the pipe fittings, it never was going to work, was it.

A few days later Rob started to feel a severe pain in his right leg and began taking painkillers. He had a graze on his knee, could this have allowed harmful bacteria in? But from where? The river water in the bilges or the black water tank? And how serious was this new problem?

We were so glad that we were nearby to *Zoonie* while this work was being done so we could check everything as it was installed, and it was just as well we were near a hospital.

This is a letter I sent to family and friends to bring them some extremely worrying news about Rob…

9 July 2017

Good morning all,

We hope you are well.

We want to let you know that Rob has contracted a type of streptococcus bacterial infection that can damage the heart muscles, and as he was found to have a heart murmur during the thorough medical examination he had when we applied for our visa extensions, they have decided to keep him in at Whangarei Hospital for the moment and feed him intravenously with penicillin every four hours. The regime has to continue for two weeks but he may be able to return home to *Zoonie* in that time with a semi-permanent drip inserted.

He developed a pain in his right calf muscle that turns out to be cellulitis, possibly from a graze just below his knee which happened when he was cleaning the bilges, and the bacterial infection may have come from there. He is responding to pain treatment although he finds putting his foot to the ground difficult and even his fingertips are hurting.

This means we will not be flying home as planned on the 17th of the month, and we will cancel the flights and get Rob through this before we make any plans for journeys further than to our favourite bars.

We understand this will be worrying and disappointing for you, and we are so sorry about this.

I will write again soon and keep you up to date on his progress. Be reassured he is being cared for by an amazing team of people.

Lots of love,

Barb xx

Living back on *Zoonie* in a New Zealand winter

12 July 2017. Rob was admitted to Whangarei Hospital three days ago so it's just Zoonie and me perched up here. As the New Zealand weather deepens towards mid-winter thunderstorms, frequent showers and cold nights are the norm. The wet on the grass and in millions of puddles matches the river water. Zoonie wobbles ever so slightly in her cradle as the wind whips around her elegant hull and slams against the mast. A chain rattles as a neighbour lowers his new engine into place, and the dredger, being pushed by a chunky little tug, rumbles upriver to work in the Town Basin.

When Rob was taken poorly, I developed tunnel vision which focused just on him. Yesterday, getting back to the marina, which was in darkness, I tripped over a kerb, falling flat on my face on the gravel yard ground, and finding the incident so bizarrely amusing, as I scrambled up brushing my hands together and sorting myself out, I could hear my own laughter. Adrenalin kept me going for the first 24 hours, and now I am settled into the easy routine of visiting Rob twice a day, with the added variety and challenge of getting Vicky through her Warrant of Fitness (WoF) before he comes home, by way of a distraction.

Tomorrow Vicky, our Volvo, goes to have her replacement headlights fitted followed by her re-test to get through her WoF (like our MOT). Fingers crossed. Then I'll have to see if Rick can do anything about her thirst for coolant, which is even greater than ours for good beer! I think I should enrol her in AAA, Alcoholic Automobiles Anonymous!

It's all down to me as Rob continues his treatment in hospital.

Before I go to see Rob, I am hoping for visits from Steve and Bruce. Steve is coming to measure up for a wooden shelf so we can install the new fridge parts, and Bruce will hopefully apply the Coppercoat, if it's not too cold for it to cure. Once that is on, we can put Zoonie back in the water, and Brian at the Town Basin Marina is saving a berth for us whenever we want.

Much depends upon the outcome of the TOE (transoesophageal echocardiogram) — an ultrasound scan to look at Rob's heart to see if the antibiotics have done their work and whether the two bacteria vegetations have further damaged his heart valve.

16 July 2017. Bruce arrived with his tubby little white lady Staffy companion. He is hoping to start work on the anti-fouling job this weekend by filling the osmosis holes Rob ground out and sealed before his illness.

Skipper released on good behaviour

21 July 2017. Rob is back on board Zoonie where he will receive his daily dose of antibiotics from me, once the district nurse has overcome her fear of climbing up Zoonie's ladder and has shown me how to do it! He will visit the district nurses once a week for a check-up and blood tests for the next four weeks, until 18 August, when his six weeks of antibiotics will be complete. Then three days of blood tests and a further TOE at the end of August, to see how the antibiotic v bacteria battle is coming along.

His discharge letter confirmed he is not fit to fly yet, at any level, including sea level! Nice touch of humour from the doctor, and no escaping aboard Zoonie, then!

Just as well we had applied for an extension to our visas a few weeks ago because of the work we needed to do on Zoonie.

The normal world is out there

23 July 2017. I have spent the past two weeks passing along a tunnel, I thought, as I poked my head out into the cockpit this morning to be met by sunny blue skies, for a short period anyway. Rob is now back on board and we are emerging quickly back to our normal lives, Whangarei-bound as we are.

*The district nurse climbed bravely up Zoonie's ladder this morning for the last of her two visits supervising me, in my role as 'Hot Lips' Houlihan from M*A*S*H, feeding Rob intravenously with his antibiotics. That done, Rob decided the game plan for the day would start with a gentle walk around the Hatea Loop, stopping on the quay for a restful coffee.*

Mo agreed to help with loading new batteries for the standard boatyard currency of Steinlager Classic. He hauled the old ones onto the side-deck by hand and then employed the generous laws of gravity to help them to the ground ten feet below.

Now, Mo is a strong – but not a big – person, and we shared a fear that gravity might take over as the battery disappeared over *Zoonie's* topside taking Mo with it, so I was given the dubiously enjoyable task of holding tight onto his leather belt and leaning backward against *Zoonie's* coach roof to counterbalance the combined weight

Gripping Mo's pants

of Mo and said battery. This we did four times, and by the time we had finished I was getting quite used to holding onto the pants (US meaning) of a man who was not my hubby!

It's a funny thing, independence; before Rob was ill there were many day-to-day tasks of shore living (driving, ordering and paying for things, carrying money) that Rob had taken over from me after we started out on this trip. Suddenly, with his hospitalisation, it became necessary for me to take them all back on board, and it gave me much delight to realise I could still not only do them all but also enjoy doing them all. I still hold the car key! For how much longer, do you reckon?

6 August 2017. Yesterday we climbed to the Mount Parihaka lookout, once a stronghold of the Hatea Māori tribe. A vast array of plants are starting to flower: glossy-leaved camellias, rambling jasmine filling the air with their fragrance from flowers in indirect proportion to their size, busy lizzies, snowdrops, lilies, geraniums and magnolias all bursting forth. You know how I love the challenge of the steep valley we have to scale, with its busy stream and indigenous forest and the sounds of human activity as good as a million years away; it is an escape to see what New Zealand once looked like all over the islands. Rob clicked on the torchlight on his iPhone and we crouched down and tiptoed tentatively into the old gold mine on our way back down again. No pit props here, just solid dripping rock and puddles. The single tunnel entrance soon opened out into three dinosaur claws, and we turned back to the warm daylight. Maybe we'll explore a little more sometime.

In the meantime, there are just four issues still to sort on Zoonie, starting with an incorrectly installed fridge compressor, which Rob has now turned around, then cabling to the bow prop having been crossed over, so the controls work in the opposite order, easily solved by uncrossing them.

Thirdly, the new macerator pump for the black (poo) tank does not work for some reason (can't say I really blame it, what a job), but we need to get that system working in a world of ever more stringent and necessary environmental regulations. The new pump is on order.

And fourthly, Alex from WMS, our engine people, came aboard first thing last Friday and discovered the engine was not quite in line with the prop shaft. This came from Rob finding it was very hard to turn the prop by hand when one should be able to do it with one finger. A careful nudging of the engine on its adjustable mounts and the desired effect was achieved.

Finally, Zoonie was back to the same state of readiness as in February before our land trip, i.e. ready for sea.

At last, *Zoonie's* launch day

12 August 2017. Mo re-launched Zoonie and then we gently slid her around from the hoist bay onto the pontoon for the night, and Rob and I moved her upriver this morning, UNDER HER OWN POWER FOR THE FIRST TIME SINCE WE ARRIVED LAST NOVEMBER!

Next week we have a busy one with visits to the hospital every day, the most telling being Thursday when Rob checks in at 7.30 am for his TOE and again at 1.00 pm for a chat with the infectious disease doctor. We should have more news for you then, and let's hope it is positive.

Zoonie's repairs being complete, now we were naturally hoping Rob was on the mend too, but…

20 August 2017. Yesterday, while coming down the steep path from the Parihaka lookout once more, Rob felt tingling in his left arm, a pressure on the left-hand side of his chest and muzziness in his head.

"More so than normal," he bravely joked before speaking with Dr Harriet by phone and giving her details of his symptoms.

Immediately she quietly said, "I think you should come straight back into Emergency."

We both silently feared what might be coming up; Rob was clearly seriously unwell, and our future was suddenly stripped from our control. Would he survive even? I deviated from that train of thought pretty quickly.

One step at a time, my common sense told me.

He was re-admitted, and various tests were carried out. Dr Harriet explained that the results established the antibiotics had killed the bacteria, which was good. But the bacteria had formed a mat on Rob's mitral valve, and as it disintegrated, tiny bits of debris were floating around in his blood system, causing havoc in the form of mini strokes.

Some of the doctors felt Rob should be flown home for an open-heart operation to replace the damaged valve (having been told he cannot fly?), but Dr Christine stepped in and pointed out the remaining bacteria could break free at any time and he needed to be under medical care until either that happened or they replaced the valve with a porcine one (grown from pig cells).

He is having a full dental check today, to see if the bacteria could have come from his teeth or gums, which apparently is a possibility with endocarditis, but Rob keeps his teeth pristine so we both think that that is unlikely. More likely, but possibly unproveable, is it came from the river water he had to clean out of Zoonie's bilges after her submersion. Which in turn caused the cellulitis infection in his leg and the bacteria growth on his heart valve. We've ruled out the source being the black water tank wash as Rob wore overalls and gloves and there was an organic bacteria digester in there anyway.

An MRI scan and photos of his heart's vascular system were all completed ready for the surgical team in Auckland to prepare themselves. He will be operated on ASAP, to either repair or replace the valve, and will then stay in hospital down there for around a week before returning to Whangarei.

I shall be staying with friends, Andrea and Mark, who live walking distance from the hospital, for the duration.

We had both been feeling anxious about the outcome of this week's tests and the possibility of not setting sail next year knowing he had a faulty valve which could become infected again. So, this decision of his doctors is the best we could have had, and we are so grateful.

He is back in the same room of the same ward he was in before and has gained a reputation in the hospital Emergency Department and on the ward as the sailor with the interesting heart problem!

One district nurse felt that *Zoonie's* near sinking that kept us here was an example of things happening for a reason. I think his leaking heart valve may have remained an unknown weakness had we remained at sea, that may or may not have become critical. After all, the bacteria infection most likely came from the river water inland, far from the sea. What do you think?

21 August 2017. The car keys are still in my pocket in readiness, and if he gets to fly to Auckland on the Air Ambulance helicopter we have admired so many times as it landed on the roof of the building opposite his bed, I shall be just a little jealous…

That was the week that was

I followed Rob's ambulance down to Auckland City Hospital, although I never did catch up with it, using the driver's direction, given to me as Rob was prepared for the trip.

"Take the Port turn off and then Wellesley, and you come up by the hospital." Perfect.

23 August 2017. "Hi Mark, how are you?" I asked as we hugged on my arrival to stay with our friends for the duration of Rob's hospital confinement.

"Agitated at the moment," came his troubled reply. "Luca has brought in a bird, and I hate it when he does that."

"What sort of bird?" I asked, as deep-chocolate, shiny-coated Luca the cat lay stretching and satisfied in a beam of sunlight on the living room carpet.

"A dead bird."

We both enjoyed the humour of that remark.

We had last seen Andrea and Mark for a long weekend a few months ago, having met them on a shared afternoon swimming with spinner dolphins in Niue. Since then, our life has been taken over by Zoonie's flood and Rob's health issues.

Rob was installed in Ward 41 in the biggest Cardiac Unit is Australasia, and Boris became his medical consultant. It seemed we had to start all over again on the thinking about whether or not to operate. Boris felt the best outcome would be to remove the vegetation and repair or replace the valve, but his team were toying with the idea of further antibiotic treatment using penicillin. This line of thinking really concerned me. Rob was harbouring a ticking time bomb with the mini strokes, and even in hospital he could have had a really serious one and they might not have been able to save him.

The next morning, after Rob had had his visit from Boris with no real progress on their decision making, we enjoyed a coffee and shared a piece of cake. Suddenly Rob complained of dizziness and blurred vision, and I pressed the alarm button. The nurse took on board the problem and disappeared, and soon Boris returned.

"My team has decided an operation is the best option as there is no point in continuing passive treatment when there is the risk the vegetation will give off more harmful particles at any time." (My thoughts entirely.) "We have a space this afternoon; have you eaten since breakfast?"

That piece of cake delayed the operation by a few hours, but within minutes of the decision Rob's chest and 'other' hair was being shaved and we were being rushed through the pre-op briefings. Rob's occasional odd sensations were for the first time referred to as mini strokes.

The time flew by, and soon I was sitting in the waiting area outside the four operating theatres while Rob was having that life-saving procedure. Mr Parma Nand had introduced himself to us as Rob's surgeon and set to with his team for what turned out to be a three-and-a-half-hour operation. It was reassuring to know he is a leading heart and lung surgeon, and in his gentle, personable way he went to great pains to explain everything that would happen to Rob. Like me, he understands the need to be fully informed even though the details were a bit alarming.

Andrea and Mark arrived to sit out the remainder of the wait with me, and soon the call came. Mr Nand confirmed the operation was straightforward, the remaining bacteria mat removed and the valve repaired – perfect, the best outcome. Rob's own valve had been stitched and secured within a permanent Dacron band that would maintain its size so it could open and close properly (the same material as *Zoonie*'s mainsail, a quirky thing to have in common).

During the night I slept in my room in Andrea and Mark's home while a few members of the 130-person highly skilled nursing team in the unit attended Rob. His nurse was pleased that Rob was the first post-op patient she had sent on to the regular ward within the

same shift as his arrival from the operating theatre. Rob was being progressed through recovery at the same rate his body was repairing itself, and as he was so fit, and not yet sixty, that progress was rapid.

Rob was sitting in his bedside chair the morning after the operation looking bulldozed but happy. "I woke up, so that was a bonus!"

He was rigid with tubes after machines had enabled him to breath and his blood to circulate via

Bulldozed but happy

external means, his heart stilled for the procedure. Well, it would have to be, wouldn't it, when you think about it. *Budump, snip, budump, snip* just would not work.

Most people leave hospital about a week after their op, and Rob was no different. The day after his release he walked a circuit from Andrea and Mark's, which included a gentle hill. I loved and admired his determination to speed his recovery along; he was showing an inner strength I hadn't seen before.

31 August 2017. On our final evening with Mark and Andrea it was my turn to cook. The tempeh and black bean chilli done with, Andrea presented Rob with a chocolate cake and one candle to celebrate so much. The saving of Rob's life and our stay with dear friends on the other side of the world from home were appreciated one hundred per cent.

The next day I drove us back to Whangarei to the Distinction Whangarei Hotel & Conference Centre, which I suggested to the insurers because it is on the flat and easy walking into all the town facilities for Rob (and nice and close to *Zoonie*). From our ground-floor window overlooking the marina we could see *Zoonie* moving minimally with the wind and tide, itching to travel, just like us.

Daily, I went aboard to run the engine, turn the props, do some maintenance, sort things out and collect items for our use, but the registrar at Auckland City Hospital told Rob he was not to go on board because of the 'fall' risk she perceived.

"FOR SIX WEEKS? YOU MUST BE KIDDING!"

Rob nearly hit the ward ceiling, so I asked for a three-week compromise and we got it, although the prospect of six weeks in a really nice hotel had a certain appeal. The patient was getting better.

Looking at *Zoonie* from cloud nine

2 September 2017. I tried the spa bath in our ensuite last evening and made an unsurprising discovery. It is over a year since I have had a bath. Disgusting, you might well think, and I can tell you my heart leaped when I spied the hollow white fellow lying in the corner of the bathroom. I gently squeezed about half of the little courtesy tube of bath gel into the tumbling hot water and slowly laid myself down, relishing every millimetre of warm soapy liquid.

After a few minutes of familiar soaking, I pressed the soft 'on' switch and waited. Suddenly a loud subterranean gurgling started and water shot out from under the eight little nozzles in the bath walls, pummelling my extremities. It was delicious. I relaxed and let my eyelids fall. A few minutes of this liquid massage later, I opened my eyes to find a cloud of creamy white bubbles about to cascade over the side and onto the floor. Wow, a little bath gel goes a long way with this game. Is this what it feels like on the top of cloud nine?

It was a wonderful stay in a really nice hotel, marked by gentle walks in the morning, then a job for me on board painting the inside of all the heads cupboards in *Zoonie* while Rob slept, and finally meals in the restaurant in the evening with our friends.

I really admire the way Rob sensibly pushed himself, following all medical advice, back to being his normal self. I didn't need to do much beyond the odd suggestion about light activities. He was an easy, smiling patient for the medical staff, which helped them to be very open with us on what was going on. Their policy of short hospital stays appealed to us both pragmatically and philosophically, as Rob knew he would heal better out of hospital, and he was better and more quickly able to return to his pre-op level of fitness the sooner he exercised in the fresh air and let his body rest when it asked.

This is from Rob: "You were positive like me, and your caring nature towards me reminded me of how you used to look after your mum. You were stoical, if that's the right word, and the way you are reinforces how we are good as a pair." As an afterthought, "and you always remember to ask the questions I forget, with your enquiring mind."

Chapter 2

Our Return to the Normal World

Soon Rob was deemed fit to fly so we immediately arranged to fly home.

Walks in forests of rustling leaves with grandchildren and dogs were in stark contrast to the pantropical life we had left behind.

Two months on home shores flew by with Rob looking and behaving more his normal self all the time. Then soon we were flying again, back to *Zoonie*.

As we crossed the south-west corner of Australia I was waking up to a new day, or so I thought. 'Breakfast' arrived, but then our cabin manager over the tannoy said he hoped we'd enjoy our dinner. That's where I lost the 12 hours, somewhere near Perth. Perhaps we'll find them if we go that way next year.

Back on board at last

26 January 2018. You'd be proud of us for what we have achieved in this first week since we have been back, all in readiness for moving on along our circumnavigation. Jeannie and Merv collected us from the airport then came to dinner last night, and we decided to use their visit as a target time before which we would complete various jobs.

Apart from our day downriver with our mechanic, these have included a large hand and machine sewing job; out came the hand sewing machine (no need for electricity, so we could use it at any time at sea), recently bought in Whangarei.

We bought a replacement flexible solar panel for the bimini (cockpit roof) before we left for England, but of course it is a different size to the one that is on there. We unpicked the Sunbrella fabric frame that held the old one in place, and I took the two sections of fabric onto the pontoon and gave the inside of them both a thoroughly good scrub to get off the hundreds of little circular mildew growths.

In this heat they dried in no time, so then we laid the new panel on the fabric and drew around it, adapted the old Sunbrella frame to fit, sewed it on by machine and, Bob's your uncle, job done. The old panel had been attacked by the elements and was underproducing its max of 30 watts, so the new, more robust, one should hopefully give us up to 48 watts. We need it as the replaced fridge compressor seems to have an electricity addiction!

While chatting with Jeannie and Merv about their travels last night a whole new idea for our passage around Australia was born. They spent eighteen years on their trip all around the Pacific Rim, stopping over in places like Japan for a prolonged stay so Jeannie could practise nursing there while Merv returned to New Zealand to carry out building projects. Not an unusual practice for cruising couples to work from their boats online or ashore.

Circumnavigating takes as long as it suits the sailors unless something unexpected happens. This journey around the world can take from sixteen months to ten or so years, and the average, if people are not working in the countries they visit, is around three and a half years.

For us, as well as the delays you have already seen, dear reader, please bear with because there are places to see and things to do that are not on *Zoonie's* direct route home. They are the essential asides that enriched our whole experience of travelling around our Earth, in the evening of our lives, with our working years behind us, aboard our lovely old yacht. We want to make the best use of our remaining years because, as we have so profoundly been reminded, none of us know what is just around the corner, do we?

When Jeannie and Merv sailed to Australia they took the south coast route via Melbourne, Adelaide, and countless nice little anchorages along to Perth and the west coast, and Merv suggested we think about doing the same.

Although we shouldn't have had to worry about cyclones at the time of year we would be sailing west, there was only a short window of six weeks to cross the south coast with favourable winds behind us, before the low-pressure systems, typified by clouds and unsettled winds, would start whizzing clockwise up from the Southern Ocean as the autumn progressed. The predominant winds were from the west until an anti-clockwise-turning high-pressure system, characterised by light winds, settled weather and minimal clouds, moves over the area, when the winds allow sailing westwards, provided the centre of the high is to the south.

Captain Cook and Matthew Flinders knew the area and charted the coast for the benefit of future mariners. It all sounded like a great adventure and an exciting prospect to us.

We are now approaching the southern winter and the end of the cyclone season when the weather is less stable and cyclones at their most likely in the places we plan to visit first. We'll never forget the weather last March and April, will we!

Shakedown cruise

22 February 2018. We're heading for Great Barrier Island to check for any problems aboard, on Zoonie's first venture offshore since the start of our troubles in March 2017.

23 February 2018. The anchor went down at 5.30 pm in Kaiarara Bay, under the soulful wooded gaze of Mount Hobson, after a pleasant motor sail with light winds lasting ten hours. The chart plotter showed a hardware fault with the AIS which will have to be fixed.

We are waiting with Zoonie for the urge to go ashore and explore to become sufficiently strong and overcome the pleasure of just sitting at anchor once more. We usually make sure her anchor is secure as well as take in the new surroundings, especially now, after such a traumatic few months.

The wind blows and the sun shines to give us plenty of electricity. Two pretty little chestnut brown teal ducks are alongside, and they're so tame,

I wonder if they had been bred in a captive breeding location, as they are nationally endangered. I read somewhere that there is an abundance of birdlife on Great Barrier Island, but what we are noting is the variety and not any abundance of any particular type apart from pretty fantails, beaks loaded with juicy bugs, gannets crashing into the water and ever watchful sacred kingfishers. The little teals' predators are skuas, who lie in wait for them to come ashore and then attack them. So mean.

25 February 2018. The urge has arrived and we're heading for Mount Hobson, Hirakimatā, the Sacred Mountain to the Māoris, at 627 metres.

Along with James Busby, Captain William Hobson, namesake of the mount ahead of us, drafted and corrected the highly contentious Treaty of Waitangi.

Mercifully the day was cloudy and the ground dry. The path was good and well maintained, and standing on the stout bridges let us imagine the route of the mighty kauri trees as they tumbled noisily downstream, their long lives severed by two-handed saws operated by intruder lumberjacks. The remnants of two of the kauri dams remain.

The water would build up behind the dams, elevating the trunks from the uneven riverbed, and hundreds of folks used to gather to watch as the spring was pulled from the trap door; with terrifying thunder and ground vibration, the load would be released. What a spectacle!

Regular climbs to the Parihaka lookout back in Whangarei had kept us reasonably fit for this seven-kilometre climb up and down, across slips and finally up many hundreds (someone counted 2,600) of wooden steps, as steep as a step ladder, to the tiny wooden platform on top, from where we had fantastic 360-degree views from the blue South Pacific Ocean in the east to the Hauraki Gulf south-westwards, from the northern tip of the Coromandel Peninsula to the Poor Knights Islands in the north.

The raucous cry of the brown parrot, the kaka, that tuneful call of the tui and the frantic twitter of fantails filled the lush re-growth of bush as we returned downwards.

We lingered in post-industrial Whangaparapara Harbour where once noisy timber extraction and milling and bloody whaling were the order of the day; behind the scenes, kauri gum digging, gold mining and the smell of illegal stills filled the air. The latter is where I'd have been.

From Port Fitzroy back to the main(land)

I think it was partly the radio broadcaster's mention of the words 'Cyclone Hola' that made Rob and me realise the protection of Kaikoura Island (Selwyn Island), between this narrow inlet at Port Fitzroy and the Hauraki Gulf, might not provide enough shelter to keep *Zoonie* safe.

9 March 2018. There was little wind as we motored into the Hauraki Gulf, but further offshore we picked up a very nice south-easterly and Zoonie sailed under full rig towards the distant craggy shadow of Bream Head. Bream Bay was so named by Captain Cook as his capable crew caught between ninety and one hundred bream while the Endeavour was anchored there on Christmas Day 1769. Unsurprisingly he made no reference to the significance of the day, since, in his many years of travel, he found most religions were dark and incomprehensible. Like Cook, I prefer to look from the outside in when it comes to religion, but I imagine some of his crew might have felt the need to acknowledge the day.

Under the blue skies with the perfect 12- to 15-knot wind it is difficult to believe a third cyclone is bearing down upon New Zealand's shores in what appears to be becoming a pattern of fortnightly intervals. There is yet another storm showing on our GRIB files for the end of this week.

This post-La Niña weather is proving very destructive, not only for humans but also, of course, for seabirds. Their food supplies, small fish and krill, are unused to the rising water temperature, and so the birds are being forced further offshore to feed. Along with this year's brood of eggs having been destroyed, they are very stressed, and a sharp decline in numbers is pretty inevitable.

Cook knew nothing of cyclones in his lifetime, as they were defined in the modern era, but he did know the seasons are reversed between the north and south hemispheres, and he will have had a barometer on board to measure changing atmospheric pressure, but without the advantage of weather forecasting in the 370-ton, 106-foot-long *Endeavour*, he and his crew simply dealt with what came along (just as we do when crossing oceans). No doubt some of the severe gales he wrote of during his coastal surveying at this time of year were cyclones. His seamanship and mutual trust in his men and anchors must have contributed to their survival, and, of course, the fact that *Endeavour* was a flat-bottomed collier who could take a sandy beach made maintenance and repairs straightforward.

On the leaving of New Zealand, temporarily

Preparations were then well underway for *Zoonie's* season in Fiji on our convoluted circumnavigation. How could we rush Fiji? We will never sail this way again, dear reader. This was Rob's wish, and I can understand it, as I know how deeply fond he became of New Zealand and its people, where he came so close to losing his life.

Milling in Marsden

20 May 2018. It is turning chilly now as the New Zealand winter approaches. I caught a fleeting glimpse of Rob disappearing into the aft cabin with the duvet under his arm and thought, goody, we'll be snug now. I was recently greeted in the saloon with 2°C, so Rob became accustomed to reaching for the Eberspacher heater, near his bedhead, which does the work until the sun gets up.

We have delayed our departure date numerous times purely because of the weather, but it did allow us to help Randall and Alison, whom we met in Whangarei and who are fellow circumnavigators, celebrate their tenth anniversary at sea with a meal in the Land and Sea Cafe by the marina. Ten years… I wonder how many we will achieve.

(Alison and Randall are still on their world odyssey aboard *Tregoning* in 2025.)

North to Minerva Reef

13 June 2018. 29° 38' 81" S 178° 07' 91" E.
You may have guessed we are now at sea, leaving Marsden two days ago with a few others as planned, including Tregoning with Alison and Randall

on board and Hannes and Sabine aboard *Cayenne*, whom we first met in Bora Bora on our way to New Zealand, and we look forward to seeing *Cayenne* again in Minerva. That's the thing with circumnavigating: we are on a conveyor belt of similar-minded sailors finding our ways around the world, and many times we meet up again with the same lovely people, mostly by chance, sometimes by design.

The weather forecast predicted a window of six days of favourable and light winds before the next tropical depression arrives, and with 800 miles between us and Minerva Reef, where we can wait it out if necessary, we are trying to maintain an average speed of 5.6 knots to arrive six days after our start and four days from now.

15 June 2018. Yesterday, in perfect conditions, the Diva (the alter ego of *Zoonie's* cruising chute, the gorgeous fulsome blue sail at the front, above the foredeck, her stage, who can be as temperamental as the finest operatic diva) gave us ten hours and 70 miles of 6–8 knots of speed, but today the wind has gone light and even she cannot perform with so little brass in the band. So the engine is back on with the hope that later we will be able to use some of the winds that are on their way and *Zoonie* slides serenely across the deep-pile blue ocean carpet once more beneath the celestial fire burning in the hearth of the heavens. Thank goodness diesel engines are happy to just plod on and on and on.

I awoke just before my watch was due to start to a loud mid-pitch moaning from the propeller shaft/gearbox area in the bilge. So Rob and I searched for a cause but established everything seemed OK; there was no excessive heat, smell or water ingress. The shaft bearings were getting their sea-water lubrication OK. Could it be volcanic activity in this volatile area? But the noise subsided and peace returned.

On such calm nights as these, while *Zoonie* rolls along gently under a nicely purring engine, my attention is drawn to the sky above. Stars at an altitude of around 20 degrees send their reflections to *Zoonie* over the slight wavelets, whilst those that peep through nearer horizon level tease me — are they stars or ships?

When I ventured out on deck in the morning it was to find another surprise: a booby bird had shared my watch and left an incredible mess all around the mast to be cleared up after breakfast. So rude.

16 June 2018. We are over halfway to Minerva Reef now and hope to

A generous booby bird…

arrive there on Tuesday ahead of the low that is coming. Then, once that has past, it should give us nice southerlies off its tail end which we will use to cover the three/four days left to get to Fiji. Well, that's the theory.

It is getting warmer in the saloon as we move nearer the equator, 25°C at the moment, and thoughts are moving towards reducing the layers of clothing; it's all good.

Later on:

Still motoring, Zoonie is bang on course with no resistance from the waves to her 1500 rpm movement through the water at twice walking speed.

She is speeded up a little and slowed down by the coming and going of the tide/current. A fingernail moon and its celestial friend Saturn reflect on the silken water. Rarely have we seen the perfect sunset with no clouds to dim the beauty, and today was no exception. As soon as she had gone, fog patches rolled in from the east and south, the closing of the solar stage curtains.

Sitting on the cockpit seat with my arms on the coaming (sides) that surrounds it, I stare down at the wash Zoonie is sending from her side.

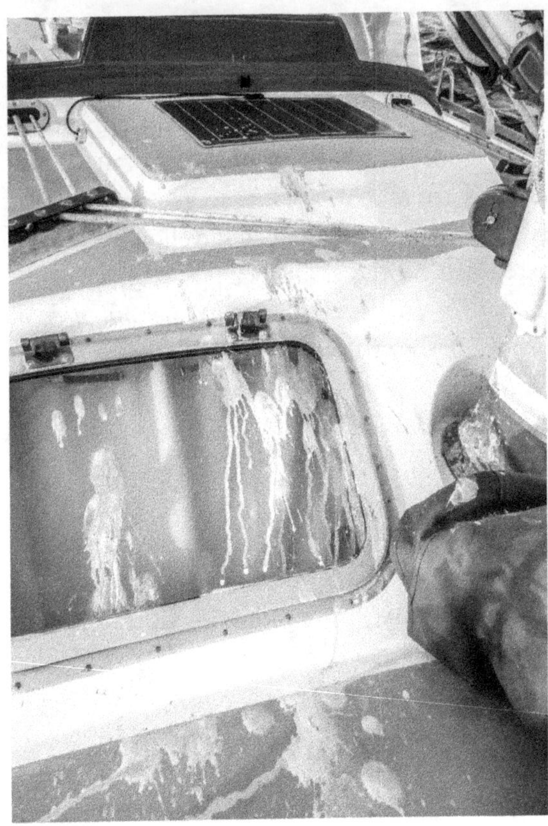

...leaves its calling card

Like a virgin bride she is pulling a gossamer veil studded with millions of tiny phosphorescent sparkling diamonds across an ebony black star-studded carpet that covers the immense 4,000-metre depths of the Fiji Basin. My mind wanders, as it often does, to where we will live when we get home and what our house will be like. I fancy a little semi-rural cottage with a welcoming garden where we can lose hours among the leaves and birds. We each own a house and we're renting the two out to add to the funds for our odyssey. We will sell them both on our return.

When I came on watch again at 4.00 am the celestial performance in the night sky was at its climax. Three satellites arced across the black curtain and many more sat stationary, glittering like wealthy wives at a charity gala. Around 5.00 am the early dawn filled the eastern sky with primrose yellow and spread its reflections down to the sea surface. Would it be a cloudless sunrise as well? There was a narrow layer of broken cloud in the way, which in the end added to the sense of anticipation and drama. Camera and I waited.

Bright flashes of stationary light, some big and worrying (would I hear of a plane crash in the area?), took my attention for a while. They may have been a meteor shower, although I have never seen one so cannot say for sure. One low-level plane flashing red was probably en route from Tonga to Auckland.

Where stage performers love an encore after their performance, the sun on this morning demanded it before. We waited and waited, like fans at a concert, for the star's arrival. At last it emerged in a halo of flaming orange, its body dressed in brilliant palest yellow as it rose slowly and then disappeared behind the clouds.

17 June 2018. Our fear of the low at the outset has become a calm anticipation with the hope we can use the wind we get. We should be well to the north of its track. As I write this at 9.22 am, we have 278 miles to go to Minerva. At 135 miles covered in a 24-hour period, that should get us in early afternoon on Tuesday, but we shall see.

My nerves in Minerva

20 June 2018. Zoonie moves very gently at her anchor in this amazing lagoon (every ocean should have one) alongside our dear friends Hannes and Sabine on Cayenne who arrived just before us. Rob will dive down today and see if there is anything wrapped around their prop, as Hannes thinks there may be, because of a strange noise they've been hearing too. Maybe the same as ours, which strengthens the idea of it being volcanic in origin. Hannes cannot dive himself as he is short of one lung.

21 June 2018. Alison and Randall, who left New Zealand with us, are well west and plan to keep going for Fiji. They will have weathered the low passing through last night and hopefully pick up the southerlies that are due to cover this area from midnight tonight. It is on these winds that trail the low that we will set off early tomorrow for the last 400 miles.

Rob caught a beautiful squid this morning. Its mate stayed with it while it was hooked, and it kept shooting out black ink, which looked very dramatic in the pale blue water. I landed it in a bucket so Rob could remove the hook before it went back to its mate in an array of changing colours. What amazed us was how it changed to the exact colour and pattern of the artificial bait next to it in the bucket. Beautiful creatures.

23 June 2018. On her way north just 25 miles south of Minerva, a yacht yesterday reported volcanic activity. The boat stopped in the water, unable to make forward progress even at 2000 rpm, and amidst

Rob checks *Cayenne*'s prop

the sulphuric smell of rotten eggs they turned right angles to the left to escape the highly aerated water.

We also smelled sulphur on board and just hoped it had travelled with the wind and not that we were sitting in a cauldron about to boil over. Our suspicions were confirmed: the rumbling sound was from beneath the Earth's surface, and we were unnerved, briefly. But where was the eruption? Near us or miles away? We could do nothing but hope our luck was not about to run out. We were used to facing problems as they arose and not worrying about them beforehand.

We were enjoying our brief reunion with Hannes and Sabine because from here they were heading further west, and who knows when we would see them again.

We were both delayed for two days due to the arrival of another weather system in the direction we planned to sail, and as Hannes' worries about a fouled prop were happily proved to be unfounded by Rob's exploratory dive, we decided to relax with a walk together on the reef.

We went with Hannes in his aluminium-bottomed RIB because the coral would be a lot less kind to our soft-hulled dinghy, and we wore thick-soled sandals to protect our feet from the razor-sharp edges.

As we paddled on the reef such a flat scene surrounded us as goby fish dashed into and out of our gaze more quickly than I could photograph them. The reef is strewn with mussel shells, various colours and shapes of coral, skittering camouflaged crabs and little pools with tiny caves, each with its own sea urchin partly revealed and part hidden, reaching for any tiny morsel passing by. Perhaps most spectacular were the turquoise-lipped clams, their soft feeding tissues reflecting the colour of the water over white sand.

Rob wandered to the far side of the reef, about a quarter-mile across, and paddled in the Pacific where the waves break in white foam. He could see the bottom where he was walking, but he then came to a deep blue fissure in the reef that went down into the depths to 638 metres. There he saw a big 60-centimetre oval fish with a yellow chin surrounded by a dozen or so smaller fish keeping it company.

Same departure, different destinations in Fiji

25 June 2018. Cayenne is following just a few minutes behind us, both keen to get a good day's sail under our belts before night-time.

The Diva completes the scene and is happy to compromise on her usual insistence on an empty stage by letting us use a little of the mainsail to steady Zoonie in the lively seas. Couldn't have the Diva falling into the orchestra pit or, even worse, the audience, could we!

We lost sight of Cayenne at around 4.00 pm, on a slightly more westerly course towards Viti Levu as they are eventually sailing west from Fiji.

27 June 2018. Early in the morning of our last day at sea, as I came onto my 1.00 am watch, I felt we needed more than the modest 5.5 knots we were doing to make Savusavu, our port of call on Vanua Levu, in comfortable time, to be checked in today, before the weekend. To advance our ETA, more than 6 knots are required, please, I requested of the invisible wind gods.

Thinking the procedure through, I gently released a little of the genoa furling line to let more of the sail out to increase Zoonie's speed. I then took the winch handle and tightened in the sail to make sure it all caught the wind till we were getting a bare 6 knots. Just a little more out then. Using the same procedure again brought the speed up to 6.3 knots, and her motion was still comfortable in the bumpy sea. Any more and she would have been at risk of a broach, coming side on to the advancing rollers and being turned over. And I didn't want that on my watch, oh no! As it was, the stronger pull forward kept her bow up and her steering secure.

The next day we said goodbye to the beautiful big ocean after 1,200 miles and entered the bay on Vanua Levu. We were secured to a buoy at 3.45 pm. Less than an hour later the Savusavu health and biosecurity officers arrived.

"How are you feeling?" the young Indian gentleman asked.

"Fine, thank you."

And that was personal health done, nice and simple. (Pre-Covid!)

In friendly Savusavu, everyone walking the pavements made eye contact, smiled and said "bula" (hello, welcome) as we made our way to the supermarket. That done, we bought two colourful sulus to wrap around our waists like long skirts, to respect their ethnic identity when we visited the more traditional islands of the eastern Lau Group. Since then, our sulus have been used for tablecloths, evening skirts, cockpit screens and windbreaks. Uncut and unshaped fabric has so many uses.

After some three weeks exploring the lovely island, from the Cakaulevu Reef in the north to the sugar cane factory at Labasa, and a snorkel at Jean-Michel Cousteau Resort to a guided tour around a typical Fijian village, to name a fraction of what we got up to, plus socialising and the inevitable round of repairs, we were more than ready to start a cruise to the outer islands of the Fiji group.

We spent three wonderful months exploring Fiji, fulfilling Rob's wish for his first season back at sea after his illness. Though filled with quite enough adventure and discovery for another book – buddy sailing with our friends Alison and Randall on *Tregoning* at the beginning and with new friends from our Savusavu stay, Mark and Teri aboard *Wavelength*, for most of the time – this is not getting us any nearer to *Zoonie's* voyage home. So I will just tell you about one nineteen-day spell we spent with the remarkable people we found on the exquisite island of Fulaga, nearly the southernmost island in the eastern Lau Group, just to give you a taste of the unique friendship and sense of community that Fiji offers.

Daring the tumult entering Fulaga

Arriving with the sun behind us in the north-east, which was useful, showing clearly the rocks and coral beneath the surface to avoid, we would be entering the passage into the sheltered lagoon in the last three hours of the ebb, with the strongest possible tide against us. This would be interesting!

We watched Mark on *Wavelength* make her turn in and proceed very slowly. I took over the helm from the autopilot a mile from the start of our entry waypoints. Waves were breaking high and white over the reef which extended as an arm out to sea on the left side of the passage, scooping us into the turbulent water.

12 August 2018. It's midday so the sun is high. The maelstrom swirls and leaps around like a whirling dervish and is playing ping pong with Zoonie's hull and rudder, one minute swinging her bows towards the angry reef on one side and then the other. The vast surface area of the reef is a kind of tooth decay yellow, as I point Zoonie in a direction I am not entirely happy with. Wrestling with the wheel I try to at least keep her equidistant from each side of the 50-metre-wide gap, and after a few tummy-churning minutes we are in the main passage. Phew, I am hoping it will be plain sailing from here, but no; a quick look at the stationary reef and then the speedometer tells us we are almost stationary. Our speed has slowed from 5.4 knots to 1.1 by the outpouring tide. So, with revs increased to over 2000 rpm, we crawl over the powerful ebb and no doubt burn some carbon build-up off at the same time. I like the bright side of things best.

Safely through the passage, we have a couple of miles to go to the village anchorage of Muana i cake (pron. thake).

Fulaga Lagoon is vast with acres of the most beautiful grades of blue and turquoise water, dotted with little palm-tree-decorated islets with overhangs above the water where waves have eroded the limestone over millions of years.

The old chief is dead

13 August 2018. They don't know who the new chief is yet as he will be chosen by the clan elders of the village sometime after the initial mourning period of vakabogidrau (lasting one hundred nights) is over. The old chief, Taniela Bese, who ruled from 1999 until his death a month before our arrival, succeeded an isolationist leader before him, who banned cruisers from visiting the island, so it's thanks to Bese we are allowed in.

Groundbreaking Taniela Bese could see that there were mutual benefits from welcoming us lot. Our visits are without religious, political, colonising or commercial elements. We bring no disease (hopefully) and seek only friendship and enlightenment, and any fruit and veg they would like to sell to us.

Each cruising yacht pays $50 (£19) at their sevusevu (welcome to the village from an elder), which goes into a fund to benefit all the villages on the island. The fund is drawn on to finance official business expenses and trips to Suva, the nation's capital on Viti Levu, of the chief and his assistant, plus school needs and church requirements.

Fortunately for us, out of this union, there comes also the richness of mutual generosity, admiration, affection and long-term friendship.

We are introduced to villagers and their way of life

An elder, Tai, and some other villagers met us, all introducing themselves with a warm handshake while saying "pleased to meet you" and asking "what is your name?"

Grey-haired Tai was shortly taking some of the younger generation of men out to a distant island across the lagoon for a day of cassava planting on a patch of good soil. The cassava root is boiled like a potato and adds starch to their diet. It is also yummy if sliced after boiling and fried into chips.

But before leaving he presented us to Bill, Taniela's grandson, a man of late thirties / early forties who is never far from the next joke. He came across from Suva in February to join the family team in looking after the old chief who was in his mid-nineties and declining fast. Bill led the way up the narrow, foot-smoothed path towards the village, chatting as we went. He was looking forward to the end of the vakabogidrau so he could shave off his hair and beard and wear anything but black, as it attracts the wretched mosquitoes, *scratch, slap!*

Mark and Teri had already arrived by a different track from

their anchorage and were enjoying their sevusevu with Mika, the temporary chief and nephew of Taniela Bese, so we stood in the shade of a breadfruit tree awaiting our turn and chatting with Bill who had donned a sulu for the formal meeting.

We were invited inside the neat hut to sit cross-legged facing Mika. He spoke some Fijian, and Bill handed Mika our $50 for the village funds, the kava root we had bought in Savusavu for their much-loved drinking ritual, and our ship's papers and Fiji Islands cruising permit. The last two items are not usually required, but a few weeks before a local fisherman found a big stash of cannabis buried in the sand above an anchorage, took it to the village where the police and Customs were advised, and two yachts were impounded and their crews were arrested.

Formalities over, Mika went back to his chores while Bill introduced us to our daytime host family: Mereh (Mary), a teacher in the kindergarten school with thirteen in her class, and her husband, the handsome Jone, a skilled wood carver (matai).

"This is 'Madame Speaker'," (Bill's nickname for Mereh) "who is happy to be your host for your stay here. Now that your sevusevu is done you are free to move around the island and village, take photos and fish if you wish, you are very welcome always."

After some more chat, Mereh commented jokingly, "You must believe less than one per cent of what Bill says," and the friendly banter between the two was ongoing.

Poor Mereh, since we hadn't announced our arrival in advance, she only learned she was hosting us about ten minutes before we arrived; fortunately, she didn't mind, but it meant she hadn't had any time to prepare food. She is not paid for her hospitality.

Mereh and Jone's daughter is at school in the capital, Suva, 200 miles away from her parents. She lives with Mereh's sister and is missed greatly by her family. (They have had a little boy, Pate, since we left.)

Mereh's parents live on their farm in the hills behind Suva, but visiting them by the once-a-month supply ship is prohibitively expensive, $119 each way (it was $135 until recently!), and then one has to pay extra for luggage and supply one's own food and bedding for the night passage, and, of course, stay somewhere for a month until the next supply ship voyage, with the same expense for the return trip. So they see their mainland family once a year, the same as us; when we travel across the world, they travel across the Koro Sea.

But Mereh chooses to live the island life. "Every day in the city we have to earn a lot of money and everything costs money; always there is this pressure. The city doesn't compare with the peace and beauty here. I like the sense of community where we all look out for each other."

Later the same day:

Mereh steps out for a few moments to pick some lemongrass, before scrunching it up and popping it into a jug. She then fills this with water she boiled in the cool of the early morning and stored in a thermal flask. We sit cross-legged on the honey-gold pandanus matt, chatting and enjoying fresh lemongrass tea and coconut milk bread made at the same time as the boiling water. The birds sing in the trees and the scent of the frangipani blossoms fills the room from the tree just outside one of the three doors. What a wonderful place.

The house has attractive bowed ends to reduce resistance to cyclone winds, and the walls are draped with colourful cotton hangings and supported with six stout, round tree trunks, which double as comfortable backrests. Mereh cooks on two cookers, one a gas oven with hobs and the other a single, much hotter, primus stove. Away from the house is a little shed with a proper toilet and lots of containers of rainwater where they have hand showers. Washing up is in a bowl on a bench just outside the house, and clothes washing is done by soaking in a large container, just as I do on Zoonie. There is no need for a fridge as food is taken fresh daily and cooked to preserve it. This way all the families have a constant supply of cooked food ready for their meals.

Coconut and banana palms sway in the breeze above us, and papayas and breadfruit are in abundance on their trees. Villager and new friend Zu wove us baskets from green pandanus leaves and fills them with a variety of produce.

Then we are all invited to take kava with the ladies, and a young man hosts the mixing of the crushed kava root inside a fabric bag with fresh water in the big vesi wood bowl (tanoa) that has been made by one of the village wood carvers. An elder sits and watches to make sure the mixing is in the correct proportions. "High tide, low tide or medium tide?" we're asked, meaning how full do we want our half coconut cups (bilo) to be on each round.

Kava is drunk socially, as we might drink beer down at the pub, and we carry some on board to give as gifts to village chiefs as it is also important as a ceremonial drink. It is illegal to import the root into the UK as food or in any food product, so we'll make sure it's all been distributed before we get home!

Will I ever get used to the dry, slightly aniseed, peppery taste, I wonder, as I sip the liquid. Embarrassingly I unintentionally make visitors and villagers laugh when I pull a screwed-up expression on the very first round. By the third round my lips are tingling and my throat is numb. Everyone is affected with varying amounts of the drink, which supposedly has mildly sedative and anaesthetic properties. I feel no such effects except the enjoyment of being included in this, a favourite cultural practice!

My unusual birthday celebrations

The 14th of the month was special to me as it was my sixty-sixth birthday (siganisucu), and so I re-used Zu's palm leaf basket to carry the plastic oval plate of sliced chocolate cake oozing (due to the heat) with melting chocolate icing and dotted with squares of flapjack up to the village.

We walked on to Mereh's house, casting 'bulas' all around to all ages of villagers. Some of the villagers whom we had met the day before came to us, "Barbara, Happy Birthday!", followed with big hugs.

Mereh had baked some coconut bread first thing, placing the dough directly into a dish of fresh coconut milk, which helps the loaf stay moist as it cooks, a kind of steaming method.

"Doesn't it soak into the dough?"

"Noooo," she replied.

It was delicious, light and delicately sweet.

"Bill and Tui are coming to take you on a tour, Barbara. We thought you'd like that."

We had only been there two days and already Bill, Tui and Mereh had made plans for me.

After a look around the village school and shop, Bill and Tui Bill's friend and the children's choirmaster, led the way through the vegetable garden, behind the homes, teasing each other all the while. ('Tui' is widely used in this region: as a name, to refer to 'chiefs', both genders, and as a nickname and term of endearment. It is also a type of bird. In this case it appeared to be his proper name.)

"Tui is from the Solomons, so he knows nothing."

A bit like the Irish/Anglo banter, but Tui gave as good as he got.

"And Bill comes from the city, poor thing."

We ascended from the garden, scrambling through thin undergrowth, to the cave of mysterious skulls and bones. And then, "whoa!", a pile of around thirty skeletons' bones piled up underneath with the skulls on top. Some skulls looked out at us accusingly from ledges on the far wall. The skulls were whitish with some pale green algae on them in the dry, airy cave.

"Even my grandfather had no idea of the origin of the bones, so they go back many generations," Bill said.

"Could they be Tongan warriors defeated in battle, Bill?" I wondered. "You could send a sample away for analysis, and that would give their age and probably their origin too."

Maybe I crossed the mark there because I think the cave is sacred (tabu), a prohibited place and entry is forbidden, or maybe they are comfortable with the mystery; it is a western trait to want to solve mysteries rather than retain the magic of them. I wondered also if they were cannibalised remains, as is likely if these bones belonged to invaders. Bill smiled a lot but is none the wiser than us and is happy to keep it that way.

Back to the village for the evening, where Mereh's grandmother made me a beautifully fragrant garland of wild rose blossoms and frangipani flowers, and Mereh tied it carefully around my neck.

We feasted on pumpkin curry with onions and fried spices, rice, Chinese cabbage in coconut milk with noodles, and we drank fresh coconut water, straight from the nut.

Next everyone sang 'Happy Birthday' while Mereh struggled to get the candles to stand upright in the cake slices; I blew them out and made a short speech before the chocolate cake and flapjacks all vanished in a flash.

The boys disappeared to have showers while the evening kava session, which I was to lead (!) was set up by Jone, Mereh's husband. Practice makes perfect, I thought.

Between each round of kava, we would join in a discussion and tell stories and anecdotes, and this exchange is called a talanoa. When I sensed there was a lull I would say "Taki" and the kava master would pour another round into the bilo and hand it to each of us in turn. Before taking the cup, we clapped once with cupped hands to make a resonant sound (cobo) and then again three times as we handed back the cup. I loved this living culture, still an important part of their daily routines.

I have no idea how many rounds we shared, but when Rob and I saw the light was fading on my wonderful day, we said our farewells and with Peter and Martina, our new Australian friends from the highly appropriately named catamaran *Havachat*, made our way back to the dinghies in the finest, most refreshing rain that only became heavy after we were at the beach and able to shelter in a store shed. We had seen but not met Peter and Martina earlier in our Fiji journey and now found ourselves anchored beside them.

A fun day with the villagers

17 August 2018. When there are enough cruising yachts at anchor, the village organises a beach party, and as we approached in the dinghy, Tui was up a palm tree securing one of the lines for the tarpaulin shades. Bill was helping, so I joined in, before playing catch ball with some of the village children. This was a great day out for them as they were on holiday and the cruisers had brought ashore paddle boards, kayaks and balls for them to play with.

Martina and I sat for a long time with Bill and Tui showing us how to make the table tops and then our own plates out of coconut palm leaves.

It was lovely to see the fusion of cruisers and villagers laughing and

Beach party fun with our Fulaga friends

chatting together, children all playing together and then the lovely array of village dishes and cruisers' contributions to make this a wonderful party, sans frontiers.

Better than the best fairground ride

True to his generous nature, the next day Peter radioed us to ask if we'd like to join them in their big, powerful dinghy to go and snorkel the main passage where we had entered and another passage to one side.

We didn't need to be asked twice.

The turbulence at the entrance, caused by the water from the two passages emptying from the lagoon as the tide fell to its lowest, like milk from a basin, was still too rough, so we sat there in the dinghy and waited a few minutes. Soon there were lots of smooth-surfaced circling eddies as the tide prepared to turn, but the waves were settling down nicely as we fell into the water.

Then the fun really started.

21 August 2018. The new flood tide is gently moving us into the safety of the lagoon. It is like flying in water, and we have a quarter-mile to go. Beneath us vast, pristine coral colonies support their varied habitats. A pile of upturned beaten copper cup shapes stacked one on top of another at least 30 feet in diameter and an olive-green cabbage coral with its uplifted leaves more like 50 feet across greet us; this really is a vast and colourful forest.

The current is building rapidly now the tide is rising, and I make a mental note of the timing to use when we eventually plan our departure. There is no chance of us turning around and swimming against the force of water; it is not even possible to stop and stare. As we speed along above the submarine world, up to 30 feet below us, we move our heads rapidly from side to side just to take in as much as we have time for and use our hands like paddles to stop us being shoved against the sharp surfaces.

All too soon Peter was back in the dinghy he had been towing by hand, and that was a sign for us to join him. Then to our relief he suggested, beaming, "Shall we do that all over again? The water will be clearer this time."

He wasn't wrong, the water looked polished, and in the perfect clarity we saw three sharks, a giant potato cod and lots of other fishes we had seen before, but this time in flowing shoals.

We flew up the main passage again and then the side passage before climbing back into the dinghy. What a gift. We would not have tried what we had just achieved in our dinghy, and so we may well have missed the whole experience if it hadn't been for our friends. Back on board we showered and sipped the hot chocolate we always enjoy after a snorkel.

Farewell party

27 August 2018. "Bula, Mereh, how was school today?"
"We spent all morning trying to remember what they learned last term!"
Well, that rang some bells, from my teaching days!
"Rob, you shall be king!" Bill exclaimed as we sat ready for the kava session at our farewell party. That meant he should say "Taki" to the kava master to start the next round.
The session had started gently with Jone doing the honours and dispensing the drink to us, then gradually fifteen or so others joined us,

seeing from the path outside that a party was underway. Children came in and shook hands with us, some of them knew our names by now and we theirs.

It was an interesting time because we had some discussions about life in Suva versus life here. Tui and Bill became serious over the tensions with Indian Fijians. Bill said that indigenous Fijians don't see skin colour as a basis for prejudice and resentment, and Tui told us about the hostility from Indian residents on the main islands that both of them had experienced.

"I understand. I have read about some of the issues," I said.

Some of the young girls stay on in Suva and marry there, finding jobs in shops and offices, whereas it is harder for young men to find jobs, and the pressure to earn money is something they are not used to.

Tangy took over serving the kava. He was so very polite each time he gave us our cup: "Bula, Barbara, and vinaka" (thank you).

He went on to explain, softly, "Why would I live in Suva and have to earn money when here I can work for all I need?"

They are blissfully unambitious and place little value on money, which is so unlike the world we have grown up in.

Sometimes the conversation would quieten and Bula, the oldest villager present, would give me the wink, and I would nudge Rob to call "Taki", which would immediately liven things up again.

Some of the expanding group shifted to one corner and started playing a noisy game with the RNLI deck we had presented to Mereh. A little boy fell fast asleep on his mum's lap despite the loud slapping down of the cards. Many skewer-like cigarettes were being smoked, and as the doors were closed against the cool of the evening the atmosphere was becoming heady. A fusion of western and Fijian music was playing on a little speaker, Bluetoothed from Mereh's phone.

I caught Mereh's eye to say we were ready to feast, Bill having told me this was the form, and Rob and I ate alone, being watched by some of the ladies. I asked them to eat with us but this was their custom, so I had to put up with my feeling awkward. We were equals, and I loved their company.

"We have something for you, but I need to finish it. Can we meet you at the beach at 12.30 tomorrow, Barbara?"

28 August 2018. We waited on board the next morning until we saw them arrive and motored ashore in the dinghy. Mereh unloaded a plastic box with some more of Jone's lovely coconut, grated fresh that morning, and we transferred it into our box. Then from her backpack she pulled a pandanus mat – yes, a real pandanus mat – trimmed with brightly coloured wool (her own work) for us to keep. I was overwhelmed with pleasure. This new mat of ours, made with such care and precision by these clever village women for us to keep forever, was stunning.

"Will you leave today?" Mereh asked.

"There is a 25-knot wind coming soon, so we'll probably wait over in Sandspit until it has passed," Rob explained.

We thanked them, also for the breadfruit, Chinese cabbage and papayas, and after big hugs stumbled back to the tender, blinded by tears and lost for more words.

(The beautiful pandanus mat now graces the kitchen floor, and as it reflects pale golden light I think of Mereh and Jone and their lovely community. Mereh and I chat on Messenger from time to time.)

Chapter 3

A Windy Passage South from Fiji

A massive, virtually stationary high-pressure system covering all of New Zealand and Fiji and much of Eastern Australia was giving plentiful ESE to E winds, and we just wanted to get out there and go sailing. We knew this non-stop passage could be subjected to the strong winds that come up from the Tasman Sea as we approached New Zealand, but would the high stay with us, all the way, keeping the lows at bay?

On this, our last trip in to Suva, the clearing out process was done quickly, then Rob fixed the inner forestay in position and hanked on the orange storm jib (last used for the passage from Tonga two years ago), and I did a big bake, hardboiled some eggs and stowed moveable items below for the passage, which we expected to take around nine days.

13 October 2018. We passed fearless surfers who were enjoying riding the steep waves as they break on the seaward side of the reef at the entrance to Suva Harbour.

Zoonie crisps along at 6.5 knots with the wind 60 degrees from her port bow on a course just west of south, 212°, enabling us to sail between Beqa and Kadavu islands. The wind is a generous 18–20 knots, and the bow wave is washing the very muddy anchor clean in no time.

Come with me on this incredible passage

A few hours later we prepared for the night by reefing *Zoonie* well, losing nothing in speed in a wind that was showing all the signs of being on the make.

By watery sunrise the wind was filling to 27 knots as *Zoonie* entered the uncluttered weather arena of the sea between the South Pacific islands and mainland New Zealand. The water beakers that stand in their wooden holder just in front of the compass in the cockpit were rimmed with salt from the flying spray; perfect for margaritas.

At night the stars gave way to dark scudding banks of cloud, but they were mostly innocent of sudden strong winds; the steady trade winds were hogging the skies.

Progress was good but not without a little discomfort. After one deluge of water into the cockpit, soaking the cushions and us, we retreated into the peace of her saloon and watched the proceedings from behind the glass windows.

By the next day, the wind was a full 31 knots, and *Zoonie* pounded the waves as they pounded her back: a marine boxing match. A quick jab from *Zoonie* met with a mean upper cut from a raging wave on her topsides. You would not think they could be made by liquid alone.

She had never been in such conditions before. The tops of the bursting waves were so far above us; the sea level was literally flying in fractured and tumultuous rage overhead.

White veils of water erupted from beneath her bows and went her entire length, blasting her big windows, so vision through them was bizarrely made perfect for a fraction of a second. Would they hold? Could *Zoonie's* watery opponent actually smash one? If so, could we fit the wooden dummy windows, which we had made back in England, in time before *Zoonie* took fatal gulps of water? Could the bilge pump work well enough to keep *Zoonie* afloat in the meantime?

I wondered how long that amazing foresail would last, constantly pulling 13 tons through the water and holding tight to the full force 7.)

Oh, for a drone camera.

Henry, the wind self-steering gear, was doing a valiant job. As a gust suddenly knocked *Zoonie* off course, the genoa would flap and the combined force of Henry's rudder and *Zoonie's* natural tendency to come to wind would lure her back onto course so the genoa could fill once again, in an act of inanimate teamwork that we mere mortals below truly appreciated.

But we were superficial pawns in *Zoonie's* contest with the sea: useless passengers watching her incredible engagement with the elements.

As I rested my body – not my mind – in the down-side berth, looking up through the big side windows at the tons of green/white water ploughing down the side-deck above my head, I could see that at times we were submarining. You can really feel her movements when lying secure behind the lee cloth and not having to hold on. *Zoonie* sometimes lifted over a wave and was suspended for a fraction of a second, her front half flying in the air, the sea's punch under her chin, with me thinking, oh, oh, there's only one way from here, and down she'd go to a thump that shook her from mast top to keel. Even her sea-kindly hull shape could not make good of this maelstrom.

Rob was amazing. He had to go out on deck in the wild weather, once to unjam the Furlex reefing drum right up at her bow and another time to tighten some halyards which had stretched from being saturated and vibrating constantly. He'd go out just in his briefs and lifeline because he knew he was in for a drenching and would return down the companionway ladder glistening top to toe in seawater.

We would both venture into the cockpit to reef or ease the genoa, and on this day, as we did so, we both saw at the same moment the six-inch seam tear near the luff of the genoa.

Zoonie's lovely 6 to 7 knot progress was under threat.

16 October 2018. "We'll roll it up completely, and I'll set the storm jib," Rob said straightaway. All he had to do was to hoist it by hauling on its halyard at the mast base, but, of course, Zoonie was moving a fair bit so it wasn't easy. As the little orange sail rose, I tensioned the sheet to stop it flapping and then, when the halyard was taught, winched in the sheet so it pulled, but, oh dear, we were down to 3 knots of speed.

By this time the companionway steps, handholds and floor had a thin layer of seawater spray all over them that made them as slippery as ice, and I kept thinking I needed to wash them so they could dry.

Down below life went on. By this time both the wooden washboards were in place, securely tied down, and the hatch cover was fully closed, and it was just as well because waves were now breaking over her stern port quarter and making it into the cockpit where they drained, too slowly in my view, down the drains.

Suddenly there was an alarming crash as a ton of water hit the washboards. Not a drop came down below, but I watched through a head-sized slit I'd made between the hatch cover and washboard as the liquid mass swirled around the cockpit floor, washing the portholes and making the steering column up to the domed compass cover look like an isolated lighthouse.

When the waves were at their height and filling the cockpit, Rob discovered that the rush of water was funnelling down below through the two air vents in the open cockpit lockers, above the side seats.

We had never had this happen before and, judging by the new and permanent stain the seawater trickle left on the wood, neither had *Zoonie*. Rob stuck duct tape over the openings and over the speakers in the cockpit.

Our wind generator plus a little daytime UV on the solar panels kept the batteries charged to 100% with over 13 volts, and, in case you know little or nothing (like me) about electricity, that's good. In fact, it's perfect.

Our hands were becoming sore from gripping the slippery handholds so tightly, and we wondered if anyone else had taken the same 'perfect' weather window as us.

Was there anyone else out there?

Zoonie changes her rig

I didn't like our reduced speed and neither did Rob or *Zoonie*. "Hun, what about unfurling just a little genoa, up to where we can let the split stay in the furled part?" I suggested.

Well, *Zoonie* showed her appreciation by surging from 3 to nearly 7 knots in the 30-knot wind, and that's where she stayed for days to come. Effectively *Zoonie* was now sailing under a cutter rig, with two sails in front of her mast and all her sail area kept nice and low. The tough little orange storm jib was set behind the reefed genoa and the mainsail was smaller even than the fore-sails, so all three pulled well.

Our bodies were aching from bracing ourselves inside *Zoonie* as she ploughed on with determination on her own route, direct to Bream Head off the Hāátea River, despite our trying to keep her on a southerly course to 30° S and due north of North Cape. The chances of a low passing across north New Zealand, while we hung about was decreasing as the

Zoonie's cutter rig

days went on. This magnificent high persisted and resisted any encroaching systems. And *Zoonie* seemed to know it, staying a steady angle to the wind. (I love her. As ever, keeping us safe.)

The forecast showed more of the same bountiful wind supply with possibly a brief reprieve, in which we hoped to tidy up and wash the woodwork clean of salty moisture.

The reprieve didn't come. We were just starting to move over the flat seabed, or abyssal plain, known as the South Fiji Basin, and I wondered if this factor might reduce the tempestuous sea. It was running at five-metre swells and moderate waves and was unlikely to lessen until the wind did. Suddenly we were startled when the bilge pump alarm went off. Checking underneath the sink at the lowest point of the bilge, *Zoonie* had around one foot or a gallon of water swishing about. A quick taste check confirmed it was seawater. Well, there was plenty of that around!

17 October 2018. At 10.45 am or thereabouts I was standing on the third step of the companionway keeping an eye on Rob as he adjusted Henry from the back of the cockpit when, with a suddenness we had not experienced before, Zoonie was shoved sideways by a marauding slapping wave, just looking for mischief: the sort that can open up the seams of a wooden boat.

My hands lost their grip, and I spun around and off the steps, hitting the floor on my back – noting how clean the headlining of the saloon ceiling looked as I passed – and slid head-first down the 11-inch step into the chart table footwell as *Zoonie* pitched upwards. A loud crack, and then, mercifully, it all stopped.

I was in a short snooze.

When I came round, I noticed I had something broken on my chest.

Have I broken my glasses? I thought, but the shattered pieces of plastic were white. My skull had smashed the double three-pin power socket beneath the chart table to smithereens.

I feared I might have an injury or injuries that would render Rob single-handed as I slowly sat up, checking for snapped bones, dragging myself onto the saloon floor and leaning against the seat front. Miraculously all seemed well.

That morning, I had dressed in a fuchsia-coloured T-shirt, which was handy because I noticed blood dripping onto it; had I worn a white one, the dramatic effect might have caused me to faint, as I had before on similar occasions. (I can taste the metal sensation in my mouth just thinking about it.)

Rob came down the ladder, his task complete. "I've tumbled," I mumbled. Rob was alarmed and concerned. "You could have broken your neck!" he said while parting my hair to inspect the cut. "It's not very long, so I don't think I'll need to shave your hair and apply Steri-Strips." Did he sound a little disappointed? Yes, he did. He tended me lovingly, mopping up the mess with antiseptic wipes and words of encouragement, while I was feeling a golf ball-sized bump swelling rapidly on the other side of my head, to match the cut.

The incident meant it was imperative to spend the morning recovering by languishing on the leeward settee, like Manet's Olympia, while Rob administered mugs of coffee laced with rum, plated flapjacks and medicinal squares of Cadbury's.

By the afternoon I was back in harness, no stuff and nonsense on this boat! Surprisingly the wind was easing down to the low 20s, and the sea showed the signs of smoothing as well.

Zoonie was still creaming along and approaching 30° S, and it was becoming more obvious that she was right in trying to head direct for Bream Bay. She knew better than us, and as there was no low to worry us, we allowed her to have her way. (I remember we had Muse playing loudly and appropriately for some of the time.)

Zoonie's fabulous progress in these conditions for over four days and nights gave us confidence. We always knew we would have spells of lively weather – this is our chosen life and we accept and deal with what comes – but what was new was the water pouring into her cockpit from the STERN.

Two days later, as the conditions were clearly settling down, I suggested to Rob, "We've got the spare genoa on board, why don't we take both foresails down and rig that one?"

To do this lengthy job we both needed to be on the foredeck while *Zoonie* motored under the autopilot, head in to wind so as to minimise the motion caused by the moderate sea state.

The storm jib was unhanked and stowed and the inner forestay repositioned in its home, leaving the foredeck nice and clear. I unfurled the tired genoa so we could lower it down the forestay, me easing the halyard and Rob pulling it down. I dragged the foot along the side-deck so it could be folded like a fan from each end and then rolled over itself towards Rob to be bagged.

This bagful replaced the one containing the spare genoa, which we had never used and which we still keep under the dining table on passage along with the spinnaker to bring some weight back from the bow.

I then stood in front of the forestay so as not to get knocked by the flapping sail and fed the sail up the roller reefing groove as Rob hauled on the halyard by the mast.

It was lovely out there. Bright sunshine glistening on the beautiful sparkly waves under a clear blue sky. Shearwater birds swooping low over the waves, completely disinterested in us.

We were delighted at how white and perfect the spare genoa looked as it rose up the forestay. It was clearly a lightweight one with thinner seams and only a single row of stitching along them, so we wondered at what max wind speed it should be stowed. (Later, Phil at UK Sails in Whangarei suggested 15–18 knots. Oops, we flew it at 14–22 knots, so that was a test for it, but we did anticipate a declining wind force, which was already happening.) The whole pleasurable exercise took only 45 minutes and brought *Zoonie* back up to 6 knots.

There was a chill in the air now, and we had to hunt for warmer clothes and our slippers! But things were getting easier down below as *Zoonie* sped along on an almost even keel in a half-metre swell, and we could walk around without looking like gorillas. Porridge and coffee infused with a tot of rum was called for to start the day.

19 October 2018. We have 400 miles to go to the waypoint off Bream Head, and at the current speed of 6 knots it will take us 66 hours to get there. Zoonie broke her speed record today with a run of 152 miles and a maximum of 8.1 knots briefly. Without a swell and heaving waves to impede her progress she just sped along.

Relief permeates the atmosphere on board, and as we laugh and joke over the smallest things, we realise how tense we have been over the past few days, in anticipation of this historically tricky crossing. Now the end is in sight, and although we never take anything for granted and try not to tempt providence while at sea, we are really starting to look forward to our arrival after one of Zoonie's finest and most eventful sails, and one of our most challenging!

After a perfect (and unforgettable) 1,000-mile beam reach we were greeted into New Zealand waters by a single albatross gliding around us for a few minutes, in which time it did not flap its wings once. I emailed Customs to give our position and ETA.

20 October 2018. During the night Rob awoke me by leaning forward to kiss me on the forehead. I knew when he did that everything was OK.

"We need to put the engine on, love; wind's down to 4 knots and falling."

My hopes of flying the Diva as the wind backed to NE were dashed, but it did make life easier to not have to mind any sails. Also, the cockpit was dry now, so we sat up there for the hour before sunset and had some interesting discussions over a gin and tonic.

"As the old genoa has thrown its sheets to the wind, we could use the fabric to make anoraks?" I thought aloud, inventively.

"No, Barbara."

Notice the use of my full name. Rob knows I feel I'm being chastised when it is used.

"A sunshade to go over the boom!?"

"No, Barbara."

"Duffle bags?"

"I'm going to the loo."

He escaped, phone in hand, for a few peaceful games of solitaire, while I went on scheming. Sail bags, shoulder bags, Hydrovane wind steering gear cover… I'm not going to waste it. I'm not.

We were beginning to feel really fit. My head was healing nicely four days on.

Unsurprisingly we had both lost some weight; great exercise without even trying, needing to brace oneself in the constant motion and sheer nervous energy expenditure. The only relief from this was to lie down in the berth and relax totally, just letting *Zoonie* rock one to sleep.

21 October 2018. One of the million horizon scans revealed another sailing boat. So we called them to see how they were doing.

The 15-metre dark-hulled Mirabella has a family of four on board who are heading for Opua to clear in. This is their first voyage across these waters, and they had been dreading it because of all the terrible stories they had been told. They are so excited to have had a "fantastic" sail down and even more so when we told them they had whales blowing in front of and behind them. False killer whales are all around us in small pods as we near the end of our journey. It seems there are scary stories about most parts of the world's seas and oceans.

The on-board music changed from Muse, to fit the boisterous conditions, to Clannad, to mirror the silky surface of the sea reflecting the opaline clouds above.

On the afternoon of what we knew would be our last day on this passage, I leaned over the side of *Zoonie*'s bows to see if her *'Zoonie'* logos had survived the lashings of the sea, and I was pleased to see they were both intact.

We arrived in Marsden Cove Marina with 1,142 miles under our belts at 8.12 am on 22 October after 8 days, 23 hours and 18 minutes at sea and only half a teaspoon of blood lost.

Two months later, after rekindling our life of maintenance on *Zoonie* and socialising with our dear friends, *Zoonie* was up on the hard, thoroughly cleaned and with her new genoa bagged in the fo'c'sle (the triangular cabin at the bow historically called the forecastle). She was ready for us to leave her, have a look at Australia and fly home, while the cyclone season blew itself through.

Chapter 4

Our Australian Tour

To Australia. First stop: Sydney

We met up with Alison and Randall for an evening exploring The Rocks.

The Rocks is now a popular area for locals and visitors to meet and chat in the numerous bars dotted between stylish modern and restored homes and hidden drainage.

Our second spell with our dear friends was spectacular. Aboard their yacht, *Tregoning*, anchored in Athol Bay, we watched the globally popular Sydney New Year's Eve fireworks show around the iconic bridge unfold.

4 January 2019. North to Jilliby to visit Jane and Greg, whom we had first met during the 2014 ARC Portugal Rally, and since in Lanzarote, and more recently in Fiji, at their rural retreat.

Together we sweltered in 40°C in the Hunter Valley while tasting wines, watched saltwater crocs sidewind like swimming snakes towards us across the lake at the Australian Reptile Park and mingled with kangaroos and koalas, who seemed entirely relaxed amidst the curious humans. Evenings were delicious in the warmth and shade of their veranda, watching kangaroos boxing and birds enjoying their numerous feeders while we sipped our sundowners and shared many anecdotes.

7 January 2019. Southwards now to Newcastle to visit Martina and Peter, whom we met in Fulaga, Fiji, and here I fell over with the bike I was about to ride, on an uneven pavement, hurting my foot. Not wanting to jeopardise our planned trip on The Ghan train, where moderate fitness is required, I tightened my laces, took some painkillers and practised walking without a limp. We swam, dined, and picnicked with Peter and Martina on the shore of Lake Macquarie during a concert.

The memory of our wonderful times in Fulaga came flooding back: Mereh and Jone and the other village people aboard Peter and Martina's catamaran, *Havachat*, after the sandspit beach party, when we danced around the aft deck and into the night.

Canberra is a bizarre place

13 January 2019. Crossing the green coastal belt on the train, south-west towards the capital, we happily ate our lunch, brought to us airplane-style by stewards who also pushed nice drinks cabinets on wheels. The green urban and suburban areas were soon replaced with sheep stations, wide open spaces and fewer trees.

The grass became sparse and peregrine falcons hovered above their prey awaiting their opportunity. Wind turbines turned lazily on the limestone plains near Goulburn, and frightened sheep ran away from the train as the lady driver took us onwards.

Michael was a breath of fresh air. His free culture bus tour took exactly an hour, and he talked for the duration, giving us a humorous and light-hearted account of his city. Five million trees were planted to create the 'Bush Capital' which surrounds the artificial Lake Burley Griffin, created by stopping up the Molonglo River. The name of the lake comes from the couple who started designing the city back in 1911, Walter Burley Griffin and Marion Mahony Griffin. Their design emphasised and reflected the achievements and needs of the first white Australians. The present layout indicates the ambition of the politicians of the time.

Canberra is located inland, miles from anywhere already developed back then, to protect it from risk of invasion; with WWI looming you can understand that. It was slow to develop because of the two world wars draining the male population and finances. Also, as time progressed, the Australian conscience was beginning to realise that, without any thought of consultation or discussion with the indigenous clans that lived there, the planners had plonked their new city on ancient and sacred Aboriginal meeting places. Public opinion, which expressed unease about this, had to be listened to and the rights of the original inhabitants acknowledged; a slow, painful process which is an ongoing struggle.

A special exhibition at the National Library of Australia building brought us close to one of the historic people I admire so much, who was in the same activity as us but in a much more important and globally significant way: the courageous discoverer Captain James Cook. His journals, navigational equipment, and his own findings in the form of the cowrie shell and bamboo stick charts of the Marshallese islands were all on display. The islanders had to remember these charts when they navigated the islands of the Pacific as the charts themselves were too precious to take to sea. We saw these early charts in a number of museum locations in the south-west Pacific region.

People criticise Cook for opening up the world to the European invasion that was so destructive; I do believe that if he could see now what his discoveries led to in the way of settlement, conflict with indigenous people and destruction of their race, culture and beliefs he would be deeply disappointed.

An indigenous encounter

---

15 January 2019. We had the good fortune to spend a day with Tyronne Bell, a gentleman elder of the Ngunawal people. Tyronne's great-grandmother was a native princess who had a daughter with an English explorer who had previously assured her he could not have children. Along came Tyronne's grandmother, and when Tyronne's mother was four years old she was taken from her mother's arms and raised the European way, miles from her home and family. One of the Stolen Generation.

We sped along the Tuggeranong Parkway towards the Namadgi Visitor Centre, Rob and I perched on the rear side seats of the white troop carrier, with Tyronne driving and at the same time telling us about himself and his ongoing work towards greater recognition of his nation within the modern Australian government.

The weather had been unusually hot and dry, and it was searing as we parked the vehicle. Tyronne told us about some of the plants in the visitor centre garden and their Aboriginal uses in medicines, cloth making, weaponry and food, including the grass straw that when blown creates a whistle that attracts snakes so they can be killed and eaten.

Tyronne explained that despite the fact he was taking us to a national park on his nation's land, he had to collect a gate key from the office before driving to the rock art site. Although title to many areas of land distant from Canberra has been given back to the rightful indigenous owners, Ngunawal Aboriginal businesses have no access to private land but can negotiate with the owners of the land to conduct cultural activities. However, while a ninety-nine-year leasing agreement is in place over the Namadgi National Park land in order that the Aboriginal clans can run their businesses, as Tyronne told us, it is virtually null and void as his father did not sign the agreement back in the 2000s. So, here non-clan people were operating the visitor centre, and Tyronne did not possess his own key.

"I'm really sorry, but the park is closed due to the risk of fire, so we cannot let you in today."

I felt tense and frustrated for Tyronne. He now had to rethink our day in a situation that was out of his hands. Maybe he had sensed I am passionate about the state of modern-day Aboriginal people and would have loved to have followed his story further, here on his land.

Unable to visit the rock art site, instead we set off for a short walk to see two intentionally cut 'scar trees'; the bark of one tree would be carefully peeled off and would once have been used as a canoe, and the central vertical layer of the heart of the other trunk would have been made into a shield.

A hot walk around the Black Mountain, where the giant Telstra Tower was built without permission from the elders, gave Tyronne an opportunity to explain.

"We are the people of the rocks. This is the meeting place of the men, women and children where we have always come together to perform cor-roborees, discuss all matters national, and enjoy celebrations. It is at Black Mountain where we started the initiation of our young men into adulthood,

The infamous tower

then followed the old pathway to the final destination of *Ginninderra Falls.*" *The women had their own area across the valley.*

Onwards we sped to a garden at the National Arboretum, Canberra, that Tyronne had designed himself in the shape of a beautiful butterfly, symbolising the cycle of life, transformation and rebirth in their creation stories. It was planted with native plants and grasses and defined with carefully placed stones. Tyronne mentioned his connection with a designer who had exhibited at the Chelsea Flower Show, and I thought, what an interesting way to tell the story of his people abroad, through a blend of their horticulture and dreamtime stories. Brilliant. Tyronne suggested we keep in touch so that next time he can take us onto his national park and show us where and how his family and clan have lived for thousands of years. We welcomed the invitation, and in parting outside the YHA he pleasantly surprised me with a kiss on the cheek and a hug goodbye.

We're going on The Ghan train!

There was hardly a sound outside as I left the Adelaide Parklands Terminal station lounge, crowded with fellow adventurers sipping bubbly and orange juice, for the sweltering, sun-filled platforms for a look around. Our resting train was so long it took up two platforms. Its one-kilometre length housed thirty-nine carriages including the engine, two power wagons, a motorail wagon with four cars, crew quarters, dining carriages, lounge carriages and our twenty-seven guest compartment carriages. But really, she was a potential travel powerhouse, as she sat in silver silence for a few moments more before starting out on the 1,851-mile journey to Darwin.

She wasn't sleek and modern-looking but tough, strong and capacious, and I could not wait for her to be moving, with us on board.

20 January 2019. At ten past midday, as the sun started its descent, we crawled slowly forward and started out on our 2,979-kilometre journey northwards.

Pink dust roads disappear over the hills to who knows where. Vast harvested fields with a few sheep and cattle cleaning up the residue of the crop munch away, oblivious to the red dust twisters that rose like smoke plumes around them. Prickly spinifex dot the red earth, and two grey kangaroos look in astonishment at our shiny silver snake moving slowly past.

Puffy green crown-on-stick trees sit in the beautiful warm ochre earth. The occasional olive grove slides by and in the far distance mysterious arid mesas, flat-topped and eroded volcanoes, the Adelaide River and arable hills all now way behind us.

As my eyes dart from side to side, I am reminded of the concept of time we feel when we start a voyage on Zoonie. Whatever we are doing, however we pepper our day with events and tasks, Zoonie sails on 24/7, along her singular path carrying us onwards in our chosen direction. And so does this redheaded, silver-backed desert snake, The Ghan, from very slow to an average of 85 km/h up to 115 km/h and ever onwards, regardless.

Moonshine at Marla was our first magical stop.

21 January 2019. We have covered 1,082 kilometres from Adelaide and are tapping on the door of the Northern Territory. Now, at 3.45 am, we are stopped in Marla. Up until 1980 The Ghan train would turn right here and follow the ancient Aboriginal Oodnadatta Track eastwards, then south of Lake Eyre to Marree. But in a couple of hours it's north indirectly all the way to Darwin.

It's still dark but the inky blueness contains a beautiful full moon rising above our comfy carriages. Hundreds of little white lanterns have been set by hiding rangers' hands, providing an illuminated pathway for us as we step carefully down onto the warm red soil of the country, home for eons to the most successful group of humans in history. Two stacks of substantial logs are piled into burning cones, providing warmth in what our little booklet suggests would be 'crisp air', just a short distance from wooden tables and benches. In fact, it is already pleasantly warm and warming up quickly as the beloved Earth moves towards the hidden sun.

Muted conversations don't prevent us from sensing the vast, still quietness of this remote and beautiful spot. Just a hundred people live here permanently, and we are up and about before almost all of them. A 4x4 pickup rests discreetly behind some bushes, the rangers awaiting our slow departure. How I would have loved to have met them.

Beautiful cirrus clouds shoot upwards across a blue sky, and circular, soft-grey coloured spinifex grass 'nests' are trapped amidst neat little trees on red-rust ground. All along the sides of the track, in areas where the soil has been scooped out and used to raise the track level, there are dry, cracked 'pools' which obviously fill with rainwater occasionally, and one can imagine the animals and birds that crouch around the edges for a welcome drink.

Leaning fence posts, cattle grids, herding pens and various breeds of healthy-looking cattle were the first hints that we were approaching civilisation. On the outskirts of Alice Springs, having trundled through a gap in the MacDonnell Ranges, we motored very slowly over a few level crossings where the poor motorists had to wait for 20 minutes or so as we slithered by.

Alice Springs Desert Park brings together some of the many species that live in the vast red centre of Australia that otherwise we could only imagine were resident. It is an environmental and educational facility which both enlightens the likes of us and carries out research projects to better understand the nature of the central desert.

Members of the Arrernte clan run the park, and we spent time with both a ranger and the director of the clan while we were there. The ranger took us round the various pens and paddocks; an emu strutted about behind a fence and a dingo relaxed in the shade of a hollow log.

His neighbour, a bustard, looked at us agog; he might have wondered why we were walking in the sunshine when the temperature was 45°C. Our planned walk through the Simpsons Gap was cancelled for the same reason, the extreme temperature, so instead the director, in a cool lecture hall, told us about the marriage laws between clans, designed an eon ago to prevent inbreeding.

Back on the train humanlike forms, neckless head on hunched shoulders and bodies swathed in cloaks of ochre, look as if they're doomed to wander the forest forever, solitary and moronic. They are in fact termite mounds. The biggest of the hundreds we view from the carriage window have unwittingly become partners to the Aboriginal people in their burial practices, once the termites have moved on.

These busy little builders dine on the sweet centre of tree trunks, and once they are hollowed out Aboriginal people use these trunks as coffins. Their artists paint beautiful dot and swirl pictures on them, doubtless telling a story about the deceased in their designs. After a corpse has decomposed in the ground, the bones are retrieved and placed in the memorial poles.

Then the top is knocked off a big, derelict termite mound, and the poles containing the bones are respectfully placed upright within the mound. Finally, stones are used as a lid to prevent animals breaking into the vertical grave.

Later, the full moon arced over us in the night sky, a heavenly headlight sending a shining line down the back of our wheeled snake as she sped more quietly on her new tracks through changing countryside. I lay in bed watching the semi-blurred scenery passing by. Gone was the hot red centre and the nests of spinifex; gone were the views of the distant hills. Instead, the sun of the new day painted a pale lilac glow through a woodland of trees; the lower trunks of which were charred after a controlled 'cool burn', designed to keep the undergrowth low and thin and prevent the risk of all-engulfing fires. They know it all – these clever indigenous people.

Then into the tropical climate of the 'Top End' of the Northern Territory with luxuriant green woodland all around. This area is fed annually by the generous monsoon, which raises water levels in the rivers by five metres in places and fills the scooped-out pools at the side of the track with water. To travel on The Ghan at the height of the monsoon and see birds and wildlife around you taking a drink must be a lovely sight. We were travelling at the anticipated start of the monsoon.

22 January 2019. Rob awoke and climbed down his ladder to have a look outside our window with me. Two beautiful sand-coloured Brahman cattle with their floppy ears and humped necks stared at us as we passed and word has it the largest herd of camels is in Australia rather than Africa now.

Our amazing trip is coming to an end and we'd do it all again just to see those earthy scoops full with rainwater, walk through Simpsons Gap to get a sense of country geology, ride on a camel as a reminder of the essential work done by these princely ships of the desert, and maybe take a fixed-wing plane flight over the MacDonnell Ranges to see the bigger picture. (Ooh, the last one was a little ambitious.)

Darwin delights

Darwin is named after Charles Darwin, as you will probably know, and is nearer to Jakarta, capital of Indonesia, than it is to the national capital, Canberra. It was the commander of HMS *Beagle*, John Clements Wickham, who in 1839 named the arrival port of his ship Port Darwin, having had Charles Darwin, the public father of the theory of evolution, aboard on two previous voyages. In 1869 the growing settlement above the escarpment here was named Palmerston after the then British prime minister and was finally renamed Darwin, like its port, in 1911.

23 January 2019. The location of our accommodation, The Adina Apartment Hotel, away from the bustle of the town, means the whole area is peaceful and safe for children to run around. There are privately owned apartments all around, and members of the public, along with their lovely dogs, as well as visitors enjoy the bars and restaurants in this inclusive area. Our room is blessed with a fine view over the area and the estuary towards the Timor Sea and, best of all, a BATH. I was into that welcoming receptacle approximately 15 minutes after shutting the room door, and I lost count of the number of soaks I had in our five-day stay.

The Ghan trip included a half-day coach tour of the town with Warren, a quietly spoken, kind-natured man, the sort that makes me feel pleased for his partner. He talked interestingly and almost continually while driving us all around Darwin, perfectly safely.

Within a few minutes of being aboard not only had we seen a few wallabies but the rain started to come down; it was the first day of the monsoon. Warren released us into the Darwin Aviation Museum (raised spectacularly around a B-52 bomber which has eighteen civil and military aircraft nestling under her ample wings) for an agreed period of time. The noise of the rain on the metal roof rendered conversation impossible and was far louder than the recorded sound of the 1974 Christmas Eve Cyclone Tracy when she hit the city with devastating force. Darwin has been flattened four times in recent history: three times by cyclones and again during a Japanese air raid in 1942. But like the phoenix she rises from the devastation every time.

The next morning was heralded in under a pretty mother-of-pearl sky, and we had to be up and ready by 6.30 am for our visit to Kakadu National Park.

Wonderful wetlands in Kakadu National Park

We were fortunate once again to have an intelligent and engaging driver/guide for our day of adventure to and around Kakadu, a world heritage site and Australia's biggest national park.

25 January 2019. Michael is an animal lover and is mortified every time we come across roadkill. "I just hate to see that," he says as we pass a decomposing wallaby, "but it's an inevitable part of our pace of living, isn't it, guys? If we drive, we sometimes kill." I so agree; it is so sad.

There were lots of very shy, pretty mid-brown agile wallabies around too, of which Michael spoke affectionately.

"I used to have one as a pet, and he was a good pet and loved buttered toast. Sometimes he would disappear for a few days then return and hop onto my bed as if to say, 'Come on then, get up, I have something to show you!'"

Finally, we arrived for our trip on the Yellow Water Billabong with Dennis, another fulsome character: "That's Dennis with two Ns because that's how you spell Dennis."

'Dennis with two Ns'

As we slid along the water towards the billabong towards South Alligator River beyond, we had to pass through a small channel. "Prepare yourselves, ladies and gentlemen, we're going into this small channel, and people on the outside may experience branches."

A comedic "ooooh" came from some of us gathered.

"Goomagen is our name for the freshwater crocodile, which grows to three metres long. Say 'Goomagen'."

(My spelling.) We all obliged. "Ginga is the much bigger saltwater crocodile. Say 'Ginga'." Again, we obliged.

"The little Goomagen can escape from the Ginga by slipping between the Melaleuca paperbark trees. In the dry season Ginga sit on the walkways waiting for one of our creators, the Rainbow Serpent, to come through. The Rainbow Serpent flies along the rivers, gorges, streams and creeks. He doesn't like loud noises or crying, that's what we were always told as kids, or it would take you away, the old people would say."

A general tone of agreement and understanding followed.

"We're going in between two paperbark Melaleucas at the end of this channel now."

In their uneven and peeling bark, they towered above us, raising our gaze as we emerged to see a goshawk circling and a group of black-and-white magpie geese gliding over the billabong ready to land.

The area opened out to a wide vista of lush shiny green floating reed and lilies, dotted with trees that withstand being partly submerged for half the year. In the branches of one a black cormorant stood, his wings outstretched.

"He's showing you the size of his last catch," Dennis explained to the delight of the group.

In the far distance were umbrella-canopied kapok trees that stood majestically above and behind the rest; the first we had seen since our journey on the Ecuadorian Amazon.

The lily leaves are totally waterproof. "Women use them to line their dillybags when they are carrying water from the creeks. Lily roots are really good bush tucker."

On our coach journey back to Darwin, Michael told us about how some clans were run by women, and those were always civilised and well organised, and they "forged successful ways", which ensured their survival.

A spell at home

After a few days mooching around Darwin at our own pace and swimming around the harbour/lagoon inside the crocodile barrier, and a final bath (of course), we were ready for our flight home.

Worry not, dear reader, we are getting near to sailing away!

Back in Dorset after spells in Oakham, Scotland and Norway, material for another tome, our few remaining days before returning to New Zealand were spent walking along the lovely beaches and through the fabulous countryside with Gary, Emily, Henry and Ruby.

At the time, in April 2019, a year seemed a long time to wait before we would see them again. Little did we know then it would be over two years because while Covid did not delay *Zoonie's* progress, it did stop us from flying home.

Chapter 5

Our Voyage Home Finally Begins!

Preparing to leave New Zealand

15 May 2019. Rob and I volunteered to take some school uniforms and games kits up to Vanuatu for a post-disaster trust, set up when Cyclone Pam hit the small island nation on 13 March 2015. We will deliver them to the SHARM Foundation in Luganville, for distribution to local schools, and maybe establish a nice connection with some Vanuatuan folk. Our American friend Gail from yacht Cetacea, moored near us in Whangarei, helped us bring three big boxes to Zoonie in her car, and they now occupy the forward heads.

Andrew in Vanuatu Immigration is happy to receive our photographed inward documents and wishes us a safe sail north to them.

We can now allow ourselves to feel excited — we are really homeward bound. We will head north to Vanuatu, in a similar direction as last season to Fiji, but this will only take about ten days, and we won't be returning to New Zealand.

From Vanuatu we hope to explore New Caledonia before setting off westwards to Bundaberg on the east coast of Australia. Then southwards to Tasmania, for Christmas with Ken and Bron of yacht *Nichola*, whom you will meet soon.

More westwards for the crew of Zoonie then, transiting Australia's south coast to Western Australia, including the Bight, just as Merv had suggested. We'll be inching nearer to home with every mile covered.

I always feel a mix of fear and yearning to be back at sea. I think the fear is not so much of what might happen to us, because that would make me fearful of every day of my life, but instead the anxiety seems to be lodged in the period leading up to departure, because as soon as we are back at sea we settle into our happy routine, the three of us taking on the oceans in a mental state of preparedness, respect and interest. And the more we do that, the more I remember past successful passages and how we coped with the challenges and how trustworthy Zoonie is under extreme situations.

This was the start of the second half of our odyssey, and we were certainly ready for more lovely people and great places and, of course, SAILING!

20 May 2019. Tomorrow night we'll be at anchor in peaceful Urquharts Bay, making sure the watermaker works and the batteries charge OK, and just easing ourselves away from all that has been dear to us here over the past two and a half years. But for now it's a final evening with Jeannie and Merv.

This morning we came across seven little blue penguins in two separate groups while making our way to Marsden Cove Marina, and after securing Zoonie on her berth we've just spent the afternoon wandering over familiar ground along the beach to One Tree Point, to the sound of paddling seagulls, calling oystercatchers and a flock of white spoonbills sifting the waterline sand with side-to-side movements of their bills. There were many kingfishers busy feeding too.

Weather-wise, there was a system whizzing around to the north; it gave the yachts at anchor in North Minerva Reef a stormy night as it moved slowly to the east. Another low then crept up the Tasman Sea, and when it passed North Cape, we looked to leave for the distant shores of Vanuatu.

14 June 2019. We are now over halfway to Luganville on Espiritu Santo, Vanuatu's largest island and our landfall, so we can clear in. The island is in the north of the group, so most of our onward cruising will be to the south before we cross to New Caledonia and then Australia, once more.

Two wandering albatrosses and their shearwater chums kept us company for a long way, their flight in contrast: the deceptively easy gliding of the albatross pair to the occasionally stiff-winged flapping of the shearwaters. They also glide but look to me as if they are constantly practising to be like their big companions.

The wind was on the rise, so two reefs went into the genoa and, in gratitude, Zoonie showed a max speed this morning of 8.2 knots. By now we had attracted five albatrosses, and on reading the bird book I discovered that many species of smaller albatross, mollymawks, show fatal interest in longline fishing boats; maybe there is a little hope for them and their survival. (It is depressing to think their fate rests in the hands of greedy and often illegal commercial fishing. I vote, I subscribe, I sign to help NGOs, like many others, but will it save them?)

The wind maxed at 30 knots with a rough sea and breaking wavetops. *Zoonie* was sailing parallel to the waves, rising as each one passed beneath her and just occasionally falling off one with a crash. It was white-knuckle progress.

Noon marked the apogee with the blow soon moderating to a pleasant 20 knots. Still *Zoonie* sped onwards, as if she sensed our need for speed, while Rob and I sheltered below, grabbing what sleep we could.

The next day:

15 June 2019. The wind is below 20 knots, so we have sneaked a little more genoa out, but it was a struggle: a combination of a new genoa shape on the forestay and possibly an accumulation of salt in the drum. Usually, the wind pulls it out, but Rob had to crank hard on the winch after his inspection of the drum revealed no particular problem. It is much easier now, just needed some exercise, I guess, the genoa drum as well.

The wind is doing exactly what it says on the computer screen, and we are optimistic Zoonie and Henry will soon be reunited with their old friend the Diva, the cruising chute.

16 June 2019. Bliss. There's 8–10 knots of wind behind the beam out there, so the Diva fills her lungs giving us 5.4 knots of speed, and now for elevenses. This brings back happy memories of our Pacific crossing when the blue-frocked Diva pulled us across thousands of miles in comfort, taking the roll and letting Zoonie stay nice and steady. Can you love a particular sail from a yacht's wardrobe? We do.

By now *Zoonie* was above 30° S and beyond the full effects of any lows tracking from the Tasman Sea across the top of New Zealand, which were now well and truly behind us.

I so much prefer the gentle ride and efficiency of the Diva compared to goose-winging the genoa and main out either side, both held rigid with the boom and genoa pole and preventers, passing all the discomfort onto the hull. The Diva just flies high like a kite and moves from either side to counteract the roll of the hull. It takes 20–28 knots of wind

Rob prepares the yellow 'Q' flag for our health check

to get 6–7 knots of speed from goose wings but just 7–12 knots to achieve the same speed from the Diva.

I was making notes by moonlight as the Diva swayed from side to side until in the early hours she collapsed and then filled and banged taught, straining her seams. Was that a one off or a warning? She collapsed again, and Rob and I shot up and snuffed her into her bag and dropped her back into her dressing room, the fo'c'sle, for a well-earned rest. All on her own she had given us 100 miles in 15 hours.

By early evening we were 39 miles from the Tropic of Capricorn, 23° 30′ S, so very nearly back in the tropics and lovely warmth. I asked Neptune when he was going to send us the SE trades; he told me to be patient.

20 June 2019. The moon rose early in an orange glow in the east and lit up the night sky. A little spider had ambitiously started spinning a circular web between the aerial post and Hydrovane, and it shone like a CD in the moonlight with the spider in the middle, waiting.

Just before 5.00 am the wind was great for sailing: 10–17 knots just off her stern. A little too much for the Diva, but the new genoa was giving us a constant 6 knots plus, so that was good, and we can relax below.

We spend the morning passing Aneityum (prev. Anatom), the first inhabited island in the 84-island archipelago, all dark and moody in the distance. I wonder what the villagers are up to.

A few metres above us, frigate birds hover menacingly over a flock of sooty terns fishing below, ready to steal their catch. Terns show no interest in us, and they have to be careful not to encounter the sea for too long as their plumage becomes waterlogged. They have to sleep on the wing, imagine that, and young terns can spend the first three years of their lives at sea until they are old enough to breed.

Sooties are also known as wideawake terns because of the incessant deafening cacophony of noise they make on their breeding colonies at night, no doubt catching up on all the gossip. So, they go to sea to get some sleep!

That night we had a visitor who sat on the end of the boom for a rest.

Boobies can grip rope with their webbed feet; they just hadn't done so on *Zoonie* before. It was a male brown booby bird, as only they have blue faces.

Another took up position behind the top of the mast, perching on part of the wind direction indicator, which I later found on the side-deck. Not a big problem because we rely on the central pointed arm which was still intact.

All down *Zoonie*'s starboard side the next day were conical volcanic atolls and flatter 'lava flow' islands. Slowly *Zoonie* was climbing further up the chain in the direction of Espiritu Santo and specifically its main town, Luganville. But first we had to navigate through the Selwyn Strait in the middle of the night.

From the eye of a blue-footed booby bird in flight, a group of the northern Vanuatuan islands together create a ring around a large bay. Starting on the southwest is Malakula. (The island is so named after some clan members got French sailors to sit down on some nice furry leaves and then proceeded to get them drunk on kava because they wanted to get rid of them. When they sobered up, the sailors discovered the leaves contained a strong skin irritant, so they ran around yelling "mal au cul" (pain in the arse). Love it.)

To the east is Ambrym, which has the Selwyn Strait lying between it and the thin, north to south, Pentecost island. North again and joined with a subterranean link to Pentecost is Maewo island of a similar shape, and west of that, Ambae with its live and very active volcano. (Not that the booby knows the names, of course.) Its caldera glows orange, and our booby avoids flying over it. It made UK news not so long ago when all the inhabitants had to be evacuated twice because of dangerous eruptions. West again is Espiritu Santo and to the south Malo island, north of 'Pain in the Arse' island.

As the booby looks around, he clearly sees the islands in the moonlight, the water shimmers between them, and white lights, some along the shores and others further up the slopes, gradually go out as the night progresses, the kava sessions finish and sleep time ensues.

But wait, spies the bird, there is something in the water between two of the islands. A tiny vessel making a dead-straight wash with just one little sail flying at the front. Two people are moving around in the middle of the craft. "I think I'll go and take a look; maybe I can rest a while and relieve myself." And so, when we came to change sails, we found the entire mast base area, the deck and one big front window were covered with stinky white guano that was beginning to stick stubbornly in place.

Dawn spreads its watery light, and the booby admires the pale blue sail flying off the front of the boat as it rocks very gently from side to side sending both the people on board into restful sleeps, at different times, of course. The booby bird, feeling much lighter and decidedly hungry, flies off to join its buddies for some fishing.

Zoonie is on rails again, the islands protecting the 'bay' from the effect of the trade winds on the water. The blue sail has gone, and a white sail is poled out with a little of the white sail behind the mast too, for balance. A perfect run across the bay.

First landfall

The end of the crossing was in sight now. The gap between where a long, flat tree-covered shoreline changed to a lighter shore in the further distance was where we turned left into the Segond Channel. Just another six miles or so to go to our anchorage beyond the town, into a little bay where we dropped the hook into sand and mud at nine metres' depth. We had covered 1,247 miles in ten days, one and a half hours and used 91 litres of fuel on our return voyage so far.

23 June 2019. There are only three of us in the anchorage off a pretty resort near Luganville, and we must stay on board until we have been visited by Customs and Immigration sometime tomorrow. I sent the inward papers from New Zealand and they replied, so they know we are coming, and now we're here!

Tomorrow night is the start of the week's markets, held on Monday, Tuesday, Thursday and Saturday, and we will be there with bells on. I can't wait to get my hands on some nice papaya again.

Andrew – a friendly face of officialdom

I should have twigged when Andrew signed off the VHF with the words "You can come and pick me up" that he was coming by road and would need a lift to *Zoonie*. Soon a uniformed figure was leaning against a palm tree on the resort frontage, so Rob and I dashed through the process of unpacking and inflating the dinghy and lowering the motor onto the stern in a quarter of the normal leisurely pace.

I didn't know until he stepped aboard and introduced himself that he was the chap who replied to my email from New Zealand enclosing the inward papers and wishing us a safe voyage.

"Would you like some water?" I asked.

"Do you have any coffee? I haven't had any breakfast."

So, while he tucked into his daddy-bear-sized bowl of porridge, Arnott's Kingston choccy biscuits and a mug of coffee, we chatted.

He told us where to find the immigration office, and 30 minutes later we crossed the bridge over the wide and clean Sarakata River and started to absorb the atmosphere of the busy street. In Luganville

75% of businesses are Chinese owned, leaving just the 24-hour fresh fruit and veg market in Unity Park, the administrative offices, local craft shops and tour operators in local and national ownership. Vanuatu gained independence from a confused mix of British and French governance on 31 July 1980 and is now a republic.

It was lunchtime and we were hungry.

The Natangora Café boasts it is the oldest in town having been around since 1990, and we made for its shady interior for a light but pricy lunch of consommé followed by fish nuggets, rice and salad, washed down with local Tusker beer (£32 for the two of us). The locals looked in but walked on by.

Back along the eastern half of the street we climbed the steps to the immigration office, then just a short distance to go to Customs along a mercifully tree-lined road, giving some shade from the 27°C in the sun. It was nice to see Andrew's friendly face again, and he took our green inward cards and said he would have our Inter-Island Cruising Permit ready for us at some point within the 24 hours before we planned to leave.

So, to the market, where papaya, tomatoes, bok choy and bananas, all in measures of 100 vatu (64 pence), filled our bags and a taxi whisked us back to the resort.

A detour into the lovely cool bar for some Tusker beer (feral boar with double curly tusks) and free WiFi, which extends to *Zoonie* thanks to a boost from the WiFi bat.

A dragging yacht

28 June 2019. Around 8.30 am this morning, a mighty and sudden gust of 29 knots hit our little fleet of, now, nine anchored yachts, bringing with it a mantle of rain and wind, which lasted for the best part of the day. Rob was making his way to the companionway for a look out when he saw a 47-foot Beneteau, which had anchored uncomfortably close the evening before, shoot backwards past us just a few metres away, dragging his anchor. I grabbed the foghorn and gave him a good blast with the hope of getting him on deck at least. Whether he heard it or not I do not know, but eventually he appeared, his vessel having found a new location, this time very close to two other boats.

He was the only one to leave his tender in the water the night before, and we wondered if he even knew the blow was due, even knew when he started dragging, even knew he was aboard a yacht anchored off Espiritu Santo!

The wind eased by this afternoon and we have benefited from the 100% battery charge the Rutland Wind charger had given us, then as the rain continued for a few more hours, Zoonie is now shining in the sunlight from her thorough wash off. Gifts from the skies.

By contrast that night was blissfully calm and the masthead anchor light of another yacht sometimes found its way through our cabin porthole and through my eyelids, illuminating my dreams. The gentlest cool breeze would come over us, and we awoke to the smell of woodsmoke and sodden earth and the usual barking of dogs and cocks crowing. Heaven.

Our taxi driver the next day was a friendly and curious chap; just as well because we had four 20-litre diesel cans to fill. We exchanged questions freely and he complained that although he pays his taxes he doesn't know where the money goes. "Certainly not on the roads!" Sounds familiar.

Later, while decanting the fuel into *Zoonie*'s tanks, Rob spotted a dugong, a sea cow similar to a manatee but with a whale-like fluke unlike the manatees' spade tail. He wasn't the only one we saw.

A short taste of village life

1 July 2019. Lily and her driver are due to collect us in their van at 1.30 pm and take us to her Leweton Cultural Experience for a look into their traditional way of life. So, knowing our time here is coming to an end, we took a walk along the beach this morning, where the locals are fishing and swimming. Swallows by the hundred duck and dive all day long; maybe they are helping keep the mosquito population at bay, because since arriving we have not seen a single one.

On arrival at the village Lily introduced us to her friend, our host, Celia, who prefers the name 'compound' instead of 'village'. "We don't live here, and the area is not big enough to grow any vegetables, so instead we like to go to the market to buy food, where we can meet our friends."

The area is made up of an arena with shaded seating, what used to be mutually exclusive men's and women's communal huts, and a swimming pool for the water music demonstration, all set in neat gardens.

Celia, who was standing in front of her fire, told us she came from Mere Lava, in the Banks Islands group to the north, twenty-eight years ago.

"The hospitals and schools meant we could give our children a better life, and there is a wider choice of food," she said, as she handed us some freshly grated coconut and tasty roasted plantain.

But in exchange for civilisation, they gave up their longevity and the independent purity of their culture. Two sisters sitting opposite us in the women's hut are sixty-five and sixty-one. Their father was still thriving at 102, "because he has never eaten processed food or drunk alcohol. Today our people are dying at a younger age."

These days, when their education in English as well as their own language and other subjects is complete, many of the young people in Celia's village work in and around the town. Often the men come home for supper and then go to one of the many kava bars for a drink in the evening; in the past her people used to only drink kava during ceremonies as part of their tradition and not as a leisure beverage.

In the men's hut we watch the young chief making kava

Kava in the making

from fresh root grated with a limestone from the shore. He squeezes the liquid from the grated root into a cup and then strains it three times through coconut husk matting before diluting it with fresh water. It has a fresher flavour compared to Fijian kava, which is dried before the mixing begins.

Celia leads us back to the arena with her youngest of five children and the other pre-school youngsters who love to take part in the lively dancing by first the women, with us joining in, and then the young men armed with spears; tourism ensures the carrying on of traditions, an uncomfortable and fragile fusion with the modern world!

Last in the bag of cultural delights is the traditional Vanuatu Water Music. The ladies, standing in the pool with cupped hands giving a resonant beat and splayed fingers skimming the water, make a liquid moan, like rubbing a wet finger on a shiny surface. Then there was the slapping and splashing, telling the stories of cascading waterfalls, rain on the roof, thunder, water rippling over pebbles and boiling water. Using water as a percussion instrument, like a military drum, is as novel to us as it is refreshing to the ladies. Water is all-important to these people.

"Without water, peace and unity cannot exist. Water is life," Celia philosophised.

Our visit concluded with the ladies singing a farewell song and then everyone, even Lily's baby, wanted to shake our hands.

During the night we were awoken to the sound of *Zoonie's* standing rigging rattling despite there being no wind; an earth tremor with a magnitude of 7.2 resonated through the area. We waited for any voices or sirens, but fortunately there were none, just dogs, barking their warning.

Northwards from Luganville

2 July 2019. Reef hopping again, just like we had in Fiji, and the passage through the reef was not too difficult, giving 2.2 metres below the keel and comfortably wide. As soon as the water deepened to 20 meters we turned right on Rob's direction and moved gently into the area between two wooded islets. Down went the hook and 60 meters of chain, which I laid out by going slowly astern back the way we had come in. Then when all the required chain was overboard a firm but not too strong burst astern to bury the hook in the sandy lagoon bottom.

With a forecast for strong winds in a couple of days we treated ourselves with the first snorkel of the season and then pondered the need to find a more secure sheltered anchorage. There were copious sea slugs, the 'bêche de mer' of olden days, and pretty pink anemone fish.

We left early the next morning, at the same state of the tide as when we arrived for safety, and headed northwards up the coast to Hog Harbour, a nicely sheltered bay with a small resort on the shore and hire cars parked outside grass huts.

3 July 2019. This time our snorkel revealed recovering coral: one can tell from the soft new coral growth and the presence of feeding fish. It's amazing how every location produces something different. Here we saw some colourful washbasin-sized clams. Within slits in the big, rounded coral heads were their mouths, open until we passed and then snapped shut, with spines around them like (some other) old granny's whiskers. I can only imagine what they looked like if they ever came out of their crevice homes. Hope I never look like that!

While motoring out of the bay the next morning a turtle came along to see us off and a black butterfly flew alongside *Zoonie* on our way to Port Olry, where we have been anchored for the last five days. A single dugong stayed around us all day and every five minutes or so would just break the surface to exhale, swim along a little, take a couple of breaths and then roll forwards for a dive with its tail curving upward just before it disappeared.

Rob and I went for a snorkel and hovered above a giant coral head as another turtle emerged and languorously moved away giving a lovely spell of viewing. There were scrapes along the coral from where the parrotfish nibble specks of food, and familiar barred wrasse and triggerfish, bannerfish, fusiliers and a big pufferfish which constantly changed colour were added to our mental collection. There is a lot of cyclone damage on the reefs, but recovery starts straight after the storm has passed, and we feel we must be optimistic. Poor ni-Vanuatu people, as I have learned they call themselves; if it's not earthquakes and cyclones, it's volcanic eruptions. Their cheery nature is an embedded part of their survival instinct.

The SE trades run hard through these islands, and when new friends Bron and Ken, aboard yacht *Nichola*, who arrived after us, came aboard for their first visit, they reported 40 knots of winds and standing waves just outside our anchorage. We had reefs and islets around us, but it was really the lump of limestone next to us called Thion island that made this anchorage so sheltered and calm.

As the rain poured down, fishermen in their dugouts with outriggers returned after their day of subsistence fishing. At least the rain was warm.

When the weather finally cleared, we carried out our plan to visit the village of Port Olry, about a mile from us.

8 July 2019. Climbing ashore for the first bit of walking exercise since leaving Luganville six days ago, we found a young villager in the shop who sold us a loaf of bread that looked very much like the ones I bake on board. A building brick. Upon my asking, he said the population of the not-so-little village is around 4,000 and growing. It is the second biggest village in Vanuatu.

There is a big school and a college where children are educated right up to university age.

Eleven fishing boats go further offshore than the little dugouts and cast lines astern dropping 250 meters to catch big red fish, poulet (chicken) fish, down in the depths and export it to Port Vila for good prices.

Friendly villagers called greetings from the dark shade of their homes, and a young mum kindly gifted us papayas and limes, cut straight from the trees in her garden, with her mum looking on from the doorway, tending the two young grandchildren. Such kindness remains with me.

Closer to our boats we visited nearby Thion island to hunt for the freshwater lake so Bron and Ken could get some fresh water.

There are cattle there, we noticed, from the very fresh dung oozing around my sandals, and new barbed wire fencing. Cattle ranching is big business on this island for the Vanuatuan economy, and the meat is largely exported to the Japanese, who like its high quality. Clearings provided grass for the cattle, and the lake a source of water.

The lake was easy to find, lying beneath a vertical wall of limestone, and Bron and Ken collect fresh water there regularly now and take a nice dip at the same time.

The wind is still howling, so as to our departure… best hold this space!

Our penultimate day in Port Olry

11 July 2019. Yesterday our little dinghies sped across the blue bay, only slowing down when we entered the narrowing river as we were unsure of the riverbed.

A likely landing place among the waterside jungle of banyan, hibiscus, mangrove and palm was a pretty clearing with the ruin of a home set in a cleared parcel of land above the riverbank. People lived just down the hill in a traditional woven bamboo hut, but this building has concrete walls set with stones, suggesting foreign hands thought they were building it to last. Many such ruins exist from the pre-1980 independence years, and after that year settlers from Australia had to go home, leaving their tropical paradises behind.

The enclosure was fenced, and behind it a small plantation dotted with piles of de-fleshed coconuts told the story of an income at least partly from copra.

Back in our tenders we made our way towards the old wharf, on the beach near the well-spread village, and wandered up past grazing horses to the track. Outside one hut, fresh green woven baskets filled with papayas, breadfruit and bananas were being loaded onto a pickup truck to go to market. A smiling old man came towards Bron and me and gave us each a grapefruit as a gift with a beaming smile. We chatted briefly and shook hands with him and lots of other folk of all ages. Those grapefruit were so sweet they needed no extra sugar.

Punching towards Maewo island

12 July 2019. There were 55 miles between us and the north end of Maewo to the east, and the chunky sea foretold the strength in the wind. Early on we actually managed to fill the reefed genoa and a handkerchief of main with a beam wind for a few minutes before the wind did a backward flip of 90 degrees, to head us, and away went the sails, but not before noticing the seam above the 'O' for Oyster logo on the main had opened completely.

The seam repair we had done in Guadeloupe, having seen the gap during our Atlantic crossing, was only one row of stitching per seam! The sail will have to come off, probably in New Caledonia for repairs, and until then we can use it reefed in to the end of the open seam.

Ken and Bron's *Nichola* is a spirited steel 32-footer, and she gained on us under sail while we were faster under motor, so we were never far apart, until later on during this long day, when we decided to anchor in daylight so we could be a beacon for her to sail towards.

The waves hit *Zoonie* on the starboard bow and she pitched over them and into the troughs, shooting white spume outwards sideways.

We needed to locate *Zoonie* to the left of where a waterfall enters the sea and we would find black sand and mud, but in the failing light, where was the waterfall? We saw a flat area of rock and it looked like water passing over it, so there we laid the anchor and rolled uncomfortably.

Rob was feeling the strain of the incessant strong winds and seemingly no escape from them in what should have been comfortable moorings on the lee (windless) side of the islands. I knew he was deeply saddened to leave New Zealand, for perfectly understandable reasons, and this was just more mental anguish on top.

Two hours later *Nichola*'s steaming lights appeared, and she tucked herself in to shore from us and rolled even more. This all boded for an uncomfortable night ahead and an unhappy hubby on the morrow.

A bite-sized piece of history

Cook spotted Maewo in 1774, but, like French naval officer and explorer Bougainville six years before him, he did not land here. And neither did we; the water was in such turmoil, our first landing on the island would be much further south. Instead we spent an unsettling night at anchor.

The landscape is rugged and narrow, no more than five kilometres across, so not much protection from the trade winds even on the leeward side where we were. Also, with 177 inches of rain each year it is the wettest of the Vanuatuan islands, so few foreign settlers came to live there.

Back to our southward passage

Rob awoke with a thick head, bunged-up nose and feeling hot and sweaty – oh dear, was he going down with something, or was it a lingering problem from his heart issue in New Zealand? I awoke feeling like a well-rolled Havana cigar. We were both keen to get moving.

At the advancing light of dawn, we headed south towards Narovorovo with the hope of a sheltered bay. We were not disappointed; in fact, we were elated. The village area looked like a park, well grazed by the cattle, and the top of the beach was bordered with beautiful mature trees including giant, ancient banyans with their generous shade-giving canopies and mangoes bearing what promised to be a good season of fruit, just not quite ready yet.

Village elder Alfred came down the beach along with a delightful throng of children keen to help with the dinghies. Alfred showed us all around the village, gave us the freedom to stroll where we wanted and introduced us to some of the ladies and young men. The river was not used as drinking water because of the grazing cattle; instead drinking water is piped down from further upstream. The washing is done here, though, with children rubbing clothes against wooden washboards while sitting mid-stream and then drying it by laying it out over the clean, warm volcanic beach stones (pumice), all in the essential spirit of play. Ken and Bron gained permission to do theirs the next day.

The ladies of Narovorovo

14 July 2019. Alfred told us there would be a market around 4.00 pm and we would hear the bell being sounded (long empty gas cylinder, hanging from a tree) when the time was right. But the sound was not forthcoming, so Alfred called to us and waved us ashore.

While waiting, Alfred introduced us to Lilian, a widowed grandmother, who with the help of her granddaughter was preparing the evening meal. The little girl aged about eight was slicing choy by holding it in her hand and using a machete with confidence and precision. I was a little alarmed, but she knew what she was doing. Lilian had peeled taro root and hollowed out the centre, keeping the outer layer to use as a lid. She would then put coconut milk in the hollow, replace the lid and roast the roots until they were cooked through, roasted outside and steamed inside. Sounded delicious.

Close by other young grandchildren were playing on the level concrete surface of the grave of her late husband, Michael, and her son sat on the tomb, grating coconut flesh into a bowl. I was reminded of Fulaga last year, when Jone used to grate punnets of the delicious pure white flesh for us. Happy memories.

Piles of chopped kava root lay drying in the sun ready for their own use and export to the cities.

We cooled our feet in the river, chatting to the girls and learning about which was their favourite subject at school. Rob was relaxing, enjoying the calmer conditions.

Each village is arranged slightly differently in the way they keep their animals. Here the cattle and chickens wander free and keep the grass short and well fertilised, the chickens clearing up the cow dung as they peck around, each hen with her brood of chicks, while the pigs are fenced securely in the coconut plantation behind the village where the men tend the new crop. Copra is big business because of the growing demand for healthy oils, and within the village are lime, lemon, avocado (later in the year), grapefruit and banana trees. What a wealth of delicious, healthy food, just outside their huts.

(This is why I do not think of these people as poor. When we were there, their produce was naturally organic because they do not buy any fertiliser; they didn't need it, having naturally fertile soil, although outside powers are trying to change all that by encouraging the import and use of their chemical products.)

The village homes were laid out in neat rows, and a communal cookhouse and bread oven were in daily use, sending out delicious aromas to where we were anchored. A young villager opened the shop for Bron to buy a few items, and then we went into the meeting room to join some ladies who were also waiting for the market produce to arrive.

I sat down between two ladies and we started chatting. Sarah is a trainee primary school teacher with forty-eight children in her class.

While we talked a young lady offered us cooked crayfish from the river, spread on roasted coconut flesh and topped with coconut cream. It was flavourful. I mentioned to Sarah the items we had brought from New Zealand to give to villagers who might need them. Stationery and writing materials, spectacles, bras and a big bag of clothes.

"There are many old ladies here in the village [of 200] who need glasses," Sarah said. I was relieved and delighted. We arranged to bring them ashore the next day.

After a relaxing, still and restful night, Sunday dawned with the sound of chanting from the Sunday school taking place under a giant banyan tree above the beach. The 'gong' summoned folk to the church service. Sarah was amazed when I told her there were three or four services on our little island in Fiji. "How boring!" she exclaimed at the thought of sitting through more than one service.

She had only been living in her home for three months, and next to it was her mother's old house where she was born and raised.

"The old ladies are keen to try the glasses," she said, and I only hoped they would enrich their lives; what must it be like to have to give up reading because of failing eyesight?

While in her teens her father obtained a job in the government on nearby Ambae, but Sarah left there to return to her birth village when her teacher mother was dying. She clearly loved and missed her mum. Her new home was decorated with all the colourful wall hangings her mother had bought in readiness for Sarah's marriage. On this island marriages are arranged, not always with happy outcomes.

Sarah confided, "I have my two children and my new home and maybe a job, so I am happy." She had a wistful look in her eyes, and I felt for her.

"Nice clothes," she said almost to herself as she slowly went through the bag, and when she came to the stationery, "Ah, good, pencils. The children keep asking me for more because they eat them!" She had prepared a snack of roasted wild yam with coconut cream; it was very welcome and much tastier than pencils!

Sarah loves her teaching job and the children, but the government is delaying making it a formal position. Sarah explained there is much self-interest and nepotism in government and the good jobs go to friends and relatives of the officials, so she is afraid her job might be taken from her. If they do come good for her then much of her income must go to the village funds or she will be shunned. It sounds as if she is between a rock and a coconut palm tree to me.

After she gets back from school, she spends her time making the beautiful pandanus mats we have seen many times before. She weaves in different coloured stems and uses dyed chicken feathers as the fringe. It takes a week to weave a two-by-three-metre mat, and her current one will grace the main room of her new home.

Sarah is the proud owner of the first house in the village to have a solar-powered TV, and in the evenings her main room frequently fills with children watching TV programmes. A lovely, intelligent and forward-thinking lady.

She walked with us back to the beach and called her husband over to meet us before we left.

Light winds to Ambae

15 July 2019. Zoonie's log records winds of 5–8 knots as we follow Nichola across to the little island of Ambae, where the sleeping volcano, Manaro Voui, suddenly awoke from its slumber in September 2017 and again the next year in August 2018. A pyroclastic cloud and toxic fumes forced the 11,000-strong population to scatter to other islands until the activity died down.

We are discovering natural beauty, kind and friendly people, well-groomed villages and lovingly tended gardens wherever we explore. If one or two villages appear to be litter strewn it is packaging from trade products exported to them which they would not have had a use for in the past. The natural compostable rubbish that comes from their home-grown products is either burned on a daily basis or rots down over time, but modern rubbish does not decompose in the same way. If a very few villages appear untidy it is hardly their fault.

We approached two bays on the north-eastern tip of the island and anchored to the right of a high rocky promontory, with plenty of room, in Vanihe Bay. The water was calm and the heavy black sand provided a secure holding, and within minutes both dinghies were in the water ready for our first visit ashore.

The very short journey around the heavily wooded headland to the other bay was awe inspiring. Beautiful mature and healthy trees of many kinds clung tightly to their unlikely bed, and hundreds of fruit bats voiced their disapproval of our motors by wheeling and diving above us, making a terrific screeching din. Satisfied they had made their anger felt, they returned to their upside-down position in a fine-leafed pine tree, their blonde bellies and brown bodies visible against the soft green foliage. As we reached the end of the cliff face crabs of all sizes scurried up the burnt ochre rock. We could see this would be a spectacular place to snorkel.

For fun, really, we lined up the dinghies with the two triangular transits and, leaving the green buoy to starboard, motored cautiously into this new haven. The second pole had lost its triangular topmark, but thoughtful locals had kept the undergrowth at bay and the pole was clearly visible.

Edison and his village friends sat near the quay, and we chatted for a while. He told us 8,000 of the islanders had returned as complete families, leaving 3,000 still abroad, many with children at the high school in Santo. (Luganville, where we had cleared in, is also known as Santo, as is the island it sits on, Espiritu Santo.) He had been back for seven months after his stay in Narovorovo. He gave us permission to walk where we wanted, and we strolled to the well-equipped hospital and spoke with some of the staff there. A desalination plant and small field of solar panels provided by Japan were out of action for need of maintenance and spare parts.

Legends are commonplace in these islands where natural processes are all powerful, and people have created their own explanations for events over which they have no control. One legend concerns the Lombenben volcano, also known as Manaro Voui, and its lakes.

The cultural hero of the island, Tagaro, who is thought to have arrived from Samoa around AD 1400, may well have found inhabitants here already. Carbon dating suggests the Lapita people were in the area before 500 BC. The legend tells how Tagaro removed the volcano from Mount Lombenben and planted it on Ambae, then drowned the three main fiery vents by submerging them in water, the two largest of the three lakes within the caldera representing Lombenben's eyes.

That evening Ken and Bron came to us for supper, this alternating of evenings on each other's boats was becoming a delightful habit. We sat in the cockpit supping gin cocktails when we witnessed one of the most stunning sunsets we had ever seen. The white gold of the sun's body, as it sat for a fleeting moment on the horizon, diffused its golden light across the heavens towards the paling blue sky at the end of its own daytime beauty. On downwards at fiery speed, it seemed, so others far away would witness its glory while its final ageing fuchsia rays changed places with the falling blue. A glorious inversion of colour on the celestial palette, for which there are hardly sufficient words to say.

16 July 2019. We were ashore early, bats allowing, to save the midday hours for a snorkel. The charming lady in the shop came up with fresh eggs but no bananas, so we went on a walkabout up the track leading away from the village and back towards our bay. Back near the shore and laden with a few bananas and coconuts Ken and Rob had plucked from palms near the road, we met a young man helping a little old lady who was clinging for dear life on to her Zimmer frame. Her pretty face revealed a life of struggle which was now replaced by a dependence on her family to look after her, and judging by the tenderness the young man was showing her, she would be alright.

Our first snorkel was around 'Bat Hill', and no sooner had we plopped into the water than Bron and I spotted a ray, with a black-and-white striped tail, lying on the bottom. It was a first for us to skirt the submarine rock of a volcanic cliff, and it was fascinating. Many brightly coloured lichens clung to the rock, and we explored right into one cave, finding grooves carved into the rock, each becoming the home of an urchin. I was relishing Bron's company; we were so alike we thence called each other 'Sis'. I was feeling the warmth of her company, and it was a chance gift.

In the evening it was Bron's turn to delight us with Mexican wraps for supper, but not before Rob announced he would do no more fishing and handed over all his fishing gear to Ken, who was so pleased, he thought Christmas had come early.

"They look so beautiful when we land them but soon lose their magnificent colour because of what we have done," Rob lamented.

I felt his sorrow, and it was unusual for him to be so candid, but he didn't go as far as excluding fish from his diet.

Since the age of seventeen I have been vegetarian, because I didn't want animals to be slaughtered for me. Before we set off in 2015, I chose to eat fish that we caught and killed on the circumnavigation, only because it would be a valuable source of protein for the long weeks at sea. But with plenty of eggs and cheese keeping well on *Zoonie*, I was beginning to want to revert to my previous diet, and this may have influenced his decision.

Asanvari on the southern tip of Maewo island

17 July 2019. Deputy chief Albert strode down the beach to greet us and gave us freedom to wander all around Asanvari, back on Maewo, a sheltered anchorage compared to the one at the northern end.

Was this greeting of us sailors a routine to be found on all the remote Vanuatu and Fijian islands? Or was it the watchful eyes of the locals who were curious about us? And did this agreeable greeting occur the world over? We assumed it was typical of the islands, and I cannot say for the rest of the world; it certainly enriched our experience as independent visitors.

Albert then called over young Martin to lead us through the village to the school area. There were plenty of children around to help with the dinghy as they were on their lunch break. Passing homes along the path, people would call "hello" from the dark interiors, and we saw their crops in different stages of ripeness: papayas, bananas, pineapples and root vegetables, so there is always plenty to eat.

The soil track opened onto the football pitch, where some children joked at Martin with his adult followers, and then we walked between school buildings to the open playground area and surrounding homes. A chance encounter with headmaster Fred gave us the opportunity for a chat while one young boy clung to his leg, maybe his son.

Arriving at Loltong

18 July 2019. Entering the anchorage facing Loltong on Pentecost island, we had to get two triangle-topped marker poles in line with each other, and these were located next to the giant banyan tree, of course! I hadn't expected the further marker to be just behind the nearest one and located in a cave, but we soon spotted them and the reefs on either side of us, between which we safely passed. I do like a challenge!

Although the presence of the reefs broke up any swell such as had made life a little uncomfortable in other places, here the wind rushing down the hill from the Pacific beyond and to the east caused strong gusts in the anchorage, but as the holding was heavy sand, we felt secure enough.

Three weddings, one ceremony

Shortly after our arrival we saw there were three weddings in progress, this being the first day of celebrations before the second ceremonial day, and we were welcome to visit and watch the proceedings. On this island, despite being part of the same mountain chain as Maewo and there being just six miles across the strait separating the two islands, the marriage tradition is quite different. Here couples can choose each other; if the woman does not like her suitor, she can reject him, and vice versa. I wondered if Sarah knew this and whether the difference has happened since her marriage a few years ago and if it will spread to Maewo.

How two different sets of customs could exist so close together seemed strange and suggested little connection between these two islands. Multiple weddings are not common in Vanuatu, and I regret not finding out why this particular triple event was taking place.

When we arrived, there was much fun and joviality ashore with crocodiles of people weaving around the nakamal (communal house), in and out of the doors, and a party was in full swing. Bron was loading two swim boards onto their dinghy. "We haven't used these for ages, and the children will love them."

She was not wrong there; a little lad grabbed one, delighted he had beaten his mates to this prize, and soon two of the lads were whizzing around on them in the shallow water of the bay.

Roger came to meet us on the beach just as a supply ship arrived, lowering its front ramp while it approached the hard, flat sand. Villagers escaped the excitement of the wedding to help unload the fuel drums and building materials, sacks of dried food and boxes of breakfast crackers. Ken wondered why they ate so many breakfast crackers when their fresh bread is so good. We bought a loaf that was still warm and smelled of the wood-burning oven it was cooked in.

It was a lovely, busy day for a walk through the village, where panga-loads of family visitors from other parts of the island were arriving for the celebrations. On the water's edge chunks of meat hung, red and dripping, from trees ready for the hangi ovens the next morning. Inside the big nakamal hut huge pits will be lined with hot stones and the meat (beef and pork – we heard their final squeals that morning), wrapped in banana leaves, will be laid in them and covered with palm fronds and cooked for at least three hours.

We shook hands with a couple about our age, and they turned out to be Roger's parents, Mary and Solomon.

"You met our son Roger on the beach," Solomon said. News travels faster than the internet on these islands!

He explained that today meetings were being held to decide the dowry of the brides and tomorrow would be the ceremony, to which he invited us.

Back on the beach another ship had arrived and two more yachts. We had been the first into the anchorage with *Nichola* following, and now a yacht I recognised, *Mirabella* with her family of four, had anchored near us. She was the yacht we called up as we approached New Zealand last October after that amazing 1,000-mile beam reach. We chatted with André and Eva, his wife, and Amina and Jaël, their two daughters, while clinging on to *Mirabella's* toe rail, on our way back to *Zoonie*. A brief but sweet reunion.

(André and his family are friends to this day.)

Next morning, I was up early making mini scones in the cool of the dawn.

19 July 2019. Ashore we perched on a low form next to Roger to watch the proceedings, having handed my plate of scones to one of the three brides who, along with the other two, was sitting on her pandanus mat with her family and all their worldly possessions in a heap behind her. The brides and older generation ladies looked pretty in their square-necked white-and-blue Mother Hubbard dresses, a common style brought to the islands by the French missionaries. The women like the patterned material, which they can use to make matching garments for the whole family. The dresses have puff sleeves with many pleats in the boddice and full skirts with flaps over the hips allowing a draft to fill them and keep the wearer cool, and the ladies can fling them around as they dance. I wondered where all the traditional grass skirts had gone.

The grooms wore T-shirts and shorts and stood holding the pig pole at the end of their row of squealing porkies. If one could bring back ancestors from the past just for this occasion, what would they think? Not that there was any lack of colour, just the noticeable absence of traditional clothing.

There were three rows of ten pigs of various size, colour and shape, all in different moods ranging from snoring to disgruntled fighting, along with finely woven and purple-dyed pandanus mats, gifts for the new homes. Many of yesterday's celebrants were looking a little the worse for wear after

Blessing the wedding gifts

a lengthy session on the kava, and today the atmosphere had taken on an almost solemn tone.

An elder gave the grooms their talking to, in front of the gathered audience, about how to behave towards their new wives and how they could no longer rely on their parents as they were now a family themselves. Then all the guests wove around the three rows of pigs and mats, giving their blessings to the couples by touching each bristly hide and fine weave. All the while the smell of cooking meat and taro came from the big hut.

Jacob came from a traditional village two kilometres away, Labultamata, and explained how he had chosen his wife after falling in love with her. Disputes between couples were settled by the chief and his council, and he inferred that in free-choice marriages divorce was not allowed. Does this mean that in arranged marriages it is allowed? The laws were complex, and I was only just beginning to understand them.

These snippets of cultural protocol, freely given, enriched our experience of Vanuatu, and I so hoped they could hold tight to their beliefs and practices despite the intrusion of the modern world.

All was quiet ashore that night, and there were few lights on as the four of us tucked in to our supper on *Zoonie*.

Down the western side of Pentecost

20 July 2019. "We'll catch you up; I'm going to try for fish now I have enough line," Ken said as we moved out of Loltong Bay, back down our black chart plotter line and into a silky-smooth ocean.

"I've caught one, a nice big poulet for our tea!" Ken's jubilant voice rang over the VHF. "Don't know how much line went out, but it was over 200 metres." And that was just outside the bay!

It was a calm, almost cloudless day; a reprieve from the fresh trades that were tiring and irritating in equal measure. Behind every sandy beach along the coast were settlements and thin plumes of smoke ascending as the villagers cooked, baked and cool burned the shrubbery.

Flying fish spun away from us, the oceans' mini fighter planes. They emerge from the water, tap it hard with their tails while their 'wings' are slanted, and then when sufficiently elevated to glide, they level their bodies and their 'wings' and they're off. What we take as an amusing sight is, in fact, their escape from a predator – on this occasion, us.

Passing a jungle headland, we came into Batnavni Bay, still offshore from Pentecost island, where a herd of six spinner dolphins showed us where it would be best to anchor.

An hour later Ken and Bron arrived, and we went ashore to explore the sprawling village that was gearing up (actually, tidying up) ready for the Independence Day celebrations on 30 July.

Ken brought ashore a coral trout with massive eyes he had caught, and as it was so big, too big for the four of us, he offered it to a young lad.

"Go on, take this to your mum, and tell her you caught it off the beach." The lad understood the joke and dashed off with his prize in a carrier bag. We wish we'd been there!

Young Susan came forward to greet us and introduced us to her mum, who opened her shop. Susan then sent her husband off to collect some coconuts and papayas, which we loaded onto the dinghies having made payment.

Susan's family ran out of money, so she was unable to finish her studies, but her brother is at university in Beijing learning Chinese history and hopes to work in the diplomatic service in the Vanuatu Embassy there.

We were on a mission to find another shop for any edible produce and found one which belonged to very friendly Ben. He introduced us to his wife and friend Brian, who was sitting in the shade of the shop veranda watching his mobile phone screen.

"Come and look at this," he beckoned, so Ben hastily brought together enough chairs, and we sat and chatted while some young children watched. Brian had retired from a career in teaching followed by a government ministerial position, and he was very concerned about the growing foreign presence in Vanuatu. Not the all-pervasive retail presence in the shopping areas of the big towns but the massive financial loans given to the Vanuatu government for the building of the vast new customs compound in Luganville, on the first island we had visited, Espiritu Santo, and also the sports complex in Port Vila where the government cannot afford the cleaning and electricity bills.

He showed me an interview between a government minister and a British journalist who asked such questions as "Why were these places built?" and "How is the government going to pay the loan back, and could there be a strategic reason for the buildings?" The government minister could not, or did not dare, provide an answer.

The Luganville customs compound and substantial wharf is adjacent to an area of water large enough for a fleet of ships. Brian suspected a foreign government might have designs on taking over at least one island in the area for its own use, and he feared for the future of the young children who were listening to our conversation.

On returning to the dinghy, we found some bananas from the family of the little boy who had presented them with 'his catch' and escaped back to *Zoonie* to relax: to sit a while and watch the dolphins, a dugong and two turtles around the boats.

The night turned out to be the mother of roly nights, and at 2.50 am I had to break up the romance between the two wine bottles waltzing on the galley floor.

21 July 2019. The tiring boisterous trades have re-established themselves with gusts of 20 knots from nothing pushing us around as the seventh hour approached, and we were relieved to get underway once more, 17 miles down the coast to Homo Bay.

We entered Homo Bay and motored right across to the other side, following *Nichola* in for a change as they had been here before.

Rob was getting weary of the strong winds, and they were affecting his enjoyment of the whole Vanuatu experience; that and his reluctance to leave New Zealand combined to darken his mood for a number of months.

Our fruitful search for a calm anchorage

Back underway the next day, as we moved across the Selwyn Channel (through which we had passed on our way to clear in to Luganville), despite everything, it was pleasant to be making progress under reefed genoa again, sailing and watching *Nichola* making strides ahead of us.

Predictably the wind was gusting to 27 knots at times, as it funnelled through the strait, but we thought it was starting to die down as we came into what we hoped would be the lee of Ambrym island at the beginning of a long day of testing out FOUR anchorages for comfort and secure holding, all to no avail. We should have been relaxing in sheltered places in the lee of the islands, but the pesky wind just reached right around the shores of the little islands, disturbing all chances of peaceful anchorages in its path.

Finally, and with a degree of desperation because of the advancing hour, we decided to try Craig Cove. *Zoonie's* anchor dug well into the black sand opposite the big market building. At last, this bay was pretty, sheltered and very CALM!

Volcanic Ambrym – a misnomer?

Somewhere off this rocky bay in August 1774, on his second voyage of discovery, Captain Cook ordered his men to drop the *Resolution's* anchor, having previously visited the islands of Erromango and Tanna to the south. He reportedly had a brief communication with a group of natives apparently from another race (lighter skin and finer features typical of the Melanesians of Papua New Guinea) who came out from the land in numerous outrigger canoes.

They offered him yams, saying "am rem", meaning 'your yams', and as they ate theirs, they said "ama rem", meaning 'my yams'. Cook may have thought this was a good enough name for the island or thought they were saying the name of the island itself; either way that was how the name Ambrym came about.

His log tells of the coastal scenery being 'most luxuriant', and it still is. A tropical jungle of mixed foliage looks magical as it sways in the breeze. Cook considered his survey of the group to be complete here and next headed towards New Zealand, but we decided to stay a little longer before heading south to Epi and then Port Vila on Efate island.

We went ashore as a foursome for the last time, knowing that Ken and Bron were planning to move on the next day and our company cruise would be at an end. Our sorrow over our parting was assuaged as we were already looking forward to seeing them again in Australia where they had invited us for Christmas, handily for us en route to our planned sail westwards to Western Australia.

A group of women were trying to unblock a water pipe in the village; one lady was pushing the piston pump up and down while another had made a hole in the pipe (!) and was trying to extract the black rotted mass from inside. Ken went to the pump tray and started to push his palm down on the mesh over the drain outlet, when suddenly clear water started gushing out of the hole. Cheers of jubilation soon stopped when it blocked again. The pipe must have been broken where it went underground.

Happy trucks of local youngsters bounced along the earth tracks; they smiled and waved at us as they passed.

24 July 2019. At Ken o'clock (6.35 am) this morning we watched as Ken and Bron had to work together to clear their anchor from around a rock and make their way west towards Malekula island. They are heading in the long term to Luganville to clear out and then to Cairns on the east coast of Australia.

We have been watching the weather, and tomorrow we will leave, if only to make progress south.

Chapter 6

Alone Again in Vanuatu

South to Epi island

---

25 July 2019. At 6.20 am this morning, Zoonie poked her bow out into the trade winds once more, but this time they maxed at 20 knots, according to the log. Unfortunately, because of our heading, towards the wind, Zoonie could not sail, and since the autopilot was on strike again, we took turns at the helm. Twenty knots of wind we couldn't use was so frustrating. Mercifully for us lazy helms folk, the journey was only 26 miles and the experience was pleasant with warm winds, blue skies and a bluer sea beneath.

I relaxed back, leaning against the cockpit coaming and sitting on a comfy cushion, while my right foot rested at the bottom of the wheel and occasionally made a little steering correction. I watched the confused sea state and took the odd photo.

Motoring *Zoonie* gently through the channel and reefs between Lamen Bay and Lamen island just off Epi we could see three moored yachts in the distance, in what turned out to be an expansive bay with a very gently shelving seabed. A familiar shape caught my eye as a manta ray leapt from the water to our right and did a spectacular flip, and as soon as we were at anchor two turtles came to inspect us. I liked this place already, and the animals lifted our spirits.

Numerous fires smoked in and around the village. Like the Aboriginal people, they do cool burns every day to keep the undergrowth around the trees clean and short and to control the mosquito population that carries malaria and dengue fever. Despite visiting many villages, we only came across mosquitos and their bites in the capital, Port Vila.

Epi's colonial decline started during the global depression of the 1930s and was followed by a number of catastrophic cyclones affecting business and trade and then finally concluded with Vanuatu's independence in 1980.

Another brief history for you

Let's go back in time to the late nineteenth century, when many Europeans, especially the French, arrived and the fight for land started. Cattle stations and coconut plantations were set up, pushing locals off their land, and Australia became fearful that Epi would become an annex of France, making their own access limited. So, in 1878 an Anglo-French agreement, which lasted for a century, was established to prevent this happening.

The settlers thrived at the expense of the ni-Vanuatu, who died from diseases and the effects of the introduced alcohol. The locals' chances of working on the plantations were limited as many French plantation owners imported cheap labour from the blackbirding trade.

One of the worst incidents of this cruelty happened at the hands of Epi resident Dr Murray who owned the labour ship the *Carl*. Well, about ninety villagers in canoes were enticed alongside the *Carl* with the offer of trading goods. Dr Murray ordered their canoes to be sunk beneath them. Some escaped but most of the survivors were brought aboard his ship and locked below.

For two nights a battle raged as the captives tried to escape using their bunks as battering rams, only to be met with pistol fire from Murray and his men. On the fourth morning the remaining survivors were ordered to the deck, and, miraculously, five were uninjured, nine were slightly wounded but sixty were dead. Then a historic cover-up quickly took place, with the whitewashing of the ship after an inspecting officer from HMS *Rosario* failed to notice the injuries on the remaining captives and the bullet-damaged quarters.

Despite this hideous secret eventually reaching Sydney, justice was not done as Murray escaped, avoiding a trial, and his two fellow murderers were acquitted, following a public outcry over them being charged, let alone convicted. Morale among the islanders at that time must have been lower than the low tide.

Epi – our last remote island stopover

The village at Lamen Bay on Epi is called Vaemali, and the island is the first and last stop out of Port Vila on Efate for cruising yachts travelling north and south respectively.

The sunset over Lamen Bay was beautiful, and small outrigger canoes were a long way out to sea as darkness fell, catching fish on lines. Each day islanders come across the bay from little Lamen island to Vaemali for work and school, and in the olden days they would sail home in the evenings in their dugouts using freshly picked banana leaves as sails to catch the island-filtered trade winds. That must have been a pretty sight. I saw an old photograph in the museum in Port Vila of one such dugout sailing home; it was such a romantic image.

26 July 2019. As the dinghy touched the sand at Vaemali on Epi in the late afternoon, Thomas took our dinghy painter and introduced himself as the chief, and then we met his wife, who brought us the most beautiful hand of perfect bananas in exchange for our gift of a coil of rope. He showed us the shop and gave us freedom to wander where we wanted.

A little further along we chatted with Charlie, a retired teacher, whose tottering grandchild clung to his trousers for support. Charlie also is worried about the ulterior motive of the massive Chinese investments in the region. He commented how his fellow islanders have struggled since the British left. "The French, they took from us, but the British gave us a way to live."

In fairness, the French did expand their cuisine, bringing grapefruit as a crop, referred to here by the French name pamplemousse, and the delicious white French bread and croissants that add to the enjoyment of food for modern ni-Vanuatu and us visiting sailors.

We knew these would be our last meetings with local villagers, and we were savouring each one. In fact, this would be our final encounter with the natural and unpretentious Pacific islands, which we had enjoyed so much, from the Marquesas to Vanuatu, over the previous three years. We would miss them but take with us such happy memories.

The next day saw us sitting out a blow with five other yachts, our plans for a 'Ken' departure gone with the wind. I worked on my Ambae blog and baked a cake. The constant pressure of the trade winds and the messy sea state are certainly a challenge for the cruising yacht. Perfect if the vessel is shooting through south to north, but a different story if a cruising circuit is involved.

I listened as wind started easing to gusts and broached the subject of a night crossing over the 80 or so miles to Port Vila, the capital of Vanuatu on Efate.

Rob prefers to avoid night watches on short passages, but for us to arrive tired at a new port with falling light after a day of sailing is not a sound idea, whereas arriving at first light in the morning, having had at least a few hours of sleep, makes better sense to me. Also, cool night-time sailing avoids the heat of the sun and allows for the potential, at least, of some rest.

28 July 2019. Fortunately, Rob agreed, so we will leave at 5.00 pm today to arrive the day before the Independence Day celebrations.

Zoonie's good effort to Efate

Zoonie quickly turned what had been an uneasily anticipated passage, what with the state of the main, into a thoroughly enjoyable one, and I fell in love with her all over again for it. The main was reefed because of the split seams, but the foresail was reefed also, to keep her speed down to 5 knots, even though we know *Zoonie* does not like being slowed down, so we would arrive in daylight at the waypoint we had placed off the peninsula, where we would turn for the harbour of Port Vila.

She rolled along, nicely close-hauled and just to the right of our desired course, and the sea was reassuringly comfortable, suggesting there were only light to moderate winds out there. The night sailing was proving to be a steadier option than daytime, when diurnal wind patterns become established around and over the islands, to do with the difference in air temperature over the sea coming into contact with the warming land temperatures; at night the temperatures are more equal.

Zoonie tucked 50 miles under her sailing belt before the wind turned to face her and said, "No more by that means, lady," so on went the engine, and we furled the jib at 3.30 am.

29 July 2019. Helming, steering by hand, was a pleasure under the starlit sky in the cool of the night, and dawn started chasing away the dark around 5.30 am. The channel is well marked because container ships and cruise liners use this port, and nearing the shore I spotted what appeared to be a massive quarantine buoy. We knew the anchorage was anywhere immediately around it, but I hadn't expected such a big, bright orange buoy at least 27 feet across, until we got a little closer and saw it was an all-orange yacht! I don't know if I could live on a vessel where everywhere you looked was orange. The actual quarantine buoy is a tiny yellow pillar buoy.

We anchored temporarily on coral, not a secure holding at the best of times, and with the promise of moderate winds in a couple of days we were not happy. The alternative was to pick up one of the many substantial Yachting World Marina buoys at £10 per day on the other side of a shallow reef, for total peace of mind, and a few hours later that was what we did with a little help.

The kind lady on their radio said that Moses would be waiting to give us a hand with the mooring, so we motored gingerly into the lagoon between pretty Iririki Island and the town, through a little channel over the reef where Zoonie's echo display recorded a butt-clenching drop in figures, in metres: 28, 23, 17, 14, 9, 6, 3, 1.9, 1.2, 1.1!!! The depth reads from the keel down, which makes sense as that's the part of her that would touch first, so we really had 3.1 metres from water level. As we passed over this pale green stretch, I was watching the decreasing numbers at the same time as our progress towards the deeper blue water; that helped.

Rob sorted out the two mooring lines to go through the rope loop Moses held up while I kept *Zoonie* nosing into the mooring as best as I could, and in a matter of moments, we were secure amidst the loveliest birdsong.

The delights of Port Vila

The first great pleasure of the archipelago's main hub was, of course, the Independence Day celebrations in Independence Park. On 30 July 1980 Vanuatu shook off the shackles of British and French rule, and many of the ni-Vanuatu residents have had mixed feelings over the issue ever since. Many older folks are worried that the new independence has brought the vulnerability of exploitation by foreign countries more powerful than this small archipelago can cope with. The young have limited opportunities because of lack of investment in education and careers and a small job market, and they feel frustrated as a result.

Their path to full independence is paved with sharp rocks, and I wonder how free of outside foreign aid they can ever be with the frequent natural disasters they have to deal with.

We walked slowly up the hill beside the parade ground with the crowd, looking for a spot where we could view the proceedings, and came to a TV van that was recording the event. In front of it was a gap, so we stood next to seated folk as dignitaries stood to make their speeches and army officers very slowly raised the Vanuatu flag.

Back down the hill at the bottom of the park all the food and trinket stalls were laid out and we could have bought anything from burgers and chips to lap lap and rice. Lap lap is the national dish and is made from grated manioc (cassava), taro or yam roots, staple crops of the area, just as we grate potatoes for hash browns. The gratings are squeezed to a doughy paste, laid on wild spinach leaves and soaked with coconut milk then topped with either meat, flying fox bat flesh or seafood, wrapped in banana leaves and cooked amongst hot stones in one of their ground ovens. We tried some topped with crayfish and it was delightful.

Edgar's soft voice of welcome

It was a good workout up another hill towards the Vanuatu National Museum, and we were grateful of its shady interior, a reprieve from the humid heat outside.

Instantly we were submerged in ancient traditions. Men commonly used to wear a namba (penis sheath) in ancient times on Malekula island (remember the 'mal a cul' (pain in the arse) French soldiers). The namba custom has now largely died out except in a couple of isolated villages in the south of the island.

Although we didn't visit, we were relieved for the local population to learn that cannibalism also died out in the 1960s on Malekula, but evidence of another tradition can still be seen.

A few old people have extended skulls, after their heads were bound when they were babies. The centre of a person's being was thought to be in their brain, so by 'stretching' the cranial cavity it was thought the person would achieve greater intelligence.

5 August 2019. I was leaning over a glass table containing shells upstairs in the museum when I heard the soft voice of the curator, Edgar, say, "I am about to start a little cultural show in a moment, if you would like to join us."

Well, that's like offering a dog a bone to me, so I scuttled after him back down the stairs, making a note of where to resume my gazing.

On the floor was a large shallow wooden tray covered in a thin layer of sand. Sand drawings, I thought, great, a treat indeed. A young lady came

A sand drawing in the making

out of the office, knelt on the floor and gave the tray a sharp shake so the sand settled into a fine, level layer ready for her index finger to 'draw' a continuous line, starting with the straight lines of a grid, like graph paper, to assist accuracy. Her finger then 'drew' a lot of sensuous curves without leaving the board until the picture was finished. I could see, amidst the numerous lines, the shape of a heart in the centre, and she finished by drawing an 'I' on the left side and a 'U' on the right side. I love you. A great activity for the grandchildren, I thought.

Then Edgar gave the tray another quick flick to level the sand and drew firstly a turtle and then a typical French blackbirding ship that brought terror to coastal communities and drove some of the natives into the hills to live in hiding, exiled in their own land.

He told us the story of Roi Mata (more about that soon) and then played a percussion instrument while singing the Vanuatu national anthem followed by the British national anthem. I asked him about present marriage rules, and he confirmed that couples now marry from choice but divorce is strongly frowned upon.

"All the entities that supported the couple in their union in the first place would be likely to follow the separated couple with bad luck for the rest of their days."

I valued his show as it came from his heart, and it was so nice to meet someone who knows how important it is to pass down the colourful history of these islands.

Roi Mata's reign

The tomb of Roi Mata, with his excavated skeleton along with that of his beloved wife, tells the story of a man who landed in south Efate with the intention of conquering the island, but later he turned out to be a peacemaker.

We set off in our hire car to explore the rim of Efate island and came firstly to Havannah Harbour, steeped in the history of Roi Mata. Roi Mata was a term used for centuries previously for the accepted leader in the central islands of Vanuatu. This last Roi Mata became the most famous of all.

Another short, potted history coming up.

Picture the scene, when sometime during the sixteenth or seventeenth centuries a fleet of big outrigger canoes with triangular sails makes its way northwards towards Efate island, crewed with men keen to find new lands to settle. Pandanus mats fill the holds of the canoes along with building materials, tools and weapons, food and water, and their precious ceremonial clothing and head masks. In the first canoe of the fleet are two brothers from a high-status family, henceforth known as the supreme chief Roi Mata and Roi Muru his warrior chief.

The outriggers ground onto the coral shore at the southern-most tip of the island, Maniora, where there is now a spa resort. From there over the next months the two men led assaults on this island and its many off-lying islands until Roi Mata was recognised as the new leader by the previously waring villagers.

Roi Mata did not agree with village fighting village, over land, women and water, even though his record of invasion was a violent one. Once hostilities had settled, he introduced a new system which linked villages through marriage between high-status families from neighbouring clans. The marriage of the women from these families to men of the same-status family in nearby villages served to maintain links between villages so war would not be waged between them.

The system still functions today, and we met numerous women throughout the islands who came from another island to marry and live with their respective husbands' families. Although there are still land disputes after a volcanic eruption destroys one person's productive land, these are sorted by the chiefs of the combined village councils.

At Manga'asi, on the shores of what is now known as Port Harbour, a village was known to have been inhabited from AD 500, and here Roi Mata decided would be the ideal place to settle. After his conquering start he ruled the island with benevolence, and under his leadership the village grew and grew.

The people of Efate became united, and the economy thrived on the productivity of peacetime.

Offshore from his home village there are three islands: Lelepa, Moso and the much smaller Eretoka or Hat Island, so named, in modern times, because it looks like a broad-brimmed hat. Altogether this area is known as his Domain, where he lived and ruled for around fifteen years.

Sadly, his brother, Roi Muru, was a jealous person, and one day while they were on Lelepa island he shot Roi Mata through the throat with a poisoned arrow. Roi Mata's mortified followers carried him to a deep cavern of compressed ash and calcium called Feles Cave near the island's main habitation, Natapao, where he died.

High up within the cave are black wall paintings of men, fish and birds, which date from about AD 900. Since Roi Mata died there, it is now a place of national significance, and he is remembered as the man who shaped present-day Vanuatu with peace and unity.

His body was laid carefully in a canoe and taken back to Lelepa Landing and then on to his village, Manga'asi, to his young wife and family, and the other members of his court, for the one-hundred-day-and-night mourning period. Tragically for his family and courtiers, it was decided by the elders of his village that he would be laid to rest on Eretoka with his eighteen courtiers, their twenty-one wives and Roi Mata's own wife, all of whom were alive at the time they were buried, effectively ending his dynasty. It gets even more sad.

When the time came, the men drank a lot of strong kava to make the terrifying experience less frightening, but the women were not given this option and, according to Edgar at the museum, Roi Mata's wife ran as fast as she could into the bush to escape. What must she have felt? The loss of her beloved husband and then facing being buried alive… Did she believe she would be reunited with her husband? Was her fear balanced by this thought? Maybe she had children. Nevertheless, she was brought back and joined the rest of the funeral party as they made their way to Eretoka.

After the mass burial, the mourners danced over the grave and then decorated it with a big stone. The story was carried down through the generations, who treated the grave site as tabu, a forbidden area. But was it true?

In the late 1960s a French archaeologist, José Garanger, decided to test the history and spent some time locating and excavating the grave site. He found the forty-one skeletons, and Roi Mata was clearly distinguished by his ornate necklace and the many rings around his ankles. The bindings around his wife's wrists and the position of her bones confirms she tried desperately to avoid being buried alive.

Here we were, centuries later, standing where this tragic turn in history took place in surroundings that have changed little over time. We were privileged.

The Cave of Swallows

Onwards through the sprawling village of Ulei, built amidst the abandoned Havannah Harbour settlement. (The name Havannah came from the first British warship that regularly patrolled the archipelago.)

Back in the 1800s this was the island's main settlement, until a combination of drought, falling world cotton prices (when the US resumed production after the Civil War), cyclone devastation and malaria forced the settlers to set up the new capital on the shores of the protected bay at Vila.

All around remains the evidence in the form of runways, wrecked planes, jetties, a museum and ruined buildings of the WWII US presence, but we decided to view them only if they appeared; our main interest was in the island, its history and its people.

So next on the list was the Valeva Cave at Siviri on the north coast, where a local guide, David, had an interesting story to tell.

To tell the story of the cave it is essential to understand that some of the islands were isolated from each other and were not always peaceful. The big island of Nguna that lies across Undine Bay to the north through history had been a home to warfare between the hill dwellers and the coastal people over the theft of fruit and vegetables from gardens and trees, superstitious allegations of causing injury and death by sorcery, and the availability of water – and that is where the cave comes into the story.

David explained that back in the dangerous times of blackbirding, the people from Siviri village, where he was born and bred, and the Nguna islanders moved up into the hills on their respective lands to hide from the marauding French ships, so for a while the coastal villages were empty and the exiled villagers lost their access to fresh water. Not wanting contact with the existing hill dwellers of Nguna, the exiled Nguna coastal islanders paddled their canoes across to Efate under cover of darkness to search for water. They watched as swallows disappeared into the rocky undergrowth and then emerged from a different point. On further searching they found the cave and its life saving lake of fresh water, and from then on shared it with the swallows and the Siviri villagers, paying compensation to them for the water.

An expedition of scuba divers is once thought to have travelled five kilometres into the cave before turning back, but we just took a few paces into the cool watery interior with David.

Our next stop was an idyllic little garden area between Siviri village and the waters of Undine Bay, where we watched a big herd of narrow-beaked oceanic dolphins gradually making their way down the bay about 20 metres beneath our beautiful lookout. Straight opposite, in dark shadows, Nguna was brooding under its white layer of cloud; it would soon become our offshore companion where we were going to stay for the night.

We had paid 1,000VT (£7) each for access to the garden area, and it really was ours for the time we were there, quite alone. After lunch at a picnic table, with the benches fastened to young sandalwood trees, we scrambled down the steps to a little walled terrace just above the water for a snorkel. No need for the changing room, we were soon making our way in sandaled feet across the carefully and thoughtfully smoothed limestone rocks before launching ourselves into the deliciously cool and clear water. Through our goggles we saw familiar fish in the caves and submarine alleyways of this limestone reef.

Doroline's dream

About fifteen years ago a young girl was travelling with her mother and father from their home on Malekula to Port Vila. (In accordance with tradition, her mother had long ago moved from her birthplace on Ambrym to marry.) She was on her way to the college in the capital to study foreign languages and business. Her name is Doroline.

During the course of her studies, she met a young man, Tony, who was training to be a teacher, and they fell in love. Doroline is a bright and loving person who thrives in the company of other people and animals, and Tony was an equal, so they made their lives together, but this did involve sacrifice for her. When their sons came along, they decided that she should 'stay back' in the home to be a home mum, and so the fruits of her studies were put on hold.

After Tony fulfilled teaching roles at two schools, including one on watchful Nguna, they settled in the little village of Emua, on the northern shore of Efate, where Tony's parents lived in a house overlooking the beach, Undine Bay and Nguna.

Soon Doroline's thinking was turning to what she could do to occupy her healthy mind and help the family and village at the same time. She had a dream and was formulating an idea when, in the market in Port Vila one day, she overheard a young man talking. She approached him and asked if she was right in thinking he was a builder.

"Yes, I am Brian, the builder from the Banks Islands."

"I would like you to come and build me a guest house, please."

That same evening Brian, Doroline and Tony sat down at her home table to draw up some plans and list the items needed in the construction. Brian would return with the building materials, which included sheets of flattened and woven bamboo for the walls, roof shingles made of woven palm leaves, planks of wood for the floors and various other lengths of wood for the uprights and wall supports. The guest house would be one room, about 12 by 12 feet, with a full-length veranda at the front. It would be built on a family-owned strip of land between their home and what used to be Tony's parents' home. In accordance with tradition, after his father, Raymond, died, their home was demolished, so now Tony's mother lives with them.

The build took just a few months because the roof and walls were prefabricated, and during the process Brian taught Doroline how to do a lot of the work so that she can manage her own repairs.

Doroline was proud of the little house, which was built in the Melanesian style. She set to decorating the woven walls with pretty fabric and making sheets and coverings for the beds and covers for the cushions. In one corner of the bedroom there is an airing cupboard

Doroline and our Melanesian retreat

where the wall is just one thickness of the woven bamboo. The corner cupboard she 'screened' with fabric and it is used for sheets and blankets.

Soon Doroline was in business. Tony looked after the advertising on the internet, and her first guests arrived. Doroline is very flexible in that she is happy to cook an evening meal as well as breakfast, and if the visitors wish for a ferry to Nguna and a truck to the top of the volcano, she is happy to organise that and any other trip, walk or flight the residents might choose. Then disaster struck.

Cyclone Pam hit the island with winds up to 320 kilometres in March 2015, and the conventionally built house next door, also used for paying guests, was flattened. But Doroline's house stood virtually undamaged, and she was letting it out very soon after the devastation. There is a gap between the walls and the roof of about six inches, and the walls breathe through the woven bamboo. There is also a gap underneath the building, which itself stands on stilts over a foot off the ground. So, the entire building breathes and gives in a strong wind, like the bamboo homes we had come across in Ecuador, and is refreshingly cool and well-ventilated at all times with its louvered windows on opposite walls.

When we arrived, we parked the car in the pretty lane outside just as Doroline was making her way towards us. Her previous guests had only just left so she used the word "sorry" a lot when explaining we could see the room but she hadn't got around to cleaning it yet. We said we understood and she needn't apologise, until we realised that some people here start almost all their sentences with "sorry".

"We'll walk down to the bar/restaurant and have a beer and be back in an hour or so, if that's OK?"

We sat on a high bench overlooking the water to Nguna with two ice-cold Tuskers, which after the snorkel tasted sublime.

Back at our tropical beach-front retreat, a trail of roses and hibiscus blossoms paved the way to our room for the night. Some of Doroline's guests stay for as long as a month; now there's an idea.

Not only were there fragrant flowers on the ground, but we had our own frangipani tree and a pretty, carefully laid out garden with coral paths bordered with variegated-leaved hedges, and beautiful shells decorated the veranda balustrade and acted as soap dishes in the shower and outside washing area.

A little procession comprising Doroline, Tony and their young son, Morris, came with our supper of salad, fish with wild yam, boiled rice and stewed fresh vegetables, and beans. How easy for her to cook a little more of what she was doing for her family to provide us with supper; that's what I would do.

We lit the citronella mosquito candles and relaxed over cups of coffee with hot water taken from the big thermos flask while listening to the evening sounds: a tiny crying baby, adult laughter from next door, yellow-faced myna birds and the ubiquitous crowing cockerels, cicadas and chatty dogs. The sounds of peace.

Trouble was, I didn't want to miss anything in this one-off magical experience, so my subconscious would not let me sleep for long.

The night began with a struggle to get completely covered by the purple mosquito net so we wouldn't be eaten alive.

"We'll start with the flaps at the bottom," Rob said. But then, by the time we had spread it out around the bed, the gap at the bottom had opened. Rob scrambled around trying to pull the gap shut, getting more and more frustrated all the while.

"OK, we're going to move it round so the flaps are at the top." We pulled and pushed and huffed and puffed and laid back only to find the top corners didn't reach the bed. So, we pulled them down and tucked them under the pillows, which meant we had the net over our faces. It all worked pretty well in the end, after a very discombobulated Rob rolled over into the land of nod.

A deliciously cool breeze wafted over us and silence reigned, except for the lapping waves and the distant roar of surf on the reef, but they were soothing sounds. Sleep enfolded us until all at once something upset all the village dogs, who set off a cacophony until, with a single, long-drawn-out howl, the matriarch or alpha male silenced the lot of them, and we went back to our dreams.

Next, in the early hours just before dawn, were the cockerels, who even get on Doroline's nerves, but it was all part of our one night in a Vanuatuan village. A gong was sounded at 6.45 am and again at 7.30 am to get families up, workers off to the bus to Port Vila and school children off for the short walk to Manua School.

Over our breakfast of a fried egg with white bread and doughnut followed by banana and papaya, Doroline told us about her plans to recall Brian and with him build another guest bungalow on the site of her late father-in-law's house. It would make good use of the space which has been respectfully empty for a while.

Doroline pointed to the small area of carefully placed coral in front of the house before the beach. "We were married there last year." How lovely that their lack of convention is part of modern village life, here, anyway.

Tarmac and trees

The fact the Chinese have tarmacked the entire island ring road and are in the process of building sturdy new bridges over the many rivers that run down from the hills (for whatever reasons) has changed the working lives of many islanders. Instead of migrating to the capital for work at the beginning of the week, staying somewhere in the city and returning home at the weekends because the pitted earth road meant the journey could take many hours, if it was achievable at all, they can now catch a work bus and return home every night.

The east coast is, of course, the Pacific Ocean coast, which announces its arrival with swell and constant breakers bursting into white foaming masses on the reefs. We stopped briefly to take it all in, and it reminded me of the Abel Tasman Coast Track on the South Island of New Zealand, around Greymouth and Hokitika.

Giant banyans stand on either side of the road watching over the travellers passing underneath. Further back in the fields smooth and pale-trunked she-oaks display on their bare branches clusters of tiny scale-like leaves that look like sycamore seeds. They are thought to resemble the feathers of the cassowary bird (a big flightless bird that looks like an emu), which has the genus name *Casuarius*, so the alternative name of the tree is *Casuarina*. Pretty and feminine, don't you think?

A dip in Eton's blue hole

We sped on past vast plantations neatly cleared of undergrowth, and in between them and the fields of fat cattle that lay contented in the sun, the wild flora was smothered by the 'mile-a-minute' creeper. (Bitter vine, *Mikania micrantha*, is a rapidly growing vine that covers all other growth and was planted by the Americans during the Second World War to camouflage their machinery.)

I was thinking it would be nice to find Eton's blue hole, the Blue Lagoon, for a cool dip.

The bottom was pure white sand, hence the delicious blue colour, and the hole is fed by the sea, so there were nice fish to see. We did a leisurely face-down exploratory circuit of the pool, roughly the size of two tennis courts, and then ventured into the channel that led out to the sea. Off the distant entrance is a protective reef which kept the water nice and flat where we were swimming, but we could see the Pacific rising up and breaking on the far side, and it looked as if it was much higher than the water that we were swimming in. We ventured to the far end of the channel where large fish, including sharks, are known to gather, but I hoped not that day.

All was well and we turned back, cruising down the other side of the channel, just to be thorough. We had been swimming for around an hour before returning to our little car and deciding it was time for a beer, to get rid of the salty taste in our mouths, you understand!

Delivering our charity goods

Rob's back went into spasm as he winched the dinghy up the evening we were back on *Zoonie*, so we had a quiet day on board the next day with him taking the max dose of ibuprofen to reduce and limit the swelling, and paracetamol and codeine to deal with the pain.

He managed to limp ashore the next day, carefully, as we had a pre-planned meeting for a coffee with Steph of the SHARM Foundation and her husband, Rod, where we handed over the boxes of donated school clothes we had brought up from New Zealand.

They are both concerned about the future of Vanuatu's youngsters. There is a high birth rate, of which a big proportion are babies born to single mothers, and 45% of the population is under fifteen years of age. What to do with all the young lads that are leaving school with no job prospects? Rod understandably foresees social issues such as gangs and a continual erosion of social stability.

Steph set up a project to provide young men with chainsaws and the necessary training on how to use them so they could saw fallen trees into marketable lengths of wood, but then the chief of the village put a stop to the idea and the saws were taken away. Many of the supplies sent to schools 'disappear' for a profit, and any excess of supplies are warehoused rather than shared around. Money rules everywhere, it seems.

Many chiefs are now very wealthy from selling, for example, land rights, business licences, etc., and there are many instances of financial aid not getting to its intended destination. When we were travelling around, we rarely met any chiefs, they were always "away" or "not here at the moment". Sometimes if they are old or ill they move to the town to be near health facilities. Others are so wealthy they live in apartments on the Gold Coast of Australia, leaving their village way of life lacking authority and funds.

Chapter 7

Now for New Caledonia

25 August 2019. As Zoonie nosed her way seaward at 6.00 am having just lost sight of the town, Rob and I were looking at exactly the same spot in the water when a young humpback did a full breach just a few metres away. Wonderful, although I did wonder if there were more with the same intentions, nearer to us or even directly beneath!

Sliding south down the tropics

Zoonie soon settled into her groove. The 22-knot wind filling her headsail, and her kerchief of mainsail supporting her from behind the mast enabled her to pursue a course to the waypoint, off the pass between the Lifou and Maré islands of the Loyalty group. We passed between them after 240 miles of sailing. As the wind was now becoming less constant, and wanting to get anchored inside a reef in daylight, we started the engine and motored the remaining distance to the Havannah Boulari Passage which leads through the New Caledonia Barrier Reef, the second largest double barrier reef in the world, where the two reefs grow alongside each other.

27 August 2019. The white lighthouse on the reef to the right of the entrance channel confirms a night-time entry is feasible into Goro Bay on New Caledonia, but, as you know, we always err on the side of caution if possible. So we motored along in the flat water, leaving a green buoy to starboard in the middle of the lagoon to avoid a shallow area, continued on past Cannibales Point (!) and anchored in Goro Bay, on sand in 15 metres, just off the old nickel ore loading wharf, with its two rusty gantries still pointing upward. On the top of one of them was an osprey nest, where the single fledgling was being encouraged to take to the air by its parents.

Nowadays the nickel ore is processed at the quarry on the other side of the hill and is sent by conveyor belt, laid through corridors cut in the red rock, to the modern wharf in Prony Bay.

It's grand to be at anchor once more, by ourselves, with just the birdsong around us and the distant roar of the surf on the reef. Occasionally a vehicle goes by on the road that hugs the shoreline, but by evening we're alone, and it is wonderful.

The next morning, we set off early for the 41 miles to Nouméa, passing the elegant hills, denuded of kauri and other building-material trees and eroding dramatically in places, revealing dried-blood-red scars amidst the dry shoreside forest. The conveyor belt I mentioned was clearly visible as we passed Prony Bay.

The channel markers were all in place, which was just as well, as the day was grey and rainy, and visibility limited. A ship passed us confirming our forward course for a few miles until she disappeared through Canal Woodin. Little crests and rims of white showed us where the numerous coral reefs were to our left, but most were marked anyway. We moored alongside the outer wharf of Port du Sud Marina; *Zoonie* felt strangely constrained being tied at both ends after months of just a bow restraint.

28 August 2019. Anne Marie eyed the only bio product I had on board, a pathetic and doomed quarter of white cabbage I found lurking in the bottom of the fridge a couple of hours before.

"I can make a salad, and we'll eat it today."

"I have to take it," she said with an expression of reluctant duty.

"I could stir fry it tonight?"

No chance, I thought, as I unpegged the bag wherein cowered the victim.

"Keep the peg," she said, as I popped the cabbage into her plastic bag.

A waste of food and plastic, I snarled mentally!

Her colleague, Carolyn, had given us the name of the sail repairer, and we called him to arrange collection of the mainsail. My rusty

French came in handy as I chatted with Yves. Early the next morning a familiar voice whispered in my ear, "There's no wind, hun," so up we got up before 5.00 am to lower the mainsail and bag it ready for Yves.

Notes from a time warp

30 August 2019. François is a keenly intelligent man who was born in Paris of a Vietnamese father and a Polynesian mother. At one year of age, he came with his parents to live in New Caledonia and grew to love the country. His education and location taught him English and French, and along life's path he has learned and retained as much knowledge about the geology, flora and fauna of New Caledonia's Great South as you could want, and enough to do conducted tours for the world's top scientists, geologists and botanists. So, the five of us were very fortunate to have him as our guide.

The five being, apart from Rob and me, Robert, a retired history teacher, from Brooklyn, NYC, and Takahiro and Azusa from Hokkaido, Japan. So, François' commentary was given in perfect English and then Japanese, which was great because the latter repetition gave me time to make a few notes. Our host constantly involved us all, and as a result we were soon chatting with the others and encouraging Taka and Azusa with their minimal knowledge of English.

We drove away from Nouméa through dry forest around Mont-Dore, named because it looks golden with the evening light shining on it, and stopped in a viewing area where François gave us an insight into how New Caledonia was formed and why its geology is unique in the world.

New Caledonia was part of the land mass known as Zealandia which broke off from the supercontinent Gondwana between 79 and 83 million years ago forming a cluster of islands of which New Zealand and the island group of New Caledonia are the areas above sea level. The isolation of this island group preserved the pre-existing ecosystem, allowing it to remain largely unchanged. Amazingly, the endemic plants are pre-dinosaur, without predators and still thriving. (Today, the remnants of the ancient supercontinent Gondwana comprise Antarctica, South America, Africa, India, Australia and more.)

Surrounded by a protective barrier coral reef, the largest island of

New Caledonia, Grand Terre, measuring 400 by 40 kilometres, lies in the biggest lagoon on the planet. We were visiting at the end of the cool dry season, which runs from June to September. Over 800 mother humpback whales come to the safe shallows of the lagoon with their calves in July, and that is when the farmers plant their yams.

Along with the considerable ancient biodiversity endemic to the island is the variety of ores and minerals that have been found and exploited, especially over the last 160 years, including nickel, copper, iron, serpentine, pink bauxite, jasper, jade, sapphire, manganese, chrome and fluoride, to name but a few!

As François explained the geology to us, honeyeaters sang from a nearby toothbrush tree in between poking their sharp, curved little beaks into the flowers. The earth gets so hot in summer that plants growing near the ground cannot have flowers or spores; instead their stamens grow extra long within the protection of the leaves and form seeds and then fruit at their ends.

We stopped at the Blue River National Park entrance amidst a wonderful plantation of kauri that are being grown commercially in some parts of the forest. A fifty-year investment before they can be felled suggests a good future for them. Ironically, their commercial value, which once nearly caused their extinction, is now ensuring their continued existence.

Onwards and upwards for us to the wetlands and the sunken forest created when the Rivière Blanche (white river) and Rivière Bleue (blue river) were backed up to create the Lac de Yaté (Yate Lake), now a popular leisure activity area. We saw osprey nests perched at the top of the bleached trees, and peered into pitcher plants to see the half-digested flies inside. François gave us another lesson on the local flora and how it survived the hungry jaws of the dinosaurs. The diverse flora of the island remains 75% endemic species.

The pleasure of seeing a half-Vietnamese, half-Polynesian man showing two Japanese youngsters, at the start of their life's varied path, around his south-west Pacific home, after the turbulent history of their nations over the last century, was not lost on me. Travel, the great peacemaker.

François stopped on a roundabout; it didn't matter as there was no other traffic on this red earth road at the time.

"It's not raining too much, would you like to walk down to the bridge? I'll meet you on the other side; we cannot take vehicles over it."

We chatted happily, the five of us, as we walked the short way down to the wooden Pérignon bridge in the drizzle. At least it was warm.

François came to pick us up, having driven through a shallow part of the lake. The dam was built in 1958 for hydro-electric power and is now also used in the nickel mining industry. The Pérignon bridge we had walked across is made entirely of rubber oak trees, as they do not rot — useful, as it is often submerged in the rainy season.

We pulled in beside a tiny sign saying 'Cagou' and started out on a little walk through the pretty forest along a well-worn track, and I cynically wondered if François was 'having us on', doubting the likelihood of seeing a rare cagou bird in this vast forest, despite them being unafraid of humans. Imagine a bird the size of a Tower of London raven, its colour similar to a pigeon, with long orange legs and a matching beak, topped with an over-the-top wedding fascinator crest, and you might be getting the idea.

Their lack of shyness and the fact they have lost the ability to fly and lay only one egg each year are all factors attributable to the lack of predators on the island. Likewise, the plants have no thorns and their foliage is soft, without the need for prickly leaves to deter predators.

Forty years ago, there were only sixty cagou left on the island after the predation of humans and dogs, but now due to careful protection there are over 1,000 and the population is growing. Despite François' optimism, our hopes were fading as we finished the forest loop and started back along the road to our vehicle. We peered into the dense woodland, and there I spotted one. François immediately started upturning leaf piles at the side of the road, which brought the little fellow out. They are territorial and any trespassing cagous might well be killed in a bloody fight. The long grey feathers lying down its back are raised at times of threat into a beautiful crescent, enough to shiver the timbers of any intruder, me included.

During our amazing day with François, we had seen and/or heard the blue goshawk, the falcon, the whistling kite, the yellow-bellied robin, the red-headed honeyeater, the second biggest pigeon in the country and, of course, the cagou.

The struggle of the indigenous Kanak people

An afternoon visit to the unique Tjibaou Cultural Centre gave us an insight into the culture and history of this troubled country and its indigenous Kanak population.

"No people could behave with more civility than they did," Cook said of the inhabitants, who were generous in supplying the mariners with fresh water.

However, the colonial experience for the Kanaks under French rule had been a particularly violent one, and in June 1988 independence fighter Jean-Marie Tjibaou did his final act towards his vision by signing the Matignon Agreements, effectively bringing peace to his country. But distant militants on Ouvéa island misunderstood his motives and intentions, and on 4 May 1989 he and his friend and fellow political mover Yeiwéné Yeiwéné were assassinated during a visit there.

3 September 2019. At present the country is under a three-separate-ballot referendum system to review the independence issue. The first referendum in 2018 resulted in a small majority to stay with France, 56.7%, to 43.3% for independence.

Since then, the second referendum in 2020 was nearer the Kanaks' target: 53.3% voted to remain and 46.7% voted for independence. Had the increase in votes for independence continued to the final vote, the result would have been closer than ever to New Caledonia becoming independent, like her neighbours; instead, the Kanak people were dealt a pair of terrible blows.

First, Covid-19 killed 280 Kanak individuals, which initiated their traditional mourning period lasting up to a year, during which time they are restricted by custom as to the activities they are allowed to take part in, so they were not allowed to vote.

Second, their request to have the ballot delayed until the end of their mourning period was denied by the French authorities, in violation not only of the Kanaks' obvious interest in the referendum but also of their traditions and the spirit of the law surrounding the matter.

The results, although expected, must have been a dreadful blow to them. I couldn't believe it until I researched the reasons.

96.5% voted to remain with France and 3.5% voted for independence during a 43.87% turnout.

All that is left to them now is to take part in discussions over the new status of New Caledonia as a French overseas territory.

I fear the rights of the Kanak people could continue to be challenged by the wealth to be made from the mineral-rich ground alone and the continuous influx of French expats, who under the present rules are given the vote after just ten years' residence.

Backtracking to Prony Bay

Yves took just a couple of days to re-stitch every seam of the mainsail, so then we only had to wait for a strong south-westerly to fade and we would leave Nouméa after nine days of shore-life to do a little exploring.

6 September 2019. Under engine and a blue sky we left Nouméa and retraced our route to Prony Bay, securing Zoonie to one of the six buoys in Anse Majic.

7 September 2019. The weather could not have been kinder this morning as I packed the rucksack with food and water and Rob inflated the dinghy. The chart plotter and our pilot showed a wharf just inshore from Zoonie's mooring. All we could see was a pile of rocks, but as a little tinny (small aluminium boat) arrived earlier and was moored on a water bottle buoy nearby, we took it as the place to go ashore.

Birds were all around us as we trudged along the winding rusty (literally) red iron path. They perched in the spindly trees of the scrubland close by, singing away, telling us we were heading in the right direction.

This is the dry season with summer approaching, so the fire risk sign is set on 'très elévé' (very raised risk), and judging by the burned ferns lying close to the ground, just two tinder-dry branches rubbing together in the wind would seem risk enough of ignition. I was taken by the painstakingly careful way the path had been cleared and edged with stone in places; not only a back-breaking task but also gloves would have had to be worn as many of the rocks were sharp. I wondered who had done this and if the path had a previous use. The original builders, keepers and telegraph office staff would have come up by foot before the advent of 4x4 vehicles in the last twenty years or so. Or did the indigenous Kanaks come to this glorious spot throughout their history?

The climb was not long or far from Zoonie back in Anse Majic, and we arrived at the round house lookout after an hour and sat in awe at the fact we could see waves breaking on the barrier reef and Île des Pins nearly 60 kilometres away.

We climbed onwards, up the path to the Cap N'Dua lighthouse, built in the 1890s when the dangers lurking beneath the waters around New Caledonia were already well known. Despite the maritime knowledge, we had effectively come to a wilderness, in part, anyway.

Wilderness is defined as an uncultivated, uninhabited and inhospitable region; a neglected or abandoned area. There are no towns, villages, or shops here, and there are certainly many once-used and now-neglected and abandoned areas, especially in the numerous small scale mining operations. A wilderness indeed.

Moving on, this time aboard Zoonie, to our right a covered conveyor belt of the Vale nickel mine stretches across the countryside, bringing the nickel export product from the processing plant to Prony Port and the waiting ships. The whole site, including the factory and associated residue area and the accommodation buildings, is being carefully monitored for ecological degradation and chemical contamination. The results are mixed and the study ongoing.

8 September 2019. Suddenly there is movement in the water ahead, dark fins just cutting the surface, languid in their movements until they spot us, and then we are joined by a herd of seven spotty-tummied Indo-Pacific bottlenose dolphins who play and explore Zoonie's hull before losing interest and moving away; I don't think we were going fast enough for them!

A little further on a huge yellow-and-black-striped sea snake was sidewinding its way across the water from Casy islet to the mainland, a distance of about four kilometres. "I'm glad he didn't emerge from around the outboard this morning," Rob commented, remembering the baby sea snake that had been asleep under the fuel tank of the outboard in Fiji last year until Rob started the motor!

We tied to a buoy in Baie de La Somme, which is so named after the ship that arrived here on 9 October 1869 to load timber and transport it to the head of the bay. She struck the Recife de l'Aiguille

Zoonie amongst the pines for one night

just off the bay, which is now marked by a red-and-black pillar buoy, and was stuck there for 50 years until she was re-floated.

It is a beautiful wide bay with a handful of buoys at one side under the outcrop of pine tree-studded land. A resident dark-hulled schooner with a couple and a vocal dog aboard rests in the middle of the bay, and a river mouth to the other side, where the fallout of mud and sand has left a raised bank marked, conveniently, with thin wooden posts or withies, would be a good place to explore.

Where have the whales gone?

We hadn't been there long when a big white catamaran came around the headland and the skipper called across in good English, "These are private buoys for the whale-watching boats. You can stay tonight, but we will need that buoy tomorrow. You are OK for one night."

"Did you see any whales today?" I asked, and he shook his head, a look of regret on his handsome face. He then motored away to pick up another cone-shaped buoy before taking his punters ashore.

We pondered this mystery of no whales when there are usually hundreds as we emerged on another beautiful, calm, sunny day from East Bay.

In fact, there were six whale-watching cats that used the buoys and operated from July, when the whales arrive to raise their new young and to breed, to mid-September, when the mothers and their capable and sufficiently mature calves return to the Antarctic to feed on the abundance of cold-water krill. I didn't know until I read the sign that krill is made up of ten different kinds of crustaceans. You learn something each day in this game.

Whale watching surveillance covers 90 kilometres by boat in the south lagoon every day. Normally, they could expect to see twenty to fifty humpbacks. The next day they would see some of the same and other new arrivals as well. This year they have seen as few as one in a day and never more than five.

The air temperature is 4–5°C cooler here now than is usual at this time of year, so the water is cooler too, maybe too cool for the babies, so have the mothers taken them further north into the tropics? More alarming is: have the mothers failed to breed? Are the males still producing live sperm?

Baie du Carénage

You may know the term 'careen'; it means to turn a ship on its side by running it onto a beach to clean and repair it. This bay takes its name from this process; it is an ideal location for careening as there are no coral heads and the rocky reefs are clearly avoidable. Where the Carenage River flows around a vast muddy/sandy bank a number of ships can be beached, or careened, at the same time. We decided to anchor rather than beach *Zoonie* there!

11 September 2019. A lone lady from the sole moored yacht rowed her dinghy, before sunrise and at a completely still time of day, towards where two rivers meet at the old carenage bank. Above her the perfect cobalt blue of the sky was broken by a helicopter trailing one of the counterbalance frames they use when a wind turbine has to be lowered and looked at. Two-bladed turbines are used here as they can be easily lowered before cyclones and for maintenance and repair.

Mangroves hugged the rocky shore as she rowed, barely producing a wake to disturb the red muddy deposit that marks the tidal range. A pile of what looked like rocks from a distance turned out to be the old thermal water baths where work-weary folks could relax and clean up. They are built of brick on a rocky reef around the rising warm water, and nearby her dinghy floated over another reef with warm water bubbles where rock oysters and little black fish were living and thriving in the warmth.

I will forever remember that personal excursion.

A walk on the mine side

Our walking shoes tied firmly on, we were ready for a planned three-hour round trek along one of the many excellent walking tracks in the area. It started with a shady welcome where the thermal spring has been tamed within a recently restored square concrete pool with wooden slatted seats in it and picnic tables around; a perfect spot to cool off and relax in the warm waters before returning to one's boat or vehicle.

Bold and pastel colours abounded at our feet. Hard, dark rocks with soft green/white putty-like seams in between that we could not understand. Blue algae polka dots against the red rust of the rock, and the odd black rock in weird wind-eroded shapes. The most obvious places for mines were on top of the hills where, after the deforestation of earlier times, the soil layer would have eroded away, leaving the rock ready to be extracted.

The mine we found showed where spades had cut down into the rock from the outer edges of the hilltop, leaving a level, smooth area of ground with vertical sides and some initials carved for posterity. One day, the activity stopped, mid-slice, while there was still more usable rock left. What happened and why and where did they go? I like mysteries.

Rob chipped away at one brittle stone, and a razor-edged lump broke off, the colour of jade, a thousand little pieces squeezed together. Jade is found in this area and it is a very similar colour and opacity to my Māori fish hook pendant made of Hokitika jade, known as green stone or pounamu in New Zealand.

Zoonie **explores further inland**

While anchored, *Zoonie* was undergoing a thorough spring clean, inside and out, involving bouts of thorough washing, polishing and painting interspersed with relaxing on board, baking, writing blogs and emails and waiting for the odd blow to pass through.

After a few days of toil we decided to explore further up the bay in *Zoonie*, and we had heard of a special place. Although conscious of moving on to Australia soon, we felt a few more days in this rare place would be alright. We anchored as close as the depth would allow and used the dinghy to creep further in.

17 September 2019. In the Bay of a Lonesome Pine (my name) is a perfect spot for small and shallow draft vessels like catamarans. With lines into the mangroves and a dogleg to break the wave force, no sea swell could possibly reach this area, making it a perfect hurricane hole.

Ashore we soon found evidence of a camp used certainly in mining times with a rusty boiler and some familiar precise stonework with smooth-faced rocks providing an elevation from the ground for buildings. The site has also been used since, judging by the crude shelter, with five coins on the wooden counter and a tent containing a man's clothing in it.

Off came our shoes and socks so we could paddle across the slippery rocks of the shallow Carenage River. A Frenchman strolled across at the same time in his flip-flops, and we shared a greeting as we dried our feet on our hankies.

We walked on, savouring the shade and forever in awe of the diversity of plants and birdsong. Soon we came across another blue river, the colour made by the nickel-laden rocks as well as other chemical elements, no doubt. There was a nice spot on the high bank where we could sit and relax and have a drink of water. Opposite was a lovely copse including a straight-trunked kauri in the middle. There was a good-sized house in the centre of the copse with neat walls around it and outside seating guarded by two enthusiastic dogs. The bigger of the two barked his question incessantly, "Who are you and what do you want?", while his little friend just stood and looked inquiringly at us. "Well, are you going to come and make a fuss of me?"

There was no vehicle on the well-worn track outside the house, and nobody responded to the dogs' enthusiasm. To cross the river at that point would have been difficult. In times past there was a suspension bridge – we could see this from the remnants of the iron channels for the cables in the bark of the tree.

Someone had told us that a French chef lives there who has worked in various prestigious places around the world and who is willing to cook a meal for punters with prior notice. He also had a tinny and two canoes moored downriver, so I guess he was into the opportunistic tourist business too. Pity he wasn't there; he sounded very interesting, and we were hungry.

Back on board, *Zoonie*'s spring clean was almost done, and we were entering our third week away from civilisation. Supplies were holding up, and I had added to them with bread, cake, flapjacks and numerous one-pot-stew-type suppers. Rob will be looking forward to some meat again, I mused, as I soaked another batch of TVP (textured vegetable protein) in a hot, tasty solution.

Time was moving on and our minds were turning towards our next passage. We needed to return to Nouméa, stock up with food and watch for a weather window, clear out and set off for Australia, onward and homeward, but not quite yet.

Casy, our very own Isle des Pines

We had spent twelve fascinating days in Baie du Carénage when *Zoonie* poked her nose out into Prony Bay once more. We were en route to a mooring buoy off the west coast of Casy (a governor in the French Empire). We had spotted the buoys when we were approaching Baie de la Somme Bay in what seems many moons ago and thought an exploration would be fun. Where the seabed is mud and sand it is fine to anchor because no harm is being done to the habitat, but where there is coral, rock and seagrass these must be protected, so the government has laid free and regularly maintained mooring buoys, ideal for us because the holding in rock and coral was not good anyway.

Sitting in the cockpit, planning our stay over a glass of wine, a long streak of pale green in an otherwise denser green water to *Zoonie*'s side caught my eye, but I thought nothing of it – a patch of sand, maybe.

Rob had mentioned seeing some metal bars and an old sinker near to ours when he was picking up the buoy, but it wasn't until I sat back into the water from *Zoonie's* stern boarding ladder and turned my masked face through the surface into the depths that I discovered to my surprise a 50-foot yacht lying on the bottom right near to *Zoonie's* stern. I couldn't be sure then what length it was; that came out later when we discussed it with a local couple who have visited here over the years.

The mast and spars were laid along the deck, making me think she was the victim of a disaster and was being salvaged when she was left on the old mooring. She may then have fallen victim to a cyclone and sunk on the spot, beyond hope of being raised and restored and has lain there ever since. The shoreside noticeboard showed an aerial photo, and one can see that she originally sat upright on the bottom before giving up all hope of being rescued and thus laid herself down easy.

25 September 2019. Rob is hull cleaning. I can hear him as I type, gradually swishing his way around, and when he gets a little further towards his start point, I will put on the kettle for a well-deserved coffee. He is not alone as there are numerous parrotfish watching his progress with an eye out for titbits from the meagre scrapings. A period upstream in largely fresh water does wonders for getting rid of saltwater growth.

All the walking, exploring and snorkelling led us both to have some of the best nights' sleeps for a long while, and soon we were ashore once again on a papaya hunt, this time the other way around the islet for our last south-west Pacific island jaunt.

26 September 2019. We oohed and aahed at the rock formations, admired the flowers and collected some shells and coral to place on local canine hero Mousse's memorial at the shore end of the pontoon. Sixteen years ago, when the owners of the resort on the island were packing up ready to depart permanently, their faithful hound refused to leave, so they moved away anyhow. Word spread along the cruiser grapevine, and visiting yacht crews started taking Mousse food. Local cruisers visited him regularly, and a local vet agreed to treat him when he was ill.

Mousse would wander down the jetty when a cruiser arrived and eyeball them until they came ashore, then he would lead them on a conducted tour of his islet. Until 2017 when he died, he showed hundreds of cruising yachtsmen and visitors around his terrain. What a dog!

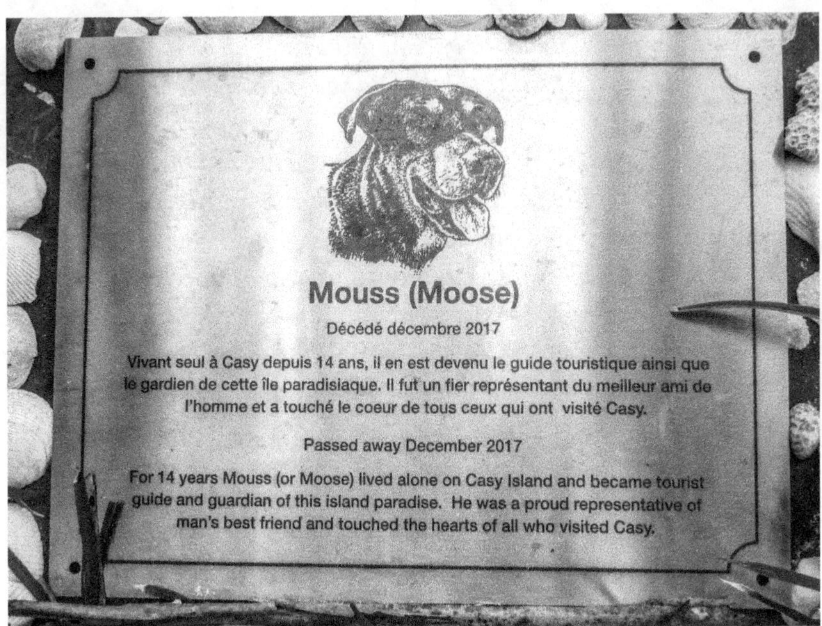

Sole inhabitant Moose

Getting ready to leave Nouméa

We arrived back in Nouméa harbour and anchored on the very edge of the mooring field in Eugenie Eleanor's Baie de l'Orphelinat (Orphanage Bay) near Port Sud.

Happy that *Zoonie* was secure, we motored the tender into the marina to see if they could squeeze us in while we prepared our departure, but as it was lunchtime we decided to have a beer before going upstairs to the office.

28 September 2019. After a few minutes a familiar sunglassed man walked towards us. "That is your dinghy, isn't it?"

"Yes."

"You know you cannot just come into the marina and tie up your dinghy; it is not allowed." His tone was aggressive. Clearly to him seeing us sitting here in the bar beneath the office, sipping a beer, was a sure sign we were up to something illicit.

"Maybe you remember that three weeks ago we were clients of yours, and this morning we telephoned you and Rob asked you if you had any

berths, and you told him to call back at 2.00 pm, so here we are!" Always best to simply state the facts, I think. Did you note my emphasis on 'you', pinning him down!

"Oh, I had so much on this morning, can you remind me what I said?"

So we did, and it suddenly became OK to leave the dinghy there.

From our pleasant spot on the edge of the mooring field we watched as dinghies disappeared into the private marina opposite, which we had noted on the way in, so we went and took a look. A few dinghies were tied up at the fuelling jetty, so we did the same, and I went into the office there and spoke to a very nice young man, who said we were welcome to leave it there for a small cost and advised that the supermarket was just over the other side.

So, we victualled up in an upmarket Casino store that supplied the many luxury apartments in that area of town and then had a delicious and relaxing coffee, where the café boss was happy to provide his internet password, before returning to *Zoonie*. Rob then took the diesel cans across to fuel up, and so two major jobs were completed just a few yards from *Zoonie*.

We were expecting to take around a week for the crossing, and reading the books and nosing the charts was helping us feel prepared mentally for this next passage. A familiar mixture of excited anticipation and a hint of trepidation settled in my mind for a few days, but as time marched on this faded and then I couldn't wait to leave, return to our own little bubble on the ocean, become students once more of the elements and far from the troubled world of humanity.

The next day sunglassed man from Port Moselle Marina confirmed that, having given them three weeks' notice of a berth request, they could, in fact, change the 'maybe' into a berth number, and we made our way around there, if nothing else, to make the lengthy 'clearing out' walk via Immigration to Customs and then the harbourmaster just a little shorter.

Chapter 8

Embracing Australia's East Coast

1 October 2019. The weather was total blue, and the sea agreed that all was well in the 12-knot wind, but it didn't last and we didn't mind because, as you know, Zoonie likes a blow. Her mood rubs easily off on us, so we were both delighted as the wind rose gradually but determinedly to the top 20s.

Within 24 hours we had a wind of 26 knots gusting 28 knots and a delightful speed of over 7 knots. The day was bright and sunny but the night was cool, and out came my leggings and NZ black-with-gold-polka-dot slippers for the watch periods. We delighted in our zero-carbon footprint and our zero-chemical overboard regime. All our wash powders and liquids on board are now chemical free, and only organic waste goes overboard. Our electric power comes from the bountiful wind and blessed sun.

Zoonie whizzes along, bounding forth to Bundy (Bundaberg), tight as a well-turned nut, working with the waves which were coming to her port stern quarter atop the three-metre swell as an efficient machine, and she continued to do so as she had done for four days as we crossed the Coral Sea over the New Caledonia Basin.

One night Rob saw a brilliant flash of light shining down onto the foredeck for about a second. It was too bright to see if there was anything above it being its source, and it reminded me of the strange phenomenon of lights sometimes experienced by mariners when leaving port or far out to sea. (Our friend Neville de Villiers in New Zealand saw them as he left Sydney years ago and this was not the only time we witnessed bright flashes of light at sea.)

The following evening a feeding frenzy took place near us with birds above and dolphins below, working together for their supper.

Appetites assuaged, some of the dolphins came to us for a visit. The sun was nearing the horizon, and as I have done so many times before, I could not miss recording the beautiful scene; after all, no two sunsets are exactly the same. Imagine my surprise when, without my realising, the dolphins were still with us, leading us westwards to Australia.

A lesson in tiller steering

Five days out, and the wind was weakening. It was with a mixture of relief and regret that we adjusted *Zoonie's* rig to suit our failing source of power. Around midnight, the clattering of the genoa sheet in its block helped us make the decision to furl the sail safely away and start the engine. Rob set the autopilot and disconnected Henry the self-steering gear, and as a last check I went to make sure the wheel was unlocked and free to move.

The wheel usually has a little play in it when on auto steering, but this time it went too far; in fact, it went on full lock without changing *Zoonie's* heading. In a little moonlight, we dismantled the pedestal it is attached to and found the chain was off the cog and the cable on the starboard side was loose.

So, just before midnight, with his head torch on, Rob handed me the entire contents of the lazarette, which I laid along the side-deck. The steering quadrant was underneath a wooden hatch, and as soon as Rob lifted the hatch we saw the splayed ends of the snapped cable, showing us, immediately, the cause of the problem.

The knowledge that the autopilot was working independent of the wheel and would now be one of the alternative means of steering – which also included the emergency tiller, Henry and his Hydrovane rudder, and the bow thruster – was reassuring.

Initially Rob thought that by connecting a continuous line, attached to the end of the emergency tiller and through blocks to the cockpit, would enable us to hold the main rudder still and leave the work to Henry, but as there was now virtually no wind, we would need to keep the engine on anyway to proceed, and so might as well use the autopilot and rig the steering ropes for when we needed to take over the steering while approaching land.

It may sound strange, but I felt we were absolutely secure despite being almost 300 miles from the coast and sitting above a depth of 1,986 metres of water. We knew the weather was settled and calm, *Zoonie* was not going to sink and we could drift for as long as it took to get sorted out, which wasn't long, but perhaps, even more importantly, we had time to mentally prepare and discuss our arrival procedure under the new circumstances.

5 October 2019. Nearer to Bundy, of course, we will need to steer up the channel and into the marina; so, how easy is it to steer with the lines?

In the light of the waxing moon, miles from land, we have been experimenting, and we both found it was no problem at all to steer Zoonie, and what's even more helpful is to know that the knot Rob has now tied marks her rudder midship point. Because the tiller sits backwards over the rudder, whichever side rope we pull, Zoonie will turn that way (unlike a tiller on a dinghy). That was a new experience for us. I like new experiences.

A few hours later and as a precaution I

Rob fits the emergency tiller

emailed Bundy marina about our situation and asked if a tow could be made available should the conditions require it.

Then we got on with the task of enjoying the rest of the crossing.

The weather continued to be beautiful, and we had two consecutive nights of rare perfect sunsets without a whisper of cloud anywhere near as the blazing sun sucked the light into its fiery furnace.

By now we were leaving the favourable easterlies, riding along the top of a high into a wind vacuum, so we had to continue motoring, which always troubles me because of the carbon footprint effect, but at least we had sailed for well over half the distance. Small groups of false killer whales moved gently away behind us, and more pods of dolphins appeared as we neared the coastal region.

Last Pacific offshore day

6 October 2019. Sadly, this is our last day out of sight of land in the great and beautiful (in my view) Pacific; after our departure from Bundaberg, we will be coast-hopping southwards to Tasmania for Christmas and then west along the south coast of Australia. Sailing close to land, with all its hazards, is not as relaxing as the freedom of the ocean. I do love a wide, deep ocean.

The wind is piping up as we pass between the off-lying Lady Musgrave Island and Lady Elliot Island, blowing from the north across the Bundaberg River mouth while Zoonie slowly makes her own unassisted way in, her rope steering system working well.

Pam in the marina office suggests we anchor for the night just by the marina as it is the Australian celebration of the Queen's birthday, meaning our clearance will not be until tomorrow. At least that makes the initial stage easy.

Rob goes forward to get the anchor ready, and Zoonie turns perfectly into position. Down hurries the hook with a good bite into the muddy bottom.

7 October 2019. How handy it would be, I was thinking, if we could just up the anchor, do a little circle in the river and go straight into a really convenient available berth just behind us and not have to make two moves. Bless her, Pam was thinking along those same lines this morning, and she has allocated us Black 6. "I just want things to be as easy as possible for you," she said with conviction.

An abundance in Bundy

Aimee from Bio and Leah from Immigration descended upon us within a few minutes of our arrival in Black 6 and were quick and efficient as well as friendly.

Then Colin of QuinRig advised us that his lads (son Jesse, who'd trained at Spencer Rigging in Southampton and Cowes, Isle of Wight, and fellow employee Danny) would be coming up from Mooloolaba (emphasis on the 'loo') to remove a mast on another vessel the following week and would do our steering cable job and a rig check at the same time.

So, we were free to explore. The new Bundy marina is sat alongside the Burnett River, with good holding for anchoring on either side of the river on approach. The land was once sugar cane plantations (there are still a few to supply the local Bundaberg Rum Distillery), and I could picture a 'blackbirder' in the offing as it prepared to anchor and disgorge the next load of stolen ni Vanuatu and New Caledonians to work in the fields back in the day.

A regular marina courtesy bus service ran, surprisingly, on each Sunday to the Shalom Market, in the grounds of a private school, where local farmers bring their wonderful fresh fruit and vegetables. The timetable and itinerary for this trip really depended on the driver, and ours was Paul, who had his priorities exactly right, because he shortened the market trip and pulled up in front of Dan Murphy's, the biggest off-licence you can imagine, where we were able to stock up.

Three days later Jesse and Danny arrived with the shiny new steering cable. For all we knew the old steering cable was the original, and the manual suggests regular maintenance and replacement every two to five years. *Zoonie* is thirty years old!

17 October 2019. It was blowing a hoolie as Jesse hauled brave Danny aloft for the rigging check. All was well at the top of the mast. It was the shorter inner stays that go from the side-decks and foredeck to the first spreaders (renewed in the UK in July 2015 before we left) that were found to have been overtightened at some stage and had started to spring their strands. You can see daylight between the loose strand on the baby stay and the core. They could not replace the rigging at the time, so we agreed to have them back on board when in their neck of the woods at Mooloolaba.

Let's get things strait

19 October 2019. The shags on the fairway navigation marker were either still asleep or yawning as we passed by, and shortly afterwards Zoonie was under full sail and heading directly for the northern entrance to the Great Sandy Strait at 5.1 knots in sunshine and under a clearing sky. We had an easy 23 miles to go to the fairway buoy at the entrance to the Burnett River, which leads to Bundaberg: a nice little hop to regain confidence in the steering system.

So, *Zoonie* is effectively embarking on the first day of her semi-circumnavigation of Australia, which will take about a year, before we leave next October from the west coast to cross the Indian Ocean. Not before we spend three months or so back home, of course. (Or so I thought at the time.)

On Sunday, 20 May 1770, Captain-to-be James Cook and his loyal crew in the good ship *Endeavour* were heading north and passing the tip of Break Sea Spit, as he named it, which runs NNW from the top end of Fraser Island, then known by the Aboriginal people as K'gari (and now officially known by the original name) and only named Fraser Island long after Cook's passing by.

He had just named Sandy Cape at the top of K'gari and shortly before that, Indian Head: 'a black bluff head or point of land, on which a number of Natives were Assembled, which occasioned my naming it Indian Head.' (Taken from *Captain Cook's Journal During His First Voyage Round the World*.)

By the afternoon of the next day, they were near to clearing the east side of Break Sea Spit when Cook sent a boat ahead to sound the bottom and thus chart the northern extent of the spit. When we were planning our route to Bundy with the help of Cook's work, the pilot book and available advice, we determined that a safe passage in would be between Lady Elliot and Lady Musgrave islands, to keep us well away from this dangerous patch of water.

By the evening on Cook's voyage, they were well into Hervey Bay, which we were crossing on our trip, Cook heading NW while we pointed in the opposite direction, SSE. 'We discover'd from the Mast head land to the Westward, and soon after saw smooke upon it.'

Aboard *Zoonie* 249 years later, we were seeing descendants of Cook's 'Boobies' (booby birds, see below) socialising with the shags, and we were hoping they would not want to land upon *Zoonie* for reasons you will well understand, but Cook came up with an interesting comment and deduction:

'For these few days past we have seen at times a sort of Sea fowl we have nowhere seen before that I remember; they are of the sort called Boobies. Before this day we seldom saw more than 2 or 3 at a time, and only when we were near the land. Last night a small flock of these birds passed the Ship and went away to the North-West, and this morning from half an hour before sunrise to half an hour after, flights of them were continually coming from the North-North-West, and flying to the South-South-East, and not one was seen to fly in any other direction. From this we did suppose that there was a Lagoon, River, or Inlet of Shallow Water to the Southward of us, where these birds resorted to in the day to feed, and that not very far to the Northward lay some Island, where they retired to in the night.'

He was right about the river, inlet or lagoon, and that is to where we were heading. Cook's next landing was 46 miles north of Bundaberg; at 5.00 pm the next day they were 'abreast of the South point of a Large open Bay where I intended to Anchor.' I like his professional use of capitals for nautical terms.

Endeavour anchored in Bustard Bay, named as such by Cook because of the numerous birds of that type in the area, in particular the 17.5 lb bird that graced their table that night.

Flocks of shearwaters and terns fished together as we crawled up the shallow channel to anchor off Sandy Point with some very threatening cloud banks gathering in the distance. The wind was fresh, but a sand bar protected us from swell and waves, and *Zoonie* sat happily as we watched sheet lightning over the mainland while listening to the

England v Wallabies rugby match in the Oita Stadium, Japan, on our little black tranny. We beat them 40–16.

20 October 2019. This morning three little birds, either tree martins or welcome swallows, were sitting on our handrail as I emerged to inspect the day. We made our way southwards towards Kingfisher anchorage where there is a resort and more protection from the fresh SE winds.

The scenery around us is so similar to The Solent between the Isle of Wight and Southampton Water that I wonder: if Cook had explored into the waterway he accurately guessed was there, would he have agreed with my comparison? The tides behave exactly the same as in The Solent, which is a comfortable familiarity. The rise and the ebb of the tide happen at both ends, meeting at Boonlye Point here and Cowes in The Solent. The Great Sandy Strait is longer than The Solent, providing around forty miles of enclosed waterway while the Solent has just over 30 miles, but the same brisk transit can be enjoyed by entering one end at the start of the rise and exiting the far end during the ebb: favourable tide all the way!

The channels were easy to follow today on the tablet, which acts as a copy of the chart plotter in the cockpit, and we gave ourselves the advantage of deep water by travelling two hours before high and anchoring north of the little jetty in 6.6 metres, knowing the spring tides were approaching and the water would drop around 2 metres. We are expecting strong winds tomorrow, up to 50 knots, so Rob has let out 35 metres of chain, giving her a longer take-up time on the curve of the chain, the catenary, which might exceed the duration of gusts, and to put more weight overboard. The inner end of the chain is fixed to the inside of the anchor locker by means of a stout rope that can be quickly cut if we need to ditch the anchor, if it's snagged and cannot be retrieved, for example. We also factored in the direction in which the wind would push her, to make sure we were sufficiently far from the sandy beach to not bottom on an ebbing tide. Ooooh, no thanks.

We went ashore quickly to the resort to book a guided day excursion for the next day, and then we took a leisurely stroll up through the wooded hill beside the resort for a fine look down on *Zoonie* in her anchorage – always a pleasure. I took photos of plants with the curious bottlebrush-like fruits, *Banksia* shrubs, named by Cook after his friend, patron and botanist Joseph Banks.

Fraser Island

In 1836 the *Stirling Castle* brig was under sail and bound from Singapore to Sydney with eighteen crew and passengers on board and under the command of Captain James Fraser when she hit a reef in the Great Barrier Reef and was irreparably holed. The crew along with Eliza Fraser, the captain's pregnant wife in imminent likelihood of bearing her fourth child, took to the ship's lifeboat and pinnace. The crew in the leading boat towed the captain and his wife and their small group towards Brisbane, but since the second boat was taking in water, the crew cast it off to beach on K'gari, possibly for their own best chance of survival.

At some stage they were taken in by local Aboriginal people. Captain James made himself unpopular by refusing to work alongside the natives and died in mysterious circumstances either by starvation or from injuries or both; either way, one crew member said it was "natural causes". (Not a popular man with anybody, it seems.)

Eliza, who had given birth while in the small boat, where the infant drowned in the scuppers, decided it was better to work with the ladies of the clan and stayed with them for

Mrs. Eliza Fraser, the wife of Captain Fraser, lived with the Aborigines on Fraser Island for about 9 weeks. Debilitated after the shipwreck and subsequent voyage to the island in an open longboat, during which she gave birth to a baby which drowned in the scuppers, she suffered badly when put to work with the Aboriginal women. She was taken off the island by the tribe when they made their annual migration to the mainland and she was rescued from a corroboree near Lake Cootharaba by a former convict. She later returned to England, where she set up a tent in London's Hyde Park and charged sixpence admission to those who wanted to hear her story. A film was made of the Fraser saga starring Susannah York, John Waters, Trevor Howard and Noel Ferrier.

Mrs Eliza Fraser

six weeks. Then the clan took her group to the mainland with them for their annual corroboree where she was 'rescued' by either John Graham or David Bracewell, both convicts, and taken to Sydney.

In Sydney Eliza set up a charity to raise money for her three children back home and then secretly married another sea captain, Alexander Greene, six months after James' demise, and together they returned to England, the £400 charity haul tucked safely inside her bodice.

She appealed to the Lord Mayor of London to be allowed to set up another charity for her 'penniless' children and their widowed mother.

Ambitious Eliza then embarked on talking tours of the UK and eventually Australia, telling various stories about her capture and 'ill treatment' at the hands of the 'cannibalistic savages' in order to raise money. She soon twigged that the more outlandish her stories were, the more money she made, the effect of which was fatal for many of the Aboriginal people living on K'gari.

When colonists and settlers migrated to the area they would take hunting trips, often on religious holidays like Christmas and Easter, to kill as many natives as they could, based on their Eliza Fraser-induced fears. Her claims eventually led to the massacre and dispossession of the island's clans.

It is, then, hardly surprising that she is now part of Australian folklore.

Eliza was run over by the wheels of a carriage in Melbourne in 1858.

21 October 2019. Our blue high-wheel-arched 4x4 coach bounced and swayed along the deep-rutted and very dry sand tracks. We needed to wear seat belts so we would not be shot upwards and bang our heads on the coach roof. Branches screeched along the windows, and we rocked from side to side in true trade-wind- rolling-sea style.

Peter explained that there is a freshwater lake underneath the island, possibly resting in a basin of rock, like the jam in a doughnut, the volume of which is seven times that of Sydney Harbour, so all over the island this pure fresh spring water fills lakes and runs downstream to the sea. This would have made it an agreeable place to live for the Aboriginal people before the arrival of white settlers, when, from 1860 to 1992, the island was stripped of all its useful wood: Australian kauris, brush box trees, she-oaks, hoop pines, paperbarks (Melaleucas) and turpentine trees (Syncarpia, satinays). The latter with their open bark were so rot-proof they were used in marine projects like the Suez Canal and the rebuilding of the River Thames docks after the Second World War.

This and the after-effects of Eliza's stories could have caused the permanent decline of the Butchulla people, but as recently as in 2014 certain native rights were given back to the indigenous people to permit hunting, fishing and taking fresh water. Already much of the running of tours and maintenance of the island is down to members of the Butchulla clan – a move in the right direction.

Back on board *Zoonie*, a lovely way to round off the interesting day was watching two whistling kites buzzing a beautiful white-bellied sea eagle above us. The contrast in size and colouring confirmed it was an eagle, and the grace with which is soared and swung without moving its wings to avoid the kites was memorable.

Some tricky navigation ahead

It was only going to take four or so hours to navigate this southern half of our passage down the Great Sandy Strait and get from our Kingfisher Bay anchorage southwards to Garrys Anchorage where we could find enough water for *Zoonie* to go through low water safely during the night. Since we were passing the mid-tide point at Boonlye, we set off two hours before high water so we would benefit from the last two hours of flood and the first two hours of ebb for the last stage of the route.

After that, all thoughts about tide times were put on the back shelf since my concentration rested on following the dashed pink line on the chart plotter from the top of the screen downwards along the sometimes uncomfortably narrow channel. Vast areas of water were all around us, as in The Solent, but by wearing my polarised sunglasses I could see the paler greenish water showing where the submerged sandbanks lay, and they were usually well marked with green and red channel markers.

22 October 2019. The GPS heading, the green line on the plotter, has a delayed reaction to course changes, so as soon as I can I follow a heading from the chart plotter by lining up Zoonie's green line heading over the pink dashed line or the next waypoint Rob has previously set, then I take a compass reading, which has a more immediate response to a course change and is a backup in case the chart plotter freezes, as it did once on this journey (fortunately where there was plenty of water and a clear course for the next mile, so Rob had time to turn it off and on again).

When we set off there was no wind, but as we turned to port after the two reds into the channel it was around 17 knots on the nose and the sun was well down in the sky. At one point Rob became agitated as he thought we were moving out of the channel. I showed him we were well within the markers in a wide part of the channel with plenty of water, but this did little to convince him. Rob is still suffering mental strain for his own reasons, so Zoonie and I just plodded, quietly, onward.

Halfway up the tiny channel to Garrys Anchorage our anchor went down in 3.4 metres at 5.35 pm. We rewarded ourselves with a well-earned G&T. It was dark within 30 minutes.

The next day was a long one. It was just a short distance back to the main channel, and we headed south to Inskip Point in Wide Bay Harbour, at the end of the strait, to wait out the remaining fall in the tide, and then at the start of next rise we would set off to motor along towards the Wide Bay Bar.

This sand bar outside the passage between Fraser Island and the mainland to the south shifts on a ten-year cycle. To obtain the best waypoints for our crossing we phoned the nearby VMR (Volunteer Marine Rescue) who texted back the co-ordinates for us to use.

While we relaxed on board we chatted with Nick and Susie on *Water Music*, anchored near us, and Susie commented that they and the other thirty-odd boats would be dealing with crossing the bar in the morning; however, we had four good reasons to do it this evening.

First, we had already decided to and were comfortable with our decision. Second, the depth of water would be half a metre deeper on our evening as the tides were moving towards neeps, where the height of tide, the difference between high and low water, is at its least. Third, the sun in the morning would be low in the sky ahead of us, whereas with our evening choice it would be tucked out of the way behind *Zoonie*. Finally, the thought of negotiating a confined passage in the company of many other yachts did not appeal!

At 3.30 pm we recovered the anchor and set off, feeling that the trickiest part of our passage down the Great Sandy Strait was over. We had around us some unusual dolphins. A youngster was charcoal coloured but the adults were pinkish. Our reference book, Hadoram Shirihai and Brett Jarrett's *Whales, Dolphins and Seals*, identified them as Indo-Pacific humpback dolphins, and our latitude was near their most southerly range, so we were, indeed, fortunate. Our heading was 080° compass.

It felt good to be approaching open water again, but we still had this hurdle to cross. The depths were comfortable as we motored on down past the Inskip Point leads, otherwise known as the Mad Mile, where we turned to a heading of 050°, but in a westerly wind and with an opposing rising tide there are sometimes standing waves here, hence the nickname.

23 October 2019. "Ready?" I asked Rob as I turned Zoonie right through almost 90 degrees onto the required course for the next mile or so. It was a good course we had been given; we had over five metres all the way across the mid-blue colour on the plotter and were soon clear, with our chosen anchorage nine miles distant and reassuringly visible.

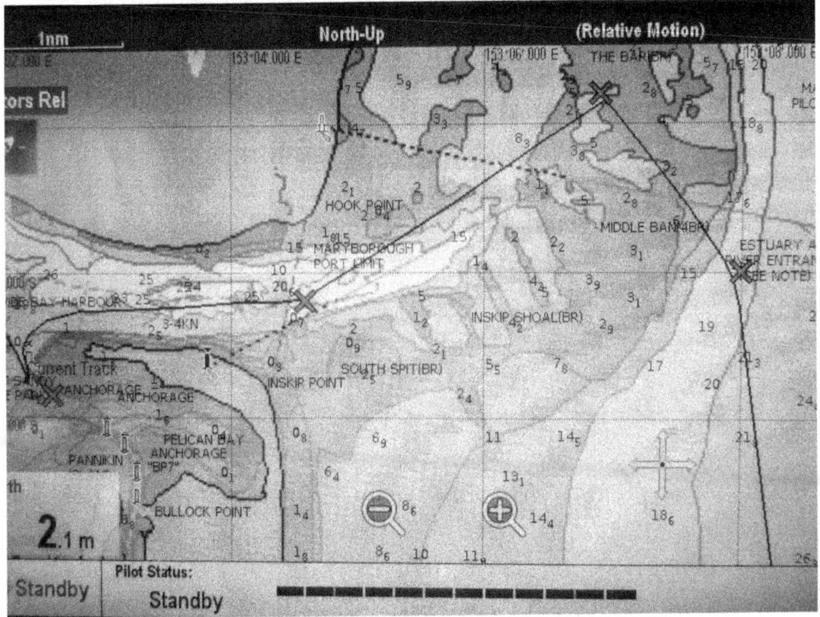

Along the Mad Mile

Two hours later we were anchored in Double Island Point bay, named by Cook.

A short quote from Captain Cook shows the logical way he named places:

'Tuesday 27 July 1802. At half past nine [am] we hauled close around Double- Island Point, within a rock lying between one and two miles to the NNE.' (Wolf Rock.) 'It is a steep head, at the extremity of a neck of land which runs out two miles from the main [land].' Captain Cook's description fitted the Point perfectly.

The anchorage was like the blue-sleeved, gentle arm of a protective mother, enfolding us, and since the wind was still in the SE the roll was minimal, but we weren't sure of the bottom. We didn't feel the anchor bite the seabed in the darkness, so we set the anchor alarm to tell us if *Zoonie* was moving beyond the length of chain plus her own 40 feet. She jiggled about on the circumference of her range but had not moved far by the morning.

As we predicted, by the time I looked out of *Zoonie*'s big side window just after 6.00 am, there was an armada of white sails heading towards the point, some passing inside of the rock and others taking a much further offshore route. We merged in with the fleet, a little like turning right at a busy junction, and headed south on a smooth snakeskin sea, with just enough wind to fill the sails.

Pantropical spotted dolphins came to see how we were getting on, and just before entering the harbour an adult humpback whale rolled over revealing the white under its fins and belly. Again, Rob and I were looking at the same spot of water at the same time to see this beauty. Their migration back to the Antarctic was nearly finished, so we were lucky to see this one.

Mooching around Mooloolaba

---

27 October 2019. As I write this Zoonie is happily sitting alongside her own pontoon at a luxury residential address opposite Minyama Island in Mooloolaba Harbour, courtesy of Lynne and Geoff who own and live in the house; I don't think she has ever been so sophisticated. There's even carpet on her landing stage!

It is not only humans who enjoy this Australian East Coast seaside resort; we awaken on Zoonie in the mornings to the sound of the local myna birdsong, while paddle-tailed bush turkeys pick over the tinder-dry undergrowth for grubs, and ospreys nest happily on the tops of poles within easy reach of interested eyes and camera lenses.

The young of today play water games and whizz around the canal next to Zoonie on their sail boards, exercising and practising under adult instruction, maybe to be tomorrow's lifeguards. The lost fishermen of yesterday are remembered in bronze, and families and couples of all ages who love to be beside the seaside are here, either on holiday or living in the apartments, of which there are many, or in spacious homes on the leafy, wide-streeted suburbs.

Jesse and Danny from QuinRig came and laid out their toolkits on Zoonie's freshly carpeted pontoon and replaced the five shrouds that were in the invisible process of becoming undone as single strands of steel were breaking beneath the swages.

Australia Zoo

29 October 2019. I don't think I would be far wrong in saying that the late and much-loved crocodile hunter Steve Irwin's ethos in life was to love, understand and respect the animals with whom we share the world and by extension to take action to protect animals in the wild, by stopping the human behaviour that causes them extreme harm and the real threat of extinction.

With over a hundred bush fires burning throughout Queensland and New South Wales at the moment and the devastation that will inevitably cause to wildlife, especially the animals that cannot escape the inferno, like koalas, the role of Australia Zoo in protecting indigenous species is as vital as its work in protecting foreign species. One known colony of over 300 koalas has succumbed to the fires already, and they are predicted to get worse.

The afternoon may have been very hot, but seeing the animals so relaxed was contagious. Rob loves giraffes, so we hung around there and enjoyed their elegant movements; that was except when the youngster disapproved of the keeper's near proximity and chased him away. They can move very quickly when they need to.

Seeing adults with their babies is always a good sign, since they are obviously contented enough to breed, and especially the white rhino with her baby gave us some hope for their continuity. Even the quite long, hot walk to the far end of this enclosure did not put people off making the effort to visit the endearing meerkats; their lookout movements remind Rob and me of our watch-keeping 360-degree horizon checks when we're on passage.

Beautiful Brisbane

6 November 2019. From the rooftop dining area and pool in the youth hostel where we are staying for five days there is an amazing broad view over the city skyline, which we enjoy while eating breakfast and later, after a hot day of exploration, while swimming to cool off and relax.

Brisbane is blessed with plenty of green spaces, and one of the oldest and most carefully preserved is ANZAC Square. ANZAC formally stands for Australian and New Zealand Army Corps (1914–18), but the informal and more appropriate meaning is anyone from Australia or New Zealand, because here the Boer War, Second World War and Vietnam War fallen are also remembered.

Two hundred Aboriginal people served in the Boer War as trackers in South Africa despite not being recognised as Australian citizens, and it is likely that some were not allowed back to their native homeland because of the White Australia policy of the time. Indigenous intellectuals and academics are busy researching the history of their people and writing books about their past within an ever-changing society of mixed opinions and politics. Also, it is a pleasure to hear radio interviews with indigenous people who are living and expressing themselves and their origins within contemporary Australian society, not forgetting, of course, the ongoing struggles of people such as our friend Tyronne Bell, of the Ngunnawal people, with whom we had spent time in Canberra, who is fighting for the restoration of land titles around his own and other centres of modern civilisation.

The weather was still clear and blue for our five-day stay in the city, and I mention that for two reasons: first, it is the best light in which to appreciate the modern buildings because most of them are more glass than walls; and second, by the day we left, Brisbane central business district (CBD) was becoming engulfed in the acrid smoke haze from the bush fires raging not far away. The koalas in the wild could all have done with a flight arranged by Flight Centre to airlift them out. That is exactly what happened for some lucky ones, so I have heard.

9 November 2019. The City Botanic Gardens are a wonderfully peaceful alternative to the noisy, bustling street life of the city just a few paces away and Brisbane has plenty of open spaces where busy city-dwellers can relax and unwind. The birdlife in the botanical gardens is delightful, with the blue-winged kookaburras calling, bush herons chilling in the shade and an extensive ibis colony nesting in the treetops. (I was so surprised to see them, I thought they had escaped from somewhere!)

A fire-licked weather window to Coffs Harbour

14 November 2019. We are getting used to the rapid changes in the Australian weather, and choosing the best weather window is becoming something of an art form. This weather window promised a nice sailing breeze as we continue down the Australian east coast, followed by light winds and then a 30-knot wind up Zoonie's stern followed by a 180-degree turnabout, to the same velocity from the south, but by the time that happens, we plan to be tucked up in Coffs Harbour.

After a predictable morning, the sailing breeze started to fail and we motored towards the dramatic ledge where the famous East Australian Current gave us a little over 2 knots – not to be sniffed at when it amounts to nearly 50 miles every 24 hours on top of Zoonie's own speed.

Great swathes of mustard scum covered the water, and we could not make out whether it was pollen from the land or some miniscule sea flora. Hundreds of small white shoe-shaped cuttlefish shells floated past, and I wondered what had killed them at such a young age; could it be related to the fires?

During the night I listened to Radio Australia while I was on watch. The Port Macquarie Koala Hospital had put out a request for $25,000 to buy watering stations to be distributed in the bush so a variety of wild animals could have a life-saving drink. In view of the unprecedented early and extensive fires and the global coverage of the unfolding tragedy, in a very short time they raised over $500,000. A heartwarming spec of hope during the catastrophe.

'Ember Alert' from sky-born sparks and 'Watch and Act' were just two of the warnings, bush fire terminology, constantly being heard on the radio. Sometimes people leave it too late to escape and they just have to take cover and hope for the best.

The new day dawned to the ever-present sulphur grey skies from the wood smoke. The smell was not one of a happy campfire but of death and destruction, and it was depressing. *Zoonie* was covered with tiny black bits of carbon, despite being miles out to sea, and goodness knows what effect this acrid, particle-filled air will have on the lungs of all air-breathing creatures, animal and human, in the long term.

Around us were lots of sleek black false killer whales gliding elegantly through the water. Terns and sooty shearwaters skimmed over the calm of the morning, but as the afternoon approached the barometer was falling and the sea was definitely building, the waves getting bigger from the north-east and the swell lifting *Zoonie* higher and pushing her along with the bountiful current, helping us in our race against time.

By mid-afternoon there were lots of whitecaps (breaking crests to the waves), and *Zoonie* was speeding along at 9 knots with a poled-out genoa and reefed main. Wonderful progress. So bizarre: death and destruction to our right, yet perfect sailing conditions for us.

Then, at last, with the clock approaching 10.00 pm, we turned between the two headlands of Coffs Harbour – Muttonbird Island on the right and an old quarry hill with a long harbour arm on the left – and were amazed to discover the best night-time transit lights ever. Two massive blue neon triangles that Rob had the sheer fun to keep in line, one above the other, until the red and green at the marina entrance came into view. There was absolutely no chance of losing those lights amidst the other shore lights.

As we turned in towards our berth a voice from nearby said, "Welcome." You remember those sorts of things about people and places.

The smoke hanging over the hills to the west was all too visible the next morning as we made our way ashore for a wander. We could see flames at ground level in the distance.

Rob's iPhone showed us the way to the Aboriginal Coffs Creek Walk, which tells stories of the first residents of the area and identifies medicinal and culinary plant uses. The fires must be heartbreaking for them.

The creek walk was delightful in that it explored the rural world in its natural state, and it was good to see the influence of the native inhabitants, preserving their story for posterity and for use in local schools. What must they think of these fires that they have always avoided by low-level burn offs to clear dry undergrowth?

We found ourselves ducking and diving on Muttonbird (Shearwater) Island, not as you might imagine from the shearwaters who canoodle with this year's mate out at sea, but from the scores of local 'healthies' running up and down the hill, sweaty red necks and dead serious faces.

The way into the harbour looked impressive from above. We could see why those welcoming blue neon triangles keep one well across to the left on entering; there is much turbulence caused by the rocky shore off the island on the right. Even the local fishing boat was taking it very carefully. The resident birds were pigeons, oystercatchers with their pretty orange legs, white-faced herons gliding overhead like witnesses of pre-history, swallows, terns, gulls, buntings and a peregrine falcon. Not a bad head count for a small island.

Two hundred smoky miles to Newcastle

18 November 2019. Yesterday, we picked up that fine favourable current again just three miles off the coast, but even that close in, the coast was not visible as we passed the ironically named Smoky Cape. Flocks of hundreds of shearwaters were gathered together around us, having recently returned from the Philippines in their annual migration, and were now choosing their partners before proceeding to the coast and their regular burrows, including Muttonbird Island, to mate and lay their eggs. For a while our skies were blue and the winds light.

Later, during the night, the wind bucked up to 28–32 knots, a near gale, and Zoonie was reefed right down and manageable.

Muttonbirds returning in the blue

Dolphins arrived in the hours of darkness and torpedoed underneath *Zoonie* and all around her bow, creating tunnels of pale green and alarming the phosphorescence into spots of brilliant light. That was such a pleasure to watch as we hadn't really seen this behaviour since the Atlantic coasts of France, Spain and Portugal back in 2015.

19 November 2019. A fuchsia sun and smoke-filled air greeted us today. Our clothes reek, or is it the permanent stench in our nostrils, or both? Australia really is burning big time and has been for weeks. Winds that spin around the compass don't help and send the flames in all directions, making firefighting even more hazardous.

This time *Zoonie* made a teatime entry to her destination of Newcastle, and again we had telephoned ahead and knew the number and location of our berth. Terns and gulls were having their tea as we came into this major industrial port and tied up at Newcastle Cruising Yacht Club, our home for the next fortnight.

Our friend Greg, who with his wife, Jane, we originally met on the Portugal rally back in 2014 and stayed with earlier this year before we returned home briefly, came over from Jilliby to measure up the job of fitting his Watt&Sea hydrogenerator to *Zoonie's* transom.

A few days later Greg came back with a bracket he had made to facilitate fitting the hydrogenerator, and he and Rob laboured away for a few hours. Rob had already laid all the wire through to the control panel mounted in the aft cabin.

The Watt&Sea propeller turns as *Zoonie* moves through the water and means we have plenty of electricity in the making, around 8 amps. So, when the Rutland Windcharger is producing little, and at night when the solar panels won't produce anything, when under sail we can make plenty of green, free, power; enough to keep the batteries charged and run the watermaker and autopilot.

Newcastle

Newcastle was so named at the beginning of the nineteenth century because, like its English namesake, its main industry was, and still is, coal, using the labour of convicts in the coal mines years ago.

Unlike Newcastle, UK, which has seen a decline in coal production over the last century, Newcastle, New South Wales, is now the biggest exporter of coal in the world.

At our location near the docks, coal dust, building site grit and smoke smuts covered the decks of the moored marina vessels, and I wondered how the microparticles in the air were affecting the lungs of locals and, to a lesser extent, visitors.

However, Newcastle is a city much loved by the modern population because of its diversity and opportunities for all ages: the university and colleges, a vibrant cultural choice and fabulous beaches that cater for their much-loved outdoor way of life.

Zoonie was moored where there used to be wild honeysuckle *Banksia* trees producing copious honey; the only thing remaining of those plentiful times is the naming of Honeysuckle Marina Newcastle, Honeysuckle Drive and young *Banksia* trees planted along the new pathway.

We met Peter and Martina in Fulaga, Fiji, and we were here to visit them at their Bar Beach home. The four of us went down to the bowling club one evening for a nice, cheap meal and beer, and Martina and I decided that next day we would make some strawberry jam, as trays of strawberry seconds were on sale at the local farmers market for an 'I must make jam' price.

We bought four trays, and all my jam jars from *Zoonie* were put to good use. Goody, I could now start collecting again! The two of us set up a conveyor belt process to wash and quarter the red beauties, doing the occasional taste check, of course, while admiring the view of the ocean from the kitchen window. No whales out there that day, just whitecaps.

One day we went for a beach walk with them followed by a homemade supper. As we ate the sky clouded over and we were engulfed in a violent thunderstorm that rumbled and sparked around us. We hoped that some of the torrential rain would reach inland and quench the fire, but no; the rain stayed by the shore and the lightning inland started three more fires. Nature seemed to have lost its temper.

The predicted 34°C of shimmering heat arrived; Australian ravens cawed and crowed with their distinctive and mournful downscale ending as Rob and I walked along the honeysuckle tree-lined promenade. Ladybirds were biting me for a drink; the third one took a flight it didn't expect.

Walking along the beach watching the rollers thunder to shore and then suck sand back down the slope of the beach in the powerful undertow, we decided we would swim at the Newcastle Ocean Baths instead, to cool off. They were just ahead of us, built on the promontory ninety years ago in the gentle art deco style and maintained faithfully since for the enjoyment of all.

To the home of our friends Jane and Greg

Meeting with friends we have made en route is one of the most delightful aspects of cruising, and back on board we packed lightly for our train trip to Wyong Station the next day to be met by Jane and Greg, who live nearby.

From the train window we could see areas where cool (or back) burns had been practised. The tree canopy was green and healthy, the

Shep and Murphy on patrol

tree trunks blackened by the smoke and the ground a bright green carpet of new growth.

Once inside their fenced home with the gate safely closed behind us, Shep remembered and welcomed us and newcomer Murphy just welcomed us anyway. He was not yet six months old. A rescue dog, part mastiff, part Rhodesian Ridgeback with a dusting of Great Dane, with a distinct similarity to Grommit.

28 November 2019. I cannot remember how many lovely walks we had with the dogs around the 20 acres (8 hectares) of paddock they own. The first was with Greg, and we were walking on land that had probably once been cedar forest, was then logged out and used for dairy before being sectioned off and sold, which is when Greg and Jane bought it thirty-odd years ago.

A seasonal stream runs through the land into and out of the pond, and when in full flood a good canoe ride can be had around the centre of the paddock. Last time we visited there were kangaroos around, but not this time. However, the abundance of birds is still evident, and the chorus of kookaburras just after 5.00 am is a lovely sound.

It is wonderful to just sit and chat for long, relaxing periods with our dear friends; after our excursions with them earlier in the year, we don't need to go out to look around, just being 'at home' is perfect.

On our last morning Greg and I planned a bacon and egg breakfast with muffins and local cherry tomatoes, so I got up early, just after 6.00 am, and set off, just me and the dogs, for a lingering, meandering walk in the cool, still damp of the morning. A cuckoo called, and I found part of a tiny creamy-white-with-brown speckled egg telling me the fantails we had seen were nesting.

Murphy was hardly awake and had none of his usual puppy exuberance, which involved jumping up and grabbing my hand; he was so placid I could stroke him without getting myself dotted with slobber, which was nice. I wondered, as I have often wondered before on our travels, will the environmental problems of the world affect this beautiful place or will it be very similar in fifty to one hundred years' time? I hope it stays the same.

Strong winds to Jervis Bay

Back in Newcastle we did a big shop at Coles and spent our final evening with Peter and Martina before parting at the yacht club after a drink. Where will we see them again, I wondered. Which hemisphere? As in all things there are ups and downs, and parting from cruising friends is certainly one of the downs. That's life.

3 December 2019. The wind started off being light and variable and then moved gradually 270 degrees around the compass, increasing to 34 knots, a full gale, at one stage during the night and never dropping to less than 24 knots until the second morning. A low was making its way across us as we headed south to Jervis Bay. We had predicted it, but one thing that varies without warning is the wind speed. So, we were constantly on the lookout for the changes and had to react with rig alterations accordingly.

One night we sailed through the lethal smoke haze off Sydney and Botany Bay; Rob saw the orange glow of the fires, and the next morning Zoonie's decks and windows were once again covered with sooty smuts.

An orange segment moon hangs in the starlit sky while Orion and the Southern Cross keep vigil over the tragedy.

Next morning a wandering albatross swung elegantly by *Zoonie* heading north, and when Rob was leaning over the stern to swing up the Watt&Sea two dolphins came over and looked him in the eyes, just to make sure he was OK.

Still sailing, while we approached Jervis Bay the wind veered westerly from south-west. As we have learned before, an offshore wind can send sudden, vicious gusts over the water that can rise in seconds to 40 knots and more; fortunately for us we were nearly into the protection of this vast and beautiful bay.

We picked up one of the substantial Booderee National Park pink buoys that can take up to 40 tons. Being just 14 tons, we felt wonderfully secure. The idea of the anchoring ban and the provision of these pretty and practical buoys is to protect the seabed from the scouring effect of anchor chains and allow the seagrass to flourish, and it is doing just that, providing home to numerous fish.

Before roads were built onshore, Jervis Bay served as the place where ships loaded up with produce from inland settlements bound for Sydney. With the building of Canberra as the nation's inland capital it was decided in 1908 that the capital should have access to the sea at Jervis Bay, so 28 square miles were handed back to the Commonwealth Government from the NSW Government.

6 December 2019. Our second day here and it is a much gentler day than yesterday, when Zoonie was tugging against her bridle lines onto the buoy in a strong westerly. Flies of all shapes and sizes were coming aboard for a look-see, but now, along with the semi-permanent fly screens on the windows, we have fixed nets over the companionway and open window, so we are enjoying a much more restful, less bruising day.

In the afternoon yesterday smoke from the fires to the south-west of here reached the skies above and the sea eagle was up in the sky to take a look.

Rob is overboard in his wetsuit cleaning the hull; he will be a tired and hungry bunny when he comes back on board. He seems to be more his old pre-medical-emergency self these days, and I am glad for him, and me.

Looking at the weather for our next opportunity to head south, this time to another lovely big natural harbour, Eden, it looks like an early start on Sunday, when we will leave here for the 120-mile leg.

South to Eden

8 December 2019. South, south, south, when will we turn west? Two sea eagles stood sentinel in a tree as we motored past, and then we had a day communing with hundreds of short-beaked common dolphins and their babies all around us, having fun and giving us joy while we sailed on down the Sapphire Coast. The ever-present shy albatross was continuous company. Bigger, blacker petrels than we had seen before, with dart-like wings and a flight resembling the gliding of the albatross, turned out to be Parkinson's petrels, and rich brown sooty shearwaters often accompanied the albatross. The south-east Australian waters seem to support a bountiful diversity of birdlife.

Next day we did the 'Eden Shuffle' to the south side of Twofold Bay from our first night's anchor spot, to shelter from a promised blow from that direction and prepare for the passage across to Tasmania. Clothes fluttered from their line down both sides of *Zoonie's* foredeck, the aroma of a big lasagne filled her cabins, and a fit young man could be seen rigging the storm jib on the baby stay and deflating and stowing the dinghy.

Later, Rob researched the Denison Canal, which will save us many miles to our destination of Hobart, and booked us in to the Prince of Wales Bay Marina for our time there.

Chapter 9

Tasmania

15 December 2019. We have made our way down to Tasmania and are now in a beautiful place called Wineglass Bay while a SW wind blows.

We have high mounts around us on both side of the bay; one is 619 metres high and shrouded in cloud, and believe it or not it is raining at the moment. How the poor mainland could do with this rain. Even as we were travelling down the east coast of Tasmania yesterday afternoon, with shy albatrosses sitting on the water all around us fishing, we saw a bush fire raging on the shore. It seems that no part of the land bordering the sea around all of Australia has escaped the bush fires except Darwin and the south-west area.

When we set out from Eden two days ago, we knew that we would have 24 hours of favourable weather and then up to 30 knots from the west through Bass Strait, and that is what we got for around ten hours.

Are you superstitious? I wasn't until…

The wind peaked at 39 knots when we started to smell burning — not from the bush fires either, but from on board. Then wisps of smoke came from the panel at the back of the chart table, and I noticed the front of the renewable power unit was changing shape, bulging where it shouldn't bulge. As we know, 'where there's smoke, there's fire'.

Were we to be the next victims of the strong westerlies that were fanning the flames onshore?

Rob dashed aft to stop the wind turbine that was producing so much power. Combined with the solar panels in full sunshine, they burned out the control unit, which started to overheat dangerously. Fire at sea is a terrifying prospect. I have seen vessels burned to the waterline; was this to be our lovely Zoonie's fate?

There was no time for him to put on waterproofs, but mercifully the high seas didn't drench him. Phew, an hour later the unit was cooler but of course now needs replacing. Surely there is a fuse somewhere to prevent that happening? That was a real scare, and brave Rob, as ever, was onto anything that threatened Zoonie's integrity, and it was on Friday the 13th!

We are seeing evidence of the bountiful high latitude (42° S) waters: the jelly fish are enormous, there are hundreds of short beaked common dolphins and lots of bird life!

To Hobart

We left Wineglass Bay, famous for its beautiful shape and beach, heading for Prosser Bay and briefly had the company of a big humpback whale near to us travelling north. At the time we were unaware of the bush fires that had now started along the north shore of Tasmania, but we did know that the New South Wales fires were getting a lot worse, greater in number and size, and this trend was only going to continue.

We anchored in the bay, and during the evening we watched as a thunderstorm, blackening the skies, moved around us, but yet again the rain went no further inland than the coast, leaving the land burning.

A weather terminology new to me was the 'Indian Ocean Dipole', which sends westerly winds over Australia bringing with them the incredible heat from the 'hot red centre', making firefighting around Sydney, Brisbane and Canberra so difficult. The fires we saw here were more frightening and faster moving than we had witnessed before. Even areas of the South Island, New Zealand, saw the smoke from 1,200 miles away.

But we were heading south, would that make a difference to the risk of bush fires – a cooler climate? We would see.

16 December 2019. The days are long now, and we know that we will still have at least an hour of light after our ETA around seven o'clock this evening.

Later…

We chose the Prince of Wales Bay on the advice of our friends Ken and Bron, and as we approach, the area looks industrial. Turning into the little lagoon past the zinc factory, Mount Wellington rises dark and proud to 1,270 metres (4,180 feet) behind everything. I have it on very good authority (thanks to our friend John Hoult of Gairloch, Scotland) that a mountain rises at least 2,000 feet above sea level, so Mount Wellington definitely qualifies!

It was just eight days before Christmas; would we get anyone on board to help with *Zoonie's* repairs (to the fridge, the autopilot, the cooker, and the hot water tank nut that had cracked)? We were amazed with what Hobart and our suppliers as far away as Great Britain came up with.

18 December 2019. Martin arrived with his gorgeous pure Kelpie, Zoe. Martin is a marine electrician who came at first to look at the fridge while I chatted with Zoe. He concluded the fridge would benefit from a new thermostat and perhaps even a new control unit. So, Rob ordered them and they arrived at the marina two days later, and Martin was able to fit them even before we went north to Ken and Bron's for the celebrations.

Rob then asked him if he knew anything about autohelms, and over the next hour he used his magic meters to trace the fault to the motor on the old ram, which was eating electricity but not using it as it should. A new ram was ordered (£1,550 – aargh), and that arrived after only two days from the mainland to a local dealership, just in time for us to wrap it up and give it to each other for Christmas, because that felt better than just buying it. The most generous present we have ever given each other, by far!

That evening, daytime in the UK, Rob called his old friend Teresa at Marlec and chatted first to an engineer who agreed the wind charger control and regulator unit misbehaved badly when it started to smoke and melt instead of just turning off in the strong winds. Teresa said she would contact her agent in Brisbane and see if he had one which he could send to us, all free of charge. Again, it arrived before our Christmas exodus and Rob promptly fitted it.

Plummer Mark, who had just finished for the day, was most understanding that what a couple of mariners do not want when they are at sea is a boat full of hot water, even though she would make a grand bathtub. So, he followed us back to *Zoonie*, took a look and some measurements, and disappeared back to the plumbing supplier that he always uses and returned a few minutes later with the right parts and sorted the job, bless him.

We were amazed at the efficiency of the delivery system and the promptness of the engineers; all to get it done by Christmas, I guess.

We were drawn, as always, to the waterfront at first, and then the lady in the information office suggested we explore the summit of Mount Wellington on the same day, as it might be closed the next day under the total fire ban rules. So, off we set.

On the summit we were lucky enough to see two long-coated rock wallabies just outside the viewing room windows, busily eating something in the prickly, arid-looking bushes. Looking westwards away from Hobart we could see the island is mountainous and the whole vast area of south-west Tasmania is virtually uninhabited. That is where we will be heading next, aboard *Zoonie* and in company with Bron and Ken on *Nichola*, to Bathurst and Macquarie harbours, after the festive period. But first we will be travelling by road to Bron and Ken's home, in George Town, on the north shore of Tasmania, and then back again to Hobart for the New Year.

20 December 2019. Remember Eden a month ago? Well, most of the residents have run to the wharf as the fires close in on their township, and they have now been ordered to leave under the declared state of emergency, and vessels are being moved in to enable the residents to escape. The BBC News film showed locals and holidaymakers driving their vehicles into the shallows of a lake to protect them and standing in the water looking back at the blazing beach and country beyond. Once the fire has moved through, they will return to the charred and smouldering shore. They must have wondered what would be left of their homes. The narrators of the film were referring to the fire as 'she', the fireships of the bush.

A helicopter was flying water to the hills near us today, but at the moment the skies are blue and the mountains clearly visible. Yesterday we awoke to that now-familiar smell of bush smoke, and as the morning progressed Mount Wellington and its neighbours disappeared in smoke. We kept Zoonie closed up for the sake of our lungs.

We were so fortunate on *Zoonie* that if the fires ever came close to her, we had our own floating means of escape, unlike the human and animal populations of the area, but then you never know what is just around the corner, do you?

North to George Town

Just a month before our arrival, the fields were still green in Tasmania, but as we drove northwards to George Town in Bron's daughter's car, kindly made available for our stay, up the Midland Highway from Hobart, passing the Bristleback Mountains, the only relief from the dry grass natural habitat was where the monster irrigators had rolled slowly around the acres of farmland. What was there for the animals to eat? How were the sheep surviving? How was the wildlife faring? The trees on the hillsides looked sparse, far from dense bushland; as they reached the summits, they looked like the bristles of a brush, hence the name – nothing to do with the fires.

By way of a lunch break, in Launceston, we sat in the shade of street trees outside the Samuel Pepy's Cafe and chatted about the many Devonians and Cornish folk who came this way all those years ago to settle, leaving the UK from nearby Plymouth and Southampton in the 1860s, and made Tasmania their home, naming existing and new towns to mirror their homeland, at the expense of the indigenous people and their culture.

Echidna encounter

After a happy reunion evening in George Town with our friends, Ken drove us out of town on a rural road past fields of white poppies, destined for the legal opium trade, and started climbing a hill that took a turn.

"Ah, look, an echidna," said Bron as it waddled towards the road from her side. Ken pulled over and we got out for a look. On seeing us humans the little chap made its way across the road, and we followed at an unthreatening distance. Once on the other side it found a hollow

'Our' echidna

and wiggled itself into it, so for a few moments all we could see was its lovely brown hairy coat with those amazing spines sticking out. Along with platypuses, echidnas are monotremes, mammals that lay eggs, but the name comes from their having a singular urogenital hole: *mono* = one, *treme* = hole. The little creatures have one hole through which they pass bodily and reproductive matter.

There are few left in the wild, same old, sad, story, so we were, indeed, fortunate.

Down by the riverside we stopped at Ken's old camping and swimming spot from his childhood. He reminisced on some of the stories of those happy days when wildlife was bountiful. A pretty little blue-headed wren and its less colourful mate flitted around the grasses on the banks. This was a little haven of quintessential Australia.

Low Head Lighthouse

24 December 2019. At night in Lymington years ago I would listen to the mournful sound of The Needles Lighthouse foghorn. To be more technical,

Low Head Lighthouse, Tasmania

it was a diaphone foghorn, with a satisfying 'umph' at the end of the horn. You can imagine how delighted this curious mariner was to find exactly the same type of foghorn, in operational order, here at Low Head Lighthouse on the north coast of Tasmania, locally described as the 'roar of a thousand elephants'.

Low Head Lighthouse is like a mini version of the red-and-white-striped Portland Bill Lighthouse in Dorset upon which its design was based. In early 2000 the original working instructions for the foghorn were found at Portland and sent to Low Head so a group of volunteers could restore it, and it is now the only operational G-type diaphone in the world. I love that kind of history.

Christmas and New Year, 'Tassie' style

On Boxing Day, the four of us made an early start back to Hobart, leaving the shores of the lovely Tamar Valley, climbing the Highland Lakes Road, passing familiar scenery amidst rivers of rock and towns with such curious names as Cressy, Poatina and Cramps Bay. The blue water of dammed lakes and lagoons glistened in the sun, looking beautiful, but we were saddened by the number of dead wallabies from the previous night's roadkill.

The build-up of 40°C heat in the atmosphere and the increasing power and threat of the growing towers of flame that we knew were destroying everything in their path combined to create a compression of emotional intensity towards the end of the dying year that was new to me.

27 December 2019. How will we reflect upon these terrible times in Australia, and how will the events and statistics change the thinking of those in power? Will the wisdom of the indigenous people be followed more?

Closeness to anything watery gave us some relief. A wander around the Sydney to Hobart Yacht Race yachts and ducking into the food hall of The Taste of Tasmania festival on Constitution Dock distracted us for a few hours. The area was beautified with flowers, making it a very colourful place to be. We chose our plates and drink and sat down at the tables to chat with fellow diners. As we left, we couldn't resist the fresh fruit pies; for supper we took one of each type of fruit to Ken and Bron, where they were staying at the home of Bron's daughter.

30 December 2019. There are fears of dry lightning strikes as we approach the last day of the old year. All this extreme weather is caused by four things, we learned from a radio interview with an expert on meteorology. It is not just the usual seasonal change or the long-term warming of the climate, or the effect of the natural phenomenon known as the Indian Ocean Dipole bringing strong winds from the west, but also, fourthly, the Southern Annular Mode, which last year forced the winds in the roaring forties further north. Rather like the jet stream we are familiar with in the UK, this climate driver can affect the weather dependent on its position. So much dry wind on an already drought-ridden country with the inevitable results.

You may have read that an estimated 500 million animals have died or been injured in the fires. Today we hear that around 8,000 koalas are known to have perished because they seek refuge at the top of the very trees that are burning, so sad, whereas reptiles can seek the insulation of the earth in their underground homes, and birds and kangaroos can get away. The figures will rise with the loss of habitat and lack of water, but there are many efforts to feed and water the wild animals once the fire has moved through. It should also be mentioned that 100,000 sheep and cows are also thought to have perished. There is now a challenging job for humans to clear up the aftermath. And February is likely to be even worse. It is heartbreaking, I can tell you, dear reader.

We stayed on in Hobart awaiting Ken and Bron who were sailing aboard their yacht *Nichola* from her home base in George Town Marina on Tasmania's north shore, where we had spent Christmas, down the east coast to Hobart so we could start out on our shared adventure around the south of the island to the west coast and the wilderness area of Bathurst Harbour and Macquarie Harbour, before continuing by ourselves, westwards at last, across the Australian Bight.

It was exciting to sit somewhere comfy on *Zoonie's* deck and await *Nichola's* arrival. We had kept in touch through Messenger, and it wasn't long after our final exchange, when her little mast could be seen in the fairway beyond the moored yachts creeping around towards us, before we took her lines and poured the beer.

We were on the brink of our adventure to one of the world's last true wilderness areas, south down the River Derwent, excited because our odyssey along the homeward path could continue, and this time we had the added enjoyment of sailing with fellow cruisers who are the greatest company. Spoiled or what.

Zoonie is back on track

6 January 2020. At last, we were off, and Zoonie was back on track, this time with Nichola, a yacht with an interesting heritage. Designed by renowned, prolific and versatile Australian designer and draftsman Joe Adams back in the 1970s, she is 32 feet long and has a double chine (two angles between the bottom of her hull and sides); she looks like an overgrown dinghy and sails much like one too. She is made of steel and weighs just seven tons – half Zoonie's weight. No wonder she is fast. Joe Adams vessels were made in all materials, including ferrocement, and there are hundreds still around.

We followed Nichola to Alexanders Bay on Bruny Island for our first stop. It was so calm in there that despite Ken picking up the empty

Still waters

The team at our first stop

mooring on the advice of the police on their launch, and despite us tying up alongside, the mooring line to the buoy remained slack all night and into the next morning.

The next morning, we moved on down the channel between Bruny and the mainland, past the vast salmon farms, and into the D'Entrecasteaux Channel, which led us towards another peaceful spot for our second night, this time in the Pigsties, a recess in Recherche Bay.

7 January 2020. Seals are bizarrely lying on their backs in the water with their flippers sticking up, relaxing with their heads down looking for the odd passing fish. It's partially cloudy and cooler as we approach the Pigsties, and beyond us there is snow on Mount La Perouse, brrr.

The entrance is very narrow, with a rock in the middle of the channel. Nichola nosed her way carefully in and we followed her wake until she anchored and we rafted alongside again; it is so handy to be able to climb directly onto each other's boats.

All around us is lush green woodland, so different to the parched fields we have been seeing. Maybe the fires have not reached this far south. Ken, using Rob's gear gifted to him in Vanuatu, has caught himself three carpet sharks (or was it the same one thrice?) and put them all back where they belong.

Three capes in one day

South East Cape at 43° S is one of the five southernmost capes, and two of the others are further south, South Cape / Whiore (New Zealand) at 47° S and Cape Horn at 55° S, but we will not be rounding those: too chilly!

South East Cape, the most southerly cape in Australia, South Cape (Australia), and finally South West Cape are the three local capes we will bag on this day. We have a perfect day to see them, but the weather does not always provide such good visibility.

We were back amongst the shy albatrosses, gannets and shearwaters as we listened to a Mayday being dealt with somewhere on the west coast of Tasmania which delayed the weather forecast but resulted in a happy ending.

Tas Maritime Radio broadcasts weather bulletins three times a day.

It is modelled on our own Shipping Forecast but is run by volunteers who do a very professional job, but not without the occasional humorous interjection.

8 January 2020. Water was breaking over Maatsuyker Island (pron. Matsiker) as we passed, and it gets some pretty hellish winds, as you can imagine. One report stated 56 knots; fortunately, we were safely tucked up at the time.

The coastguards who man the lighthouse and weather station have to be prepared to stay there for six months at a time if the weather is bad and they cannot leave by sea; to do so they must wait until the weather improves. A sense of humour is essential to relieve their isolation.

One weather report went thus: "Maatsuyker Island, they won't know what's hit them, its calm!" And on another occasion: "Maatsuyker Island, this must be a misprint, CALM!" *Zoonie* and *Nichola* were evidently calming the waters.

The main fishing around Tasmania seems to be crayfish; we have to be on constant lookout for their buoys with the thick ropes tying them above the pots on the rocky seabed below. I wouldn't like to do this trip under engine at night.

Well offshore, seals poke their heads up to see us pass, and the southern swell builds and heaves towards the coast in long pale

Rounding the capes with *Nichola*

*green/white mounds that crash to destruction on the rock cliffs in magnif-
icent style. And that's on a calm day.*

Now, you might think that with a headwind against us along the
south coast, as soon as we turned around South West Cape we might
be able to sail with the wind on our beam, but it headed us, veering
north as it went, frustratingly in the direction we were heading for the
last few miles before the entrance to Bathurst Harbour. *Nichola* was
more ambitious than us, keeping her sails out to catch whatever wind
they could for some forward momentum.

*It was approaching 7.20 pm and we could see the Bathurst Harbour
entrance is to the right of a low white-banded rock, and it was a delight,
after a long day at sea, making our way around southern Tassie, to glide
along on the calm water, with moleskin hills showing granite faces in
places, and slip into Wombat Cove, where we anchored in five metres of
reassuringly thick, grippy mud, and Nichola came alongside. The only
dragging here will be ourselves to bed.*

Wombat Cove to Balmoral Hill

In daylight *Nichola* moved gently away from us and we followed
her along Bathurst Channel towards Casilda Cove (number two
anchorage) where the two yachts would wait as we four climbed the
562-metre Balmoral Hill.

We all clambered into Ken's hard tender as we had to find the
overgrown gap in the rocky shoreline foliage onto the track and felt
Zoonie's little rubber duck would be too vulnerable on the possibly
sharp rocks. Bingo, after a short scramble we were on the foot-wide
track that meandered away ahead and upwards.

The hill cover looks like moleskin at a distance. The slopes are
covered with buttongrass as it thrives in these peatlands. It has a single
seed head that grows on a stem well above the leaves, and the round
seed head surface erupts into spikes, which give one an alarming shock
if they are caught by the wind and hit you. The ancient compacted peat
trapped over the quartzite rock is the base to the most beautiful alpine-
like garden of flowering plants, and we strode upwards avoiding lots of
holes on a track littered with cubes of wombat poo like unmarked dice!

The holes belong to crayfish that climb far away from the water, and while unwittingly giving the peat deposits an essential breath of fresh air along their tunnels, the crayfish gain their food by munching on the roots of plants that protrude into their little subterranean homes. A living larder.

The whole surrounding area reminded Rob and me of Scotland and has since inspired us to cruise that area at home sooner rather than later. (This we did in 2022 and 2023, and we weren't disappointed.)

The views from the top of Balmoral Hill were matched by the peaceful wilderness silence. It was hot and windless up there and much cooler down below. We gazed out over nature's pristine work, a perfect balance of climate and topography, a harmony between the elements and the flora and fauna; what could possibly damage this wonderful, isolated and inaccessible place?

There was severe weather forecast for the next day, so, in the back of our minds as we reached the summit, there was the need to move on to a safe, sheltered anchorage.

Nichola **and** *Zoonie* **from the top of the hill**

Awaiting a gale in Kings Cove

We headed for the uncharted Kings Cove with *Zoonie* at the front, finding our way down the deepest part of the channel using the chart plotter and eyeball navigation, followed by *Nichola* and then a big, very smart fishing boat that appeared to have the same thought as us: shelter. A sea eagle wheeled around above us, watching to see if we disturbed anything that might make a dive worthwhile.

As we turned the corner past Kings Point, we spotted a nice meaty-looking buoy with a substantial mooring line attached, so we attached ourselves to it and *Nichola* came alongside for a brief few hours of fun before the arrival of the storm. Tucked up in this cove not only protected us from the ensuing westerly wind but also meant we would not be subject to the long fetch of weather as it sped across the harbour to the eastern side.

Baker Bron had been busy baking scones on the passage down Bathurst Channel to the cove, and we were able to provide the strawberry jam I had made with Martina in Newcastle, so our games evening followed an English cream tea before *Nichola* moved away from us to anchor a short distance from the shore.

10 January 2020. The atmospheric pressure has dropped by a whopping 29 millibars overnight, so a day on board is called for, and Rob has busied himself sorting out why one of the 12-volt charging sockets has given up the ghost; he found the problem in a wire connector behind the control panel above the chart table, and we traced the cause of the fault back to the seawater deluge Zoonie experienced on our way back to New Zealand from Fiji. If you remember, salt water never completely dries out!

Listening again to the excellent Tassie weather forecast, a 50-knot wind is expected with a sea state of 2–2.5 metres, which, added to the swell height of 3–4 metres, will give a gut-wrenching sea height of 6.5–7 metres. It must be impressive out at Maatsuyker Island right now. The wind generator is still working to keep the batteries charged, but we have been watching it like a newborn, and as soon as the charge reaches 100% it will be turned off to prevent burnout.

The wind will persist all day and into the night; the Roaring Forties are living up to their reputation here at 43° 21' S. We have just recorded 39 knots in our sheltered spot and just hope the mooring is as substantial down to the sinker as it is on top. It is uncannily hot outside; is the north element of this wind coming from Aussie's hot, red centre pushed onward by the Indian Ocean Dipole? I think so.

By the following morning the blow had moved on eastwards over the island, and *Nichola* came alongside for a chat, lunch, games and to formulate a plan for an afternoon exploration of the nearby beach; we were all feeling a little cooped up and needed some exercise.

I was hoping for a short hike but there were no obvious trails to follow. Instead of vast vistas there were lots of mini landscapes along the colourful shoreline. Looking up the little creeks, flowing with peaty brackish water, one could imagine we were witnessing the home of elves and goblins. Lush smooth green earth curved gently down to the sandy beach, in places giving way to level rocky surfaces covered in mossy algae-like weed with tiny white flowers.

That evening, over supper, we planned a move the next day around to Claytons Corner anchorage with a view to a long dinghy excursion up the Melaleuca Inlet. Now the bad weather had passed so much seemed possible.

Claytons Corner

After inflating our tender ready for the adventure, it was a very short trip following *Nichola* around to the next cove, anchoring close by but separately because we weren't going to be on board for a while. First, we were drawn to the well-maintained jetty where we knew there was a homestead, and then on up the Melaleuca Inlet towards the camp and airstrip.

Win and Clyde Clayton moved into this home they built in the year I turned ten, 1962, and left for a retirement nearer to civilisation in 1976; they spent fourteen years in the wilderness with just a few distant neighbours to share company with on occasions.

They were both born to the remote life, and they would have found delightful solitude here. The surrounding protective trees that now tower above the homestead would obviously have been there back then and allowed Clyde and Win to cultivate some vegetables and fruit. After a few hours of toil on a sunny day, what could be nicer than sitting on their back veranda drinking a hot cuppa and watching the birds and bees visit the many blooms.

Pygmy possums found a friend in Clyde and a comfy spot on his shoulder, to say nothing of tasty titbits from the larder.

There was no one there at the time we visited, and we were trusted to enjoy their remote home and leave no trace. In fact, a warm welcome awaited us in the form of photos, memorabilia and, more interestingly, all their furniture, and the memory of a couple who would have given us an equally kind welcome had they been there in the flesh. Hikers are invited to take shelter there and sleep on the bare beds. The open fire in the living room had been used recently, and the kitchen only needed the addition of food to create a wholesome evening meal.

I imagined I could have lived there for a year, maybe, to experience all the seasons and do lots of writing. How about you?

Up Melaleuca Creek – and back through time

13 January 2020. The sun was up as we sped away from our yachty homes for the journey up the creek.

Small boats came by having dropped walkers off on their next stage, and then a bigger tripper boat approached us. "Fear not, dear friends, we come in peace and will do you no harm," the guide jokingly called over to us through his mic.

Decades ago, Huon pine logs were rafted and tied together by men working from fragile little punts while standing on the logs themselves. A potentially dangerous job, I thought, if one fell off between two tree trunks. The rafts could then be floated towards the estuary entrance ready for shipment to the sawmill.

A pair of black currawongs with white-tipped wings flew from one side of the creek to the other bank near to where we passed a beautiful lagoon, where only people from local clans were allowed to venture as the area was sacred; we would sit alongside it for our lunch later.

Then suddenly, after an hour of motoring, the very sturdy new pontoon appeared with a stack of kayaks stored on the bank. We tied up out of the way of the boats for which the jetty was built and scrambled ashore, numb bums welcoming the change in posture. Unexpectedly we came upon an elevated walk over the fragile peatland that was open to all comers and was intended to tell the story of the first inhabitants of the region, the Needwonnee Aboriginal people.

Little has been written about this south-west tribe, and the available information comes from the elders of three other local tribes. I wonder where they went? They appear to have made a successful getaway from the policy to shunt them all to outlying islands in the Bass Strait (mostly Flinders Island, according to Ken), continuing to live a content and sustainable existence for tens of thousands of years; we could certainly learn from them regarding our consumeristic and unsustainable lifestyle.

A little replica reed canoe reminded me of the ancient Polynesian style of bundled reeds that were used for transport over water, and I could just see a young Needwonnee person silently paddling over the protected lagoon to find food for the evening meal.

Continuing up the creek, six naturally rusted plaques with their pressed-out images tell the story of Parlevar, the first Aboriginal man. To make him, Moihernee, the Great Spirit, took some earth up to the sky and fashioned a man who had a tail and legs without knee joints, so he could not sit down. Dromerdeener, the Star Spirit, cut off his tail, cured the wound with grease and made knee joints for Parlevar.

Parlevar stayed in the sky for a very long time. Eventually he came to the land by walking along the Milky Way. He argued with Dromerdeener and was forced to leave the sky and come down to land at Louisa Bay on Louisa Island nearby. There he fought with many evil spirits who lived on the ground. His wife came down to live in the sea and many of their children came down in the rain.

When Moihernee died he went to the land near Cox Bight, which we passed coming around here. There he turned into a large rock that stands majestically on a point of land near the sea. Another lovely origin story I thought you might like.

For lunch we sat on the boardwalk looking over the lagoon, our feet just above the ancient peat bog, and tried to take in the beauty of the place for future reference. I wondered what secrets the bog held.

Bron came back in our dinghy with us so Ken was able to get more speed out of his two-cylinder motor, and we shared another evening before turning in early, ready for the start of the journey to Macquarie Harbour, northwards up the west coast of Tasmania, the next day, our latest adventure tucked under our belts.

Through Hells Gates to Strahan

During the scenic journey back towards the Bathurst Cove entrance, Bron was busy pummelling the life out of a pile of dough so that (therefore) the aroma of fresh baking bread filled the air as we anchored alongside *Nichola* just outside Wombat Cove. Ravenous, the four of us tucked into thick slices of her still-warm bread with cheese, pickles, olives, celery and, what's that, honey!

Nichola led the way back out to sea where we were welcomed with a fine 14-knot south-easterly and the ocean swell. We delighted in being in the company of shy albatrosses and their friends the shearwaters (otherwise known as muttonbirds, as they were named by hungry sailors and settlers), and the spearheaded gannets diving for fish. A new addition to the faunal mix was Australian fur seals that would pop their heads above water and take a curious look at us as we sped by and then swim alongside us for a while, despite being miles from the shore.

That night we sailed under a Jaffa orange moon. The wind was dropping so on went the engine, and we motor sailed with *Nichola's* navigation lights to starboard into a surreal misty calm morning.

Fortunately, we could make out the light from Cape Sorell Lighthouse, but the land upon which it sat was shrouded in smoky mist; the next few minutes would be very interesting. Unsure as to whether the Navionics charts were accurate for this area, we took bearings on the lighthouse with the hand-held compass and completed a running fix. Then, suddenly, the automatic light turned off just when we needed it, so we trusted to luck we still had plenty of sea room, and the closer we approached the more likely we would be able to discern land features.

The entrance to Macquarie Harbour has proved problematic over the years, especially in the days of the engineless square riggers and strong westerly winds, and a west to south-west swell can make the entrance a real Hells Gates, as it is called. Many ships have foundered with the inevitable loss of life. That is one of the reasons a rock training wall was laid at the beginning of the twentieth century, to smooth the waterway at the entrance and give ships somewhere sheltered to anchor and await better conditions or a pilot to guide them, hence the name Pilot Bay and Pilot Beach.

We were lucky the swell crashing on the rocky shoreline outside had enough south in it to not enter the channel, and all Rob had to contend with were currents that could send *Zoonie* off course as we approached Entrance Island.

Hells Gates was named not only because of the natural circumstances of weather and tide but also the appalling conditions the arriving convicts knew they would encounter at the penal colony on Sarah Island within the harbour. News reached England of the brutal regime inflicted on the convicts, and they must have led lives of utter dread as they were herded from England's shores across the world to this beautiful place, made fearful by the discipline metered out by the commanders and governors.

How different today, when people like us and fare-paying passengers choose to come and experience the rugged south-west of Tasmania.

We went ashore at Strahan to find out about fuel and see what the town had to offer. In the information centre one of the ladies gave us a long story about having to get a permit to explore the Gordon River, beyond Sarah Island, an area covered with largely untouched temperate rainforest. The pricing of the permits seemed to be done in such a way as to make as much money as possible out of visitors or to deter them from coming, so we were temporarily put off. No one likes to feel they are being taken advantage of, do they? We found another way.

Sarah Island

We had waited for the twin troughs of a low-pressure system, which had held Tasmania between their scissor-like grip for 48 hours, to move east before our much-anticipated southern Macquarie Harbour expedition could begin.

The evening before, Rob and I had gone for a shoreside walk and found a resort where we knew we could buy the two black-and-white charts of Macquarie Harbour and the Gordon River drawn by local architect and businessman Trevor Norton. The lady there was aghast when she heard about the cost of a permit to visit the Gordon, as if it was not the normal way of things. She suggested we take ourselves up there on an experience now and pay later, if necessary, basis, so that is what we did.

Just before we set off a little blue penguin surfaced beside *Zoonie*, a complete surprise to us to see one so close to human activity.

There was a stiff breeze against *Zoonie* as we motored south, the air full of the excitement of adventure. We do not often have people aboard to share our lives on *Zoonie*, as you know.

We knew Ken and Bron well by then after twelve days cruising together in Vanuatu and spending Christmas and new year with them and found our foursome to be an easy and thoroughly enjoyable group.

After five hours of motoring, I turned *Zoonie* into the bay that has Sarah and her two outlying islands at the head. The first, Store Island, where free women were housed in a cave to do the island's laundry and nurse the sick, and the second, Grummet Island, a graveyard for the many convicts who died here and a night-time prison for the worst male offenders – imagine that, sleeping among the dead.

We made our way carefully to the single little buoy that we could pick up, provided there was enough room around it for *Zoonie* to swing. The depth gauge dropped to 0.9 metres, but as the tidal range was about half a metre, we figured *Zoonie* would be fine even with just one foot beneath her.

Before white man's arrival, Aboriginal people living in the temperate rainforests of South West Tasmania for 35,000 years at least, who have always been terrified of out-of-control fires, learnt how to fight fire with fire; they farmed the land sustainably and used small local fires to reduce the flammable brush around the trees, taking only what they needed to survive.

When we first stepped onto Sarah Island, what struck us immediately was how tiny it was to be the scene of so much suffering. Only about 1,400 metres long and 600 metres wide. The first thing tasked to the convicts was to clear it of vegetation, including the valuable Huon pines, many of which can still be seen in the water and were used as the slipway base for the shipyard. In clearing, the island was then exposed to the strong winds brought by extreme weather systems, so a windbreak fence was built right across the north side of the island.

How the barren landscape and its brutal history compares to the varied heights and greens of today's vegetation. It is a beautiful, natural and diverse garden now just as it was before, silent and peaceful and, understandably, as far as the local Aboriginal people are concerned, haunted.

Life on the penal colony of Sarah Island

The story boards told us about the extreme pain of life on Sarah Island, so I thought I'd tell you some stories of a more humorous, hopeful and human kind.

William Sylvester was a convict gardener on the island and became known as 'the streaker of Sarah Island' when he ran naked around the settlement in an attempt to scandalize the wife of Dr Garrett and her sister. These sisters weren't popular, and Bill was responding to bribes from the commandant's servants to get rid of them. I'm not sure if he was successful, but his punishment was to be relegated to a timber gang, no doubt amidst much mirth and cheers, but maybe that was his intention anyway.

George Millar was lashed with the 'cat-o'-nine-tails' twenty-five times for breaking into a solitary cell when it was occupied. Later research revealed the occupant was a certain Mary Anne Furze! Hope she was worth it.

On the hopeful front, one of the few successful escapes was engineered by Richard Morris, John Newton and Thomas Crawley, and it is recorded as 'dead in the woods' because they were thought to have perished in the dense bush between the shores of the Gordon River and the hinterland. While working as lime burners, up the river, they managed to steal a boat and row it up the river as far as they could get.

Before leaving the boat, they posted a witty hand-drawn sign on it reading 'Now for Sale'. I liked that. Morris was supposedly seen in Oatlands, a town a third of the way up the modern Midland Highway between Hobart and Launceston, around 100 miles to the north-east, two months later; so, he had won his freedom.

One freeman who chose to come to the island to build ships of his own design was Master Shipwright David Hoy, who turned the convict shipyard into the most productive in Australia at the time. He specialised in building fast ships, which local masters found hard to handle. In total, from 1828 for five years until the colony closed, the yard turned out thirty-one whale boats, ten launches, two gigs, six long boats, six skiffs, three cutters, nine punts, nine yawls, one shallop and six sundry vessels.

The skills thus learned by the convicts would stand them in good stead for their eventual release, but for a few that time was just too far away; they had to at least try a bid for freedom. You may have twigged the disadvantage to the authorities of producing ships that were so fast: they could not be caught by conventional vessels and were very handy as escape vessels.

No less than the governor's yacht, *Penelope*, a fast sailor built in the yard, was used in a bold and cheeky escape attempt to Jamaica by three convicts. Ten other convicts stayed on at the yard after its days as a penal colony ended in 1833 to complete the building of the ocean-going 121-ton brig the *Frederick*; generous of them, you might think? They were last seen disappearing over the horizon to Chile, 10,000 miles away, in 1834.

Walking by the ruins of the main buildings, in places showing the precise care with which they were erected, I imagined Bill streaking past in his attempt to shock the doctor's wife, causing a ruckus of cheering and merriment, I hope, and then, of course, the dragging of re-offending convicts to the post to be flogged, sometimes to death, for misdemeanours such as allegedly telling a lie, shoving a fellow prisoner off a jetty and, of a more entrepreneurial type, selling brooms and soup. It was a brutal regime but not without lighter moments.

After the convict era came the Huon Piners, the second conservationists after the Aboriginal people. Understandable, don't you think, that these tough but sensitive and listening men saw the rivers of the south-west as *their* pathways; if they weren't ex-convicts themselves, they were almost always descendants of them, and it appears that even though their fathers' situation under the penal system might have been dire, they did not share the commonly held view of the wilderness as a terrible, hostile and inhospitable place. In fact, it was a place with which they lived in harmony for 150 years, a peaceful and generous place to live compared to life in Hobart, or back in England, for that matter.

Perhaps partly because of the solitude, some Piners didn't marry and have families, and as felling the mighty pines became outlawed, both these factors combined and led to the decline of these interesting men, who learned to harmonise with their environment just as the Aboriginal people had.

What has been lost from the wilderness, I think, is people like the indigenous population living out there in a mutually beneficial relationship with their surroundings. Today, humans seek a superficial, temporary relationship with wilderness, by walking through or, like us, by dipping into the location and history, preserving what we find in the lens of a camera as the romantic artist did back in the day, to trap a visual image as a moment in time, not a refuge for living.

This spasmodic relationship with the land may in some ways be a good thing, laissez-faire, leave well alone that will allow nature to continue to recover and evolve, to be supported by the tourist industry; surely better than leaving it vulnerable to being exploited by governments with a solely commercial, self-serving policy. Passive tourism is better than physical destruction because it wants to admire what is there and not change or take from it.

Aboriginal people would like to return one day to live on their traditional lands, and maybe one hope for the survival of this country is if they do. What do you think?

Four go up the Gordon River

The big grey day tripper catamaran, *Spirit of the Wild*, which was moored at the Sarah Island jetty the day before, overtook us on her way up the Gordon River to Heritage Landing, where we hoped we could moor. She soon disappeared around one of the many gentle bends in the river.

We were amazed at the depth of the river: in places it reached over 30 metres, unsilted by human activity as is so common elsewhere. Anchoring would have been impossible with the steep-to banks. All along the riverbank little tinnies motored gently along parallel with the shore, the occupants fly fishing and waving to us as we passed.

18 January 2020. The density of the trees is a real treat, having seen so many areas stripped of their entire crop. But it is not just the density, or the fact they march right down to the shoreline, just as the early navigators saw them, or the multitude of shades and hues of green, but also the diversity of tree types. We are trying desperately to discern the celery-topped pines and the mighty Huons, the blackwoods and paperbarks, and many others we know are in there, but in the end, we are just enjoying the sheer abundance, from our vantage point deep in the river valley.

Looking at the timetables on the brochures of the two big tourist cats, we tried to work out when they would be away from the Heritage Landing so we could tie up and have a look around the rainforest walk. To confirm I radioed the skipper of the *Spirit of the Wild*, and he agreed they would be clear by 1.30 pm. So, we made our way downstream from where we had been hovering, and Rob circled *Zoonie* in towards the jetty. This wasn't going to be easy, because the piles and lines were arranged for a high freeboard cat, not the likes of a sailing yacht.

Bron and I struggled to get a bow line attached at first, but then working together I slung the line around the smooth, fat pile and Bron caught it, so the bow was safe. Ken had jumped ashore by this time, ready to take a stern line from Rob.

The 600-metre boardwalk rainforest path led us through a tiny section of wilderness, but it was a taste of the dense interior. It was very dry for a rainforest.

Imagine trying to make an escape from Sarah Island through this undergrowth as Richard Morris and his two mates did.

We were struck by the lack of bird sounds or presence in the forest, but then you can read that 'a riverine forest offers little variety when

Zoonie **alongside in the Gordon River**

it comes to food and shelter'. The birds we saw were along the river: shags, cormorants, kingfishers, currawongs and sea eagles feeding from the water.

Our minds were turning now to our departure from Macquarie. *Nichola* would sail up the coast and follow it around along Bass Strait to complete their circumnavigation back to Low Head and their mooring in George Town near the mouth of the Tamar, while we would head for Portland on the south coast of Victoria and back on the mainland.

Chapter 10

Australia's South Coast Beckons Us

Leaving Tasmania

In the new dawn we were making our way back to Strahan when our separate thinking came together; the weather conditions would be perfect the next day, but they were also perfect right then. With the favourable weather windows being so short we could not afford to delay; the sooner we got there the more comfortably we would miss the predicted 40-knot northerlies.

I nudged *Zoonie* alongside *Nichola* to drop Ken and Bron off to take lines. We exchanged hasty hugs and gas bottles, because Ken's had more in than ours, and we were off at 12.15 pm with 278 miles over the ground distance and two days ahead of us.

Tasmania fell away in the mist behind us, taking *Nichola* with it, while we pointed *Zoonie* towards Portland; not to the Portland Harbour we are familiar with in Dorset (where *Zoonie* now lives) but its counterpart down under on the Victoria state coast of Australia. From there the south coast to Western Australia would be in front of us.

To Portland

19 January 2020. Zoonie leans under the pressure of a 16-knot SE wind, her working sheet creaking in the winch. Dolphins welcomed us back to sea and we could see Nichola approaching the rock training wall about an hour behind us, as they had done a quick shop. From then on, our paths have separated but we can still see her white sails, well into the evening. We are back among the world of the albatrosses, and we're happy sailing on, aboard our gorgeous home.

By midday the next day we had started crossing Bass Strait and were leaving the continental shelf in a 3.5-metre sea state, when suddenly one of those bigger-than-the-rest waves thumped *Zoonie* on her side, deluged the windward deck from bow to stern with liquid anger, sending her into a spin, then all went quiet for a few moments as the sea said, "Oops, sorry about that!"

20 January 2020. There are many seabirds over the precipice of the shelf beneath Zoonie's hull because that is where huge shoals of fish live: gannets, shearwaters and sometimes albatrosses fishing the same waters.

It is bright but with total cloud cover, and there is a chill in the air brought northwards by the Southern Ocean swell well to the south of us.

The Watt&Sea hydrogenerator is working well, keeping the batteries at 100% and providing the power for the autopilot to work 24/7. Mary on Tas Maritime Radio welcomes home all the fishermen who call in their safe returns to port, and she notes down the location of those who are anchoring out overnight in some sheltered cove. "Thanks, George, you have a good one."

So, they are settled for the night, but I only wish my tummy was. For the first time in ages, I have nausea and an overactive tum. The motion is not uncomfortable even though Zoonie corkscrews her way north-west, shoved onward by a quartering swell. It must be a bug; well, I cannot be pregnant!

Out beyond the continental shelf, shown by the crammed lines on the chart plotter, over the deep ocean and flat sea floor, the swells are further apart and more forgiving. Give me a deep ocean any day.

Zoonie has produced between 4.9 and 8.2 knots of speed on this, her best sail in months.

With the help of fisherman Mark, we tied up off the long hammerhead pontoon at the outer end of the marina in Portland mid-afternoon, having averaged 6 knots under sail and sailing 254 of the 278-mile journey. A nice 48-hour passage.

Hairdryer winds the next day made short work of drying the washing, and I gathered the articles in, for fear of them being blown away.

The busy westerly wind having arrived forcing us to stay put, we set off one morning for a good look around the town. Despite the size of the harbour and the generous distance from the harbour mouth, many of the moored vessels had doubled up on their lines in case chafe caused breakages and set them free.

23 January 2020. Just in front of us was a fishing tinny, belonging to Mark, who shortly after we arrived came along the jetty, tapped on our hull and asked, "Would you two like to come to dinner tomorrow evening?" Mark didn't even know our names at that stage, and when he came to collect us, he said, "I do this whenever there's a new yacht in the marina; Sandra's quite used to it." And so started a lovely evening looking at photos of their family history of crayfishing. "There's a strict enforced quota on catching crayfish now, and most of the locals are reaching theirs for the season."

We said our farewells to this kind couple after yet another short and sweet friendship, having spent a week enjoying shore life.

A short hop along to Kangaroo Island

28 January 2020. We left at the civilised hour of midday and had a nice sail southward to clear the headland, but as we turned west the wind was on our nose, so it was on with the iron topsail.

During the night the wind dropped away to nothing, so we were motoring with 1700 rpm pushing us along and still only making 4.4 knots against the tide. We moved Zoonie out to the 500-metre contour searching for a favourable current. It was frustrating for a while, all this effort and not much progress, but it was also warm with a lovely clear sky and sparkling sea.

The continental shelf along the coast we were sailing by drops from a depth of 150 metres to over 500 metres very quickly, and along this steep wall giant crabs and rock lobsters thrive, so the chart plotter display describes this entire area as a fishery for those two species, which meant we could expect to come across vessels fishing in the area with pots going down hundreds of metres. We were under engine, and, of course, at night, without a moon, one cannot see the water ahead. I humbly asked Neptune if he would kindly pull any such dangerous buoy with its attached line out of *Zoonie's* path, and unbelievably he obliged. By this time the wind was too weak to lift a leaf.

1 February 2020. We arrived here in American River on Kangaroo Island the day before yesterday, after a 50-hour motor sail from Portland in light winds that were barely in the right direction for sailing. Knowing our weather window would be short-lived, it was important to maintain 5 knots of speed at least, and this we did by finely tuning the engine revs to what we could get out of the sails, which was fun and really worked, saving fuel where we could.

There was plenty of wildlife about under the blue skies, hundreds of dolphins feeding with the diving birds and our dear friends the dignified sky masters, shy albatrosses, watching over our modest progress all the way and settling in groups on the water in the evenings, their watery roost.

We are reliant for the first time solely on the Navionics charts on the chart plotter as we don't have paper charts for this small area. This is how many seagoing vessels do all their navigation nowadays and so far has served us well used in conjunction with the overall layout of a large-area paper chart. However, I like the immediate access to details of an area that paper charts give, and, of course, they are always a backup to the electronic charts.

The night watches went quickly with copious cups of tea and dozens of trips up and down the companionway ladder for an all-round check. At one stage the fishing boat lights appeared to be travelling with us as if we were towing them, and one vessel appeared to be towing numerous illuminated lines; we kept well clear of him. He may well have been one of the two seismic vessels testing for oil, towing twelve 4-mile-long cables behind him and harming most sea creatures around him with his sonic blasts.

In the afternoon we had headwinds and a current against us of 1.2 knots. The temperature was nice and warm, the skies all over blue, no clouds allowed; the marine entertainment was great, but what we needed most was PROGRESS. It seems at the moment that the weather windows are short and lodged between extreme weather patterns.

In truth, we were not sure of our destination, having choices of mainland ports in South Australia and offshore Kangaroo Island, the latter being en route and, with the short weather windows, the shortest route in and then onward to Ceduna. The forecast told of a powerful front coming in on Saturday, in two days' time, followed by a big low passing to the south bringing rain and westerly winds, so we had needed to be somewhere protected by then. Kangaroo Island it would be.

To get nearer the island we had to cross back over the continental shelf, but the chart information said we were entering an ESSA, Environmentally Sensitive Sea Area, where marine activities like fishing are strictly limited; maybe no more fishing boats, then, but we could sail through.

Throughout our last day on passage the barometer was dropping continuously, so we knew we could trust the forecast; the question was, would we make the narrow river entrance before dark or have to anchor in the bay outside overnight, slotted in between the fish farms?

Kangaroo Island appeared low on the horizon within a strange mirage that looked like a wall of water all around us. A smoke haze, Rob thought, but it seemed to be the wrong colour, more like a reflection of the ocean, or, Neptune forbid, an approaching tidal wave? Thankfully not. We had planned our arrival approaching the channel between the island and mainland carefully to coincide with the start of the rising tide, as the ebb can produce a tide rip which runs at 4 knots against us, just like the Needles Channel between the Isle of Wight and Hurst Spit.

We had a welcome video chat with oldest son Richard and the boys as we crossed the Eastern Cove with the sun setting, giving us a race against failing light. The miracle of telecommunications, keeping us in touch but reminding me of how we missed them.

The mirage continued making out-lying rocks look as if they had a waist and the shoreline quite indistinct. The chart plotter showed a well-marked channel dredged to three metres, so with a height of tide of, at most, one metre, we could expect one to two metres below the keel, as the keel is two metres below the water's surface.

I hugged the numerous red channel marker posts a little too tightly, as at one stage the depth went down to 1.3 metres below the keel, and that was on high tide, so, mental note: on the way out I will give *Zoonie*'s black line a little more space to our right and be on a nearly full tide.

We found a nice spot amidst some moored yachts in the channel to anchor and had supper in the cockpit surrounded by the beautiful setting. We had arrived at Kangaroo Island.

The next morning Rob discovered that the engine was 145 hours overdue for an oil change. "Ooh, that'll be black oil then, hun," I commented as he disappeared aft clutching the pump and looking like a man on a mission. (Engine oil changes from amber to black over usage.)

Outside I could see the wind was rising and opposing the strong tidal flow out of the harbour. The neighbouring yachts were pressed forward over their mooring lines despite the strong tide pushing them the other way. I started to think. *Zoonie* had 15 metres of chain out to the anchor in only 2.9 metres of water. With the chain creating such a shallow angle with the seabed, if she were to change direction when the tide turned, her keel could easily catch the chain as she swung and lift the anchor out. We had gone through the night OK because there was little wind.

It was 11.45 am and we had three tense hours ahead to low water at 2.30 pm, during which I kept regular lookout using the moored yachts nearby against the shoreline as transits.

This combined with the fact the engine was now empty of oil and unusable created a degree of tension in my mind, as you can imagine. Rob did the fastest oil and filter change ever, which included fitting a new water-cooling pump impeller, and made a rather worrying discovery. Not only had one complete flange on the old impeller come off and disappeared into the system, and hopefully out the other end, but the inside surface of the pump was not the regular smooth surface it should be and would have to be replaced ASAP.

Later in the morning Rob called Carol, a volunteer on VHF American River Radio, and she immediately asked where we were.

"You're not safe there under anchor. Pick up the buoy marked 'Cotton' opposite the jetty; it will take 50 tons and you'll be fine there."

Carol also told us how the beautiful island had lost 50% of its bush and ninety homes and the fires had consumed so much wildlife they were still assessing the damage. As we approached we saw intact countryside, so the damage must have been on the western side. The residents must have been in a state of shock. "With big fires come big rains," Carol said, the voice of experience.

A quick look through the binoculars showed me the buoy was right behind us, but it was low water and we were surrounded by sandbanks, so where to safely take *Zoonie* without grounding? However, all's well that ends well, and during a few sweaty moments, after I directed *Zoonie* gradually nearer with the tide pushing her one way and the wind the other, Rob did a great job of picking up the line lying on the water from the buoy.

But more fun was yet to come. Carol was right, the thunderstorm arrived in the afternoon and lasted overnight, bringing that phenomenon, feared by all mariners, of fork lightning. With *Zoonie's* mast being the highest in our area we decided prudence was in order and secreted three iPads, two phones and the handheld VHF in the oven, hoping they would be spared and still give us the means to navigate if the chart plotter should get 'cooked'. We'd heard numerous cases of yachts being struck, but few, if any, of the crew suffering the same fate, so deemed the small risk was one we could deal with.

1 February 2020. So that is where we are now, securely attached to a stout mooring buoy in the river, feeling mighty safe and comfy and waiting for our favourable weather window to arrive in four days – five days after our arrival – so we can set out and head for either Streaky Bay or Ceduna, both back on the mainland and at what are thought by mariners to be good stepping-off points to cross the Bight, with the weather, as always, calling the tune.

The forecast is for a southerly backing to south-easterly with a five-metre sea state at the start, dropping gradually as the high spreads over the Great Australian Bight. Nice offshore winds. I wonder if we will be in time to use this high to cross over the Bight to Western Australia. We shall see.

We are watching amazed as the busy little cormorant fishes just beneath the water surface while a domineering (both in size and attitude) pelican

The cormorant and the pelican

keeps a close eye on his fisher. The cormorant raises his head above water so the pelican can grab the fish from his beak and swallow it. Interesting that these skilled birds are willing to work on behalf of others.

A little ornithology from Matthew Flinders

Matthew Flinders explored the island back in 1802 and made two interesting discoveries.

First, the vegetation that was growing was young and all the old trees were lying on the ground, leading Captain Flinders to believe they had recently fallen foul of a bush fire, caused either by two branches rubbing together during the dry season or by lightning strike.

Second, he came across many old pelicans sitting on the beach of a lagoon he named Pelican Lagoon. They were surrounded by bones, those of young pelicans that may have been caught in the same engulfing fire while their parents were fishing at sea. This led him to think the pelicans were past the peak of their existence there. There were a few around us but I wondered how many perished in this recent fire.

Ceduna bound

We were ready to leave the next morning and I had a brief chat with Carol via VHF. "You'll be OK until you're nearly out, then just by the second marker post in, you'll touch bottom…" (pregnant pause) "… ah but it'll be all good." I wondered what she meant by that, was there a secret solution to lifting grounded yachts off the bottom? We were about to find out.

Rob let go the buoy that had kept us safe and secure, and this time I motored out a little further away from the markers in what the chart plotter showed to be the deep channel. The high tides here are much higher at night; I guess the air pressure, wind and temperature combine to suppress the rise during the day. Gingerly we progressed with comfortable depths of 3.4 metres plus for most of the passage out to the bay.

Approaching the second red marker the depth gauge dropped until it read '00.00' measured from the bottom of the keel to the seabed, and *Zoonie* slid gently to a stop.

I turned the wheel so when she did move, she would be lying across the channel. Rob was hanging determinedly over her low side, the engine was on 2000 rpm and with a little help from waves and the wind against her side, lifting her, after a few minutes of gazing at my transits of the marker posts against the shore, *Zoonie* very gently bumped her way across the sand until she was clear. Maybe that was Carol's local knowledge: the effects of wind and tide.

We left behind us a distraught island. One farmer had spent decades building up his sheep station. When he drove out after the fires to see how his stock had fared, he turned a bend to find 8,000 sheep burned alive. Poor farmer and four-legged souls.

4 February 2020. Zoonie now speeds along Investigator Strait with her full genoa and reefed main, Adelaide and Port Lincoln to our right, starboard, side.

Thistle Island and Thorny Passage were named by Matthew Flinders while he was ashore with Mr John Thistle, master of the Investigator, but his naming Cape Catastrophe came about following a tragedy that befell John Thistle, along with the six other members of his crew.

Tragedy for Matthew Flinders' crew members

On 21 February 1802, Mr John Thistle and six crew members from HMS *Investigator* went ashore on the mainland aboard the ship's cutter, *Lady Nelson*, in search of water and an anchoring place where they could safely secure the ship. Matthew had known and liked Mr Thistle for many years; he was a valuable asset aboard the ship. As were the able seamen with him, all loyal volunteers to the cutter's compliment.

At dusk the white sail of the cutter was seen heading for the ship, but then it suddenly vanished. Lieutenant Fowler set off straight away by himself to see what he could find in the darkness, while the remaining crew shone a lantern for him from the ship. He returned alone noting the dangerous rip tide he came close to en route, which could have accounted for the loss of the cutter. Over the next few days searches were carried out. The upturned cutter was found battered by the rocks, and when the *Investigator* eventually sailed away the mast and sail were spotted floating in the water, but of

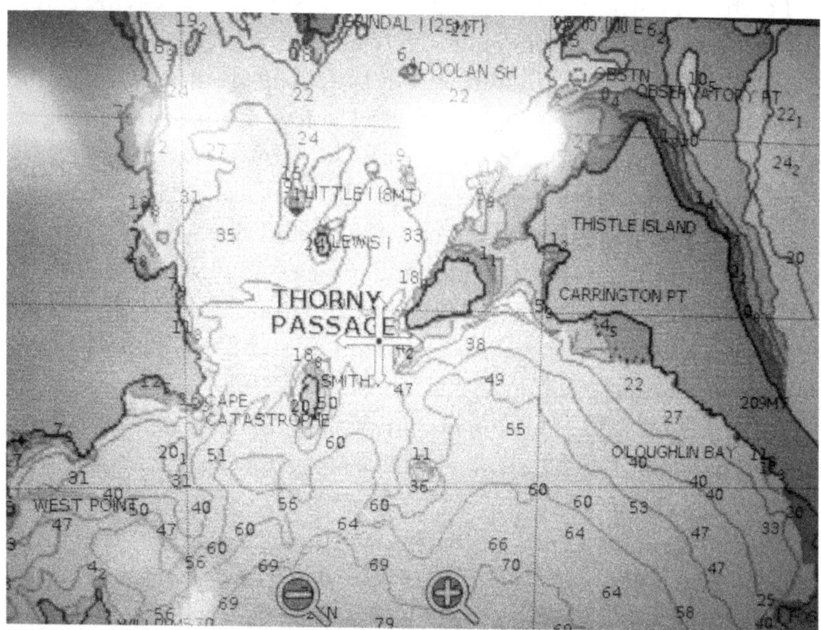

The area where the cutter *Lady Nelson* foundered

Matthew's valued master and crew nothing was ever found. Today charts are marked with the little wavy lines in that area to warn of the dangerous rip tides, upcurrents and whirlpools. Their loss bore heavily on Matthew's mind and no doubt on the morale of the rest of the crew. You can just imagine how devastating it must have been, such a well-knit crew, so far from home, to lose those brave men and friends.

Before the voyage, Captain Flinders had been sent by the Lord High Admiral of the United Kingdom to chart in depth this area along the south coast of Australia, and it was while the *Investigator* was anchored off Spithead, in Portsmouth, before leaving the UK that Mr Thistle decided to while away some of the waiting time by visiting a wise old man, a clairvoyant named Pine. In Captain Flinders' own words from *A Voyage to Terra Australis*:

'The cunning man informed him that he was going out a long voyage, and that the ship, on arriving at her destination, would be joined by another vessel. That such was intended, he might have learned privately; but he added, that Mr Thistle would be lost before the other vessel joined. As to the manner of his loss the magician refused to give any information. My boat's crew, hearing what Mr Thistle said, went also to consult the wise man; and after the prefatory information of a long voyage, were told that they would be shipwrecked, but not in the ship they were going out in: whether they would escape and return to England, he was not permitted to reveal.

'This tale Mr Thistle had often told at the mess table; and I remarked with some pain in a future part of the voyage, that every time my boat's crew went to embark with me in the Lady Nelson, there was some degree of apprehension amongst them that the time of the predicted shipwreck was arrived. I make no comment upon this story, but recommend a commander, if possible, to prevent any of his crew from consulting fortune tellers.'

The whole content of the book, published over two volumes, appears to be in the first person, written by Matthew while he was imprisoned on Mauritius.

Back to our voyage

By the next morning, *Zoonie* was surfing down the ocean swell with a bubbling bone in her teeth. Going east to west we needed to have a high moving across south of us, with its anticlockwise winds from the east sector ready to give us a shove. The present high would run out before we could really use it, so it was a case of waiting in Ceduna, further to the north-west than Streaky Bay, which would have the advantages of shortening the onward journey and give us a better sailing angle for the winds.

During the last night the wind increased and started gusting over 30 knots. At 1.00 am Rob was out on deck taking in the genoa pole ready for a course change, and the next morning found us 31 miles from the Ceduna seaward channel marker romping along under full genoa and reefed main with a ship, the *Darling River*, shadowing us. We were effectively between her and the channel marker, and it was reassuring to see her do an early and significant turn to port so she could cross our stern before making for the estuary entrance.

She overtook us and then anchored outside the fairway for two days before she could reach her berth and collect a load of gypsum from the yard, we found out later on a walk.

The moon was up and ready to guide us in, along with the well-lit ship channel, and despite daylight having gone, we enjoyed the easy approach, meandering around sandbanks to the waypoint that Rob had put on the chart plotter for me. It was intentionally in the exact location where Jeannie and Merv (*Zoonie's* saviours from her near sinking, back in Whangarei) had anchored *Meridian Passage* eighteen years ago to the day, taken from our copy of their log. Down the anchor and chain went at 11.50 pm. A good night's rest was called for.

Welcome to Ceduna

Our first day ashore was immensely successful. Having eaten our breakfast to the chilled sounds of the indigenous CAAMA (Central Australian Aboriginal Media Association) radio station, based in Alice Springs, we sped the long distance from *Zoonie* to the sailing club ramp thinking we might find someone there, but there was no sign of life. We had previously made contact with Kylie who runs the club with her teacher hubby, Brad.

So, we then took our rubber ducky, as we've heard it called around here, across to the old town jetty where once the trading ships used to tie up before the new one was built.

In the Ceduna Bakery Coffee Lounge we drank delicious iced coffee and shared a slice of carrot cake to help us take stock.

We had been in Messenger contact with our sailing friend Hannes from *Cayenne*, and he confirmed he would be arriving late the next day, travelling from the west across the Nullarbor Plain at 700–750 kilometres per day by SUV.

Next stop, Foodland, which was well stocked for all our minimal needs, then, having met up with Kylie, she gave us a lift to the fuel station, which was great, and we arranged to meet for breakfast in the community-owned Ceduna Foreshore Hotel opposite the old jetty the next morning.

The fresh breeze calmed after the sun went down, and the next morning the water was flat, so we moved *Zoonie* into a spot just off the pier and anchored where trading vessels taking on grain, salt, fish and gypsum once moored in a nice dredged channel.

Two lovely hours were spent chatting with Kylie, Brad and Kylie's mum, Val, who, up until her husband died, had a 46-foot Bruce Roberts ketch. Val came armed with a laminated chart of the local area and told us about all the best anchorages to enjoy, which she once frequented with her late husband. We didn't have the heart to tell her that when we left we would not linger in the local waters as we were passage making. As usual we could have spent a year in this idyllic spot, exploring.

Local Aboriginal children were jumping off the jetty; some waved as we motored back to *Zoonie*. The uninhibited younger generation was happy to make verbal and eye contact with us, more so than their generally reserved elders. Matthew Flinders found the same. If an intentional attempt was made by him or his men to communicate with the first Australians they would vanish, but if they completely ignored the natives, then eventually curiosity would overcome them, and that is how he learned to make the initial contact.

Ceduna has a welcoming atmosphere and is made up of a multicultural population of around 3,500, and we were heading to the Ceduna Foreshore Hotel to have dinner with Hannes, who had arrived with a healthy appetite after his drive across the Nullarbor Plain. I really liked the Ceduna Foreshore Hotel Bistro; it is open from early in the morning till late (a little like our Wetherspoons) and has a passing trade of business and leisure clients, but it is a reasonably priced venue for the locals to eat out as well. Aboriginal people were free to come and go and treated like everyone else, although they were restricted by the authorities to low-alcohol beer back then.

There were no other yachts there at the time, although Hannes did say he wished *Cayenne* was moored out there near *Zoonie*. The last time we were moored together was in 2018 in Minerva Reefs, if you remember, on our way to Fiji. We had a fun evening sharing stories of our exploits over the last couple of years.

The next morning, I was standing in the cockpit soaking up the beautiful blue around me, waiting for Hannes to come down the jetty and for Rob to collect him for breakfast on board. I was also

Happy times with Hannes

looking forward to being out on the ocean again and crossing the Great Australian Bight.

The cork popped out of the bottle of Prosecco as we shared a long, luxurious breakfast at the start of a very hot day.

During Hannes and his wife Sabine's camping tour of the country they met Rudi and Frauke at a resort being managed by the latter, and Hannes helpfully mentioned to them that we were on our way across the Bight and would call in to Woody Island, where they were based.

We had two more light evening meals with Hannes, with new topics to cover and stories to tell each time, before saying our farewells, and after hugs we made our way the short distance back to *Zoonie* in a howling wind.

(In November 2023, Hannes was making his way ashore in Indonesia to chat to Sabine back home by mobile phone. He didn't make it. His dinghy was discovered partially launched, and dear Hannes was found floating face down by the two fishermen sent to look for him by the marina manager after Sabine raised the alarm. He was a gentle, kind friend, loved by many for good reason.)

Chapter 11

Zoonie Takes On the Great Australian Bight

Bight down gently, please

There are two versions of the limits of the Great Australian Bight: the International Hydrographic Organization (IHO) includes South West Cape, Tasmania, right across to West Cape Howe, Western Australia; the shorter Australian Hydrographic Service (AHS) definition is from Cape Carnot, South Australia (near to where Captain Flinders lost his crew members including the master of the *Investigator*, Mr Thistle), to Cape Pasley, north-east of the Archipelago of the Recherche, in Western Australia.

We had already passed both starting points in the east, but would we successfully cross both versions of the bight all the way? We were about to find out!

During the southern hemisphere summer months from November to May, while cyclones bite down on the northern latitudes of Australia and cause havoc from the south-west Pacific islands to the west coast of Australia, it is possible to ride the winds on top of a high-pressure system passing eastwards to the south of the Great Australian Bight and make that progress west in relative safety.

Well, that was the theory, anyway, and we were about to try it out!

At 8.45 am we motored from Ceduna towards the winding channel, past the ship-loading berths, heading for Middle Island, 530 miles and around five days away and so named because it is roughly halfway along the Archipelago of the Recherche. If we consider the AHS definition of the extent of the bight, from east to west, the Recherche islands would be the end of our crossing. Though as international sailors, we should really strive for the IHO version, shouldn't we.

We were relying on the chart plotter and eyeball navigation, having no paper charts for this area. We had bought charts for around the north of Australia back in the UK before leaving, but then we changed our route upon Merv's suggestion and found charts were not always available abroad. Would the chart plotter be enough?

Zoonie was rollicking along with a 17-knot wind pushing from her port stern quarter, just as planned. But…

13 February 2020. By this morning, as expected with the passing of the high, the wind was dropping and moving around the compass towards Zoonie's stern, so out onto the stage of the foredeck, after too long an absence, strides the Diva and gives an impressive 'come back' performance for 47 miles.

But this afternoon the wind is veering forward of the Diva's workable quadrant, so, while being watched by a pair of shy albatrosses, we have just escorted the Diva into the wings for her own safety and reset the genoa.

The Diva leads across the bight

It's midnight and we are careering along again with the moonlight casting slithers of glass on the dark ocean.

14 February 2020. At 5.00 am we are HALFWAY across.

Today brings a Valentine's gift of a calm sea, virtually no swell and good progress with the promise of strong winds ahead, as two high-pressure systems squeeze together when we near land. Shearwater birds mass together, floating on the gentle sea in good numbers.

Once again, we are controlling our speed so as not to arrive on this complex archipelago in the dark and cannot help but enjoy Zoonie's unhindered progress on a flat sea, reminiscent of the South Pacific crossing.

15 February 2020. Early morning on Day 3, with the golden glow of dawn chasing us, we have 135 miles to go, and the barometer is still steady. Will we make it across before the strong winds arrive?

On his voyage of exploration Matthew Flinders was using the same barometer as Cook had used thirty years before. He noted that the barometer rose before a change from the land breeze to a sea breeze and vice versa, so he could use the barometer to warn of wind changes.

So we also use ours in this way, and we know a rapid drop warns of the approach of a frontal system. The barometer arm started moving left, steadily dropping millibar by millibar, so we reefed *Zoonie* leaving out more genoa than main to help pull her along the course held by the autohelm, and soon we had 27 knots of predicted wind.

Suddenly there was a flash, and it wasn't the periodic winking of the smoke alarm. Then, in the fading light of a threatening sky, *Zoonie* was lit up as if she was in the limelight. Sheet and fork lightning was all around us, so we put all our mobile devices in the oven and prayed the mast would not be struck, nor either of us, for that matter (not that I am ever one to think it will never happen to me). The wind increased to 34 knots, a full gale with rain. Ah good, I thought, that will wash some of the salt off. We had the engine running in case her engine starter battery was hit and we wouldn't be able to restart it. Once running, the engine no longer needs its starter battery.

Despite sleep being a distant prospect, we did our routine watches – at least one can relax while horizontal and tucked behind the lee cloth – and while Rob was resting, I wondered if the welcome light of dawn would come before we reached Middle Island (beyond the AHS version of the bight's western point).

The refreshing scent of pine and eucalyptus was all around, and as 5.30 am passed, the clouds to the east grew silver linings, or, more appropriately for us, 'every silver lining had a cloud'.

We were entering the weather of a squash zone and fog was rolling over the vague outlines of the distant islands with the wind doing a 180-degree turn to send us 20 knots on the nose.

Those last few miles were a scary slog, and seemed to take forever, but, at last, the lee of the islands started to offer some shelter.

One definition of the bight conquered

16 February 2020. Rob cannot use the 29-kilogram fisherman's anchor we bought from Merv as it is too heavy for him to handle and risk his already weakened back, and when we tried five times to anchor in the bay beside Middle Island using our Delta, it dragged every time, barely dropping through the seagrass, bringing up with it a massive ball. Out of the world's sixty seagrass types, twenty-six thrive here, at present on our anchor.

I was so sorry because Matthew Flinders had anchored here on two separate circuits of Australia in 1802 and 1803, and I would have loved to go ashore and explore the island he described.

His first visit was a happy and productive one. His crew soon found the beautiful pink lake, Lake Hillier, and took on board the purest white salt from its shores that only needed to be dried before it was ready for use. The pinkness comes from the algae, Halobacterium and microbes working together to produce its vibrant colour.

His seven crew members, including Mr John Thistle, who weeks later would perish in the rip tide off the then-unnamed Cape Catastrophe, were still alive, chatting, laughing and making the most of their busy lives.

His second visit seventeen months later was part of an unfolding tragedy. Lack of fresh water sources along the north coast of Australia drove Matthew to sail to Coupang (now Kupang) in Dutch-held Timor to fill up with water. As the *Investigator* moved south down the west coast of Australia, one by one his men fell sick and died from dysentery, and Matthew himself commented that it must be the water. As his ship rounded Goose Island his boatswain, Charles Douglas, breathed his last breath and was buried on Middle Island. His name and the ship's name were carved on a sheet of copper that was only found in 1999, and it is thought to be the oldest marked grave in Australia. He must have requested a land burial instead of a watery grave, poor man.

I can imagine her anchors would have been so heavy and big they would be more likely to sink through the grass into the sand than our plough-shaped hook, even though it has a long 'nose'.

So, we turned out again towards the passage we had chosen through the archipelago.

By the time we arrived in Hammer Head Bay on the mainland the day was wearing on and Rob was getting fed up with what he termed "all the disappointments".

I said nothing but I was not holding out much hope for this place either, and, indeed, as the sun set, *Zoonie*'s anchor dragged once more, this time on hard sand – sandstone in the making.

9.50 pm and the light was fading fast. "As a last attempt let's try Duke of Orleans Bay," I suggested, and we motored around there, just making out a small offshore island we needed to hug to avoid two small rocks in the bay itself.

Looking down at the chart plotter, to our black route line on the way into the bay, I was concerned about those pots with their long rope lines to the seabed that could so easily wrap around Zoonie's prop.

"Rob, would you mind going to the foredeck with a torch when we approach our inward route, please, and look out for pots."

I just had a feeling.

"Halt!" he yelled and shone the light dead ahead so I could instantly put Zoonie into neutral, stopping the prop and turn the wheel so her forward momentum moved sideways, and we watched silently as the potentially lethal two white buoys passed close down her port side. Phew. Teamwork, the mortar of our marriage, was working again.

Same thing again; it was like trying to anchor in concrete. We retraced our track and continued motoring.

Rob had put waypoints in to take us close to the mainland, past rocks, islands and reefs, to Woody Island. Hannes had let Rudi and Frauke, who manage the eco camp there, know we were coming. The thought of a mooring buoy was very welcoming.

In front of us lay two 10-mile stretches and then a few short doglegs through the obstructions.

In the pitch darkness we heard water against the rocks just feet away as we crept forwards. We took turns having one hour of sleep on each of those first legs. It was some of the best sleep; as our heads reached the pillows we were out like snuffed candles and wide awake when touched with a kiss.

I thought that to get through there, motoring through the wall of black without catching a pot, would be a miracle, and I had to temper the euphoria that we were nearly there and focus on the task in hand.

The Navionics charts on the plotter had been totally accurate.

Looking on Rob's incredible Google Earth, we had decided which of the mooring buoy lines we would pick up – the one just past the jetty. It came up quicker than we expected the next day, so I let *Zoonie* slow to almost a stop just before it, shone the 12-volt light onto it and motored just above tick over, to sit with her bow in the vicinity, while Rob picked up the line and attached it around the starboard cleat. I then shone the light up the striking pink granite rock face, just a few metres in front of us. At last, after 647 miles we could stop. It was 3.45 am and we relaxed with a gin and tonic before hitting the sack.

Woody Island

I sat on the side of *Zoonie's* cockpit the next morning admiring the honey glow of the rock wall enhanced by the early sun. I could make out some concrete blocks, moulded to the rocky surface, descending from left to right, and the weeping rust marks of the bolts that supported the original jetty that Don Mackenzie and his sons built there back in 1973 when he was given a permit to start his tourist business. I wondered how on earth anyone could build such a structure in that dangerous location, and Don himself named the slope Cardiac Hill after he and his sons lugged the massive timbers up there from the boat.

There was certainly a demand for visits to this island, the only one in the Recherche archipelago with soil deep enough to support trees. But there were also risks. The island has been swept by fire a number of times, the most recent being in 2006, and if that happens again the resort would be a total loss. Also, there is no natural water on the island. Rainwater is collected from the roof of the lodge and stored in tanks, and some of the loos are composting ones that use no water and do not smell. This is a real 'out on a limb' enterprise.

Rudi appeared on the terrace of the lodge and we waved. I called him up on the VHF and we agreed he would fetch us shortly.

When we arrived at the lodge coffee was being served, and the other visitors sat at tables and on the settees.

Les lives in Esperance on the mainland and with his business partner owns the Woody Island Eco Tours business. When he took over the lease and tourist business from Don Mackenzie's sons it was in a run-down state, but by the time he added six mooring buoys (tied to the seabed on railway carriage wheels and piles of ship's anchor chain), a liquor licence and accommodation at the end of the fast cat ride, he had sown the seeds of success.

18 February 2020. The island has a network of walks that are dotted with neat information boards, and tame birds fly close to one on their daily feeding errands. There is the beautiful rugged coastline, and the movement of the ocean around and over the rocks is mesmerising.

Les instructed Rudi, who had collected us from Zoonie earlier, that as international yacht visitors we would not be charged for the mooring for the duration of our stay. We appreciated his kindness. Not many circumnavigating yachts come south of Australia.

For the few days we were there a strong NE wind held sway over the area, meaning that from late morning until around midnight *Zoonie* pitched furiously into the sizeable waves that marked the end of the fetch over the waters of Esperance Bay. Sometimes the peaking waves were so high *Zoonie*'s bow would completely submerge, and then, as the bow sprang up, her stern would slap the water with a big bang and make her shudder all over. We watched a video of this on Frauke's phone, which she had recorded from the safety of the clubhouse. Aboard at the time, we were so used to the motion we even slept right through it, but the wear and tear on the cleat holding the mooring line was a little worrying.

After our coffee we went first through the camp exploring the accommodation that is loved by many locals from Esperance, who, having enjoyed the island as children, now bring their children and grandchildren back many times. We were glad we followed the advice of wearing strong walking shoes as the ants of all sizes scrambled for a taste of our blood, as did the early March flies, like the cattle gadflies at home, and, boy, did they hurt. There were peaked ants' nests two metres in diameter up near the weather station and right across the path, which had me running at times to get the ants off my legs and escape the ant fields.

Back towards the camp we joined the loop walk that would take us to the southern shores of the island, Twiggy's Landing and then up to the summit for a fine view westward over our next route and Esperance in the distance.

Twiggy was Don's family dog, a liver-and-white-coloured Labrador mix. On an excursion in their boat she was lost overboard, but her absence was not noticed straightaway. An unsuccessful search led the family to the heart-breaking conclusion she had drowned.

Three and a half months later a family member spotted a very thin Twiggy alive and reclusive, having supposedly survived on lizards and chicks. She was very reluctant to approach her family at first, but Don encouraged her with some food, and when she got close enough he grabbed her, and she launched into a wild display of affection and relief at being reunited. She was not the same after the experience and died just over a year later, but at least she had a year of enjoying her rescue.

Woody giants and hungry kangaroos

In our scramble over the smooth rocks that make up the Woody Island shoreline we found chitons and limpets that were at least four times the size of the ones we had seen before in Tonga and New Zealand.

Later the same day, in the afternoon, I was peeping through the undergrowth with the hope of seeing some of the illusive kangaroos; thirty were brought to the island many years ago. There was a time, after the sheep were taken off because the Recherche Archipelago was declared a nature reserve, when they would have had access to grass and oats, but the natural undergrowth has returned since the 2006 fire and the recent drought dried up lots of their rainwater puddles, so the remaining few rely on eating and drinking at the lodge, and Rudi and Frauke happily oblige with water, sheep nuts and oats, especially for the kangaroos.

Arriving back at the camp after the daily visitors have left, we were hoping we might see them in the evening as we sat with Rudi and Frauke and her son Michael, sipping Frauke's delicious iced coffee. The sun moved across the island casting shadows over the area around the lodge, and the kangaroos arrived, eight of them, and we leaned over the banister to take photos and watch them watching us and enjoying their supper. The biggest has a crumpled right ear and is shy, only Rudi can get within a half-metre of him, while the youngest was the boldest with strangers, lying not far from us and paying only scant attention to our movements.

We were planning to leave the next day, as there was lots of cyclone activity going on up north which draws up wind from the south leaving behind a favourable 15- to 20-knot wind. This time only the unpredictable movements of the current cyclone gave us our opportunity.

The next morning, we said our farewells to our new friends and headed back to the now very still *Zoonie*, the wind having dropped and veered, leaving her in calm waters. I squeezed into my wetsuit, and carrying our masks and flippers aft we were determined to explore the underwater world in the now attractive sea just before leaving for good.

22 February 2020. The seagrasses and weeds were abundant, and the submarine growth on the pink granite walls was a multitude of bright colours. The wreck Rudi told us about was there: a small wooden well-rotted vessel. We swam with thousands of clear jellyfish that had no visible tentacles and were not a problem.

By far the most interesting find on this trip was the sinker to our mooring: the railway engine wheel and ship's anchor chain. The wheel was now clearly visible at the end of a metre drag line, and the heavy chain pulled away from it, in a straight line. Frauke had done a comparison of our position with previous photos on her phone of other yachts on the

Rudi's send off

same mooring, and her findings confirmed Zoonie had played her part in repositioning her buoy during the strong winds. Mr Google will sort out the new position on Google Maps next time he passes!

Rudi gave us a fantastic send off, a knight on his yellow horsepowered mount with banner flying, and Frauke took photos from the pier.

Zoonie rounded the island, and we had two waypoints to reach before we could set the course directly for Albany. I had filled in the logbook before we departed and the barometer read 1013 millibars, but when I checked it again after half an hour, almost in passing, it had dropped to 1010 millibars, an alarming drop in such a short time considering a drop of 5–6 millibars in three hours presages a force 6.

"Rob, if that drop continues, we will have to go back. Six millibars in an hour is unthinkable."

"You must be kidding," Rob said, disappointed.

Fortunately, the dark blue pointer stayed on 1010 for the duration of the passage; so, what had caused the drop? The weather was benign with a settled cloud state and calm water, so that was not a factor. The sky was grey but not threatening or particularly dark. Maybe our location behind the island? Well, partly, I think, linked to magnetism in the pink granite.

24 February 2020. Apart from a cheeky 28-knot blast of wind between the islands as we left – maybe that was the cause of the drop – we had no more alarms until we arrived in King George Sound, when the man overboard alarm sounded just as the chart plotter turned itself off. A quick head count proved there was no action necessary, and we learned that the autopilot is disconnected if the alarm goes off so that rescue procedures can be instigated; perhaps it works another way as well and the alarm is to alert us on board that the chart plotter has died. Cool, learn something every day.

The wind was rising as we approached the Albany entrance as we knew it would; another short weather window was ending.

The Western Australian Government's Department of Transport owns and runs these marinas, and they had allocated us a nice easy 'pen' to enter. The choice of our mooring pen proved to be fortuitous when we met Mark from the sailing yacht next door.

New friends in Albany

There are many aspects of professional sailing that Mark Macrae is involved in – skippering, sail training, yacht delivery, global racing, escorting visitors like us, advice and brokerage – and the more time we spent with this congenial man the more we realised his local knowledge of sailing locations and onshore facilities in Western Australia is extensive and, for us, useful.

He came aboard for a coffee with one of the ladies who crew for him regularly, Katrina.

Back at the end of January I started making enquiries about where we could lay up *Zoonie*. Mark suggested Emu Point Slipway Services, which has a yard just around the corner from Albany and is privately owned.

27 February 2020. We went with Mark for a tour of the local area, and he introduced us to Darren who runs the boatyard at Emu Point and once sailed in the area between Portsmouth and Poole.

We agreed a price. "Is that inclusive of GST?" I asked – legally, prices quoted should include it – and Darren confirmed he could include the tax at that price.

Having firmed up on *Zoonie's* spot, we were keen to book our flights home for the start of April to see family and collect the new water pump, and we also wanted to arrange accommodation in Perth for a look-see. The word 'Covid' was being used more and more frequently in the media, and we didn't know when we might see family again without this trip. In the process we also booked a ten-day camping/hostel tour from Perth Youth Hostel to Broome starting on 21 March and taking in beaches for snorkelling with turtles, national parks, the dolphins of Monkey Mia and swimming in secret holes and waterfalls.

The clever consultant in the travel agent found direct return flights that were only £60 in total more than those with stopovers, and in view of the current global health panic the fewer encounters with human strangers the better, we thought.

While we were in Kangaroo Island, if you remember, Rob did an engine oil change and service and found the impeller in the water-cooling pump had shed one of its flanges. Also, the inside of the pump had an unhealthy-looking residue on one side, like solid emulsified oil, which meant the impeller was spinning against a rough, uneven surface. The little black foreign body had disappeared, we assumed into the heat exchanger, and we hoped it had made its way out. Naturally Rob had replaced the impeller, but the pump needed attention.

Rob again, on Mark's advice, took the pump apart to see if he could find the lost fragment and very carefully, with a torch, had a look into the exchanger. There followed a delicate surgical removal of the foreign object that could so easily have blocked the water flow, causing the engine to overheat, and with those unforgiving rocky shores so nearby, we may have been no better off than the ill-fated sailing ships of the past on a lee shore.

But something else he found that was even more disturbing was that four of the flanges on the new impeller were torn, in only 81 hours of engine use. Just as well we had a new pump on order at Golden Arrow Marine in Poole.

Vancouver, Lockyer and Mokare – the founders of Albany

In 1791 Commander George Vancouver sailed amongst the whales into the sheltered waters that he immediately named after George III – King George the Third's Sound – and approached the inner harbour where the Indian Ocean swell and free winds are left behind, replaced with a vast area of shallow water and sandbanks, teeming with seals and sea lions, which he named Princess Royal Harbour. He stayed a while, anchored off a natural amphitheatre of hills enclosing a perfect place for future settlement with a plentiful supply of wood, game and water. He then sailed on to North America and broke the news of his discovery.

Soon the whalers of England, France and America were busy in this far-away place with their deadly business of supplying the northern hemisphere's insatiable need for furs, oil, meat and bone. Whale numbers have recovered but the same cannot be said for the seals and sea lions.

Ten years later our friend Matthew Flinders dropped the hook here, off Point Possession, and carried out many observations of the magnetic variations in the area, which were affected by the granite base of the surrounding rocks. He compared the observations on board to those taken by his men from their tents ashore and took the mean between the two. 'I conceive it will not be far wrong if taken at 7 degrees west.'

Having taken on nature's supplies he continued eastwards close to the shore so that no river or entrance would escape his detection.

I digress, which, as you know, dear reader, is a trait of mine, so back to the early beginnings of Albany.

In 1826 the British brig *Amity* was commissioned to transport twenty soldiers; twenty-three convicts (cheap labour); two officers plus seamen to sail her; a surgeon; and Major Edmund Lockyer, his wife and eleven children (more cheap labour?) to establish the new settlement. He became the first commander for a period of three months.

On the way around from Sydney in November the brig was hit by storms and was forced to put into George Town on the north Tasmania coast, where Bron and Ken live and where we spent Christmas, to take on supplies and carry out repairs to her sails.

She didn't have the same agreeable sail we had across the bight, instead arriving in King George Sound on Christmas Day after a rough six-week crossing, poor things.

As she sailed into Princess Royal Harbour, she flew her colours and fired her gun and thus Major Lockyer made the first official claim on behalf of the British Crown to domination over the whole Australian continent. Heady stuff.

Soon Edmund Lockyer met Mokare of the Menang Noongar people, who learned English, maybe from Edmund or his wife, and acted as interpreter and guide, teaching Lockyer the Dreamtime stories and acting as the perfect host, showing him literally the lay of the land and the walking tracks, many of which are the modern-day roads.

Early relations between the Aboriginal people and foreigners were good, not least because of Edmund's fair-minded and even-tempered nature, but also because the offshore whaling and sealing industries did not encroach upon the available land in the area, leaving the Menang people to continue their way of life unhindered.

Birth pangs of early Albany

The nineteenth century saw Albany burgeon as a major town due to both its strategic position on the route Europeans took around the south and east of Australia and the natural resources it offered in the way of shelter, water, fresh meat and land.

The early, largely friendly, relations between the indigenous people and the newcomers soon changed when the building of fences to enclose land started and increased rapidly in what must have been an alarming sight to the Aboriginal people. They were rapidly losing their hunting and fishing grounds and thus their food supply of the past (at least) 50,000 years.

It must have been a major disappointment for Edmund to see the destructive decline in relations after such a promising start with their accommodating hosts.

In a picture of Mokare's family they were displayed in mocking, demeaning caricature at the time to re-enforce the erroneous colonial concept of seeing them as ignorant savages in need of reform and civilising.

As the facilities of road and rail transport were set in place, with communications using telegraph established by 1872 and via the telephone in 1886, by 1891 the permanent population had grown from 1,200 to 2,665.

The town prospered as can be seen in the architecture today reflecting various European styles from classical to colonial, carefully preserved to remind people of the commercially successful beginnings. The human cost to the Aboriginal people is fortunately not forgotten, nor is the understanding, at the time by only a few, of how morally wrong and inhumane was much of their treatment.

As time moved on the local Menang people were largely absorbed into the European way of life, this being one of the reasons so many died of the diseases brought aboard the visiting ships. They filled such jobs as road builders, domestic and farm servants, farm workers, interpreters, whaling teams, (kanga)roo shooters (for hides and meat), police assistants and trackers, and land guides guiding newcomers through their lands; the latter a role for which they still do not qualify for pensions even after a lifetime of service.

Also, of course, they were subject to the same harsh jurisdiction that brought so many criminals to Australia in the first place. They were convicted of various crimes ranging from theft of livestock (this after their hunting grounds were stolen from them) to murder, and their punishment went through the full gamut of prison in Albany gaol, hard labour, imprisonment on Rottnest Island off Fremantle, work camps and execution.

One industry that prevailed for much of the second half of Albany's first century was coal bunkering. The new age of steamships as well as the railway engines on the rapidly growing land network had to be supplied with fuel, and the pall of coal dust hung over the town as the lumpers worked 24/7 with their shovels in the holds of the ships and coal hulks, with then unknown damage going on in their lungs, to keep the fledgling town growing. What previously had been clear, sweet sea air over Albany was now filled with minute particles of odorous coal dust and the sulphurous smell from the smoke of idling steam engines, for half a century. Lumps of coal from those days are still washed up along the high tide line of Middleton Beach.

But Albany's supremacy in Western Australia came to an abrupt end in 1900 when the British Postmaster General decided that Fremantle would be the mailing port of the west, and all that industry was taken away; the monthly visit of the mail- and passenger-carrying ship *Australia* now taking place along the wharf in a young city 400 kilometres away on the exposed west coast. Rail links with the east soon took over from the sailing routes to Sydney on account of their greater speed and safety, and for a variety of reasons, mostly political and commercial, the town on the Swan River became the state capital, known today as Perth, eclipsing the strategic importance of Albany as a centre for communications.

However, Albany has never lost its income from the changing nature of trade. Even when Perth was growing as the state capital, Albany was pioneering the supply of foodstuff to the goldmine fields at Kalgoorlie, 480 kilometres distant, and as a satellite industry from this, to feed the miners, the fish-freezing industry grew.

A decade and a half on and the First World War made Albany the main port from which Australian and New Zealand soldiers were shipped to the battlefields of Europe; an estimated 40,000 left through the tiny gap between Princess Royal Harbour and King George Sound known as Atatürk Entrance after Mustafa Kemal Atatürk, founder and first president of the new secular Türkiye, against whose brave soldiers the Australians and New Zealanders famously fought at Gallipoli.

The success of Albany as a secure harbour ensured the ongoing arrival of settlers and undoubtedly led to the expansion of arable and livestock farming and the growth of the towns of the south-west. Today the wharves are home to ranks of silos and piles of woodchip, and the number of cruise ships visiting the area throughout the year, because of the pleasant climate, is growing, or, rather, it had been until the arrival of the coronavirus, Covid-19.

Chapter 12

Covid Changes Our Plans

Keels to wheels

6 March 2020. Two days ago, we gathered in our lines and motored out of the marina into Princess Royal Harbour, past the three ships loading woodchips and grain, and back into King George Sound, where we had entered on 24 February, and changed course for Oyster (appropriate) Harbour where Mark had told us there were three courtesy moorings. Fingers crossed the impeller would remain intact for this seven-mile passage!

The location, opposite Emu Point where the boatyard is located, is delightful, and we had the cackling of kookaburras and the squawking of Australian ravens and the sight of white-chested cormorants roosting like candles in the trees plus the languid movement of two dolphins gliding past us in the still of the evening to enjoy. Also, it was calm, so we could sleep in our own bed knowing the waves wouldn't start slapping *Zoonie* during the night.

8 March 2020. It is 5.30 am on a tranquil blue morning in Emu Point boatyard, and an Australian raven is noisily fighting its reflection in a boat window, its mate calling to it from the deck of another stranded vessel, "Stop, you numpty."

Zoonie was lifted into the yard and is now settled here for the next six months, while we explore Western Australia and go home, finally setting off again in September, this time across the Indian Ocean to Mozambique or Réunion before the next cyclone season begins.

But will Covid alter these plans? Might we become stuck in the UK while Zoonie languishes here, and just how badly will the pandemic affect us? As the old adage says, 'the show must go on', but might our show be taken out of our hands? We have heard that Covid is spreading in the UK, prompting Prime Minister Boris Johnson to launch his coronavirus action plan. Surely the doors to visitors will soon close all over the world. I feel for the people affected, and I have a pang of guilt that we are so safe, for the time being, at least.

Zoonie has been busy voyaging for seven and a half months now and has covered 6,386 miles since 19 June 2019. She deserves a rest, but for how long?

Mark has been a constant friend, helping us with errands and ideas. He sourced a fuse for the bow thruster, a totally different fuse to anything I have ever seen, and he recently visited us in the yard and, over a cup of tea, told us about another English couple, Jeremy and Kathy Spencer, who entered Esperance near Woody Island in their Westerly Solway yacht and were now nearby in the marina. I suggested to Rob we should find them, if only to congratulate them for crossing the bight.

This is Jeremy and Kathy's second circumnavigation in their dependable bilge-keeler, *Sal Darago*, and we chatted and shared our stories and routes over numerous cups of tea. They were a few days behind us in their crossing and weren't aware of the moorings at Woody Island; in hindsight, how lucky we were that Hannes had told us about them.

Malcolm (Jeannie from Whangarei's brother) lives two hours up the Perth Road from here, and on a visit to his daughter, Kylie, just around the corner from us, he and his wife Christine had very kindly brought with them their spare car for our use until we return it to them on our way to Perth this Sunday ready for our planned ten-day tour to Broome.

Walter and his Noongar people

In Perth another beautiful day dawned, as if the weather was in defiance of the global Covid crisis. We took part in this defiance by walking towards Kings Park or Kaarta Koomba, the elevated 400-hectare area of natural bushland and cultivated gardens with wide vistas, still beloved by the Nyungar people, including Walter McGuire.

19 March 2020. Around the back of the commercial area of restaurants and Aspects, a craft and design shop, in the park, is the car park, where we met Nyungar elder Walter McGuire. Our friend Tyronne Bell from Canberra suggested we get to know him, and we were delighted to spend two hours with him along with a lady from Perth called Pauline. He and his wife, Meg, run the Go Cultural tours, and he straight away told us his two daughters were both away from home. One daughter was literally on a flight back from her studies in Canada because of the plans to close Western Australia during the Covid pandemic. He was clearly looking forward to this reunion with happiness and relief.

Walter is a traditional owner of the lands on which Perth now stands, and he has a very pragmatic view of the First Nations people's experience since the arrival of the first Europeans.

"It has happened, it is history, and there were misdeeds on both sides."

His view of Perth is one through the eyes of pride in ownership and title, and his vision for the future is one of tolerance and benevolent humanity.

Walter unwraps his props

He is a warm and welcoming man who loves to tell of his history but also of the culture of his people today, both of which he is determined to keep alive. After all the cancellations he has recently received because of Covid, we will be his last tour until the global epidemic is sent packing.

A question was formulating in my mind, but I didn't want to break his train of thought, so we went on listening to his softly spoken story. Pauline read out the terms of the Certificate of Exemption, whereby First Nations people were invited to throw off all aspects of their original identity in order to become part of European Perth life. It was dated March 1951, the year before I was born. The injustice of it for me was lessened by the fact it is no longer relevant or applicable and there is some recognition of the Nyungar people as being the first, present and ongoing guardians of the land. Tongue in cheek, Walter told us of how the high-rise city buildings are built on many lakes, the water from which has to be pumped into the Swan River constantly.

I imagined the view ahead, without the modern high-rises, when sunlight glistened on the waters as the Aboriginal community paddled their canoes and fished in the clean waters of the lakes. Walter's great-great-grandmother would have been a little girl in one of the canoes or splashing on the foreshore with her siblings. She was called Fanny Yooreel Balbuk and was known as the last Queen of the Nyungar. Walter had a delightful story to tell us about her.

While growing up, she saw the first European settlers arriving to make a life in this harsh but beautiful land to which they were not suited. As a grown woman she resented the white picket fences that were erected to enclose homesteads and land across the ancient pathways her people had walked, unhindered, for tens of thousands of years. So, on her daily perambulations she would kick the fences, uproot the posts and cast them aside in disgust, much to the obvious annoyance of the newcomers.

Her actions have become a part of the Nyungar folklore and became the basis for their claim to title of the lands when they submitted it to the Western Australian Government. The terms of the title are still being worked out and the fear is that the longer it takes the more watered down they will become.

However, it was good to see Walter was making a good business out of telling his stories, or had been, rather, which brings me to my question.

"Walter, with all your tours cancelled, what will you do now?"

"I will take my family and we will go into the bush. We know how to survive and hunt there, and that's where we will be until all this is over."
I was glad for him and impressed by his versatility.

He finished his tour by singing us a farewell song accompanied by clapping two boomerangs together, then he climbed into his maroon 4x4 and sped off to the airport.

The brief start of our eagerly awaited road tour

We were off early, heading north towards Broome, taking in places of interest en route, starting with The Pinnacles Desert, eleven of us out of the eighteen originally booked, and Wokka, our driver, all quietly knowing that, with the four-square-metres distancing rule because of Covid, we should not really be there at all. However, the local organisers had not received the command to cancel, so we were hopeful that as we were effectively isolating ourselves to an area of country populated at the rate of one person per square kilometre, we might just get away with a few days, at least. Things were changing by the hour, and at least in our rugged bus we had the means of return.

The Pinnacles are 32,000 human-height limestone rocks, and scientists are not certain how they were formed. There are three major theories, and they could all be partly true.

First, they may have been the result of a period of dissolution, possibly by seawater, as the pinnacles are made of rock more resistant to erosion than the surrounding strata.

Second, tree roots possibly became groundwater conduits allowing calcium carbonate originating from marine shells to replace the liquid in them and act as a glue for sand and gravel to stick to the root forms. Wind then eroded the softer outer layer, exposing the harder calcified shapes.

Finally, and similar to the second theory involving roots and calcium from marine shells, if an excess of water in which nutrients including calcium pass through plants when they are alive, this hard calcium accumulates on the surface of the roots as it cannot all be absorbed. When the root dies, this root cast survives.

Like derelict cities and wrecked ships in the Sahara, they cover and uncover depending on the movement of the massive sand dunes. The colour of the sand around the mini monsters is yellow like Bird's custard powder, while the seashore sand is, well, sand coloured. Make of that what you will. All the theories involve sea water.

We arrived at Jurien Bay for lunch and by this time were well on the way to gelling as a group. Optimistically, we climbed back onto the coach to head for the pink lake at Lynton.

All the youngsters were from Europe, and they started to receive confirmations that flights booked for April were being cancelled; their plans, unlike their flights, were being thrown up in the air. One of the two Mels had successfully booked hers only the day before, but now just hours later her flight was grounded. The mood of excitement over the long-anticipated trip was tempered by the rapidly changing situation; borders were starting to close between countries abroad and the Australian states.

Hannah, on her fourth trip to Aussie, was determined to swim with whale sharks. Tom from France and Carmel from Belgium chatted away in French as we sped along.

Next stop on our first day was Bluff Point Lookout with its elevated views over the Indian Ocean and the beautiful red horizontal strata of the rocks. This invigorated the youngsters, who posed on high rocks with the wind off the ocean blowing their worries away, just briefly. For us it was a view of our next destination.

Wokka showed us a distant house that is now a B&B, which has a history of interest to the older ones of you who have heard of the truth-based films and musical entitled *The King and I*. Anna Leonowens was the 'I' and lived there with her military husband and four children, but this was before her position with the King of Siam. Later, after they had moved to Singapore and then on to Penang, her husband and two of her children died. She sent one of her other children, a daughter, to England for an education while her son stayed with her when she became governess to the King of Siam's children for five years.

The pink lake near her home, otherwise called the Hutt Lagoon, was very long. The colour comes from the algae that lives there,

Dunaliella salina, which is a source of beta-carotene used as colouring in the food industry; consequently, the lake is home to the world's largest micro-algae farm.

21 March 2020. By then, after hours on the road, we were in the tropics, and that evening the breeze that blew through the barbecue area at the hostel was very welcome.

We spent a comfy first night sharing a dorm with Tom and Carmel and quiet and charming Rafael from the Dolomites in Italy and prepared for an early start, heading for Murchison Gorge, where the river of the same name flows down the meeting place of two tectonic plates in the Kalbarri National Park.

Red, puffy, anxious eyes of broken plans and lost flights calmed as we moved towards our next mini adventure. Wokka hadn't brought us any negative news yet, so we were free to enjoy the moment. It was hot and getting hotter and the flies were a pain, but at least they didn't bite.

The climb down to the Murchison River bank was a wonderful scramble over rocks, through natural rock alleys and down ladders before we relaxed by the green river. It reminded me of a small-scale Grand Canyon, and the climb up was just as invigorating. But what would be the news back at the rugged bus?

Heading for the shade of a rest area, Wokka walked over and gave us the thumbs up. Spirits rose: not only was the trip continuing, but we would soon be snorkelling again.

Wokka drove forward a little then stopped and was looking at his phone. "It's over, we head back when you're ready, should take about six hours with breaks."

It was a kind of relief because the uncertainty was over and we could all start to plan our next moves. Some of our young friends would bunker down in a houseshare and others would go to the airport on the off chance. Ticket prices back to Europe were high as the sky, and I really felt for them; commercial opportunism was as sinister as the disease.

The sun was still high as we started off, passing numerous white crosses and bleached piles of kangaroo bones, the product of roadkill.

The dramatic natural colour palette of red ochre roadside, green plant growth and blue sky with its pure white bulbous clouds was a treat to the eye, and with our inevitable confinement approaching, I tried to soak it up.

Mercifully, Perth City YHA had plenty of space for anyone who wanted it, and we could look forward to an ensuite double, but the $29 was too much for Tom – a park bench it would be. I just hoped he would be safe.

The sun was getting lower and its heat less intense. The coach air con did not always work and Wokka had to contend with pleas from the girls to make it cooler.

Soon we were back in Perth, and against the rules we all met up in the youth hostel dining room for a final meal together, and Rob and I offered what support and encouragement we could.

We had booked the train from East Perth station the next morning to connect with the coach for Kojonup where we would pick up the Ford Falcon car, kindly on loan to us again by Malcolm and Christine, so we would do the last stage back to *Zoonie* under our own steam. But would public transport be running as normal?

22 March 2020. Fortunately, the links worked, and as we settled onto the coach the pristine Irish driver came within a safe distance and instructed us: "Please make it a short trip to the facilities at the back; we all like a nice trip, and I'm not a plumber. While you're making your way there, hang on and you'll survive my driving." If that wasn't enough: "The water on board is vile; drink your own and you'll live." Helpfully: "There are levers at the sides of your seats, and back you go." And finally, and reassuringly: "The damage at the back of the coach was not my doing!"

The car was parked ready for us in Kojonup as arranged, and we were glad to see Zoonie's homely hull once again in the boatyard at Emu Point. The Falcon had landed.

Chapter 13

Forty-Five Days in Lockdown

24 March 2020. Once Rob has fitted the new raw water pump, sent from Sydney, checked the exhaust elbow for wear and changed the alternator belt, Zoonie will be shipshape once more and we will know our eventual exit is assured. Border Control has told us there should be no problem clearing out of Carnarvon at the end of September, but we know we may be excluded from putting in anywhere on the way home. That is the worst possible scenario, but it is do-able. Non-stop to the UK.

Our flight booked for 8 April has been cancelled and the funds banked for use or refund at some future date. Fortunately, our families accept the situation and suggest we stay put for the duration, and we would be reluctant to return home at the moment anyway in case we could not get back to Zoonie.

One of our young friends has made it back to Germany, and we hope to hear from others too. For all of April and May there will be no Qantas or Virgin international flights, so here we are in this beautiful spot with the southern winter rapidly approaching, in isolation at Emu Point. We are so fortunate in our location and to be healthy and with friends around us while we live on Zoonie.

We hope to swim again tomorrow in the sea-swimming pen, but now it is raining and a front is passing over this weekend, so who knows... swimming in the rain, why not!

While we were on our once-daily permitted hour of exercise, we walked past optimistic pelicans awaiting fish scraps towards the wild area of the estuary as far as there was a path and where the ibis fished with the oystercatchers while the tide was low.

27 March 2020. We've just got back from our swim, the second such activity we have done. My target was to do four lengths of the offshore seawater pen, the same as last time, and I managed it, so next time it will have to be six lengths. The pen is three sided and made of piles driven into the seabed with pontoons attached to them, just like in a marina. So, there is no barrier underneath the pontoons; this means that fish are free to come and go and live in the seagrass beds down there on the bottom. We watch their daily routines from behind our masks.

28 March 2020. There is a change in the weather, as a front passes south of us, and Zoonie wobbles very slightly in her cradle. We have had two treats in the last 24 hours. Rob was returning from town, where he extended our internet account, and noticed the little café around the corner was open for takeaways. This is good because it not only keeps their business going but also pays the fishermen and other suppliers, and we enjoyed fish 'n' chips in tempura batter in the evening.

29 March 2020. I was standing in the cockpit this morning, wearing my swimsuit and wrapped in a beach towel, contemplating an early swim, when dark clouds moved over the yard. So, Rob and I went for a walk instead. We cleared the little beaches and bays around Emu Point and came to the long beach at the head of King George Sound, where there were well-spaced folk and their oblivious dogs enjoying the fresh air.

I peered out across the bay towards the horizon, our exit one day, but my mood was not one of yearning; instead, I was looking to see if the blue whale, sighted in the sound last week, was still there. I didn't see it, but it was enough to know that this example of the largest animal in the world had at least paid a visit and was maybe still around.

Keeping on keeping on

30 March 2020. Darren, who runs the boatyard here, is happy for us to stay on board during lockdown. We chatted briefly at the allotted safe distance before our morning walk. The yard is busy now with moving machinery and people working on their marine projects, in happy isolation.

Last night my limbs did not want to rest, so we discussed exercising twice a day so we would go to bed more tired. On the radio people are coming up with all sorts of ideas about staying fit and sane in the isolation and adopting a sustainable psyche. How about you all – I think you have been self-isolating a few days more than us? I have always enjoyed structuring my days, and that helps now. Also, because we have no idea how long all this is going to last, I look at each day constructively, as another day less to go to the end of the tunnel. Then, as a long-distance sailor, I like to prepare for the worst scenario in some ways as time goes on.

For example, I wrote to Border Control the other day, as us cruisers have to every three months, and asked if it was likely we would still be able to clear out of Carnarvon at the end of September to start across the Indian Ocean, and they said there was no reason why we shouldn't, but we may not be allowed into South Africa, a possibility we already understood.

There is a cooling of the air temperature now when the sun is not shining, reminding us that autumn is approaching. We bit the bullet yesterday and walked the entire length of the long beach on the sound, 50 minutes one way and a little longer on the way back because I kept stopping to look at things like little birds and sweet-smelling flowers.

1 April 2020. For Darren I imagine life is pretty normal, with running the yard, lifting boats, cleaning them off and putting them back in, and all the odd jobs and admin to do. He confirms this is so. I ask him why there are so many tinny-towing vehicles in the car park today when other days the park is empty.

"Perfect day for tuna fishing today, and lots of families are taking their kids out as something to occupy them. My daughter has just sent me some photos of the conditions out there, and they're really nice." Tomorrow strong winds are due, so they are making hay while the sun shines.

Rob has now serviced four of the ten winches and has made the concerted decision to leave the next two until tomorrow. So much safer to do when she is on the hard; we mustn't let essential body parts of these vital aids ping into the water and be lost.

Away with the birdies

---

2 April 2020. The water in the beakers on the table wobbles with every gust that whacks Zoonie on her side. We are opting for two short walks today as the thunderous clouds threaten rain at any moment and we choose to stay close to home. Perfectly aerodynamic pelicans glide in to land into the wind on the crowded pontoons like A380s on final descent.

Glistening swimmers in wetsuits emerge to grab towels, making us feel we should 'make more effort' at this alternative exercise. The car park is empty as white caps scoot across King George Sound, and hundreds of seagulls and pelicans cover the swimming pen pontoons, sheltering.

Life goes on in lockdown

18 April 2020. It is now the twenty-fifth day since our return to Zoonie after the aborted camping trip, and we are still sane. Each day has a gentle structure to it, as do the weeks. After breakfast Rob does Zoonie jobs, including now servicing and fitting a new switch to the windlass; at present it is not playing ball, but he will trace the cause, I have total faith.

I have been making strides on finishing my book of the first half of our circumnavigation, A Tale of Two Yachts, and then have other projects in mind. I wrote the story of Graham the Green Dinosaur to our oldest grandson, Henry, this morning. Graham was originally buried in the sand on the beach in Poole by Henry, and now he has turned up here! It is wonderful now that both Henry and Ruby are writing to us regularly; I feel so much closer — it really shortens the miles.

Wonderful wildlife around us

We returned from a walk at dusk one evening to find two kangaroos grazing just under *Zoonie*'s bow. A different day, a bandicoot dashed along the path away from us, ten times bigger than a mouse and prettier than a rat. Another morning there were hundreds of small blue jellyfish washed up, some still alive. Their tentacles could reach over a metre in length. They were all gone the next day.

Many sandy trails wander through the brush around here, presumably from ancient times, and lots of broken-down sheep fencing, but the natural shrub has grown back leaving just these enticing tracks. It doesn't matter at all if one gets lost because they all come out on the local roads.

26 April 2020. We do not look too far ahead as nothing is certain about when the lockdown will end globally, but common sense would suggest that opening up country borders to visitors will be the last thing on the governments' minds.

In the evening at the moment, after supper, we have a three-day cycle of games: Scrabble (very much our own rules), Tri-Ominos and 3/5 Dominoes. They all last an hour or so, by which time we are ready for a bit of viewing. At present its Howards' Way one evening and Killing Eve the next.

We wear our wetsuits now for swimming. I suddenly couldn't see the logic of wearing them in the tropics for snorkelling and then not wearing them down here at 35° S. We also wear our snorkels so we can breathe without our heads bent up while we are swimming, and so we can say "hi" to all the little fish down there. I do eight lengths at a time now and find my aching neck is pain free for days afterwards.

So far eight people have the infection here in Albany, and I guess they must be in the hospital either here or in Perth; it seems nowhere is escaping the virus.

We like cycles, don't we, and I don't just mean bicycles. Annual, weekly and daily cycles are reassuring concepts that we can look forward to, coming around again and again, with their elements of enjoyment and predictability. In our present world of uncertainty, when the future organisation of society is in itself on the change, those cycles are even more important.

On our weekly cycle here, despite the fact we are 'retired' or 'keenagers', we still work, and our work is important to us as it grounds us and gives us direction, usefulness and purpose, to say nothing of satisfaction at the end of the day. So, we look forward to the weekends when we try to do something not work related and a little different. Similarly, we look forward to Fridays, when we buy fish 'n' chips from the 'Squid Shack'.

May Day magic

On 1 May the federal government published the first easing of lockdown, in that up to ten people could meet socially provided they maintained the distancing rule. So, without further ado – we made plans.

3 May 2020. Today is Rob's birthday and the morning was spent with our English friends Kathy and Jeremy, whom we met when we were in Albany Marina, and it will go down in our memories as being our first social get together for more than a chat. We went for a lovely walk around the nearby golf course in warm sunshine, passing fields where the local mob of kangaroos relaxed on the soft new green grass. They recline just as humans would, sometimes resting on one elbow while laying on their sides, and they weren't at all fussed by us walking by.

The barbecue area at Princess Royal Sailing Club was the venue for our picnic. Sal Darago, Jeremy and Kathy's marine home, is moored in the sailing club's marina. We maintained the one-and-a-half-metre social distancing rule by sitting poised at the four corners of the lovely big table and tucked into Prosecco, sandwiches, homemade beetroot hummus with parmesan and truffle oil crisps followed by a yummy vegan chocolate and raspberry cake. The gentle breeze blew out Rob's seven candles (one candle for each decade and one for luck – Rob turned sixty-two).

Pelicans and their personal space

We were surrounded by a variety of sea and shore birds as well as the ever-vocal ravens and local magpies, but apart from the majestic and aloof sea eagles who command admiration, it was the local colony of thirty or so pelicans that I found most friendly and almost companionable, if one can get past that colossal, all-enveloping beak.

4 May 2020. I remember when we were sailing south from Panama watching V-shaped formations flying above us with the odd cormorant in position within the group and it was welcomed, it seemed, by them.

Here at Emu Haven when fishermen come ashore there is a little covered area with a green roof and a central stainless counter sloping inwards to the drain hole where they clean and wash their catch. Seeing these pelicans in small groups waiting patiently for scraps showing the height of good manners is remarkable; they are not at all aggressive but just like to keep their personal space, sidling away if one gets too close, eyeing me with those doleful eyes.

I wondered for a while why the back of their heads and necks are grey when the rest of their plumage is the beautiful contrast of black and white. Of course, they cannot reach their heads with their beak! They are big birds, they came up to my chest, and watching them take off down the fairway between the boat pens, elevating over the harbour and then banking around reminded me of what man has learned from birds in the progress of aviation.

Sometimes we watched them from on board *Zoonie* as they circled in groups overhead, riding the thermals for exercise and pleasure. They really graced this place with their presence.

A patient pelican

Goings on in the boatyard

We spent a total of forty-five days in lockdown in the boatyard, and I will remember those times with pleasure for the people we got to know, the discreet freedom the rules allowed us to move around, exercise and explore, and the work we completed.

That's not to say it's all been play here: there are a few small commercial fishing boats and Darren and John work every day in the boatyard. The two cafés have been busy providing a takeaway service which will be an essential string to their bow when they open up their table and seats again and have to reduce the capacity to comply with social distancing rules. There is a boat sales yard and chandlery and the shellfish plant that processes the oysters and mussels for which the area is famous. And, of course, the chippy!

Rob applied his usual thorough and loving attention to the jobs *Zoonie* asked of him. He serviced the windlass and by fitting a new switch, with a little help, got it running again. Four of the winches were taken apart and cleaned and re-greased by my action man ready for continued service.

The kindness of friends

Malcolm and Christine (lenders of the Falcon) invited us to come and stay in a small cottage on their 160-acre lifestyle farm/station near Kojonup, off the main Albany-to-Perth highway. They both have had careers away from the farm, so it is primarily their home, but with small-scale arable and sheep farming activities as well. Despite loving our lifestyle aboard *Zoonie*, we promptly accepted. It served as an alternative to the visit home we would have been enjoying, as well as an opportunity to spend lots more time with our dear friends. A date of arrival was set for a few days hence.

There was a mighty early winter storm brewing in the Indian Ocean to the west of us and we wanted to stay with *Zoonie* until it passed, as much to assure ourselves she would be fine when more came along to batter the coast while we were away up country as to ensure she was OK on this occasion.

The morning after the storm it was calm, eerily so, as the centre passed over us. The barometer had dropped 19 millibars to 995, and a thunderstorm complete with rain and hail joined us for breakfast. During the day there were sudden gusts of wind up to 40 knots, and we were relieved to talk with Kathy and Jeremy, who had moved from their exposed outer-pen mooring in the yacht club to a mooring buoy in the northern end of Oyster Bay, not far from us, where they were sheltered. They planned to leave soon after and head around Cape Leeuwin and on up to Shark Bay to warmer climes, as they had no heater on board and winter was approaching. We would keep in touch and looked forward to the next time.

Northwards for some station life

The white ford Falcon took off for Kojonup with a plan to visit Mount Barker for the view and the bakery near its base for some enormous Swiss rolls en route. We sped up the Albany Highway and after Mount Barker turned off for a more scenic route onto the Great Southern Highway near Cranbrook. We left the outside world behind us, just briefly, as we arrived at the end of the earth track.

Chapter 14

Living the Station Life

'Going bush' around the homestead

On the first morning at Te Opu, Malcolm and Christine's hobby/ lifestyle farm, I awoke to the sound of birdsong and the desire to explore in the cool of the early hour.

Te Opu is halfway along the straight line between Perth and Albany in the south of Western Australia, near Kojonup. On 160 acres they farm crops and sheep alongside their professional careers in education, because they like the rural lifestyle, hence the term 'lifestyle farming', but they don't need to rely on the income from the land to survive.

7 May 2020. Collie Tess was walking arthritically but purposefully around Malcolm and Christine's house, where we spent the first night, and I didn't think she'd mind if I tagged along. Last night she had barked a few times to tell the fox he was to leave the chickens well alone or he would have her to contend with. Which at the age of 17 doggy years, 119 human years, is admirable.

I met Tess on the broken-stone crazy paving path, and she showed me her shady little walk that keeps her fit before the sun gets too hot.

It being the end of the summer, the grazing and arable land is looking parched and dry, but around the homestead the cool mornings are creating dew on Christine's well-loved and cared for garden, resulting in an oasis of lushness. The house is built largely of stone and block with a tin roof overhanging generously to provide outside shade. The inviting open cellar door and dark interior had a particularly romantic French look about it; nice place to keep some wine and preserves in there.

Walking back towards the house I met Malcolm and commented on the size of the ants on the crazy paving path, and Malcolm asked, "You want to see some really big ants?" Curiosity overtook the flight instinct, and we bounced along on the quad bike down a gentle hill towards some trees and what looked like a dry stream bed. Well, the ants were about an inch long and had pink heads, legs and antennae and shiny reddish/black abdomens.

The skeleton of a dinghy next to the dam showed the harsh effect of the climate over time. The stripped plywood skin, once painted, was lying beneath plant growth next to the hull, once used by a generation of youngsters to explore the fun of life on water; I could almost hear the screams of delight and lively chatter from years ago.

The sheep match the colour of the earth, and the little flock raced towards the hopper of grain as Malcolm spread it along the ground to give them all a fair meal.

The strength of the walls around the garden reflects the strength of family love that has been present in this home for years. Their two daughters, Kylie and Tennille, are now grown and gone, not too far, with families of their own, but there are still signs of their happy childhood. The tennis court and barbecue area and a discarded tricycle help make this a warm and welcoming place to stay filled with memories. Best of all, of course, was Malcolm and Christine's company.

Our hosts asked if we would like to live in a little house, still on their land and a short distance from Te Opu, while we were staying with them, and thinking it would be fun to be able to invite them over, we happily agreed.

Rob completed the pre-existing furnishings for our own little homestead, Shipton, with a couple of chairs he found in Malcolm's wonderful Aladdin's cave of a storeroom/workshop. Washed, dried and relocated, they made excellent bedroom chairs.

Within a short time, I realised Shipton, originally built as a honeymoon venue many years ago, was also an observatory on the rural world outside, the pretty farm vistas changing all through the day as the sun moved over us and then faded in the evening, for a few minutes adding a delicious tone of pink to nature's palette.

10 May 2020. Malcolm sometimes texts us to come and witness yet another wonder. I was thrilled to see a beautiful redback spider he spotted when turning over a length of metal. She's also known as the Australian black widow because this striking female has her relationship with her husband all sewn up.

She is too busy to worry much about housekeeping (like me) and her web is a mess, made to be functional and not of 'Grand Design' style. Intolerant of any misogyny, she eats her husband once the mating process is complete (unlike me), hence the name. Her mate actually positions his abdomen over her mouth while mating to make it easy for her to feast upon him, thus lengthening the mating process, so to make more babies. She has an hourglass red shape on her belly, but neither Malcolm nor I were prepared to turn her over to see; even the picture on Wikipedia shows a dead upside-down spider.

A bite from her is unlikely to be fatal, just very uncomfortable with nausea, sweating and irritation for a few days. A horse can help. Since 1956, horses have been injected with a non-lethal dose of the venom, and the antibodies they produce are used as an anti-venom to be injected into the victim. But anti-venom is not always necessary; apparently, we are quite good at producing our own, and paracetamol helps reduce the pain. The best option, as with a snake bite, and already well known to animals and indigenous people, is to lie very still for up to 48 hours.

2 June 2020. The ground around us is greening up by the day. Early morning dew after the cooler nights and a sprinkling of rain is helping.

Rob helped Malcolm take some fence posts out of the ground so that once the track into the station is graded, rain will run off it into the dam. Brilliant. All they need now is rain.

All around is the evidence of farming over the years in the form of the old farm machinery, some dating back to the first days of settler activity, rusting and looking more a part of the scenery as time goes on. A brick chimney is all that remains of an early settler home.

A pretty little pink mottled lizard we found on the barbecue is typical redback spider food; we gently let the lid back down to hide him.

Early days in Kojonup – a short local history

One fine morning in February 1837, by white man's calendar, a group of eight Aboriginal people were walking stealthily through the lush green countryside of south-west Australia, towards a waterhole where they hoped to find some wildlife drinking, which, using their hunting skills, would provide their next meal.

Just imagine the mutual surprise and astonishment they will have felt when they stumbled onto a party of white men, led by surveyor Alfred Hillman, who were marking the road that would lead from King George Sound (Albany) to the Swan River (Perth). The party had spent the previous night at a lush green spot but found no water there. So they were grateful to these Aboriginal people who showed them the exact location of a spring of fresh water a few miles away.

Hillman was so impressed with the site of this permanent spring he wrote in his field book, 'This would be a good place for a station.' The spring is now hidden by green foliage underneath a log grating, but it's still there.

The name Kojonup probably originates from the Aboriginal word for a long- handled axe or 'kodja', and 'norp' meaning 'plenty', and the first part was most likely given to the party by those same eight Aboriginal people.

There is much hard quartzite rock in the area, known as Kojonup Sandstone, which flakes into razor-sharp edges, ideal for a cutting instrument, and early settlers found numerous axes around the land, suggesting that this could have been a factory area for making the axes that were then traded with other clan communities, also known as mobs.

Early relations with the generous Aboriginal people were good, with friendly guides helping the newcomers find their way around. They cannot have known of the intentions of the white men to claim the region and divide the area into large tracts of arable and livestock land that would be sold to settlers. Dissatisfaction amongst the settlers was abounding that the coastal plains were not as potentially productive as the rich grasslands here in the interior; the common view was that sheep would thrive and be profitable.

In September 1840 the new government held a public sale of seventeen different tracts of land around Kojonup, marked off in blocks of 640 acres, and by 1842 the sale of this, essentially stolen, land was concluded and the farming future for the investors and settlers assured. Or was it that easy? Of course not. Like childbirth, the growth of a new colony and township was fraught with pain: sudden disaster, joy and tragedy, not the least of which was the York Road poison, a plant of the pea family, that decimated the early attempts at pastoral farming by killing the unknowing grazing animals.

The toxic poison was identified as sodium fluoroacetate and it is still used as the commercially branded 1080 in New Zealand to control non-native pests, with fatal effects for native victims, amongst much opposition from environmentally concerned groups and individuals of the thinking public. New Zealand imports it from the US.

Burning up around Kojonup

The weather, apart from being dry, had been unseasonably warm, a growing trend, and so while the wood was tinder dry, farmers all over the Great Southern were applying for licences to burn the fallen trees that cluttered their land and made using the massive farming machinery hazardous. Intensive farming is imbedded in the psyche of the farmers here.

Perfect burning weather one might think, but the air became filled with the smoke from them, causing a smoke haze over thousands of square miles with the well-documented damage to the environment that has ruled out this activity in other countries, including our own.

While indigenous people the world over have wisely and carefully been using fire for small, short-term cool burning for tens of thousands of years to prevent massive bush fires, this is nothing like the modern practices of the farmers.

9 June 2020. However, when in Rome, do as the Romans do. So, Rob and I lent four willing hands in the highly social clear-up process. Christine led our little team and would decide when to move on to the next area, cluttered with dead branches of all sizes that have been drying out for a number of years.

Fire feeder Rob

We would spend a few hours picking up sticks and carrying them to the nearest blaze while chatting about this, that and the other, watching the beauty of fire crackling its way through the old wood, turning it into the purest white ash.

Eventually Malcolm would tell us the next part of the plan, which often meant we were free to walk back to the house and wait for the kettle to boil while we drank welcome glasses of water. Then we'd all sit down, sometimes outside under their pretty veranda, and chat some more over mugs of tea and a variety of small, delectable Christine-made cakes, Tess relaxing in her basket nearby. What a life!

We felt it the next morning when we got up with the aches and pains of complaining muscles, so we knew the exercise was doing us good.

10 June 2020. While Rob and I were watching a giant eucalyptus consumed in flames, we poked around a little pile of farm junk and Rob gently lifted a broken slab of concrete to find a female huntsman spider. They are venomous but, as usual, only as a means of defence. Here is a nice word for the day: they are 'sparassids' because they have eight eyes in two rows of four. Ours was about 7–8 centimetres across, but they can grow to 30 centimetres in diameter and are as common as they are beautiful. Alarmed at the sudden blast of sunlight, her smaller husband ran protectively all over her like a paler, ghostlike version of herself. I quickly took a photo and Rob gently laid the slab back down.

Family arrives

11 June 2020. Our life at the farm continues very pleasantly indeed. We have loved the outdoor exercise of log lugging and fire tending.
The burn continued for three days, and now there is nothing left to show for its long life apart from the ash that will now nourish the ground and which Malcolm has already buried with a layer of soil.
Neighbour Locky completed seeding the farm with barley two days ago. Rape (canola), lupins, wheat and oats are also common crops. It was fun to watch him manoeuvre the big machinery around the small paddock behind us. But before he started, we were able to pluck plenty of mushrooms from the paddocks and freeze lots down. I made a vegetarian mushroom stroganoff for supper when Christine and Malcolm came for a few hours of chat and games.

Malcolm and Christine come for supper

Their oldest daughter, Kylie, and her three girls, Abbey, Zoe and Isabelle, came from their farm, and we had some lovely times walking the fields with them; Grandad Malcolm provided fun entertainment by bringing out a motorized go-cart and a little tow-along go-cart. Isabelle's screams of joy could be heard from far afield as she bounced along behind Grandad, her pigtails flying, and her two sisters on the quad bike, repeating the fun her mother and Aunty Tennille had had when they were children.

3 July 2020. So, we have seen the transformation of barren fields to a glowing green and now red/brown seeded soil. We have had about half the rain hoped for during a weekend of strong winds from a storm, merging with a cold low-pressure system in the south Indian Ocean, so that moistened the soil for planting and raised the level in the dams a few centimetres, but more is needed if this year's crop is to thrive.

Chapter 15

Northwards to Broome and Back Again

The Falcon flies northwards

It seemed incongruous, but while deadly Covid-19 still gripped the world; while the regime in China was sabre-rattling over Hong Kong, and Taiwan, and threatening Australia and the US; while Melbourne in Victoria went at least in part *back* into lockdown, we were going on tour! To be precise, our faithful 110 NZD New Zealand tent and self-inflating mattress (I hoped it still would) were packed in the Falcon and once again became our mobile bedroom.

6 July 2020. Yesterday, after a couple of days planning with much help and advice from Malcolm, and a final coffee and cake with our dear hosts, we left our cosy little station home of sixty days exactly.

In a small cloud of dust led by 'our' 1995 Ford Falcon, 290,000 kilometres on the clock and freshly serviced thanks to Malcolm and Rob's efforts, we headed north. I am writing this in bed in our motel room behind a super little pub, the Settlers House York (which beckons us).

Lying in the beautiful recently named Avon Valley on the shores of the wide, flowing Avon River, the founding military fathers back in 1830 realised they were claiming ground that has been home to the local Aboriginal clans for tens of thousands of years, but they claimed it all the same.

Today most of the nineteenth-century buildings remain in use and are grand in style and well maintained. York was the first inland town in Western Australia and has seen all the wealth-creating activities of farming, mining and communications through growth and decline and back again. The town has a busy, friendly atmosphere.

Towards the gaping minefields and vast stations of Western Australia

6 July 2020. The Great Southern Highway, State Route 120, flows between vast green arable plains, their young crops on the rise; lightly wooded hills in the distance; and black-faced sheep with their lambs fenced away from the long, level stretches of road with just the occasional bends. We filled up at Northam, said goodbye to Toodyay, with its cared-for colonial architecture, and moved on towards Yerecoin, where we started to note the pattern of these small towns, with their railway passing through and the grain silos standing close by. They are the hubs where farmers get their supplies and deliver their crops.

National Highway 95, the Great Northern Highway, our smooth, easy-rider road from now on.

Dalwallinu, a place of wheat and wattle, sped by, and there were wheat fields to the horizon on both sides until gradually low bushes and shrubs started to dot the miles and red soil became the norm.

Mounts Gibson and Singleton loomed large, and side tracks peeled away to mines and more mines. This is why the road surface is so good: it has to withstand mining lorries en route to and from Port Hedland. These road trains are up to four trailers and 60 metres long and present an overtaking challenge.

There isn't much traffic, fortunately: mostly oversize loads, pick-up trucks, the road trains, hardy four-wheel drives towing rugged eight-wheel caravans or boats and a few, a very few, saloon cars like us. Pretty unique were we in our white Falcon!

We would be travelling alone along miles of straight open road when a dark dot would appear on the road in front, on our side. When near enough we would come off cruise control and prepare to overtake. I kid you not, every time we did there would be a bend, hill summit or dip ahead, so our continued progress past the vehicle was ill defined, uncertain and could lead us into uncertainty, and potential harm.

After 468 kilometres we arrived at Kirkalocka Station, where owner Blue told us how she and her policeman husband, James, bought the 190,000-acre station two years ago and still haven't seen half of it.

"Ours is small compared to those up there," she said, nodding her head northward. The previous owners had the farm over three generations, and their sheep farming overgrazed the all-year grass crop, which is now all gone leaving just bushes and dry red earth. A tragic story that resounds all over Australia.

Dark Emu by Bruce Pascoe tells of *Aboriginal Australia and the Birth of Agriculture* when, for tens of thousands of years, the first native Aboriginal people farmed sustainably and in harmony with nature. More about this book later.

A lady back in the boatyard would not believe me when I told her the farming history of the Aboriginal people.

"The Aborigines weren't farmers!"

Ignorance or wilful ignorance, I never did find out.

They considered the wild dogs a problem, so strychnine and 1080 were spread everywhere to kill them and goodness knows what else. James had researched bringing cattle back, either Shorthorns (which would colour match the ground perfectly!) or a breed I had not heard of before, impersonally called the Droughtmaster, to eat the remaining bushes. What did they want? A desert!?

Blue directed us behind the shearers' quarters and suggested a little corner next to the pet pen and between two old eucalyptus trees for the tent. The pegs went into the parched ground more easily than we thought they would, and we provided a distraction for the sheep, goats and resident ducks in a pen next door. A sign in their little paddock said they were expressly for 'Cuddles and not Casseroles', and the camping kids carefully shut the gate before communing with these gentle and friendly creatures. I liked that and I love camping; it's so 'down to earth'.

There are three homesteads on the property. The finest is rented out to passing visitors, the newest is where Blue and James live with their young children and the oldest is the original: a tiny one-room dwelling with its covered lean-to. I know which I'd live in, how about you?

Camping at Kirkalocka

So that was the first night at camp, and delightful it was too. We sat in our chairs beside the car, lemony gin and tonics in hand, watching the sun set through the bushes on the plains, and turned in, the noise of the lorries rumbling past too distant to disturb our sleep.

Across the Tropic of Capricorn to Newman

7 July 2020. Golden grasslands hold our gaze, and the Earth is being mined for her rich treasures of gold, emerald, iron ore and ochre. In addition to the kangaroo roadkill, there are now the bloated corpses of healthy-looking cattle being fed upon by, to our amazement, wedge-tailed eagles, standing hunched and hairy legged, looking at us as we pass. Pairs would be feasting on one animal, and because they're heavy and their take off is slow, many eagles themselves are falling victim to whirling wheels as vehicles pass. This is brutality to land and life.

It was now becoming decidedly warmer and sometime during the day we crossed into the tropics – warmer days but still three-blanket nights in our little tent.

We were in heavy open-cast iron ore mining country, and massive loads were being transported between sites, some taking up almost the full width of the road and causing oncoming traffic to perch on the highway shoulders like the eagles.

We were taking it in turns to drive alternate days, and 7 July was a long day, 670 kilometres long, but it got us to Newman, a newish mining town, active 24-hours a day, built for the mining men and women working shifts around the clock, many of whom sat in The Red Sands Tavern's courtyard with us, still wearing their hi-vis jackets. That beer was so welcome.

An avoidable disaster in the Karijini National Park

Tragic was an event that happened close by just before we passed by, when Rio Tinto, a global mining group, blew up a site of immense Aboriginal and anthropological importance in the name of iron ore extraction. Two caves, containing the pictorial history of the earliest known human activity, blasted off the face of the red earth.

In 2008 a law was passed that the mining of such known sites was to be done only with the agreement of the native land title holders, but the law did not mention any subsequent sites that might be discovered. Juukan Gorge in the Hamersley Range of mountains near Mount Meharry was discovered in 2013, so the management of Rio Tinto allegedly decided there was no legal reason why they should not go ahead.

Two hundred kilometres further on we arrived at the Auski Roadhouse (of perpetual light), where a young man showed us where to camp on grass. That was quite an experience; behind us mine workers, men and women, used rows of en suite cabins when they came off their shifts. The road trains also stopped for rest and recuperation well into the night.

There was a dynamic sense of different lifestyles in the camp: the busy mine workers contrasted with families on the children's school break and older couples like us, passing the time exploring this diverse and beautiful country.

Floodlights lit the area all night, and a very loud, earplug-busting generator ran 24/7 near us and just behind a massive pile of used tyres snazzily hidden by a beautiful bougainvillea. We were totally comfortable and near the loo and shower block, but I could barely sleep through the generator noise. I did dream the oddest dreams about being entrapped – they were uneasy. I was relieved it was Rob's turn to drive the next day. Bless him.

Disgust at dusty, rusty Port Hedland

On the road again, we were amongst the multitude of four-carriage road trains loaded with the recently extracted red guts of the earth, plying the road northwards to the export town of Port Hedland, which really needs to be re-named Port Redland because it is covered, head to toe, in red dust. Even the wooden buildings are painted in the same earthy red ochre colour and the red brick buildings look totally at home.

9 July 2020. Today Rob counted eighteen ships anchored off awaiting the call to enter port and load up, just to give an idea of the scale of non-stop iron ore exporting here.

We need iron ore, of course, for manufacturing all steel products; it is not that to which the local people are objecting. It is the fallout of the archaic system of loading the ore from the acres of stored piles of the stuff onto the kilometre-long trains that role it the short distance to the port for yet another messy system of loading it onto the ships which the locals oppose. In both processes tons of dust are freed into the atmosphere and accumulate on everything around, including the inner linings of the lungs of all the people, most damagingly of the children, who live here.

Our little tent is pitched and ready in the Discovery Parks site on a little nearby headland where we are in a totally different world. A number of the caravans and cabins around us are homes to mine workers and their families, so again we have the mix of workers and non-workers in a shady site with some delightful amenities including a fish 'n' chips van, arriving later, and a pretty swimming pool with views over the small estuary next to us.

From our shaded vantage point, sitting on our folding chairs by the pool, Rob and I are watching the tame little yellow-tinted honeyeater birds that keep flying to a dripping tap and drinking from it just as hummingbirds would, by hovering underneath using rapid wingbeats. Clever little birds to find the tap was dripping; I hope no one comes to turn it off. Maybe it was left on intentionally, or it has a conveniently worn washer inside.

Out across the Great Sandy Desert

10 July 2020. We are approaching the northern border of the Great Sandy Desert and white cattle graze safely behind a long fence.

A mixture of small pindan wattle trees with yellow flowers and bushes merge into areas of grassland dotted with watering holes and Brahman cattle, the most prominent breed around here. We passed through the Warralong Community area of indigenous lands and stopped at the Pardoo Roadhouse & Tavern to fill up and experience a truly delicious freshly ground coffee with just a drop of milk, supping it under the shade of some trees, dunking our own ginger nuts into it, and then sucking them dry until we'd finished and were ready to move on.

It is 30°C outside and we have a long road ahead and a choice of three camp areas to choose from for the night. I want to get as far across the desert today as possible, to make tomorrow a nice short run into Broome. The Falcon has been behaving well (fingers crossed) and, treated gently, by easing back on the gas as soon as possible during overtaking, she rarely misses a beat, except having to clear her throat before attempting anything resembling a hill. But I am a little nervy about the many miles before us, where there are no services of any kind should we get into trouble.

Low hills appear on the skyline either side of the road ahead, which become a shimmering mirage near the horizon. We know we are near our destination.

Safely over the desert

In the end we turned left down the dirt track towards Port Smith between junction numbers 507 and 508 on the map because an old gentleman back at the Auski Roadhouse had told us it was a lovely spot to relax. It was, in fact, a little oasis, built many decades ago by a couple, now in their nineties, who moved to be nearer civilisation in Broome a couple of years ago, selling the leafy site and their beautiful home complete with bird garden, hidden behind the bougainvillea, to the Indigenous Land and Sea Corporation, who have plans along the tourism industry lines for the future.

We set ourselves up next to a couple who have been coming to this spot for the last twenty years for three months of the year to escape the southern winter. The lady kindly took us to see three little frogmouth owls that are resident.

"There used to be so many more, but there is a barking owl here that eats them for BREAKFAST!"

I really liked the tufty feathers that stick out on top of the beaks of these cute little creatures.

After a light lunch of beer and ice-cream, we decided to catch the last of the high tide with a quick dip down at the lagoon for the first swim in ages, before it flowed back out a long way over the sandbanks and between the mangroves.

The range of the tides in this part of the world is pretty immense, up to 12 metres, so the rate of the flow is fast, faster than I first appreciated as we waded out to deeper water behind a chap trying desperately to push out his boat, with its big outboard motor, far enough to lower the motor and get going. At last, the water was waist deep and I took the plunge surrounded by succulent mangroves and started to really enjoy the ease with which I was making progress down tide.

"Barb, I'll be out of my depth in a moment, and have you seen how fast you are moving?"

Rob heaved me back into my own standing depth, and we wandered slowly, for the air was very hot and the water nice and cool, back towards the beach.

The only drawback to this idyllic place was the sandflies; four days later, the bites were at last losing their itch. These creatures were so hard to see I had no idea what was causing the sharp pricks until I watched really closely, and then the needle prick that was filling with MY blood was all that was visible to the eye behind my best reading glasses. Not only 'no-see-ums', as they are known, but also invisi-bums.

Broome was built on pearl buttons

The town of Broome was born in 1883 and rapidly developed into an area filled with Chinese, Japanese and Europeans along with local Aboriginal men blackbirded into forced labour aboard the pearl luggers. The industry of pearling was a dangerous one, and thousands of lives were taken when the fleets were caught in storms, their divers lost in the watery depths.

With the advent of plastic, the bottom fell out of the pearl fishing market, and all that remains of the business is the local cultural pearl industry for the making of jewellery sold commercially. But there is plenty going on in Broome, which includes both 'new Australians' and the indigenous population, and the future looks good for both groups, as tourism slowly returned and Western Australia re-opened its internal borders.

Having feasted for lunch on a delicious sweet orange from Christine's Kojonup garden, a juicy apple, two soft 'ginger kisses' biscuits and water, we decided we'd go to our lodgings, booked for three nights which became four, and see if they were ready for us.

Bojack and the boab tree

Kimberley Travellers Lodge has been through many guises since it was built over twenty years ago as a 'party resort'. Two years ago, James and Jen bought the little gem along with the boab tree of unknown age that provides abundant shade in the middle of the social area — a fine old lady who likes to dress up in her diamond lights for the evenings. If only she could speak, what tales she would have to tell!

When we arrived, fragrant, leafy frangipani trees greeted us either side of the entrance, and a dog burst forth in pursuit of his blue ball. So, we would get our daily doggy fix to boot.

Manager Scruffy (his pet name) was on duty with Bojack, his one-year-old blue heeler cattle dog. Australian cattle dogs were originally bred from the Australian wolf or dingo and an imported breed possibly of the collie, hound or terrier type. Heelers round up cattle by nipping their heels, but Bojack wasn't into nipping; however, if the youngsters become too noisy, he barks once to restore peace and order.

The road to the Kimberley

There was an air of excitement amongst us as we set off. Speeding along with a small group seemed to be something remarkable considering the closed borders and raging global pandemic, but for us it was in the satisfaction that we were about to enjoy what would have been the highlight of our Perth-to-Broome ten-day camping tour we started four months previously – pre-lockdown, when we had to turn back to Perth after two days, if you remember.

Looking at the map, we headed from Broome to Derby, where we visited the Boab Prison Tree (those trees look so cuddly) and the longest water trough in Western Australia, which can quench the thirst of 500 cattle at one slurping.

13 July 2020. Here at the Prison Tree, allegedly, Aboriginal 'prisoners', who were stolen from their village by blackbirders to be consigned to a life of slavery in the dangerous pearling industry in Broome and other north coast towns, would spend their last night in 'country'. A traumatising experience in the extreme, considering the tree was a sacred place to them where they would normally pay their respects to their ancestors; instead, they suffered the humiliation of being chained together by the neck and unlikely to ever see their families again.

Boabs are incredible little store houses. Their native name is larrkardiy. They have no tree rings and so telling their age is a matter of guesswork; some experts reckon they can live to over 2,000 years. They provide food and medicine to the knowing Aboriginal people, plus their fibrous centres make excellent rope. But beware of ever staying in the shade of one if there is thunder and lightning around, as being struck by a stray bolt flips them out of the ground and is the main cause of their demise. They are resistant to drought and fire and just shed their burnt bark when the flames have passed through.

The Kimberley is a vast region, 421,000 square kilometres and 600 kilometres from north to south, bigger than Victoria and Tasmania combined, and it would swallow the UK in just over half of a tasty gulp. With enormous cattle stations above ground and a wealth of mineral ores and oil and gas deposits down under, the clamouring for rights to export live animals and extract carbon fuels is not going to end any time soon.

Speeding on we passed numerous signs to indigenous communities that were closed because of Covid. Our driver and guide, Sean, told us of the many 'good people' who are helping the indigenous population with courses and programmes that give a future to the younger generation; so, there are many reasons for optimism.

Shall we smile at a crocodile?

Wedge-tailed eagles and whistling kites circle above us as we cross the blond savanna dotted with boabs, eucalyptus bloodwoods and pindan wattle trees adorned with their yellow blossom, when in the distance we see the flatland rising to the grey limestone cliffs of the Napier Range, our destination.

We followed Sean into Windjana Gorge and occasionally he would stop and explain the fossils in the rock and where to spot the 'freshies', freshwater crocodiles.

But the landscape talked to us itself.

The steep overhangs of water-worn rock and the residue of foliage stuck over branches way above our heads told of how deep and fast runs the Lennard River through here during the wet season, and how impossible it would be for us to visit then.

The sun-bathed permanent waterholes in the riverbed

A friendly freshie

came into sight, and we saw our first freshie, the sunlight illuminating its legs as they dangled in the pale green water beneath it. It looked so restful.

"Stay five metres away and smile, and you'll be fine," Sean had said, so double that to ten metres for me as we eyed another crocodile lying in the shallows. They have fine long snouts, and their scaly streamlined bodies are quite beautiful. They were motionless, and I was glad they remained so. They are well mannered and unthreatening compared to their lumbering and deadly saltwater cousins; mutual respect is all that was needed. So, yes, we definitely smiled at the crocodiles.

Jandamarra – the Aboriginal activist

Visiting this short stretch of the Napier Range, one must mention the legendary freedom fighter and advocate for the rights of the Bunuba people, Jandamarra, who from 1885 to 1897 was torn between his Bunuba origins and his relationship with the land-grabbing settlers and their police protectors.

Jandamarra was an intelligent and gifted man who became an outcast from his people because he ignored their ancient skin colour marital laws designed to prevent inbreeding and took whichever woman he fancied at the time. He learned English and worked on sheep stations and as a police tracker for a while, capturing Bunuba cattle stealers and imprisoning them at Lillimilura Police Station, the ruins of which we saw as we drove past.

He became fascinated by the Bunuba male world of ritual, mythology, and the laws and spirituality of Bunuba country – he acquired a cause to protect his homeland. The Bunuba elders successfully gained his support in their fight against the malngarri, the European settlers.

On the night of 1 October 1894 at the police outstation Jandamarra shot his friend and work companion police constable Bill Richardson as he lay in bed suffering from malaria. He then released the Bunuba prisoners and turned his back forever on the new world of immigrant farmers to fight for the Bunuba cause.

The white powers were very worried because the Aboriginal fighters were armed with guns, and so Jandamarra's fate and that of his warrior friends would be sealed as their own blood soaked into the hot ground.

For three years he waged successful guerrilla warfare, ambushing cattlemen and police camps to get arms and supplies. Police troopers said he took on a ghostlike quality, seen only in his tracks. He knew Windjana Gorge and Tunnel Creek like the back of his hand, and it was as if the water-eroded rock had formed caves and crevices solely for him and his warriors to hide in.

Present-day elders remember him as a great warrior and as a courageous and clever leader, who defended his people and country against growing and overwhelming odds. They also remember him as a Jalgangurru, a man with spiritual powers that flowed through him from the timeless law of their country. His ability to disappear, transform himself into a bird and protect himself from deadly weapons was legendary, for a time. Settlers could no longer recruit Aboriginal guides and cattlemen because they were afraid of Jandamarra, so the settling of the area was on hold until he could be stopped. Micki, a fellow tracker and Bunuba man who had no fear of the living legend, was recruited from the Pilbara area to track him down.

In 1896 Micki wounded Jandamarra, who managed to escape through the long grass to his hideout in Tunnel Creek, where his wife and mother nursed his wounds.

The following year Micki spotted his adversary on a rock at the entrance to Tunnel Creek. They exchanged fire and Jandamarra fell 30 metres to his death. Thus started the long road to reconciliation.

This was the outermost point of our planned trip. Soon we would start to head west around the coast, slowly making our way south to chilly climes. We would have loved to spend another two weeks exploring more of the Kimberley area but the border into the Northern Territory that crosses the area was still closed.

We luxuriated in a day off: a day of writing blogs and an afternoon swim in the shady pool, after wondering if we were late or early up because the communal area was deserted when we emerged at around 8.00 am; we were early! There was a complimentary breakfast laid on with all kinds of fillings for toast or pancakes, fruit juices, etc., which was nice, and unexpected.

Westwards to Point Samson

We dragged ourselves away from this little oasis in the heart of Broome, gave Bojack a final fussing and headed off on the road westwards, back across the Great Sandy Desert along the Great Northern Highway, but where would we camp next?

Lunch comprised of rum and raisin chocolate and a mug of coffee from the Pardoo Roadhouse, consumed as we sat and chatted about where to stay the night. We decided on the devil we knew, and I gave the Discovery Parks site at Port Hedland a ring, knowing what a nice camp it is, and we booked in with ease. Then, for the following two nights, I booked the sister site in Karratha, because we wanted to check out the Aboriginal rock art and the town of Dampier.

Chatting with friendly fellow campers, one man, camping with his wife and sons, was moved by the ruthless nature of Rio Tinto's operations. Like others we had spoken with, he felt Rio Tinto should be spending a lot more on services for the people their mining processes adversely affects.

Another topic of conversation in camp is always "where are you heading?" We were clearly grouped under the title 'grey nomads', thousands of whom head north in Western Australia away from the cooler winter. Ours was a brief voyage of discovery, whereas many around us were there for months before they would venture south and home for the summer.

On a bright sunny day in Karratha, guide Clinton Walker showed visitors the Ngurrangga rock art. Clinton knew Walter McGuire, with whom we had spent a morning in Perth, in Kings Park, learning about his culture, and both are wise men who know all about their heritage as well as the plant and medicinal values of the local flora.

Two girls in our group already knew lots about Aboriginal people and their customs and traditions, and they were intrigued by the flowers and their uses, especially the berries that were sweets to Clinton and his friends as children. Clinton squeezed the deep purple centres of the luscious red flowers known as Sturt's desert peas to reveal the inner part of the flower where the sweet nectar can be found. He encouraged the children to suck them and spit out the pips so the plant would spread; as you can imagine, the children had no problem with this. They're worth a Google as they are so unusual.

The children were drawn close around him, sensing his warm and interesting personality. He was clearly a respected and much-loved man.

Surrounded by 360-degree views over the coast and countryside, we progressed uphill towards the pictures carved out of the dolomite rock and thought to be between 40,000 and 80,000 years old. Clinton stood beside a carved record of a family with their dog, kept for protection.

The dog is a Tasmanian tiger. These carnivorous marsupials have striped bottoms and are thought to be extinct; this factor helps to give a rough idea of the age of the picture. They used to roam all over the continent and were the first domestic dog of the Aboriginal people before European breeds were introduced.

Another rock showed a giant echidna, like the one we saw in the wild in Tasmania – a big hedgehog-like creature with porcupine-like spines. There was a bounty of durable recordings of past lives out there in what looked like a hostile area but was, in fact, home for millennia to the most ancient race of humans in the world; how good it is that the knowledge of the past is being spread and preserved right now and for the future.

A beautiful beach and humpback whales

We were on the North West Coastal Highway by 6.40 am the next morning, Karratha and Dampier on our right and the ancient dolerite and quartz Karratha Hills on our left. Such an early start for the long drive ahead deserved a hearty breakfast, and we were not disappointed at the Fortescue River Roadhouse. In fact, Rob's only frustration was he couldn't finish his plateful.

18 July 2020. To make the most of our time, and as soon as we were pitched in Exmouth, we drove northwards to beautiful Bundegi Beach to see the wreck of SS Mildura, which pitched up onto the corner of the reef in 1907 during a cyclone. That event was formative in the decision to build a lighthouse nearby. She was carrying nearly 500 head of cattle, and although they were released and given the chance to make it ashore, sadly few survived.

The beach itself was a wonderful cornucopia of shells, living sea creatures and birds. Rob held a massive sea snail in its shell; we had seen others but tiny by comparison. Funny how all the emphasis is about getting offshore and seeing the reef and the whales when there are items of wonder right at one's feet.

We drove to an elevated position nearby and, along with a handful of other folk bracing against the wind, watched humpback whales outside the reef just as we had watched them a few weeks ago off Middleton Beach in King George Sound near Zoonie, on the opposite coast of the continent. Guess we'll be watching them from Zoonie next. I can't wait; maybe you feel the same, dear reader?

Back in camp we decided to try the American-themed Cadillac's Bar and Grill over the road for a country concert, beer and a pizza before experiencing the windiest night in the tent yet. The opposing sides of the tent fabric didn't quite meet, but they weren't far off and we were sandwiched in between!

The sun goes down on Hamelin Pool

19 July 2020. Extricating ourselves at daylight, we head on southwards and eventually turned right near the Overlander Roadhouse. Uncertain of where we would spend the night, we pulled into the newly signposted Bush Foundation Hamelin Station for a look-see. I fancied another station stay as the one at Kirkalocka is still a happy memory in my mind.

The brilliant white paths are made up of miniature cockle shells, their dwarfism caused by the high salinity of nearby Shark Bay, home to Hamelin Pool. Black dots of roo poo contrast on the paths, and we are hopeful we might see some kangaroos enjoying the land they have lived on for eons.

This whole area is a place where there are no barriers between one's links to ages past and the wonderful natural phenomena of our present.

Driving the short distance to the lower part of Hamelin Pool, we found ourselves in the presence of something truly great and yet modest in size: incredibly rare beds of stromatolites – layers of different cyanobacteria (blue/green algae) living off the fermented

Timeless stromatolites

Sunset over Hamelin Pool

residue of the layer above and watered by concentrated seawater. They fed the atmosphere with the oxygen essential for the start of life on Earth three billion years ago, four and a half billion years after the Earth came into its hot, gaseous existence.

These living fossil stromatolites bear witness to that process.

It is completely understandable then, I think, that the Aboriginal people look upon the rocks as their ancestors; this is a place where myth and reality coexist harmoniously in the salty water.

From stromatolites to *Sal Darago*

That evening we cooked in the outdoor kitchen near the tent and I'm glad we did because we met numerous really interesting people from Western Australia; one lady travelled the world's universities in her role as an adviser to students on dissertation presentation.

During the night I had to attend to the wants of nature and was ably assisted by the brilliant white path showing up as grey in contrast to the black rocks. On the way back the starlit sky was well defined, there being little in the way of light pollution. Orion and the Southern Cross and a moving satellite, a nice collection to take back into my sleeping bag with me. Soon we would be viewing the heavens from *Zoonie*'s moving hull, I hoped.

Next day, with the tent packed away we sat on our comfy folding chairs and sipped tea while the early morning sun warmed our backs. Then as we drove slowly through the campsite, past the lovely old restored homestead, we were rewarded with the sight of three kangaroos, contentedly nibbling the local bushes and casting just a cursory glance in our direction. Another place we were reluctant to leave.

We had booked into the Denham Seaside Caravan Park for two nights, and I was tickled to discover the plot the lady allocated us was 'A' in the camp area, nearest to the town, about ten paces from where Jeremy and Kathy, with whom we spent Rob's birthday back in Albany, had tied up their dinghy to a pole, and in direct sight of their yacht, *Sal Darago*, through the dunes!

We had a good chat and a valuable exchange of info with Jeremy and Kathy at a hotel bar in town. Jeremy had been talking with an official in Réunion island, near Madagascar, on our up-and-coming route across the Indian Ocean, and it seemed a stopover there would be feasible. That will break up the voyage home, I thought.

The four of us were assisted by the fact that we had come from Western Australia, where the interstate borders had been closed for months and there was no Covid. But we knew that if the WA government was to lose its high court battle to keep its borders closed and Covid started to raise its ugly head there, then the situation at the borders could change; so, another reason we were spurred on to leave sooner rather than later.

From Denham to the dry Lake Indoon

Back towards the North West Coastal Highway, stretching 808 miles from Port Hedland to Geraldton, and soon we would have travelled the whole length. The highway was created immediately after the Second World War, from existing roads and pastoral tracks, and was moved inland between Carnarvon and Port Hedland in the years between 1966 and 1973 because of the regular and expensive damage caused by cyclones hitting the north-west coast.

The highway passes through the Pilbara region and surfacing it became essential to accommodate the growing volume of traffic from pastoralism, tourism and the extraction and export of iron ore. So, it is no coincidence that with the improvement of the highway into an all-year route, by the 1960s roadhouses were built along its length to cater for all the needs of travellers, and we visited the Billabong Roadhouse, which was established in 1962.

Roadhouses are now very much a part of the travel culture in this part of the world, and this one deserves a mention. The genuine smiling welcome from all three of the staff on duty was pleasant to start with, and the range of ready-to-eat food they had on sale was as good as Woolworths, or Waitrose back home, and it included fresh fruit salad that we had not seen at any other roadhouse.

A short distance south of Geraldton, having passed olive groves, historic settlements, dog kennels, flat paddocks of sheep, glossy black Angus cattle, horse farms, more dry rivers, a big goat farm and homesteads built from adobe bricks (just to paint a picture for you), we turned onto the Indian Ocean Drive that hugs the coast down to Perth and were glad to get away from the volume of traffic that was slowing us down to 80 km/h. We weren't used to lots of traffic!

23 July 2020. Rob was flicking through the pages of Malcolm's road map to find somewhere to stay for our last night of camping when he discovered Malcolm or Christine's brief comments to the effect '23 May 2017, very picturesque' over Lake Indoon, so that became our destination too.

There was not a drop of water in the vast and almost perfectly round lake. We pitched the tent and went for a walk. Back in the 1930s the lake was dry for a few years, so maybe, sometime in the near or distant future, folk will again enjoy boating if the rains play ball.

We started to walk right across the lakebed, where there were footprints and tyre tracks everywhere, leading us to hope we would not slip unnoticed into a mire of mud or quicksand, never to be seen again. Sunglasses, lost overboard from a boat, and the sinker to a lost mooring buoy painted the scene of fun times past. Today, and partly because it is wintertime, there were just a few of us braving what would be a chilly night in this lovely spot nestled in the Beekeepers Nature Reserve.

24 July 2020. This morning, our last in camp and so to be savoured, we lay in our snug bags knowing that the sun would warm us shortly and listened to the variety of birdsong. We chatted to a couple of fellow campers; one was there with his poorly wife taking a significant trip back to a favourite spot, and another could not remember when there was last water in the lake. I have since read reviews about the lake that suggest it has been empty for at least two years.

Our tour of Western Australia is complete

Tyres on tarmac once again, and excited were we at the prospect of seeing Mel, manager at the Perth City Youth Hostel, where we had previously stayed at the start of our abortive tour with Wokka before we were summoned back because of Covid. We booked in for two nights of nostalgia and a farewell to this part of Aussie. She was not in the office, so off we went in hot pursuit of a decent beer at The Island pub at Elizabeth Quay, one of our 'locals'.

It was good to see Mel again and chat about how her youth hostel was ticking along OK. However, the future looked pretty bleak with Australia not planning to open up until there was a safe Covid vaccine, so business was nowhere near out of the woods.

We spent our whole day strolling along the embankment, built to tame the river and provide land for the skyscrapers to be built. Walter had described the area as marshy with small lakes when he shared his Nyungar history with us on our first visit to Perth. One of the lakes still exists at the end of the esplanade, Lake Vasto, named after the Italian City with which Perth is twinned through its welcoming so many migrants from Italy. Lake Vasto is a haven for birdlife. It was sad and ironic to see a sleeping Aboriginal figure finding shelter behind the monument to the immigrants, where his ancestors would have rested in their homes in times past, before the arrival of the Europeans.

We lunched on pizza and beer at the treetop bar The Aviary, our second local, amidst many young revellers, no more counting heads and limiting numbers; the place was happily heaving.

After a few days back at pretty Te Opu, Malcolm and Christine's home in Kojonup, where the barley was well up and inspected daily by Tess, our mental transition back to circumnavigators was almost complete, and we could not wait to be out there again! We bade our friends a brief farewell as we would see them again in Fremantle.

Back on *Zoonie* the now familiar wait for a weather window, this time to get us around the south-west corner of Western Australia and up to Fremantle, was our ongoing task. The powerful lows kept marching across the area, with only a few hours between them, creating swells up to ten metres just outside. If we could get a gap of just two days, we could get halfway to Augusta, but even then we knew the sea would be challenging. All the time the weather window to the start of the next cyclone season both here and on the other side of the Indian Ocean was getting nearer.

One memorable weekend, on their way home from netball in Albany, Kylie, Chris and the girls came to see us on board. Isabelle shot up the steps at a rate of knots after her dad and was curious beyond measure about life on board, especially how the shower worked. So, I went through the steps with her turning the taps, holding the shower head and pumping out the water. She there and then demonstrated the process to Zoe, her older sister, and later, back home, to her grandparents, so Malcolm and Christine would know exactly how to take a shower on *Zoonie*!

Using some lateral thinking Rob explored the idea that the stiffness of *Zoonie's* steering wheel we had noticed even before we arrived in Bundaberg, under emergency tiller steering, was to do with the rudder stock and not the running of the cables through their conduits. Having re-greased the conduits, a useful task well done anyway, there was no improvement in the steering stiffness. Also, the rudder was impossible to move by us when we stood on the ground.

His exploration of the stock in the lazarette, the grease reservoir and the pipe leading to the nipple revealed solid grease halfway down the pipe. The rudder bearings had been lubricated with just seawater for an indeterminate period of time! Rob routed out the solid grease and replaced it with a new, more appropriate type, and all is well.

I sewed little bags from the remnants of fabric I used for Ruby's dress I made for her while in New Zealand. We filled them with balloons, tiny rubbers, little boxes of Smarties, notebooks and pieces of eight (gold foil-covered chocolate coins) because I thought the latter particularly appropriate, being sailors ourselves. We left them for the girls on the servery at Kylie and Chris's nearby home when we popped the Falcon car back into their garage, one of our last jobs before launch day.

7 September 2020. The genoa is back on the forestay and the Hydrovane rudder clings, once more, to the transom at her stern, so Zoonie could not be more ready. Our friends Jeremy and Kathy are lifting Sal Darago out of the water at Carnarvon and will fly home to the UK in a few months until they can return and sail back at a more leisurely pace, calling at places now closed to them. But for us, we are homeward bound ASAP, keeping our little team together.

Maurice is a professional rigger and a skilled sailor, and he very kindly offered to check our rig for us before we left. His friend Ian and I hauled him aloft to the masthead with him checking the standing rigging and connections as he ascended. All was well, fortunately.

Turning the corner around West Cape Howe

13 September 2020. It was lovely to be back at sea once more, with the humpbacks (not too close, please) and albatrosses. We motor sailed most of the way, to maintain 6 knots and arrive at Fremantle before the next south-westerly blow. Chris and Kylie with Abbey, Zoe and Isabelle were there waving us off and they watched from above Point King Lighthouse, where we had walked a few days before, while we slowly crossed King George Sound for the last time.

West Cape Howe was benign, lying grey and featureless in the distance, and so now we have traversed the Great Australian Bight using the longer International Hydrographic Organization definition from South West Cape, Tasmania, to West Cape Howe, Australia, and from there we had a nice offshore wind right up to the passage into Fremantle bay and Success Boat Harbour, where we moored up in Fremantle Sailing Club.

The five southernmost capes so treasured by sailors mark the most southern mainland or large island points on Earth. They comprise:

Chris, Kylie, Abbey, Zoe and Isabelle wave us off

1   Cape Horn, Chile
2   Cape Agulhas, south-east of the famous Cape of Good Hope, South Africa
3   West Cape Howe, further south than the more cited Cape Leeuwin, Western Australia
4   South East Cape, Tasmania
5   South Cape, New Zealand

So far, the fine yacht *Zoonie* has bagged two of them: South East Cape and, most recently, West Cape Howe (and a little further north around to Fremantle, although not a great cape, Cape Leeuwin). Can you feel the pride?

16 September 2020. There is a strong blow due at the weekend, so we have arranged with Border Force (Customs) to clear us out on the Monday, and Rob has gone off to rummage for a plank of wood to make a second barge board as the one we have is not long enough against the vertical piles of the harbour wall here in Fremantle marina. Also, we have moved Zoonie to a slightly more sheltered spot where there should be less exposure to the wind.

Inclement weather means we can visit the WA Maritime Museum and WA Shipwrecks Museum (perhaps not such a good idea when one is about to set off across the Indian Ocean, but never mind).

Chapter 16

The Indian Ocean Beckons

Réunion was around 4,000 miles away; a delicious ocean crossing awaited us of around a month at sea. Mr Google suggests the southern route across the Indian Ocean (ours) is for adventurous travellers who are willing to sacrifice safety and comfort for speed; well, that's us. Plus, taking weather, time of year and *Zoonie's* well-maintained integrity into account, we felt we were more than ready to set sail. The Indian Ocean for us was en route to our destination, and with the trade winds and hopefully the current in our favour, and having discovered how well *Zoonie* behaves in rough conditions, we hoped our meagre human efforts to navigate and sail her would be enough to make a safe passage. Beyond that our fate was in the lap of the elements, and we have always been prepared to accept that.

The latest news on the Covid situation told us Réunion was still open to us, so our course would take us NW from Fremantle to a point around 16 degrees south of the Equator, 230 miles south of Cocos, and then, when the moment was right, we would turn left and take the trades across to Réunion.

We were beginning to wonder if we had enough store food on board for, say, six months and decided to do a stock take. I filled in the spreadsheet while Rob called out the items, and then off we went to the shops to fill in the gaps. (We only finished the dried pasta we bought in Fremantle in 2024.)

North till the butter melts

The phrase is usually 'sail south till the butter melts', but I think a variation is appropriate on the old sailors' saying – originally for those who sailed south from England heading to the Caribbean: as they reached the warm Canaries and the butter dripped from their toast, they turned right across the Atlantic.

21 September 2020. Departure day came and Border Force were due at 2.00 pm. Time, then, beforehand for a quick walk into town with our dear friends Malcolm and Christine for lunch and a beer at the Sail and Anchor before a smooth inspection and lines aboard.

The wind at first was as patchy as a pirate's pants, and there was a fair ocean swell.

The sun rose the next morning and took a shower; at least that is what it looked like from where I was sitting.

24 September 2020. We are motoring right now in light airs that won't allow us to fly the Diva as we had hoped. The barometer has dropped 6 millibars since yesterday, so hopefully that will bring a blow we can use. We are heading for a spot south of the Cocos Islands and will turn towards Réunion when we reach the SE trades.

We had a night and day of winds over 20 knots, which would have been great had it not been for the 2-knot SW current against us that we only identified when we looked in the Indian Ocean Pilot. Fortunately, we moved out of it last night, but into very light airs! Frustrating. (Winds blow from a compass heading and currents flow towards it.)

Zoonie is presently under full sail with Henry steering us northwards at 3.6 knots. I am more than happy to proceed at the pace of Captain Cook's flat-bottomed collier, especially northwards.

Des, our weather guru, confirmed that the westerly we are getting is a gift from the low to the south and that we should move on to the south-east corner of a new high in the next three days, which will give us southerlies becoming southeasterlies and enable us to turn westwards, at 26° S, 138 miles from here. Sooner than we had thought.

Des likened crossing the Indian Ocean to eating an African elephant: one small bite at a time and hope you can arrive before you get to the elephant's posterior. Well, the approaching high on our

GRIB file looks like that part of the big fella's anatomy, so I think we should climb aboard using his tail and scramble up along his back, taking a slide down his trunk into Réunion, don't you?!

Riding the elephant to Réunion

30 September 2020. This morning, we finally, after nine days, turned west towards our destination. We have 2,768 miles to go (say it quickly and it doesn't seem so far!). We still have the pesky current taking away some of our progress, but we are doing a gentle 5 knots over the ground, so that will have to be good enough. The sea sometimes has Zoonie rolling gunwale to gunwale, which shocks the wind out of the genoa, which then in turn takes a while to recover, so we have rigged the pole on the leeward side to support the sail.

With the downhaul lines attached and ready to lower the pole, Rob suddenly exclaimed, "Oh no! Look at that; it's come off its pin!" He was referring to that which is commonly named after the part of a male donkey's anatomy that ensures their perpetuation and starts with 'D'.

Rob was holding the pole in one hand and clinging on to *Zoonie's* handrail for dear life with the other. I dashed to help and held the pole as tight as I could into the mast.

"So, we need to guide it down over the foredeck and turn it round," Rob said confidently, "but, first, could I have my hand back?" It was squeezed between the pole and the mast and neither of us wanted to lose the pole or Rob overboard. (Not necessarily in that order.)

I walked forward with the pole until I was crouched on the rolling foredeck holding this cumbersome 'baby' in my arms.

"Just got to get a screwdriver to tighten the screw holding the pole into the clip on the pole." There I was, nursing this heavyweight child, sitting on the lively foredeck in the tropical heat, somewhere a few hundred miles off the north-west Australian coast; I can think of worse places to be and worse things to be doing.

All is well now and Zoonie is sliding along, with a gentle roll, in light airs. We can still reef the genoa while it is on the pole because the sheet passes through the clip at the outer end. With the blow we are expecting, and the accompanying seas, we will need to keep power on to pull her out of troughs in the water.

We have caught hold of the elephant's tail and are now climbing along its back. Bring on the slide down its trunk. Two more days and we will be a third of the way there.

The big lasagne I made before we left will provide two more suppers, accompanied with sprouts or salad or sweetcorn, tomato or coleslaw. I put two portions of the lasagne in the double saucepan steamer to heat it up and keep it moist at the same time. Then we have sundowners while we wait. Yum, but we are ready for a change!

Music plays away gently all day as, along with *Zoonie's* naturally peaceful saloon, it helps keep our minds relaxed, and there is something very uplifting about singing along to one's favourite tracks.

It was grand being back in the tropics; from sleeping in our leggings from Albany to Fremantle, we were plenty warm enough just in our cotton sleeping bag liners. During a calm spell Rob put 66 litres of our fuel into the main tank from the cans – that is what we used trying to beat the current as we moved northwards with only a light breeze astern. Were we glad when we could turn off the engine! It was equivalent to 44 hours of our 290-hour motoring range.

While relaxing after a scrambled egg breakfast one day, Rob said, "Barb, there's a split along the mainsail seam beneath the logo." Here we go again, I thought. So, we lowered the sail and used some sticky-backed sail cloth strips on both sides of the offending seam, in two places. Makes us wonder if it would be better to have vertical seams on an in-mast furling sail rather than horizontal; the present one suffers chafe.

27 September 2020. Three other yachts are out there somewhere. They left Lombok, just east of Bali, so they will be on a course to our north for the crossing, and maybe we will meet them in Réunion.

1 October 2020. Yesterday we altered course from nearly north to west, turning Zoonie through 90 degrees to port, and the boom took the mainsail across to her starboard side with the wind blowing constantly from behind in a manoeuvre called a gybe.

By way of a welcome onto our new course, last night was beautiful. Sometimes Zoonie hissed along as if the friction of her hull was causing

Repairing the mainsail seam

the water to boil, but gradually the wind has dropped and now our progress is somewhere between 3.5 and 5.2 knots. The moon was full and shining bright, and there were two identical satellites, both equally brilliant, slanting at the same angle, similar in size and shape and about 60 degrees apart. The space station had me wondering who is up there at the moment, like us, escaping Covid restrictions. It's amazing the volume of 'stuff' we see in the sky now that is human in origin.

Another morning, I was standing on the companionway steps, head and shoulders above the hatch, having a good meerkat look around and studying the ever-changing mood of the waves, just as we do countless times around the clock, thinking, shall I let a little sail out? It would be nice to maintain a 6-knot average. But then I noticed a charcoal grey bank of cloud with veils of rain beneath it moving slowly towards us, which answered my question. I wondered whether we might soon be getting a lot more wind and maybe even some rain to wash the salt off *Zoonie's* surfaces. But no, it just petered out, sliding off to one side.

While reefing one day, we became covered in translucent crystals;

wherever we moved, our hands picked up enough salt to season a pan of porridge. I had cleaned the windows recently, single-handedly, holding on tightly, to get rid of the white streaks she suffers from as the gel coat on her coach roof slowly dissolves, while Rob tightened the ropes holding the two gas cylinders in place on the aft deck and collected three desiccated flying fish, sending them on their last flight home.

The sailing was fabulous before the blow arrived. In the early morning the moon's sun-reflected light shone on the water towards us and simultaneously shone on the space station in the sky behind us. The crew up there must get sunlight from both sides. Later in the day, under the penetrating blue sky, the sea was that wonderful oceanic blue that is impossible to capture on the camera, a treat for our eyes only.

The swell was increasing and the wave tops were starting to break and boil over forward of the tons of water beneath them. I watched as a wall of water would build up behind *Zoonie's* stern, and if it didn't break, the swell would gently lift *Zoonie's* stern high up and send her skidding down the wave, surfing. As she slowed and settled and the wall passed beneath her it would leave a deep canyon far below and behind her. If the wall or wave did start to break it was quite a different story. The force of the water often had us wondering if *Zoonie* would be pushed to either side and rolled over by the next water wall, but how could we doubt the design of her hull that swam fish-like with the force?

6 October 2020. The wind has been above 30 knots for four days and nights so far, along with its accompanying lively sea of around five metres; the elephant runs on with Zoonie on its back and a bee under its tail. We are riding the 1016 isobar of the Indian Ocean High, and there is plenty of wind in there for sailing. The reefed main is on the other side now and held out firmly with the preventer pulling the opposite way to the securing sheet, and it is working. Zoonie is goose-winged and using every bit of wind around her.

Studying my pencil plots of her progress over the paper chart, I'm thinking her daily runs (148 miles average) seem so short, then I realise the chart covers half the world! She's not doing at all badly!

9 October 2020. Two days ago, we reached the halfway point with around 1,930 miles and twelve days to go if this wind persists. I sat looking up through one of the big side windows watching the sails when a wave engulfed her from the top of the mainsail, which was reefed to halfway up the mast, and from stem to stern; the sound was thunderous and wet, and the sight of blue bubbling water careering along her leeward side-deck was impressive. I once again wished I had a drone that could film her valiant progress.

The other three yachts making the crossing are ahead of us, so we will see them when we get in.

Darren from the yard at Emu Point, watching us on Marine Traffic, says this weather system should last another eleven days. Yesterday was another perfect sailing day, and Zoonie was as well-mannered and sea-kindly as ever. I love it when she is belting along at 6–7 knots as if on tracks, with the gentlest roll to remind us we are still AT SEA.

Looking ahead

13 October 2020. I've just emailed Jerome at Réunion to tell him we are seven days away now with 1,090 miles to go, and I just hope they don't come back and say they are now closed. With three other yachts on their way as well I would think they will permit us to anchor and rest even if we cannot go ashore.

The sailing continues to be terrific with Zoonie on a broad reach, her fastest point of sail, and creaming along.

The other day I made a turmeric and dried tomato loaf that would serve better as a house brick. I definitely need some fresh yeast and cream of tartare. Sliced very thin and spread with creamy cheese or marmite the brick slices make a reasonable lunch; 'waste not, want not', my mum used to say.

The SE swell is still pushing against us, even though Des says it should be NW giving us a little help. Things will get a little livelier as soon as Zoonie is pummelled by waves coming on her port bow.

Twenty-one days of isolation and a complete cut off from world news had us quickly adapting to life in complete solitude, without external demands. We slowed to *Zoonie's* pace and wore our daily routine like a comfy house coat. We both love being at sea in *Zoonie*; the honest harmony we experience with the elements and our love of sailing enfold us only when we are offshore.

Every morning I came back on watch at 5.00 am after my three hours' rest. First thing, while still dark, I washed and then made a mug of Milo hot chocolate and sat quietly sipping while my brain slipped into gear. One morning I scooped the heaped spoon into the mug and then took a little to taste, as one does: BLAH, coffee! Just as well I hadn't poured the water. I always thought of little grandson Milo when I made my early morning drink.

Then I turned to the laptop, clamped to the table and sitting on a non-slip mat, to write emails and the latest blog. For the first time in our entire circumnavigation, I worked on the laptop until I started to feel nauseous in the irregular sea state, typical of the Indian Ocean, then I would take a break.

When Rob stirred around 7.30 am, on went the kettle for a cuppa swiftly followed by breakfast of porridge or cereal (if the brick was all gone). Then we linked the satphone to the computer to send and receive mail and weather information.

Lunch was a light affair; I usually had fruit, tinned now as the fresh was finished, eaten after I had taken my noon position from the plotter, made up the log and plotted us on the chart. Then I had a kip, Virgin Atlantic blindfold on, earplugs in, so I could just hear the music that was playing, and after an hour and a half or so, Rob and I would swap places.

Then around 3.00–4.00 pm the kettle would go on again for a cuppa, and 5.00 pm SHARP was the much-anticipated time for a sundowner, sitting on the windward settee, holding glasses of wine and looking across out of the leeward windows towards the horizon as *Zoonie* rolled that way, chatting about who's doing what and where we had got to in our books and so on. Such sweet memories.

Supper was ready around 6.00–6.30 pm and then Rob would get his head down for a while before coming on watch from 8.00 pm to 11.00 pm. My watch was then from 11.00 pm to 2.00 am, when satellites danced across the heavens in front of their starlit audience. I would often wonder, peering ahead into the pitch-black moonless night, what were the chances of sailing tens of thousands of miles, as we were doing, and not hitting anything in our path? For how long would our good fortune last?

During our watches, along with frequent looks all around the horizon day and night, we read or played games on our backlit tablets, and the time passed all too quickly.

Life on board was such an ordered routine that we both had time to relax and read, something I hadn't done much of for a long time. Also, we had time to sit and reflect on where we had been, what we had learned about the places and people. I cherished the mystery of what lay ahead beyond the next ocean, and still do, because without it there can be no adventure.

When we made landfalls in these distant lands, part of that adventure was to learn about the people who have lived there, and so, dear reader, I hope you don't mind when I refer once more to Bruce Pascoe's book *Dark Emu*. The author is an Aboriginal scholar using the mountain of white man's written, photographed and drawn evidence, plus the work of archaeologists, anthropologists, etc., to piece together the true history of the Aboriginal culture and society before the arrival of the colonialists. A story of sophisticated farming and fishing methods that worked with endemic species of flora and fauna to farm almost all of Australia over a period now reckoned to be 90,000 years.

Aboriginal society used the principles of community living, two of which are sharing excess crops with other groups and living by common laws. Their largely sedentary lifestyles, defined by staying in one location unless they were travelling to a corroboree (celebration meet up), are in evidence all over the continent.

The vast grasslands, which the colonialists thought were natural and ready for the overgrazing by their swathes of sheep and cattle, eventually killing the grass, were actually made by careful land management and husbandry of the wild animals.

Bruce first published the book in 2014 and then received a mass of information, journals, logs, pictures, etc., from his readership. He incorporated this new information into the latest, revised edition.

A great read, if you're interested.

No holds barred – but we're the ox at the back

Nothing was holding *Zoonie* back; the Diva was putting in long performances, overnighters as well, in perfect sailing weather. Her audience of two watched, along with a passing pair of Matsudaira's storm petrels, as she performed while listening to music all day from her accompanying orchestra below.

Every few days we exchanged words with our weather guru, Des in Durban, Durban Des:

Dear R&B

Thanks for the latest update.

I have asked the others [the three yachts] to meet and greet you with a cold one as you are not actually in the race – it was their call.

The Afrikaans people in South Africa have a very descriptive expression – agteross kom ook in die kraal – translation: even the ox at the back gets to go into the pasture!

You are only two days behind *Milanto* and *Sealover*. It reminds me of a criticism of sport hunting – it's unfair if the other team does not even know it is playing!

The GRIBs still show boring ESE\E 15–20 [knot winds] with no threats or abnormal weather, so you should have a pretty relaxed end to your marathon run across the Indian Ocean.

Done that, you will have to get the T-shirt!

Have a great day and stay safe.

Had we started from the same port, *Zoonie* would have been racing, all right!

Dear Des,

Looks like *Cajou* is going to win then, by 128 miles, a giraffe's neck! And we'll bring up the elephant's rear.

Zoonie is gliding over 20° 39′ 09″ S 69° 24′ 11″ E at 7 knots and bearing 273°. 0243 UTC.

Have a great day everyone,

Barb

Later on Des told us *Cajou* had arrived, spurring us on…

Dear R&B

Thanks for latest update – Réunion 500 nm due west.

Vessel *Cajou* is in and *Sealover* and *Milanto* one day out, ETA tomorrow morning. I hope they will welcome you with a cold one!

The GRIBs show ESE\E max 10 knots for the next 24–36 hrs and then filling in a bit to 15 knots max. Closer to Réunion some SE 20 knots coming through but will update again tomorrow as this forecast is a bit dicey due the activities further south.

No threats or abnormal conditions.

Have a great day and am sure you are looking forward to a change in diet – elephant is so boring!

Regards

Des

Chart plotter causes mayhem

With two days to go we had a lovely flat sea, so progress with the Diva was pretty good. *Zoonie* was doing in excess of 7 knots when suddenly perfection was interrupted; the Diva was not happy, swirling and twisting over the foredeck, upset and flustered. We were off course, the chart plotter screen displayed overall white and the connection to the autopilot was lost. I leapt to the wheel, stabbed the STBY (standby) button on the autopilot and steered *Zoonie* back onto a course that would enable the Diva to fly and not get tangled up. I didn't care what course that would be.

Poor Rob was fast asleep and hastily roused into some kind of remedial action. The chart plotter would not turn off at the device, so Rob snuffed it at the control panel, waited ten seconds and turned it back on. All was well and working again, and after a gentle talking to, the Diva was ready for another night-time performance. But the problem was far from over.

I couldn't believe it; she was cavorting up and down the forestay, her gossamer gown pulling in all manner of frenzied directions like a harbourside hussy, quite unlike her usual fulsome and controlled self. Montserrat Caballé would never have behaved like this.

"Barb, chart plotter's down again and we're off course."

My first thought was for the safety of the Diva. I flung my T-shirt on and wriggled into my skirt, no time to do the zip up – we had to get her offstage ASAP. Scrambling to the mast under the limelight of the deck light above, I looked forward and saw this unseemly sight and then noticed how my left/port boob was much cooler than its right/starboard sister. I had only managed to get one arm through one armhole. Then, as gravity took over, my skirt decided it was time to slip towards my knees, and, if that was not enough, I had completely forgotten the need for a certain item of underwear.

It took a short while, but with me holding a sheet in one hand, intermittently pulling up my skirt with the other, and Rob on the snuffer line, we let *Zoonie's* roll fling the remaining free material of the Diva's gown back and forwards, Rob pulling the snuffer bag down centimetre by centimetre until within a metre of her hem, when he went forward and gathered the rest safely in. The fact the forestay is wrapped with the genoa protected the gyrating Diva from tearing on the forestay wire, and Rob's tender care saved the precious sail from an untimely end.

Rob then looked at me and got the second fright of the night: a dishevelled apparition under the glow of the deck light.

We let the engine guide us through the remaining hours of darkness – our nerves had suffered enough.

But all was not over yet!

An hour later and the chart plotter gave up again, taking down the GPS, AIS and link with the autopilot. It recovered after ten seconds on the naughty step, and I started to wonder if this was anything to do with the fact the variation (the difference measured in degrees between magnetic north, as shown on the compass, and actual true north) over the preceding days had been between 22° and 30° W. Could this magnetic anomaly have been affecting the chart plotter?

We were able to confirm this extreme local variation from the lines of variation on one of the paper charts we have of the southern Indian Ocean, another good reason to use paper charts as well as a chart plotter. Each time the chart plotter gave up and Rob got it back I noted our position in the ship's log, and on the paper chart, ready for a possible next time!

16 October 2020. That was yesterday, and after all the 'fun' my afternoon nap lasted for two and a half hours. Last night the Diva regained her confidence and gave us a blissful gently rolling night of peace and slumber, making a 5.4-knot silk purse of progress out of a 10-knot sow's ear of wind.

This ox has nothing to beef about.

Chapter 17

Réunion

Bourbon bound, and a little sober history

In the seventeenth century, around March 1667 when he was dropping off five women sent by French Finance Minister Jean Baptiste Colbert as part of Colbert's colonisation plan, Admiral François de Lopis, the Marquis de Mondevergue, possibly in his journal or ship's log, described Bourbon, now known as Réunion, as appearing 'rather primitive with its mass of mountains and impenetrable forests'. However, he more generously added 'there are some exceedingly beautiful places, fresh air and clean water, and such a large amount of game, fish, turtles, tortoises, wild cows, goats, and pigs that anyone ought to be overjoyed at the prospect of living there'.

Typical man, thinking of his stomach. He and his ilk clearly weren't the first there. The island used to be populated by the Rodrigues solitaire (dodo-lookalike) bird too, but it was just too tame and tasty to survive for long.

France had recently taken possession and named the island after their own royal family, Bourbon, and a few French families started to settle there with their Madagascan servants, but the island had also been known to Arab, Portuguese, British and Dutch sailors for some time. It was renamed Réunion for the second and final time in 1848.

Modern Réunion is one of the Mascarene Islands, which include

Mauritius and a number of others skirting to the north and east of the submarine Mascarene Plateau. On the old trading route to the Orient, the island is at the crossroads of European, African and Asian cultures, and this is certainly reflected in the history and cuisine of its population.

Our approach to this rich location was overnight, and we were astounded by the amount of orange and white lighting there was on the east coast, the windward coast blown over by the SE trade winds. The island of 2,512 square kilometres has clearly been plentifully populated in the coastal regions for centuries. Today there are over 896,000 residents.

21 October 2020. Our marina (Darse Titan) is one of two in Pointe des Galets, Le Port on the north-west corner, sheltered from the prevailing winds but exposed to any marauding cyclones from the north and east that can engulf the entire island. We'll be gone before they start in November, we reasoned. With the climate being in a La Niña phase they are likely to be more prompt in their season and more numerous both here and in the Pacific and North Atlantic regions. Just something to bear in mind!

Two beautiful white long-tailed tropic birds came out to greet us, and at 8.45 am yesterday Angelique took our lines with a smile, a warm welcome and lots of useful information. Réunion is a popular stopover for world rally yachts and having such a sheltered marina benefits all passing cruising boats.

We had 20 minutes, Angelique said, before Customs would be upon us, so we dashed below to tidy up, get all the papers together and put sail bags back where they should be so the officers could sit comfortably at the table. I had used up all the potatoes in a curry, and with eggs and onions safely whisked into a Spanish omelette to minimise the fresh vegetables they might take away, we were ready.

A little later… *along comes an interpreter and two customs officers who declined coming aboard(!?) and weren't too pleased we didn't have three copies of the entry document they had emailed us in Fremantle which I had completed, photographed and emailed back to them. We don't have a photocopier aboard, funnily enough!*

Tempting providence, I asked, "Do you want to inspect us?"

"Do you have anything to declare?"

"Nah."

"Anything fresh, dairy, just don't take it ashore, OK?"

"OK!"

And that was that; our remaining cheddar cheese lived to see another day, the fourteen onions I had completely forgotten about — honest! — could go back to sleep in the cosy dark pillowcase, and Zoonie looked neat and tidy just for us!

To celebrate our arrival, we had a whole (small) can of beer each, with a slice of the Spanish omelette and a two-hour kip for lunch, and then Trocken wine and the rest of the spaghetti bolognese for supper.

Early to a motionless bed: after twenty-nine days at sea, satiated with oceanic beauty and the sense of peace that life out there brings, we were in fine shape, physically and mentally, but the prospect of a full night's sleep on a still bed was pure bliss. We planned to be up at the market for 8.00 am the next morning. I remembered that life in the tropics starts in the delicious cool of a fresh morning, here with the smells of bread baking around 5.00 am.

Our trolley bursting with market goodies (papaya again, we were so happy) and my cloth bag bulging with croissants and two sweet-smelling baguettes anointing my nose as they poked out of the bag at shoulder height: ah, the aroma of French baking.

Looking around Le Port

22 October 2020. Poor Rob has broken a filling, and it wasn't when he clenched his teeth on the night of my foredeck wardrobe malfunction either, it was more recent than that. I Googled homemade fillings and found superglue is not such a good idea as it contains cyanide, but epoxy filler, of which we have plenty, is a perfect alternative.

Rob is becoming more a part of Zoonie as time goes by, what with the mainsail material the same as the Dacron band around his mitral heart valve and his tooth filling now exactly the same as the white paste we use to keep Zoonie looking young and beautiful (wish it would work for me). Whatever next? I have progressed from being his nurse in Whangarei to being his dentist here in Réunion!

We took the dinghy and wandered ashore in the cool of the evening, did a recce, and saw what looked like fuel pumps in the outer marina where we could fill our fuel cans, and a chandlery – perfect, we needed a new genoa sheet.

After a little more meandering we found ourselves outside the Buccaneer Pub. Mutineers were exiled here in days of old and nourished themselves on the chunky dodos; now all that remains of the doomed birds is the beer named in their honour, undoubtedly once used to wash them down. Optimistic geneticists think they might be able to bring them back into existence, as an alternative to 'poulet' perhaps?

Feeling each day more refreshed than the day before, our minds soon turned to how best to explore this lovely, tropical island.

One Saturday evening we went to an informal gathering of fellow sailors under the hibiscus trees bordering the steps up through the grassed terraces to the roadway.

There we met our Swiss friends André and Eva Maria and their little girls from *Mirabella*, whom we last saw at Loltong, at the north end of Pentecost island in Vanuatu, and with whom we first spoke at the end of our sail from Fiji back to New Zealand. They had been in Réunion since May and the girls had loved being in the local school. They planned to sail to an island off the Tanzania coast soon for a few weeks before transiting South Africa, so we had no doubt we would see them again sometime.

Henk and Marjolein, from Naarden in the Netherlands, are planning exactly the same route and timing as us, aboard their steel yacht Jori, so that could be fun!

23 October 2020. Henk told us that he had been to the local car hire place, where they could hire a small car for three days for €102. So, off we went to book. No problem, thanks to Covid the charming guy had a forecourt full. We will be off exploring from tomorrow morning, after a fuel run to the nearest petrol station with our eight 5-gallon cans.

Cirque de Salazie

We stumbled into crowded Saint-André for a quick look around, but the centre was incredibly busy with shoppers and traffic, so hastily back in our little white car, we drove straight onto the D48 that runs alongside the Rivière du Mât towards Cirque de Salazie (one of the three long-extinct and eroded volcanic calderas on the island), fortunately leaving all the coastal traffic behind. We were by this time ready for a break, a coffee and a little history; we weren't used to traffic!

The sides of the valley were lush green, and I wondered how the trees clung to near-vertical rock. The river flowed fast beneath us, fed by the thousands of waterfalls (cascades) flowing from above after the frequent rainfall on this moisture-rich side of the island. We crossed the river over a bridge leading to a pretty little café where a red-whiskered bulbul bird was tucking into the previous customer's sugar pot.

From then on we knew that a lot of the local residents we saw further up the valley were likely to be descendants of escaped slaves, Maroons, who lived out their lives on their small holdings, growing, among other crops, maize, banana, papaya and potato, away from the pains of their enslavement. Understandable that after the abolition of slavery in 1848 most, who did not get on with their masters, joined their fellows further up the fertile slopes of their new master, the Piton des Neiges shield volcano.

The island is a mix of races: indentured Indians were brought in after the 'abolition' to work the sugar, coffee and vanilla plantations; others came from Asia, some by choice; some from Africa and its small eastern sister Madagascar; plus, of course, the Europeans, especially from France. The island had so much to offer: not just its fertility and climate but also its oceanic location, which put it on the clipper run from Europe to Asia. The East India Company exploited its value to the full.

We were heading on through Salazie caldera and its main town of the same name to a little village called Hell-Bourg because we had heard it was very pretty and should not be missed.

Everywhere was dripping, the air was dripping, leaves and caves were dripping, even the gentle local mutts were dripping, and as we climbed higher, it was also becoming cooler.

Many of the wealthy early residents, merchants and plantation owners, built summer houses up in these cooler locations, especially when the hot water springs were discovered at Hell-Bourg, and we saw numerous grand gateways, decorated with elaborate wrought ironwork, leading to flowery terraces overlooked by the villa above. We sat on the lower terrace of one which had been turned into a flower-lined al fresco café; begonias, azaleas and hibiscus blazoned forth while we sipped bottle-fermented local beer, Yab.

We progressed around tight bends, the dank mist swirling all around us, when suddenly Rob brought the car to a sudden stop, unsure of the direction of the road, and on the stone by the gate was written '26, Route de Bélier', our destination for the night!

The lady of the house introduced us to our little ensuite room, one quarter of the building, with a couple of young doctors, from near Bordeaux, who had been living on the island for three years, next door.

We had not booked an evening meal with our host, so we drove a few miles back into Grand Ilet, to a restaurant of the same name.

A diminutive chef was busy stirring his three woks and a rice steamer when we arrived. Despite his mask we could see he was smiling from the sparkle in his eyes. He was the master of all trades, and as the restaurant's eleven tables filled, he was as busy as a bee, taking orders, pouring wine, waiting on the hungry customers, tempting us with tarte aux pommes, to which we succumbed, and dealing with our bill, all with calm charm! The food was as tasty as he was efficient. Rob and I shared a carafe of good, warming red wine, and the bill for two courses and the vin rouge – €43.

Les environs de Le Bélier

28 October 2020. 6.10 am. I have just come back in from a circuit of our little patch of level mountain terrace, overwhelmed by both the sheer beauty of our surroundings and having the good fortune to awaken to clear skies and green mountain peaks set against the loveliest blue, after yesterday's mist and low cloud. Just a few little veils of cobweb mist hang around, sunlight sparkles on leaves and petals alike and droplets fall from foliage like tiny beads of molten silver. All around the garden are borders of potted and planted colourful flowering plants: orchids, amaryllis, begonias galore, azaleas, fuchsias, hibiscus and any others you

On the slope of a volcano

can identify, all in full flower and weighed down by raindrops or just on the brink of finishing their blooming.

We are perched on the edge of the Cirque de Salazie in the early morning sunlight; my dream of waking up on the inside slope of a volcano has come true.

The lady host arrived from her house a little way up the hill, smiling and carrying an armful of fresh baguettes ready for breakfast at 7.00 am. The other three couples were all walkers, so an early start in the cool would be ideal for them, and we were happy because it would give us a nice long day for exploration. The island is within the 23° N to 23° S band around the equator, so it is in the tropics, but, of course, up here, 2,000 metres above sea level, it is more temperate, and much of the ambience and architecture is decidedly alpine.

Helicopters were taking advantage of the pristine clear peaks for early morning tripper flights over the spectacular calderas. Each one of their passengers, like me, must have felt very lucky to bear witness.

Pairs of white-tailed tropicbirds contrasted against the green on the mountains in the steep-sided valley as we retraced our track from the day before towards our second overnight stay. Salazie is one of the four main villages located in this cirque and benefits from a sizeable permanent population, and the many visitors who come in healthier times. There are numerous schools, suggesting the future of the island as an attractive place to live and raise a family is secure.

The valley towards Piton de la Fournaise (a live volcano whose peak rises to 2,632 metres) is wider than the one to Salazie, and there were good sized fields and plantations, but the bends over the next few miles were every bit as hair-raising as the day before. Black and white Holstein cows and honey-brown cows grazed the lush grass or queued up to be milked, and rows of maize stood like marching soldiers across the landscape.

We drove from Bourg-Murat up, up and even further up to 2,136 metres across the flat Plaine des Remparts and parked in a car park near the Pas de Bellecombe in the pouring rain. Many cars had crossed paths with us on the way up, and we surmised they had started out early for the five-hour walk across the Enclos Fouqué (the skirt, lower slope) to reach the rim of the Piton de Fournaise for a look over the top at the moody, stinky cauldron, ever ready to explode into life. You know me. I was quite happy to stand not far from the car park and a very safe distance inland from any possible lava flow and watch the tiny humanoid dots walking to and fro.

At our second guest house the lady welcomed us into a very new reception area, complete with open plan lounge on one side and a breakfast table the other, and promptly told us the area was closed and locked after 6.00 pm and we were to use the access through the garden and around the back after then. Did she not trust us?

While fetching our bags from the car Rob came across a very young puppy in a cage tucked in a recess to the side of the house. It was one of those short-haired, grey-coated boxer-type dogs that cost a small fortune, and it looked far from comfortable with just a T-shirt on concrete to lie on. Why?

For supper we took a short walk down to Restaurant La Kaz, where the friendly young waiter, originally from Senegal and raised for five years of his youth in Bolton, Lancashire, and a fellow vegetarian (although I was eating fish on our trip, it was a temporary choice), served Rob a sweet African curry from his own region and me a vegetable stir-fry with a local lentil side dish and chips. Our liquid desert was a taste of two local rums, on the house.

Après le volcan, les cascades

We had an early, carefully measured breakfast.

"Would you like sugar for your tea?"

"Would you care for a yoghurt?"

We retrieved our packs from the room, wished the shivering pup a better life than he was getting at the moment (he would have been happier, warmer and better cared for by the stray mutts at the marina!) and made our way down the N3, over the last of the windy roads and beautiful valley views, to another right turn onto the D3.

Down by the coast and working our way clockwise towards the south of the island, we drove down a steep road to the Anse des Cascades, the Cove of Waterfalls, which were running well after the rain showers we were experiencing. At first the rain was torrential and we could hardly make out the waters of the cove except for a fisherman trying his luck beneath a black and white umbrella.

We stood on a wooden bridge, leaning over and listening to the delightfully deafening sound of frogs, but the real treat was visible when I climbed some concrete steps leading to the base of the remains of what appeared to be historical winding or pumping equipment alongside a stream. Twenty metres or so away was a stand of bamboo and on each swaying stem hung a carefully woven nest, all of which were being attended by yellow birds, Tisserin jaune, or eastern golden weavers, hovering with rapid wingbeats beneath and feeding their young before a quick rest on a nearby perch, then jetting off on another foray for food. I am not sure why it was quite so spellbinding, perhaps because I had only seen this kind of activity before on the television, but I stood for ages, and Rob joined me to enjoy the busy scene.

Mascarene swiftlets darted across the road as we ascended back to the main N2 highway towards the area I had been looking forward to: the road that traverses the Grand Brule, the ancient and recent lava flows from the Volcan de la Fournaise, a live and moody volcano.

The vegetation gave away the age of the flows. Surprisingly quickly algae and lichen forms on the recently cooled lava and then blown seeds germinate and grasses grow, followed by spindly trees. A full tropical rainforest takes over 300 years to establish.

We parked where the flows of 2004 and 2007 had rolled their way downwards to the cold waters of the ocean. It was more dramatic than picturesque, and we pondered how frightening it would have been for the people of Le Tremblet, a small village just beyond the enclos, or raised wall, around the flow.

Après les cascades, le refuge de Saint-Paul

A little further along the highway we came across dense traffic, and we sat for long periods near Saint-Joseph, Saint-Pierre and Saint-Louis. So instead of visiting these towns, we headed on along a second highway, the Route des Tamarins, no doubt built to relieve the congestion near these popular coastal towns, and soon found ourselves in the charming and historic Saint-Paul, our circumnavigation of the island nearly complete.

We welcomed the dry warmth of this sun-bathed place after the cool and moist higher altitude of the pitons. Famished after our measured breakfast we dived into a restaurant for a late lunch with a glass of red wine. A wander along the inviting shorefront and a little immersion in history was called for, and we were only too happy to escape the twenty-first-century tarmac rat race and go back in time to an al fresco museum world of pirates, French and English battleships of the eighteenth century, cannon fire, smoke, splintering wood, fountains of blood, imprisonment and slavery. Here, the more recent history of agricultural wealth made possible by slavery, and a giant pair of steel manacles, ensure that residents and visitors alike will never forget the struggle and human sacrifice that gave birth to modern-day Réunion.

Les départs commencent – South Africa opens up

5 November 2020. We have heard on the Facebook grapevine that from 9 November not only flight and vehicle passengers but also cruising yacht crews will be allowed visas when they reach South Africa, so we can move around as freely as security will allow. We plan to leave on Monday, the 9th, and will have just over 1,400 miles to go, so much shorter than the deep Indian Ocean crossing, but then I have no doubt there will be more challenges as we approach the African coast and the Agulhas Current for the last 300 miles or so.

André and Eva and their daughters, Jaël (whose birthday party we went to the other evening) and Amina, aboard Mirabella, left this morning.

It is hot here today, 28°C in our little saloon with all windows open, but we are not complaining.

There are big spaces in the marina now and the Réunion liveaboards are mourning the passing of the winter visitors; some have been here for months, including Mirabella who had to lock down on board for two months. (André and Eva were more concerned for their girls' lack of exercise than the girls were!)

There won't be many more yachts arriving from across the Indian Ocean as the cyclone season is upon us.

8 November 2020. Many croissants after our arrival – forty, in fact, at one each for twenty days – we are now preparing to leave this little gem of the Indian Ocean.

Sitting in the saloon yesterday watching the masts of our neighbours, in line with ours, jostling and jiggling around, you'd think we were all fighting for a position on the starting line at the beginning of a race, but no, the surge from the onshore breeze outside had the whole marina of yachts sliding about on their lines, creaking and groaning. The noise was disturbing. No matter what we did to rectify and tighten the lines, the effect was short-lived; the ocean would have her way. We even slept with earplugs in one night just to get some peace and quiet. But all is well again now.

"We'll pay up in the morning, and I'll take you for a walk around the harbour," Rob said yesterday. So, off we went, broad brims on against the intense sunlight, and happily paid the £455 for our twenty-day stay, chatting with the charming marina attendants in Franglais. I spelled out Zoonie's name in the French language alphabet. "Ah, so you are the teacher," he said. Well, I was once, to some reluctant learners on the Isle of Wight.

Wandering back to Zoonie we see there are some reluctant learners here too. The nautical school is busy most days with kayaking, Optimists for beginners, lovely two-masted dinghies I have never seen before and the dragon boats that require a certain discipline and team mentality a lot of these youngsters have yet to discover in themselves.

"They just can't get it together, can they," said Rob.

"I think a lot of it is that some are not concentrating," I ventured. Instead, young lads were looking all around them, their paddles randomly touching the water. Wherever they were we could locate them in the harbour and over the wall from the 'bump, bump, bump' of the drum, designed for unifying their random rowing rhythm.

Looking into the lovely clean water in this marina, and most others we have ever been to, we discovered marinas are nurseries for baby fish. Here the water is so clean that corals are gradually growing on the rocks, pontoon supports and even the rubber tyres. Lots of tropical fish thrive: the pipefishes; scissortail rasboras; Moorish idol fish that have white, yellow and black stripes; some blue-lipped mullet; and above the water red-bodied dragonflies shoot along the surface, in the evening replaced by numerous Natal free-tailed bats, native to Mauritius and Réunion.

So, whenever I am submerged in the anxiety of mass extinction, in the marine world, at least, I find hope in the marinas – secret places where Mother Nature can repair herself.

Chapter 18

To South Africa

Life in the fast lane

24 November 2020. It is quiet and cool alongside the concrete international jetty here in Richards Bay this morning, as the clock turns 5.00 am, 3.00 am your time in the UK.

Yesterday we had our Covid tests, mine down the throat, I hadn't anticipated the nasty taste to expect from the cotton bud, and Rob did a little wriggle as his went up his nostril. We should get our results today and then the clearing in process starts, which could drag over into tomorrow.

Big grey monkeys are getting ready for their daily migration from this corner of the harbour to the trees on the other side to commune with the resident local hippo.

But let's not get ahead of ourselves; back to the voyage.

By mid-November we were entering the acceleration zone around the south-east corner of Madagascar with the NE winds intensifying and whisking us along with it. We could have ventured around the north of Madagascar and down the Mozambique Channel to avoid the zone, but there is only one word to describe sailing against the wind and current in this corner of the world: dangerous. So we didn't do that.

15 November 2020. Finally, after six days at sea, we appear to have current with us for the first time since we left Fremantle.

Des sent us a route to miss the rough seas over the shelving coast, and during that night the wind rose to 35 knots, an angry gale, so a second reef went into the poled-out genoa and the main rested safe and snug inside the mast. *Zoonie's* progress was ace, but the sea was short and disturbed, so no sleep was had by either of us.

I remember getting up at 4.00 am and thinking, where are all the cushions? We had a cushion-free saloon. I soon found out when opening a cupboard to retrieve two bowls for breakfast; Rob in masterly fashion had used them to stop every single tedious rattle and thump of the cupboard contents against the doors and hull, so the only noise was from the wind and water outside.

Before daylight arrived, I had two ships who appeared to be magnetised onto us. One, the *Alpha Cosmos*, was sufficiently big to need a little time to alter course, but when I called him up, he answered immediately that he had us in his sights. The other vessel was a big white fishing boat raiding the seas' riches, who did not answer but proceeded towards us passing slowly and closely around us before going back from where he had come. Maybe a woman's voice drew him, out of curiosity.

During the day we both had blissful sleeps as the wind eased to a nice gentle breeze.

A wide frontal system was approaching in a couple of days' time, so we enjoyed the gentler weather first, even though it started with a lot of motoring.

Our constant curious peering over the blue expanse of water was repaid with numerous 'blows' from what appeared to be humpbacks; they were a long way off (thank goodness!), but we both detected their little dorsal fins.

The ocean is vast but we were never alone for long.

A solitary gannet came past to say "good morning" and then two flesh-footed shearwaters joined us and became our constant companions for at least one day.

They each had a different flight plan. One, the smaller female, would fly in a big circle around us, swooping along the wave tops with barely a wing movement, while her partner would lift and circle right and then do a long circuitous exploration to the left, searching our wake for food scraps, swing round across our stern and with a flutter of its wings land, legs down, just behind us. He soon got left behind and became just a black dot before he did exactly the same flight path again, hundreds of times, all day long and into the night. There were two with us the next morning; could they have been the same ones?

Rob took the opportunity to top up the main fuel tank from the diesel cans, and on our daily check of the emails we read Des' plan for our approach to Richards Bay and watched as the wide front moved inexorably towards us. We were all for slowing right down and delaying a day to ensure the front came across us long before we reached the Agulhas Current, but Des told us to turn due south for the next 24 hours to position ourselves in a less strenuous part of the system. So that is what we did.

As evening crept towards us, so the sky warned us of the front's arrival. Finally, it hit quite suddenly at 11.30 pm, and it was great to be able to put out a little sail and turn the engine off. The wind was a generous 25 knots plus, but the sea was short, steep and unforgiving of *Zoonie*.

Des had formulated a plan of approach. Now back on 260°, nearly west, we would continue until about five miles off Cape St Lucia and then, when comfortable, turn for a point 20 miles north of Richards Bay and ferry glide towards our destination with the help of the Agulhas Current.

20 November 2020. The aftermath of the front allowed us to continue under sail for a while, and that night the sea was an occasional miracle of phosphorescence: sparks from squid and, above, a heaven laden with stars and the Milky Way astride us.

Our angled approach meant we would not be targeting the river mouth from the deep and across the current, a potentially deadly line of approach because of the risk of being bowled over sideways; instead, we were running with the Agulhas Current.

"Best get as close to the first breakwater as possible; too far off and we could still be flipped," I ventured.

Not a problem for our leviathan friends, and not for us either, as it turned out. The current was running at only 1.3 knots, and we made our gradual turn to join it further out than Des suggested and in a rising wind. We ditched the main, thus reducing the chance of a broach, and Zoonie pottered on under her reduced genoa.

The bilge alarm went off because of the water she had taken in during the passing front. It was leaking through stanchion bases, small accumulative leaks, so Rob did a quick pump out.

"Clear all the way now, so don't fuck it up," Des warned, not one to mince words.

Rob pumping out

Being altruistic by nature, Des did not charge for his invaluable services; instead, he asked for donations just to cover his costs. We transferred some money across to his account, and in response he commented that the pockets of the bigger yacht skippers appeared to be much deeper and their funds further out of reach than those pockets of the little yachts, like us. How sad.

21 November 2020. South Africa, our planned home for the next three months, appeared as a thin line of sand dune with intermittent trees and scrub; it is the St Lucia wetlands reserve, which is teeming with plant and animal life and is a much-loved place to visit.

Later in the morning the big ships in their anchorage came into view.

"What if one is coming in and the port control don't want us in when we get there? We can't turn around or even slow down much in this!"

The prospect of flying straight by the Richards Bay harbour entrance was worrying me.

"Let's find out then," Rob replied. The lady port officer told us to proceed but watch out for the big ships.

There was one unladen vessel on his way in, and Rob set Zoonie towards the green buoy next to the beacon that marked a wreck, with a determination I rarely see in him, and we squeezed around the corner with the big feller, bone in its teeth, coming quickly up behind us.

Welcoming hands were there to take our lines, and after a beer with them in the evening, we hit the sack at about 9.00 pm and were comatose until 6.00 am, despite the comings and goings of the tug and pilot boats near us with their thumping engines.

Lines ashore in South Africa

As soon as we completed the clearing-in process and with negative Covid test results duly recorded by the authorities it was time to take *Zoonie's* lines aboard for the short journey to Zululand Yacht Club's marina, and less than an hour later we tied up with the help of local hands, for what we thought would be around a month. Most other yachts were keen to spend Christmas in Cape Town, but we preferred to keep away from crowds where the risks of catching Covid appeared to be greater, or so we thought. Also, the weather, we had been told, moderates a little as the season progresses and better weather windows can be expected from January onwards.

Mirabella, with André and Eva, Jaël and Amina aboard, whom we knew from New Zealand, Vanuatu and Réunion, was moored on the next jetty along and planned to join the group at Cape Town for Christmas. It was nice to have a chat with them in the boatyard before they left.

We try a different game

We headed north in our hire car and took a left opposite The Baobab Inn for the Rhino River Lodge on the Manyoni Private Game Reserve for a four-day safari, at a vastly reduced price because of Covid. I know

Rob loves giraffes; for me, I was open to whatever we came across but must confess to a fear of big cats, since childhood nightmares of lions lying around the tree on the pavement outside my bedroom window, ready to eat me.

We knew we were in for a treat when we came across pretty impala antelope in a group beneath the trees near to a pair of wildebeest (called gnu everywhere else but not in South Africa) sparring across the road and a family of warthogs in a thicket right beside the track as we drove to the lodge in our brand-new little white Suzuki Swift. All that wildlife even before we checked in.

The reserve was started in 2005, having previously been a cattle farm, and it covers 23,000 hectares. All the original animals were introduced, and with careful management of numbers, using birth control and exchanges with other reserves, the regeneration of the natural habitat and fauna has been left largely to the animals. "They are much better at it than humans," as our ranger, Kyle, explained to us.

Just the right number of elephants, for example, will knock over a given number of trees so they can eat part of the nutritious root system. The tree doesn't die, so the foliage now on the ground is available to smaller animals, and the grass grows in and around the branches creating an environment for a myriad of other life forms to thrive.

This mosaic of wildlife biodiversity struck us as we stood on our little veranda outside our room, listening to the birdsong and insect voices. It was as if the birds knew when their performance time would start within the chorus. Just in the grounds of the lodge we had a pair of woodland kingfishers, who lived on insects in the trees and grass, while the seasonal tributary of the Rhino River that passes by the lodge lay dry but filled with thick, lush grass.

It is early wet season when all the young are born. The lodge grounds are fenced against elephants and giraffe, but everything else is welcomed, even lions! Warthogs often pass through, on a mission, with their tails upright, or just peacefully grazing. Park ranger Jady told me about the time she was returning to her accommodation one night when she heard a warning growl and backed away from a resting lioness on the path to a position where she could pass the watching feline from a more generous distance. After dark we were escorted back to our rooms because of the puff adders who live there and other potentially challenging nocturnal visitors. Getting to bed has never before been such a challenge!

Lunch of wraps and banoffee pie was from 1.30 pm, and then we could relax until 4.00 pm when our keenly awaited first game drive would start.

Soon our group of four – ranger Kyle, wildlife photographer and all-round talented lady Letitia Cox, and Rob and me – started seeing wildlife. First, a baby giraffe with mum and an adult male – not the father but a suitor waiting for the female to be in oestrus again, and, as such, a kind of protector of her.

Waterbuck, with the white circle on their bums, as if they've just stood up from a freshly painted loo seat, were making their way to a waterhole, as were we to enjoy our first sundowners, just the four of us, out of the vehicle. We had ordered our drinks before leaving, and Kyle set them on the little table with dishes of beef jerky, cheese nibbles and tiny homemade buns and biscuits from the lodge kitchen. We relaxed and chatted, looking all around us as we stood, without even thinking if we were safe or not out of our four-wheeled suit of armour.

In the distance grey herons standing on the backs of grazing hippos fished, while their hosts lay submerged, occasionally exhaling clouds of spray, just like whales. Cicadas reminded us of the warm climate we were in, and thunder and lightning reverberated around the distant hills, as it had when we were on the Ecuadorian Amazon, swimming in Piranha Lake; I wouldn't swim here, though – a crocodile ducked under the water as we arrived.

Jady was there to greet us on our return with little glasses of sherry, and we sat around the campfire, our chairs so positioned to adhere to the distancing rules.

The thatched lodge dining room, with one side looking onto the fire and the other side an expansive veranda overlooking the slope down to the 'river', was made even more beautiful with hurricane lamps on the tables and wall lights peeping through woven reed shades. The food was so tasty and colourful, and the staff all mixed in together running the bar and waiting at the tables: one minute a ranger, the next a bartender. In the shadows Jady waited to guide us home, for our first night's sleep beneath the gently turning ceiling fan and protective mosquito net.

What would tomorrow bring? So far we hadn't seen any elephants, though we knew they were around from the radio exchanges between Kyle and the other rangers in the vehicles; it appears a herd were approaching the area, but their route was as yet a mystery.

An African bush walk with Darren and Rees

2 December 2020. It was at about this time, 4.50 am, four days ago that Rob and I made our way to the lodge for our early morning mug of tea in readiness for our walk in the bush with Darren, a ranger from another lodge on the reserve, and young trainee ranger Rees.

Darren handed Rees a gun from the rear seat of his vehicle and then gave us our brief as dawn crept stealthily around us. On the vehicle tracks we could walk abreast, but once we started following the narrow weaving animal ways, he would lead with Rees second and us bringing up the rear, so that if he needed to defend us, he would have a clear view (and shot) ahead and to the sides.

Being on foot one is nearer the ground for studying footprints and photographing flowers, dung beetles at work and small insects. Also, it was pleasant exercise in the cool of the morning and we could see the country from the viewpoint of the antelope.

But as we make eye contact, impala, giraffe, buffalo and nyala dash away from us, showing much more fear of us on foot than yesterday when we were in the vehicle.

We knew we wouldn't be getting up close and friendly with these wild creatures, and we wondered why.

"Even before white men came here with their cattle and guns, the wild animals feared men on foot with their spears, the more so when they occasionally stopped and stood still, obviously stalking their prey and making ready for that fatal release," Darren explained.

There was plenty of evidence of animal life – nature's own environmentalists. Elephants will chew the tasty bark of a tree and the

Darren explains the elephant damage that will not kill the tree

sweet layer beneath, but they know to stop short of cutting the upper part of the tree completely off the base. Part of the tree bends to the ground creating a new environment for wildlife while the remaining vertical part continues to thrive. Nature's tree surgeons.

The 400 different species of dung beetle do a fantastic job of recycling 70% of the elephant and rhino poo in Africa, dragging it below ground to return nutrients and solid material to the soil to keep it aerated and nourished. We watched them in fascination as they rolled up the sticky olive-green goo into balls and then pushed them speedily to their destination. Some of the balls were nuptial offerings to be enjoyed by newly united couples, and then there were the nursery balls, and Darren showed us the hole through which the young dung beetles crawled out of the nest in which they were born, with plenty of food, moisture and warmth around them: an ideal nest material when you think like a dung beetle.

I glanced at my watch as we strolled on, in single file: 8.40 am and counting.

We leaned over an interesting bush, and I remember hearing a distant rumble and thinking, stampeding rhinos coming our way?

No, it was just Darren's tummy calling him home for breakfast; we had travelled light and had only water to drink on this excursion, so we were all ready for some food after nearly four hours of walking in the lovely early morning.

Creatures great and small

Kyle asked us what in particular we wanted to see for the afternoon adventure, so we whispered a desire to see the two male lions that were known to be in the area and had wandered fearless through the lodge grounds just a few days before. Did I really?

(I lie, it was Rob who made the request; my childhood nightmares still haunt me.)

Kyle picked up on my desire to photograph the views of the distant scenery and mountain range, plus he wanted to show us the area from a high viewpoint, and while driving around a hill to get to the top we came across a giraffe lying down – not a common sight in the daytime, apparently.

A band of zebras had a long think before they moved off the road for us, giving us a good opportunity to study them. As soon as something of interest pops up on these drives the rangers stop the vehicle and turn off the engine, so we were with the wild animals, surrounded by life in the bush or on the open savanna, and those moments were precious because the atmosphere rolled in, accompanied by birdsong and the distant sounds of a jackal calling or hyena barking their whereabouts.

After a while we turned around a red soil knoll to see a waterhole and two sleeping lions. They were flat out but I wondered how deep their sleep was. They do well to not mince with rhino and elephants, who, being bigger and much heavier, can do them a lot of harm, and easily kill them. We could do with them leaving us alone too!

Kyle pulled up the vehicle just above them where they lay on their own rise, commanding a clear view of the waterhole below.

After a few minutes three white rhino arrived at the bank on the far side and wandered slowly, cautiously, around towards us. I'm not sure who spotted whom first, but the lions became alert and watchful. The fully maned male is eleven years old and is the uncle of the four-year-old,

Too close for comfort

and they stay together. Another vehicle arrived, so we moved on down the hill closer to the lions to give them a better vantage point; I was even less happy about this arrangement.

We were now no more than ten metres from them. A few strides down their slope and a leap and they'd be on our laps! We spoke rarely and then in whispers, but they weren't in the least bit interested in us; instead, the lions watched the rhinos who were now moving up the slope towards them in a brief stand-off.

We followed them out and around the hill above the waterhole to where a lioness was lying in the long, soft grass. For the few minutes we were there she never averted her gaze in our direction. She was watching the two males and had moved away from their company earlier in the day. She was close to giving birth herself and was fearful of the threat these big males posed to her unborn cubs once they saw the light of day. Adult males will often kill male cubs to eliminate competition for the females, and I wondered why she didn't move right away from them; maybe a case of keep your friends close and your enemies closer.

On the morning of our third day, we followed Kyle out of the vehicle to show us hyena tracks from the night before. Little did I know I was being invaded while engrossed in what Kyle was telling us.

We sat in blissful silence to watch a white rhino and her baby grazing. They de-horn them here to protect them from poachers, but as the horn continues growing, they have to repeat the procedure. The rhino is darted from a helicopter and then the ground crew can come on quad bikes, with guests if they want to, to carry out the procedure as quickly as possible. As Leticia quite rightly said, in what other part of the animal kingdom do you have to disfigure and disarm an animal to increase its chances of survival?

Once or twice, we surprised a herd of impala by coming suddenly around a bend where they were grazing. This time was quite impressive, and the group comprised forty or so adult males who leapt and grunted as they sped away. It was exciting to see how agile they are, especially when some kicked their hind legs high into the air as if to say, "Don't mess with me, buddy."

I had chosen to wear lightweight trousers that morning and did not realise the risk I was taking with the loose weave of the fabric until I noticed a tiny black object, about the size of a pin head, clasping onto my tummy when I was about to take a shower. I scraped it off to discover it was a tick, one of quite a few that Rob then kindly proceeded to scrape off my back, bum and legs, my having dealt with the ones on my front, and, I kid you not, they got almost everywhere but chose not to climb over my bust! Not mountaineers then.

Jady knew straight away what they were: the nymph stage of the tick. Cured my fear of LIONS!

Elephants galore

Tick free and wearing a different pair of trousers, we set off with Kyle on our final game drive and heard guarded radio messages to the effect that the elephants had been near the camp days before but were now moving west. Also, a young male cheetah had been spotted on a termite mound not too far away, so these two factors determined our route for the afternoon.

Within minutes we were soaking up the beauty of new (to us) birds:

two wattled lapwings picking along the shore of a waterhole, and a pair of yellow-billed storks preening themselves in the trees above.

Suddenly, Kyle brought us to a stop as a spitting cobra started out across the road ahead. We waited until it decided to continue and disappear into the bush.

Soon Kyle spotted the cheetah, lounging without a care in the world on his little hill. He was so chilled it was difficult to get a picture of him with his eyes open. We came with an open mind to this safari, more than grateful to see whatever was going on, and we remained so; however, I can see how easy it is to want the cheetah to get up and move to see his whole beautiful body, to hope the eagle would take off for a view of its flight feathers and to wish the hippo would wander ashore so its muddy rounded body would be revealed, but we were just lucky to be witnessing our own encounters with the lovely like-minded company of Kyle and Leticia.

The rangers that morning had been disturbed by the news that a young male cheetah had gone to a waterhole the night before and been taken by a crocodile. This was indeed a shame as there are not many on the reserve and the loss of this one as a reproductive male would alter the balance for a while until the latest cubs grow up.

We were heading westwards to where the elephants had recently been seen. Downwards, towards a valley of thick, lush knee-high grass. There was an air of excitement in our bouncing vehicle; were we at last going to be in luck?

Emerging from a corridor of grass and round a bend, Rob and I exclaimed in hushed unison, "Elephants!"

They were crossing the same dry riverbed that eventually runs by the lodge and the 'tail' end was being brought up by a male; it seemed to be his role as he stayed behind throughout our encounter. At one stage he became sandwiched on the track between us and another vehicle but was very calm about it, and to pass us he just wandered off the track for a few paces and rejoined it ahead of us.

4 December 2020. We were surrounded by lush green undergrowth and trees in full leaf where the massive creatures reached up to wrap their tactile trunks around their next mouthful. The matriarch was busy pushing loiterers onwards to keep the herd moving and give the two young ones space. Then they came to a temporary stop and so too did we at about a 50-metre distance. There was a little barging going on between two of them, and then one turned briskly around and effectively chased the other one back towards us. Things suddenly became very interesting. When the one in front reached us, it peeled off to our right, but the one behind just kept coming. I think maybe the chaser hadn't registered our presence because when it saw us right in front it let out a terrific trumpet alarm, ears flared, and then calmed down instantly. Exciting stuff. They could so easily harm us, but their angst seems to be reserved for their own kind.

We are all constantly being told about the threats to wild animals in Africa, that elephant numbers are plummeting, as indeed they are, and there are no wild leopards left.

Then there were the 350 elephants who died having fallen forward, tusks still on, near a waterhole. They died from blue/green algae poisoning. As Kyle said, a tragedy, yes, but out of 100,000 elephants hardly a threat to their future survival. I didn't share his optimism; as long as there is poaching, the damage to the population remains.

We moved on a little way and stopped again to see one of them reaching high into a fig tree to pluck both fruit and leaves for an alternative meal to grass. Some of the figs are unripe and will pass through the elephant undigested. The remaining food, including grass, fruit, leaves, trees, roots and vegetables, is quickly digested and passed out within 20 minutes(!), so they have to keep grazing. Other animals and birds like their droppings because they are still packed with goodness. If ripe figs are discarded it is a good way of spreading the seeds: another way in which elephants help maintain their habitat.

They were now re-crossing the dry riverbed and climbing up the very steep bank on the other side. Kyle told us that if we wanted to escape a rampaging elephant then climbing or descending a steep hill was the best way as hills slow these big creatures right down. I'll bear that in mind.

This was the entire herd of 35 elephants that live on the reserve, and they were on their way for a drink. Most of the waterholes were dug when this was a cattle ranch, and, of course, the wildlife knows exactly which ones have water in them all year. The hippos rarely budge from theirs.

We saw a male and a female nyala, the most sexually dimorphic antelope, in that they look as if the different genders are from completely different species.

We sipped our complimentary beer and wine and munched on savoury nibbles while standing in the rapidly fading light, chatting. We hadn't noticed that our big afternoon companions were purposefully making their way up the hill in our direction. Kyle was mid-story when his expression suddenly changed. We packed away in haste and climbed into the safety of the Toyota, the elephants' dark encroaching shadows barely discernible in the enveloping dusk.

Despite the ticks, it was a treat to see the effects of leaving the animals, from elephants to dung beetles, to manage these beautiful 59,000 acres of African country: a mosaic of scrub supporting young trees, mature arboreal giants providing shade, luscious grassland and flowering trees.

6 December 2020. Yesterday, back on board, at breakfast, I mentioned to Rob that the tiny red spots I could see on my front left by the departing nymph ticks were getting smaller, which was a relief, and he then asked, "How are the two on the back of your knee?"

"What two on the back of my knee?" queried I.

I was shocked at what I saw: oozing yellow pus.

"Ooh, I haven't seen those."

A call to our friendly taxi driver was quickly followed by a seat in front of Dr Roodt, who gave me a colourful description of what effects I could experience over the next few days, having instantly said, "Ah, you have tick fever, my dear…". He concluded his description with "I know all this because I have had it myself!" That was reassuring, and I knew I would once again survive a scrape with a potentially dangerous health issue, after my fall in Zoonie while crossing the Coral Sea.

"Can I drink while taking the doxycycline?" I asked.

"Yes, no problem, and the only place I want to see you again is in the local wine shop selecting the best!"

Chapter 19

Rough Trip to Cape Town

28 December 2020. We plan to leave here on Sunday 3 January and head for Durban, 102 miles south, and wait there for the next low to pass through before moving on around the coast towards Cape Town, as the weather permits. We both have rusty throats and are wondering if we contracted a bug when shopping for the new computer on Christmas Eve.

The weather is beautiful and it has been getting hotter as the summer progresses. The other day we had 39°C in the saloon and we were saved from melting point by Rob's purchase of two electric fans, a daddy for the saloon and a mummy for the aft cabin, which we have on all night.

Our Christmas Day was fun. Interspersed with chats to family we played Scrabble and a Zoonie form of shove ha'penny, which was well worth the laughs.

We're under the weather to Durban

The birds were still in vocal form, and it was before 5.00 am when we took *Zoonie's* lines aboard at Zululand Yacht Club's marina in Richards Bay and cleared the sand bar by two metres. There was no usable wind, but we did have a favourable tide of half a knot as we headed between the big ships in the anchorage towards the 200-metre contour, which was supposed to contain some Agulhas Current to help us on our way.

The day went by very quickly, but we knew we were in for a night-time approach to Durban.

3 January 2021. No worries, it is a busy shipping port so everything will be well lit up.

We hadn't been expecting the beautiful sunset that cast Durban's skyline into silhouette. The fairway buoy came up as it should, and we furled the genoa and headed for the channel marker red and green lights. Entering into the harbour we were surrounded by big ships, a car transporter, a cruise liner in mothballs and countless cargo and container ships. Rob took us cautiously towards the yacht dock where we were supposed to tie up alongside the International, now named Covid, Jetty, but we couldn't make it out in the dark and thought we'd set the anchor just outside instead. It dragged because it hooked up a black plastic bin liner. Last time that happened was in Suva. By now Rob was feeling exhausted so the prospect of another failed anchoring attempt wasn't on the cards.

Instead, we approached the jetty much further in. In the dark there appeared to be rows of boats on moorings, so as we gingerly approached what we thought was the correct channel, *Zoonie* found otherwise and dipped forwards. No problem, that confirmed where the correct channel was, so we proceeded past the moored boats towards the shore.

When the depth dropped to 2.7 metres beneath the keel Rob was reluctant to go further, so we turned around and went into one of the berths we had spotted as we passed. Nicely tied up at around 8.30 pm we thought we were safe for the night until a very quietly spoken uniformed member of the marina staff came along.

"You can't stop here; you must go to the International Jetty. I will be there to take your lines."

True to his word he helped us to moor up just a few metres from the shore. Moments later the Port Police arrived by boat, and when they were satisfied, a lady from 'health' was brought along by a security guard. Using a torch, she looked at our papers and Covid results forms and said we must wait aboard until a doctor would come down the next day to do our Covid tests, which we would have to pay for, as the first ones were five weeks old.

Our hearts sank. Would we have to do this in every port we called in to? This would put awaiting Covid results over our priority for leaving on a good weather window, breaking our golden rule. For the moment we were in and tired, staying up only to have a bowl of soup before we hit the sack just after 11.00 pm.

Late afternoon the next day Rob phoned the office and asked when we could expect the doctor. They weren't coming as they didn't think a Covid test was necessary, so we took our papers up to the office for some more form filling.

A member of the marina office staff strongly advised we should not stray far from the marina because of lack of security and the Covid risk. Sparing with the facts and with a frosty attitude to boot, we came away feeling less than welcome.

So, it was back to the boat to run the engine and charge the batteries, and not use the mains electric fans Rob had recently bought, as we'd been told we couldn't use the electric plug-ins. No reason given, so maybe because they weren't safe. We had indeed been lucky at Zululand Yacht Club.

A walk in the park

The prospect of another week in Durban, feeling unwell, maybe with Covid, floating with the decaying rubbish in the marina and unable to even think of going for a short walk was playing on my mind, so I looked once again at Windy, our weather app, and saw to my relief that the weather window that we thought had disappeared was back, and, indeed, it looked good.

6 January 2021. "A walk in the park" is how Des, our lovely weather guru, described the next two days down to East London, so we were back up to the office to complete our flight plan as quick as a couple of squirrels with their tails on fire. Departure time was set at 5.00 am the next morning, "and you must go within 24 hours or you will have to complete another flight plan." (And I might kill you, her beady eyes threatened.) Incentive enough to clear out, I can tell you.

After seven hours we were pootling along just over five miles offshore, where Des said we would find the elusive Agulhas Current, and suddenly noticed the gentle hand beneath, pushing us first by 2.5 knots and then up to 3 knots over our boat speed. The engine went off, and with her poled-out genoa full of energy, Zoonie entered the night at 8.4 knots of delicious speed. We had thought the journey of 250 miles would take 48 hours, two nights at sea, but not if this wonderful ocean gift stayed with us.

"Remember to turn for the harbour entrance when you get to Cape Morgan, 40 miles north of East London, or you will be set on past." Des's words.

Don't get me wrong, this is a tricky section of the South African east coast and has claimed many an experienced sailor, but we take as we find, having started out with due care and forethought, and this is how it was for us…

Zoonie adopted a languid, gentle roll; the waves created the music and the wind sighed as it pushed us along, and with the guiding hand beneath giving us 4 knots, we were at times doing 10 knots over the ground. Once or twice the wind held its breath and the current pressed against Zoonie's open quarter, pushing her at right angles to the current, so she was either facing the coast or the rising sun. That was a little alarming at first, but without the mainsail creating pressure behind the mast, Zoonie felt comfortable. We were being treated kindly indeed.

By the next morning Rob was feeling rough, our rusty throats back in Richards Bay seemed to be developing into something; could it be Covid after our precautions of closely fitting four-layered masks, repeated hand sanitising and keeping well apart from others?

Our second day was ageing, and I took Rob's temperature to discover it was 38.8°C; thank goodness we had only 20 miles to go.

Suddenly the wind dropped to nothing and within a few moments rose again from ahead to 25 knots. Just as quickly the sea became a blue six-foot wall of water ahead of us. The genoa was furled and engine on to battle this latest challenge. Fortunately, it started to subside after a few minutes and our progress towards East London Harbour improved.

When just off the mouth I called up the Port Authority and explained our situation. The officer instructed us to stay outside until he had spoken to Port Health, and naturally when they came back it was correctly assumed we carried the virus. We were allowed to pootle up the river to the mid-river mooring trots and tie up both ends, remaining on board until a test could be arranged the next day.

Safe distancing in the middle of a South African river

---

8 January 2021. Our location is delightful. We are surrounded by a diversity of water birds and there are steep wooded banks on either side and two bridges ahead of us, so we have plenty to watch.

The next morning Charles, who runs a local shipping supply business, organised a Covid test, the port quarantine officer phoned to see if there was anything he could do to help and Conrad from the Buffalo River Yacht Club, upon whose moorings *Zoonie* was sitting, was ready on hand if we needed him. Such kindness just when we needed it.

I inflated the tender and Rob rowed us ashore for our tests. A woman in blue brandished the required forms in her hands. "Shall I give these to your secretary?" she asked Rob…!!!

In Covid's clutches

Twenty-four hours later, the tests the results came through, which we viewed on our phone apps. Both positive and we weren't surprised. The next morning, we were ashore once more to see Dr Murray, who prescribed a new inhaler for Rob to help with his breathing and some cortisone tablets.

So, the symptoms were varied. One of mine was mental confusion (more so than normal): I filled in both forms with Rob's name, and I remember not feeling quite right up top. Not the best secretary! Another was my fingertips became more sensitive to heat than usual: normally I manage the grill pan without gloves or the handle, but I couldn't do that for a couple of days. I got off lightly, but Rob was fighting his infection by sweating and sleeping. The doc was happy as long as his oxygen level stayed above 90%. Rob's was constantly 93%.

13 January 2021. So here we are, Day 4 of our fourteen-day quarantine. Three terns are looking out from our pulpit, and the loving cormorants roost in marital pairs on the mooring buoys. Another pair reside on the port-side spreader on a nearby yacht, a spot which is also a perch for a local giant kingfisher.

It has been reassuring, the fact that our little support group came together so quickly. Conrad and his young daughter Willow rowed out to

Goodies from Conrad, commodore of the yacht club

us in a rickety tender with the drugs and a bag of goodies courtesy of the yacht club, which is usually a bustling place.

18 January 2021. The birds are increasingly happy with us here. The terns preen themselves on our handrails, a wagtail tries to come in and say "hi", and this morning a goose was standing on the cockpit coaming wondering when I was going to get up! A pair of mystery birds we cannot find in our books or on my South Africa bird app are confusing us. 'Pied plovers' is the only way I can describe them. Nothing like a little mystery to add to the mix.

Rob was still in decline. His oxygen level struggled to maintain 91% for a few days, and anything below 90% would require hospitalisation. I fleetingly wondered if his heart valve repair could be the cause, but then the immediate situation again filled my mind.

For a couple of nights, I watched him carefully to make sure he didn't slip away as so many victims seem to.

His profuse sweating, soaking towels, T-shirts and bed sheets, brought me plenty of washing to do. Unfortunately, it coincided with a few days of wet weather, drizzly rain and grey skies, so getting the towels dry posed a challenge. To prevent them from taking on a musty smell I hung six of them up in the saloon as they weren't going to dry outside.

But then all things pass, and the towels finally flew in sunshine and warmth in the cockpit.

We relished the food bag that Conrad brought along, and the juicy Queen pineapples were delicious. It isn't hard in South Africa to maintain vitamin C levels with their delicious pineapples, plums, nectarines, peaches, blueberries and bananas. We had them all, and when the cat called *Cinders* arrived, Cindy asked if there was anything we wanted at the shops as they were going there anyway.

A while later they motored alongside with three bags bulging with goodies for which they would take no payment. As well as what I have mentioned there were baby plum tomatoes, washed butter lettuce, bottles of health drink, homemade cupcakes and three get well soon cards carefully created by the children. Not only was the food welcome but the cards, cupcakes and thoughts really lifted our spirits. And although they wore their masks when they dropped the bags off, I just hoped they wouldn't catch the virus.

A recovering Rob opened the fridge and exclaimed, "It's like a market stall in here!" and he was right, so colourful I wish I had taken a photo.

It was comforting receiving get well messages from friends and family too, and as we started to feel more normal, we appreciated having been fortunate enough to survive the virus and hoped we would be much less likely to catch it again. But it was an uncomfortable kind of vacation!

Our quarantine was coming to an end, so we and Des started looking for a window to get us at least to Mossel Bay if not right around to Cape Town.

22 January 2021. The port quarantine officer warmly confirmed we could venture ashore at the end of our quarantine period today. He is a kind man who often phoned us when we were ill, just to see how we were and to offer any assistance we might need. Here in South Africa, we have found the local officials to be, without exception, kind, attentive and thoughtful.

We have chatted with family and heard from Bron's brother Brian in Cape Town; they have the red carpet all ready to roll out! So, a welcome awaits us there, which is nice.

"The only way we knew you were still alive was when you hung out the washing!" Conrad told Rob when he was ashore recently on one of our 'get fit and filled up' water runs. He and his daughters, Anna and Willow, took us up to the local SUPERSPAR yesterday, so we could shop while they did the same. So now we have enough fresh food to get us around to Cape Town!

Looking daily at the Windy app, we had thought that there was no weather window for this week, and we had given up on the idea of a four-day window to get right around to Cape Town in one hop. Then Des pointed out the imminent 24-hour window which would let us move on to Port Elizabeth, 130 miles south from here. Following on, another window appeared which could get us to an anchoring spot in Mossel Bay, just two days from Cape Town. From there we would pass Cape Agulhas and the Cape of Good Hope, the most southerly and south-westerly points, respectively, on the African coast to reach our destination. Good Hope, and such Good News.

We filed our flight plan with Conrad, and he sent it to the Port Authority where we were in East London and to our contact, John, at Port Elizabeth. These flight plans may seem tedious to some, but they are to give the rescue authorities an immediate identification of any craft that is in trouble and needs rescuing on this wild stretch of coastline. Besides, they seemed to get simpler to fill in the further we travelled and the more we completed.

We should pick up the last of the Agulhas Current for the first 30–60 miles before it heads south and then south-east across the Indian Ocean while we head in the opposite direction. At least the rain will ease the bird poo off Zoonie's decks.

The leaving of Buffalo River

28 January 2021. The river water was like a mirror as I disturbed the peace by starting the engine at 5.15 am today. We tied together the mooring lines and dropped them over the side, and I motored us slowly away from our place we had occupied for nineteen days and for which Conrad made us no charge. "You weren't here for pleasure, exactly, were you."

We were truly sad to leave behind our carers, the ones who had taken us under their wings: the goose on the cockpit coaming, the wagtail at the window, the terns on the pulpit, the cormorant astride the life raft, and especially the human ones: Conrad, the commodore, and Anna and Willow; Charles, our agent; Dr Murray; the port guys and the catamaran family. We will always have a special place in our hearts for Buffalo River Yacht Club, the place where, with the care of others, we survived Covid.

Early arrival in Port Elizabeth

Much was going on in the marine world just outside the harbour; gannets fishing is always a prelude to a good show, and soon we were surrounded by dolphins, seals, shearwaters and an immaculate humpback with not a mark on its long, smooth back.

The day was going to be a beauty as *Zoonie* nosed into an 11-knot headwind, and we soon picked up 2.2 knots of our old friend the Agulhas Current. We hurried south/south-west as the wind weakened, keen to reduce the miles to when we would turn westwards out of the Indian Ocean.

Looking to the shore we watched as the distant, faint rolling hills advanced to stands of dark green woodland above golden sand dunes for miles and miles along the coast.

By 5.30 pm we were losing the current, but with the sea undisturbed by any wind, just the gentle roll and swell from the south, *Zoonie* was unhindered in her progress.

Through the night we could see the lights of Port Elizabeth spreading around Alcoa Bay, and an acrid smell permeated our nostrils and bit into the walls of our throats. It was ore based but not like the smell of coal dust or iron ore. It turned out to be manganese dust blowing our way from where a ship was being loaded, as and when the horn-blowing trains arrived from the mines.

We found our way into Alcoa Bay Sailing Marina at 3.48 am with some dawn twilight assistance. John had informed Port Control of our situation, Covid survivors en route to Cape Town, so there was no delay there; we had done our time. We dozed off to the sounds of frapping halyards, police sirens and *Zoonie's* squeaking lines.

For the second time we thought our weather window would be at least a week away but suddenly discovered we had one in just three days, which, as I suggested to Des, could take us right around to Cape Town. Des thought it might be a little early to bank on it, but we lived in hope. It was certainly proving true that conditions for heading west around South Africa improve as the summer matures. So just a long weekend in Port Elizabeth it would be.

John came early the next morning. His very nice racing cruiser was moored a few fingers from us, and he let us borrow his vehicle so we could refuel at the nearby petrol station and do a shop at the SUPERSPAR just behind it, all while he was out sailing. We were not allowed to leave the marina on foot or we would not be allowed back in.

A historic little lighthouse is now completely diminished by the docks and high cranes of the marine shipping industry, but it would have been much sought after in the days of sail, when ships brought settlers and emigrants from Europe to this corner of Africa. Thousands would then make passage in smaller ships up to East London and Durban before heading inland to take up plots of land rendered 'available' by the governments back in Britain and the Netherlands.

From our mooring we watched the fishing boats coming and going and saw the gritty orange/black dust billowing from the open hatches of the ships and settling over the yachts in the marina as the ore tumbled off the conveyor belt into their gaping holds.

Judging by the state of their vessels, many of the boats were visitors who arrived many decades ago, tidied up the rigging and just walked away, never to return. It is the same story the world over. People get so far and then, for as many reasons as there are boats, their voyaging stops. The thought of it ever happening to us became less of a burden every time we moved on and reduced the number of destinations we had left before our project was complete.

Despite the local industry around the harbour, the fish life was abundant and numerous little colonies of molluscs and baby fish thrived on the lines and rubber tyres.

Des was cautiously coming around to our idea that we could make it to Cape Town in one.

Our ETD moved back from Monday at 6.00 pm to Tuesday midday, and we slipped lines at 11.30 am. So, our last evening in this charming place that I would love to have explored further was spent drinking G&T, playing Triominos and watching two episodes of *Killing Eve* – nothing if not inventive, we two.

Where two oceans meet

---

1 February 2021. We had only been at sea for a few minutes, on another sunny day, when we passed seven jackass penguins swimming in a closely huddled group. There wasn't much wind today but Rob poled out the genoa, and with that sail pulling and the Agulhas Current helping (as soon as we left port), Zoonie has managed a respectable 5.3 knots with the engine turned off.

Our weather window is holding and appears to extend for at least a week.

7 February 2021. As I type this in the V&A Marina in Cape Town, it is the seventh day and the wind would be against us now, but, even so, a six-day weather window is the longest yet by far.

We had been warned about the numerous ships we would come across on this busy route around the capes, and soon we were caught up in the crowd coming towards us and diverging around us as they approached from behind. Why aren't there any shipping lanes around there like in the English Channel? Maybe they have to go where the weather is giving the most favourable sea. Then there were the fishing boats, oblivious to everything except their task in hand, as usual.

For the first time ever, a ship actually called us and the officer explained the action he was going to take to pass down our starboard side as he overtook. Impressive: both considerate and professional.

At 6.00 pm we turned west for Cape Town, 281 miles away, and we knew we were in for a blow, just hoping we would be able to make use of it.

The time came to slide the main into the mast because its role as a steadying sail was being challenged by the building sea which, in advance of the blow that was coming, threatened to push *Zoonie* sideways and we didn't want that, did we? It was as if the wind was in crescendo towards the meeting of the two mighty sea masses; we were leaving the Indian Ocean and entering our home ocean, the Atlantic.

Picture this, dear reader. It's 1.38 am during the first night, and two muzzy-headed mariners are sitting on deck, under silvery moonlight and the deck light beam, trying to figure out in what order to connect the lines to the genoa pole, now that Zoonie was on a new course with the wind on the other side.

The pole had usually been rigged to starboard during long periods of easterly trade winds, so rigging the pole on the opposite side was posing a ridiculous challenge. (Could I blame Covid?)

Our ancient mariners worked away, head scratching and exchanging theories until the pole assumed the horizontal without a hitch. Soon the wind was rising and the sea was in the same mood, and within a few hours Zoonie was belting along with a reefed headsail in winds between 22 and 29 knots, relishing the freedom to do 8 knots at times under sail alone. The blow lasted 15 hours.

Atlantic Ocean, here we come!

Suddenly, as daylight arrived on the second day, we saw we were passing pairs of big pink buoys in a line at 50-metre intervals no more than 15 metres from us. A deadly drift net, harbinger of death to marine life whether suited in scales or feathers, or even fibre glass had we got caught up in it, and even worse if our engine had been on. How would such a disaster pan out for us? In the night you just cannot see them; how had we been fortunate enough to miss them so far? How much longer would our luck hold out as far as a fouled propeller was concerned? Give me an open ocean to sail across, rather than coastal sailing under motor, any day.

By 4.00 pm we were back on engine with the night looming and more than a little concerned about fishing nets.

3 February 2021. Last night we emerged unscathed again from between buoyed pots, despite being under motor, and after the blessed wind left us, everything in the cockpit shone with tiny beads of silver in the moonlight. Droplets clung on to the underside of the bimini; we could feel the chill on our skin, and everything below soaked up some of the moisture. A fog

The Atlantic – our home ocean

bank, maybe. We were in the area where two oceans meet. Was this the theatre curtain, waiting to be opened onto the Atlantic stage, leaving behind us the temperamental Indian Ocean? The Atlantic was ahead. Our home ocean. At long last.

Des suggests we head for the gap between the Six Mile Bank and the Twelve Mile Bank, where the majority of the ships go. Ooh, that could be a squeeze.

A baby buster was expected off Cape Agulhas, the most southerly cape of the continent and the recognised meeting place of the Indian and Atlantic Ocean, so we were hoping we would have made the turn north before then and receive it as a beam wind boosting us on.

I worried there was no natural luminescence in this cool water where there should be lots of nutritious food for the sea creatures. Just after midnight I noticed the enormous orange waning gibbous moon had risen astern of us. Gibbous because its illuminated (visible) area was between full moon and half-moon, and I like the word!

A seal arched out of the water to see us, all of 23 miles offshore, and a juvenile yellow-nosed albatross came to take a look. I had thought we would not see any more albatrosses, so this was a treat. I realised how fortunate we were, because modern fishing techniques are causing a catastrophic decline in these magnificent ocean wanderers.

Cape Agulhas, our third of the five southernmost capes

It's 1.50 pm and we can see Cape Agulhas 20 miles away; we wonder if we will lose the current there.

The ships are now heading directly for the westbound separation lane to the north of the Agulhas Gas Field, the oncoming ships in the eastbound lane to the south of the field. So, we draw a course just out of the westbound lane and feel a lot more comfortable. I feel a nuisance expecting these leviathans to alter course for us, but I guess it is just normal in their line of work.

4.45 pm. We are making a gentle entry into our home ocean, passing Cape Agulhas under gently purring engine. Hello, South Atlantic!

4 February 2021. We passed the Cape of Good Hope in my 4.00–7.00 am watch, its bright white flashing light the only sparkle in an otherwise sky-to-ocean grey. But soon the blue sky grew with the morning, and, as Des told us, "The beautiful scenery is there to be enjoyed."

Between a rock and hard place, literally, we made a course three miles from the shore, mostly on the 200-metre contour to avoid the cray(fish) pots laid on the rocks just off the coastline and not so far out to cause a nuisance to the ships.

Robben Island, where Nelson Mandela was imprisoned for eighteen of his twenty-seven years of captivity, appeared low on our port bow, and as we motored nearer, two bridges opened to allow us into the inner lagoon right in the city centre. Weitz from Anna Caroline (whom we had met in Whangarei, New Zealand) and a marina attendant took our lines at 1.00 pm today, after a fabulous passage of 444 miles in just over three days. We have arrived and are now in our last ocean, free to head north, and home, eventually.

Chapter 20

Taking in Cape Town

The harbour area, named Victoria and Alfred after Queen Victoria and her son, is partly what puts Cape Town on the world map as one of the most beautiful cities, and views of the clean, vibrant waterfront, with the unique Table Mountain overlooking everything, is special. The mountain is one of the oldest in the world consisting of layers of sandstone and granite; it was formed by igneous and glacial activity 520 million years ago, making it six times older than the Himalayas.

Clearing in to Cape Town

5 February 2021. Even though we officially cleared in to South Africa in Richards Bay last November, we have to follow another process in Cape Town which involves collecting letters from the yacht club and the Port of Entry Control office atop the observation tower. With the help of a Bolt car (like Uber) the process was all easy and pleasant.

Zoonie is moored against the furthest-in pontoon nearest to the harbour side activities, including the aquarium, where a sad oystercatcher paces over rocks inside an upstairs window. He is there for his own safety for some reason and would not survive in the wild.

The red Clock Tower adorning the pedestrian area at the Waterfront is the oldest building in Cape Town and once enabled the ships' captains to keep their timepieces accurate; it was an essential aid to navigation and the calculations of longitude back in the days of sail pre GPS, iPhones and quartz watches.

There is also a time ball that still falls at noon each day along with the firing of the midday gun, but as they are both set back from the harbour and the sound took time to travel to the ears of the captains years ago, they were not as accurate as the clock, although they did tell the convicts and workers when they could break for lunch.

After effects of the Indian Ocean on *Zoonie*

We needed some new rigging. Three of the stays that were replaced in Mooloolaba failed, with strands, visible from the deck, breaking clean away from the swages, and we needed sound rigging for the remaining 7,300 miles to Falmouth! The water motion in the Indian Ocean is confused because, unlike the Atlantic and Pacific oceans, it cannot run free between the north and south poles, so as waves arrive on the shores of Indonesia and northwards into the Bay of Bengal and the Arabian Sea, they flow back out to the Indian Ocean as they recede, meeting incoming waves and causing a confused ocean. For us this meant the slack leeward stays on the same side as the mainsail oscillated, turning imperceptibly but constantly, causing the inevitable metal fatigue.

So, after their inspection, while the riggers were away making new stays, it was time for us to play.

The old harbourmaster's office is like so many of the old buildings, an immaculately restored three-storey classical European-style structure painted with white borders and corners and pastel green panels. It now houses the African Trading Port, a warehouse of new and old handmade craft objects for various purposes, from supplying modern tourism to ways of expressing historic and traditional culture. I was amazed that even the clearly old and anthropologically interesting artefacts had a price tag on them. They looked like museum pieces to me.

Lazy seals

7 February 2021. We have witnessed the seals up close and scary from the safety of Zoonie and the elevated promenade.

The way they hang in the water on their backs with their heads flopped downwards, fast asleep, or lie on their special platform with their rear end over the side into the water at a right angle to their upper body is comical.

During the night they grumble to each other, or one will start a gravelly laugh like an old human with emphysema. Sometimes they will come alongside and tap titbits off Zoonie's hull, or emerge from a dive with a splash just to make one jump. They can be as languid and elegant in the water as flowing water itself, arching and rolling without even creating bubbles, but be not lulled into a false admiration because they will also, shockingly, snatch a sitting cormorant from underneath, shake it violently, and within seconds eat nearly all of it or take just one bite and leave the remainder stagnating in the water.

Two days later, while awaiting our riggers' arrival, sitting in the cockpit, it was fun to watch the goings on in the marina. Ladies in pink in their dragon boat, rowing flat out, and long RIBs with three pupils and their instructor aboard doing what must be their first, very gentle, lesson in the art of driving these inflatable boats. I remember doing my training in one as a safety boat skipper for part of the RYA Dinghy Instructor course at Calshot near Southampton. The fun part involved motoring at high speed and then doing an emergency stop by throttling down while turning left or right at the same time, so as to avoid being pooped by one's own wash.

Apart from having three steel rigging stays replaced we were also fortunate in that another vessel had required a new VHF aerial part of the masthead Windex fitting while we required the wind direction indicator part. So we used the remaining contents of their package. If you remember, a night-time visiting blue-footed booby bird decided to alight momentarily on ours, breaking it off, the arm to be found useless in the scuppers the next morning.

On top of Table Mountain

I wondered what it was like on Table Mountain; after all, we don't often come across a mountain with such a flat top, do we. What grows up there on level ground with plenty of moisture from its almost daily tablecloth of mist? We were going to find out.

9 February 2021. Eight years short of its centenary, this cable car has allowed millions of folks to make the same journey to the top. There are just two cars, speeding up and down on the same make of German cables as Zoonie's new rigging, providing an all-round view as the floor turns, disconcertingly at first, especially if one didn't hear the warning! They can take an alarming sixty-five people at once, but thankfully we were seven strong for our trip up the mountain, with the place almost to ourselves because of the lack of overseas visitors.

The substantial building that receives the car at the top looks like a pimple from a distance, but we were confident of its integrity; after all, it is sitting on a foundation half a billion years old.

Summer was on the decline and spring a distant memory, so the few flowers we saw were reminders of the masses that must look fabulous in full bloom but for us had dried or turned into fruit and seed heads. There are many paths for energetic hikers around the mountain, starting with gentle but exposed paths from the bottom that grind on up through rocky gorges to the summit and two routes to follow on the top; we took the longer Klipspringer

The cable car to the top of Table Mountain

Trail in the light breeze and warm air. I like that name, like a neat pet spaniel.

An abundance of life hides away from the drying sun. We spotted colourful butterflies and some beady-eyed lizards. There is a healthy lack of warning signs and fencing on the top; it's down to one's common sense and survival instinct to stay safe.

Rob made me edgy as he stepped close to a ravine side for a peep down one of the tracks. I called him back from the edge, even though there's always electric winches – joking.

A tiny history of South Africa

The Khoi and San, hunter-gatherer people, sparsely populated this area before Europeans arrived, and back then the plains teemed with megafauna and small animals of a great species diversity. Bartolomeu Dias sailed by in 1488, and ten years later Vasco da Gama found the first all-sea route from Europe to India around South Africa, thus opening up the commercial route for the spice trade avoiding the problematic overland journey from Constantinople (Istanbul) to Peking (Beijing) and resulting in the global economy we have today.

This southerly route is a very exposed coast in a southern storm, as happened during the Great Storm of 1865 when countless vessels, including RMS *Athens*, foundered with loss of all life. Her man-made engine block is a durable reminder of the fragility of man and a nice little target for swimmers and snorkellers, just outside the harbour. Even on the benign day we were there, the swell hitting the shore and breakwaters was impressive.

Cape Peninsula tour with Brian

Setting off with our friend Brian, Bron's brother (we had met Bron and Ken on *Nichola* in Vanuatu and toured Tasmania with them), on a tour of the Cape Peninsula, our first stop was on Signal Hill near the Lion's Head outcrop, where keen hang gliders were waiting for the opportunity to take a running jump. Rather them than me!

The coast-hugging road around the cape affords the most incredible, mind-stopping views as it clings tenaciously to the rocks or swings smoothly around sandy bays and through seasonally choked villages, which for us, because of Covid restrictions, were not busy.

We looked down on Fish Hoek Bay to the pretty little fishing harbour, reminiscent of a Cornish counterpart, and got out of the car at Simon's Town to see the marina in which Marjolein and Henk (from Réunion days) were aboard *Jori*.

The rocky Boulders Beach has been cleverly arranged with stout wooden walkways and fencing to keep people as separate from the local colony of African jackass penguins as the endangered penguins wish. Back in 1982 there were just two breeding pairs; now there are over 2,000 because of restrictions placed on the fishing of pelagic fish, pilchards and anchovies in False Bay where the beach is situated.

We walked along the boardwalk to Foxy Beach and right up to the wooden fence where there were penguins nestling in hollows under the shady bushes, nursing their eggs, while their partners were down on the cool sand near the water's edge taking refreshing dips, as were lots of human families in the neighbouring bays.

We sped on to Cape Point and took the funicular up to the old black-and-white-banded lighthouse that was built in 1859, commissioned the following year and replaced in 1919. There are three prominent headlands in this area rising to over 200 metres at Cape Point, where we were.

13 February 2021. The Cape of Good Hope is the furthest south-west headland, but Cape Point being the highest land is where the tourist activities are, including walks out to two lighthouses. The famous Cape of Good Hope is the most significant geographically for mariners, as they clear it to turn on their onward journey, just as we did to Cape Town.

From the old lighthouse we walked downhill towards the present-day white-dome-roofed lighthouse we saw on that grey misty morning, all of two weeks ago, and looked offshore towards what some think of as the border between the Indian and the Atlantic oceans. The cold northward-turning Benguela Current (which should help us) meets the warm south-flowing Agulhas Current (our old friend) in this region, hence the perceived meeting place of the two oceans, but for us and Wikipedia the Agulhas left us near its namesake cape, so that is where we felt we entered our home ocean.

Slangkop Lighthouse is the tallest in South Africa; being at ground level it had to raise its lights somehow, and in so doing it has a range of only four kilometres less than Cape Point. The long beach is true to its name and is very popular for galloping horses. To one end of it the rocky land rises dramatically to Chapman's Peak, so named after John Chapman, an English pilot, who was sent ashore from his becalmed ship in Hout Bay in 1607 to find provisions. The account doesn't say whether he was successful.

The precipitous road around the peak with its superb views on a good day was hacked out of the soft sandstone at an elevation up to which there is a granite base. Work started in 1915 and the toll road was opened in 1922. It has been closed on a couple of occasions, once in the 1990s for a number of years after a German couple were killed by rockfall. Numerous engineering measures were put in place including tough net fencing to catch falling rocks.

We had had a great time with Brian, rounded off with an evening with his family, Graziella, his wife, and Joujou, his mother-in-law, both from Mauritius, and their two Jack Russells; we sat in their garden all evening in the warmth from the wood-burning braai (barbecue) and chatted over a lengthy and delicious home-cooked supper.

Almost time to leave

19 February 2021. Three boats have left for their non-stop voyage to Brazil. As far as we know we are one of only three boats, at present, planning similar routes via St Helena and the Azores back to Europe. We know both the others: Anna Caroline with Janneke and Weitze, our neighbours here, and Jori with Henk and Marjolein, with whom we will form a trio as we move north towards Europe.

Janneke and Weitze left us on the dot at 9.30 am six days ago, on their way to Namibia, and soon it will be our turn to move on once again, but first, some wine tasting!

A weekend of wine and wonder

After breakfast Mohammed, our driver, sped us in his cherished white Toyota Corolla out of Cape Town and onto the N1 highway northward over flat plains, once home to antelope, lions, giraffe and roaming human groups of cattle farmers and hunters, the Khoi and San tribes. In the distance, high mountains, grey, rugged and dominant, drew our gaze.

We turned onto the R301, a narrower road that turns towards the east, and Mohammed told us how this was locally called the 'Freedom Road' because it was along here that Nelson Mandela made his way to Cape Town when he was finally a free man.

I showed an interest, so Mohammed asked if we would like to pause at the gate of the Drakenstein Correctional Centre where Nelson Mandela stands in bronze salute to commemorate the day of his final release from confinement on 11 February 1990. Called the Victor Verster Prison back then, Mr Mandela lived in a house there to prepare for a life back in society after twenty-seven years a 'convict' revolutionary for the anti-apartheid cause.

I remember the day well and the build up to it. Daughter Emily and I were staying with my parents at their Cornish cottage, and as the keenly anticipated moment approached, I would walk around their home chanting "Free Mandela" like so many others, my fist raised. My mother would smile in silent agreement; my father disapproved.

Soon we saw brilliant white-painted Dutch-style mansions with their curly apexes, buildings of the apartheid times, nestled amidst uniform rows of vines stretching in various directions over hills and vales towards the mountains that run down both sides of the Franschhoek Valley. Mohammed disappeared into the tram station to find our guide, Skay (pron. Esskay), who would be with us for the day, along with another couple.

20 February 2021. The Franschhoek Wine Tram is a much-loved way of visiting a number of vineyards, including our first one, the Rickety Bridge Estate. The tram rumbled and rattled slowly down the track and occasionally had to stop at a crossing to check for road traffic. At which point the lithe and energetic young man, who had just served us all with our first glass of the day, would don his luminous jacket, grab his flag, leap off the moving tram, and rush ahead to the crossing to do his visual check as the tram slowed. Then once our way was clear he would do an elaborate flourish with his flag, run to the back of the tram and leap back on board to the laughter and cheers of his appreciative audience. I wondered if he had already had a tasting!

At the tram stop nearest to 'our' vineyard an aged and faded, like me, at times, Massey Ferguson tractor hitched to a trailer with seats was ready to tow us over the rebuilt and no longer rickety bridge to the hub of the activity, and there, as we stood amidst the fabulous natural scenery, Skay delivered his brief history of the area and birth of South African wine in his slow, gentle and considered way.

A glass half full of history

While Europe was still battling with the rise of the Ottoman Empire, massive herds of elephants roamed the plains between the mountains; the first Dutch to arrive for trade and to settle referred to the valley as Olifantshoek, Elephants' Corner. Cape leopards, antelope, rock hyrax (which are small, herbivore mammals), numerous birds, puff adders and cobra, and small reptile species still live in the mountains.

After the opening of the sea route from Europe to the Orient, Dutch merchant ships needed to take on stores and water after the long sail south. At first the Khoi and San people were willing to help out, but gradually they realised that some of their visitors were permanently settling on their hunting and farming land, having seen how rich the soil was.

The Dutch used a strategy as subtle as it was cynical by pushing the two indigenous groups closer together up the valley, knowing that they would battle with each other for the remaining land. With reduced numbers they would need less land. Peace talks started and the indigenous leaders asked the Dutch how they would react if people from overseas landed in the Netherlands and started to claim land and property rights there. The Dutch reply was effectively 'relinquish or die'. Today the descendants of the 'relinquishers' live on the slopes around the fertile land and find work in the wine companies and in the service industries.

During the naissance of the grape growing industry, the Dutch soon learned that while they were good at filling in the sea to make new land, they were not good at filling bottles with palatable wine. They knew that under Catholic Louis XIV in seventeenth/eighteenth-century France the Protestant Huguenots were still suffering brutal religious oppression. Many of them were knowledgeable wine growers with a heritage of superb viticulture skills. So, intelligent and resourceful Dutch vine growers sponsored 150 French Huguenots and their families to sail to a new home on 31 December 1687, and over the next two years more came, totalling around 180 wine-making brains. In return for their expertise the French newcomers were financially supported until the profits from their work started to flow.

The French families became so successful they eventually bought land of their own and their vineyards still flourish today, fed constantly with nutrients washed down from the granite and sandstone mountains around. They also renamed the area Franschhoek, French Corner, the elephants by this time long gone.

Skay went on to tell us all about the production and fermentation processes while walking us around the stainless steel vats and also the concrete vats, which add their own flavour to the end product.

One thing we had noticed around Cape Town and in this valley

Franschhoek – wine country

is the abundance of European oak trees. The wood for the barrels is imported from Europe as the oak grows too quickly here to be of use for barrel making. Nevertheless, it was good to see the English ones healthy and enjoying the clean air and warm climate. When they are finished with, the barrels are sent to whisky and brandy makers and eventually used as plant holders for their long, slow retirement. The potted life of an oak barrel!

Our second vineyard, back over the seemingly more (!) rickety bridge to meet a minibus, was the Grand Provence, where the wines were very dry by comparison and the emphasis was as much on a shady place to relax and dine beneath the oaks in the company of numerous slender sculptures of the female form, with a gallery to soak up the artworks and maybe part with some cash, as it was to savour the juice of the terroir, the quality earth the vines grow in.

I don't remember the drive to the last vineyard, La Bri, but I do remember the tasting as it was paired with a choice of vegan chocolate, free-range dried meat 'biltong', Rob's choice, or 'lokum', locally made Turkish delight, which I tried, to savour the flavours of lavender and roasted nut. It was such a contrast to the style and content of our last tastings, and our wine taster really knew her story. It's amazingly imaginative, the different ways the vineyards can present themselves.

On our return to the marina we discovered that every single cormorant had gone. We wondered why. Back to Robben Island, maybe, for safety? Or the seals' work?

The softest settee

Landing on a soft settee is how it must feel to be a South African fur seal as it slips into the water with barely a ripple or splash, unless, of course, it has been barracked and pushed in by a temporary adversary. We have never seen them draw blood on each other, but, boy, do they squabble, day and night, until they get tired or a big male gives them a deep-belly series of verbal grunts and growls to shut them up, at which time we all can get some sleep, earplugs in for us in case they start up again.

12 March 2021. Just recently some little pups have appeared, and the number of plump seals languishing on the water-level wooden platforms provided has increased; Rob counted sixty-five the other day splayed out in envious sleep. No wonder the cormorants have escaped.

The other morning, I came up into the cockpit to see a sweet little baby seal beside Zoonie. It was practising snoozing in the water, its own personal soft settee, away from the others to avoid the risk of embarrassment should something go wrong. Its eyes were closed almost all of the time, except on the odd moment it would open them for a peak around to see where it was and that it was safe in the caressing water.

Recently, by chance, I spotted a strange shape underwater just near us that was clearly not a seal. It did not surface and looked like half a fish with its dorsal and pectoral fins right at the back of its body. It was about a metre in length, but these fish can grow to nearly five metres in length. I called Rob up into the cockpit and was thinking, could it be a sunfish? when Rob said, "That's a sunfish!"

A delightful way to end our visit.

Chapter 21

Into the South Atlantic

Let's rock and roll to St Helena

14 March 2021. The day dawned benign with a promise of blue sky and mirror calm water in our sheltered marina. Two yachts left early, Conrad and his crew from Switzerland aboard their 47-foot Hanse and Henk and Marjolein on Jori, but we took a more leisurely approach for the expected fourteen-day voyage to St Helena.

This involved moving most of the contents of the fo'c'sle onto the aft double berth and shoving two sails in their bags under the table in the saloon to level up *Zoonie's* waterline. I moved around her saloon and galley with a critical eye, looking for anything that could come adrift in the inevitable motion that was to come.

The friendly men on their daily wheelie bin round were sorry we were leaving and wished us safe passage. They offered to help with our lines, but I said there was no movement in the water so we'd be just fine. In fact, it was just the kind of berth leaving we like: quiet and just the two of us.

We were ready with ten minutes to the next bridge opening at 9.15 am, so Rob disconnected the electrics after calling Port Control for permission to exit the harbour, and I called the jovial man in the portacabin control room, requesting first the opening of the bastion bridge and then the swing bridge.

Zoonie backed slowly out of her home of the past five weeks as the lone oystercatcher was walking the rocks by the window in the aquarium; I hope they have found him a mate. We were off to catch our next island in *our* Oyster.

Only a few seals were snoozing on their wooden platform after the gas explosion on a small motorboat the day before had sent noisy reverberations through the water that even the most chilled seal couldn't stand. It was quite a bang that had me looking at my watch thinking, that's a bit early for the noon day gun.

"Barb, there's been an explosion. I saw part of a boat fly into the air in a plume of smoke," Rob reported.

Nobody appeared to have been hurt, and miraculously the boat was still floating perfectly as if it had just suffered a slight case of flatulence and nothing more, but it would be a few more hours before all the hungry seals returned.

Young families on both sides of the bastion bridge waved to us as we left, which was really nice: a farewell from strangers, so I wished them well in return and thanked the bridge operator as well.

Noon. As soon as we left the harbour wall the swell and wind became apparent, and by the time we had passed Robben Island the latter started to turn in our favour, while whales surfaced and breached and small groups of jackass penguins swam away from Zoonie, looking over their shoulders at us.

Solitary seals raced through the water quite a few miles from Cape Town, and as we cleared the wind shadow of Table Mountain the wind started rising to a near gale which stayed with us for 24 hours, giving Zoonie a fine send off.

Last night we called up one ship, bringing to the officer's notice our presence in front of him. He was trying to squeeze between us and a longline fishing vessel. He then called the fisherman to ask the length of his line. Six miles was the answer. Our early impression is that the longliners try to fish in parallel line with the regular shipping routes, thus making it relatively easy to pass them. This ship was on a course across the regular shipping route. There were AIS transmitters on the buoy at the end of the line and on the fishing vessel, which made spotting him at night so easy.

16 March 2021. 7.26 pm. At the moment Zoonie is romping along at 5–6 knots in a nice 20-knot trade wind. Let's hope it lasts.

Those dark and moonless nights

A lesson in astronomy: when the twinkling stars were out and Orion, in his celestial glory, was prominent in the sky above *Zoonie's* port bow, we could watch while we appeared to stand still and his realm seemed to turn and descend – an illusion, because it is our beautiful Earth that moves.

Rob and I are thrilled to see luminescence in the water at night and bigger, brighter sparks of light, presumably squid, in Zoonie's foaming bow wash. There are no ships now as we move gently north, just us, a pure white gardenia petal being blown across a pond 4,570 metres deep.

The nights are long, with no hint of dawn until after 7.00 am. The latitude of the sun must be ahead of us, near the equator now, as it slowly brings summer to the northern hemisphere, ready for our return!

In the hours of awake solitude in the cabin at night I use the glow from my mobile phone to write in my notebook. Anything brighter, like the phone torch or headlights, would disturb Rob's sleep, and sleep is precious out here. We have just come through 48 hours, two days and nights, of Zoonie leaping and bounding with the waves, and neither of us slept for long, so there is some catching up to do.

17 March 2021. We flew the Diva in 100% perfect conditions, the sea and clouds following us hand in hand, every blue you could imagine, and just the right blow for her performance lasting for a day and almost through the night before the wind picked up. A front is on its way.

18 March 2021. This morning started off with a miserable monochromatic sunrise and Zoonie rolling, well reefed in the wind of 16–25 knots. We are approaching the Valdivia Seamount and just hope no more of these subterranean volcanoes have risen from Cape Abyssal Plain since our paper chart was produced. The seamounts do not appear on the chart plotter so we are keeping the odd cursory lookout for breaking waves ahead.

Rob is looking forward (!) to giving Zoonie's hull a scrub if it needs it when we are moored off St Helena, because it feels as if something is holding her back, weed or maybe an adverse current.

My happy tummy has let me get on with my editing my book, and blog writing, working for about five hours a day, from before light to

I do love that sail

early afternoon, compared to the Indian Ocean where the awkward water motion would only allow me to type away below for a few minutes before nausea sent me into the cockpit for some fresh air.

19 March 2021. Last night, the wind was a pickle and had us leaping about re-rigging the genoa and its pole and then fretting as to whether we'd done the right thing. So, when the dawn light entered the eastern sky this morning, looking like a silver dagger slicing through the mantle of grey, and welcomed us back on deck to move the pole to the other side, everything felt right in the world of our own out here, 650 miles from the coast of Namibia.

We worked like a well-greased coffee grinder, Rob on the foredeck attaching lines to the pole and me on the side-deck threading said lines through blocks and onto cleats, my toes getting a nice cool wash in seawater as the side-deck dipped into the ocean blue. Then out goes the pole to the horizontal. "Yeah, we got it right again!" I yell to Neptune.

Then it was a rewarding breakfast of bacon butty and scrambled eggs for my winch grinder-in-chief and scrambled eggs and biscuits for me.

Happy living on *Zoonie*

I don't feel old at sea because I am comfortable in the surroundings, both physically and psychologically. *Zoonie*'s confines are room enough for our voyaging, and the constant moving around, up and down and balancing with the motion, keeps us fit. I may not move as quickly as I did (in fact, I have been likened to a camel getting up), but at least we are not limited by the aches and pains of cold and damp weather.

Zoonie gets greener all the time, or so we would like to think. With the Watt&Sea providing 8 amps of power, we can use the accurate electric autopilot instead of Henry the Hydrovane. The autopilot works on the main rudder, giving more muscle and speed to course corrections than Henry, who has his own little rudder and takes much longer to respond, which is problematic if there are big waves shoving *Zoonie* off course in strong winds, where steering accuracy is important.

I remember, one day, we had no wind for a few hours, so the Watt&Sea produced no power; Henry cannot steer without wind, and as we are reluctant to use the engine, we just drifted in blissful peace and it was WONDERFUL, because it didn't last long.

We left the Diva on stage one night and went below to test how long we could make two squares each of plain Aero chocolate last. About as long as a mosquito sneeze.

Rob spotted some Wilson's petrels, sweet little black birds with a snazzy wide white V across their tails. Their numbers are stable and prolific, at least they were fifteen years ago, and let's hope they are still, please, Neptune.

Looking out

During the day I would stand on the saloon seats looking forward over the sprayhood to our watery world speeding by, as *Zoonie* sailed onwards, northbound towards home, but at night the area of the companionway was my lookout post. Standing on the bottom step, clinging on for dear life, I could see to the horizon if it was vaguely visible beneath the moon. Any ships?

Shearwaters and petrels often stayed with us, checking our wake for disturbed fish, which landed on board during the nights.

22 March 2021. Yesterday I went into the fo'c'sle to ready the Diva for her appearance up through the hatch and onto her stage when I was met with a strong smell of fish.

Rob said knowingly, "I reckon it's in the bag," and he was right. As we rummaged through the folds of the Diva's gown, right at the bottom was a very dry dying flying fish (actually it was quite dead but I like the assonance) busy shedding its scales.

This night, that is barely gone, we were keeping a special lookout for Jori as she is just a few miles away from us, and a too-close encounter would be very embarrassing.

At the changeover onto my watch at 5.00 am we snuffed the Diva as the wind was picking up and the genoa was back in business. The Diva, because she is attached with soft ropes and can swing with the wind and waves, always gives Zoonie a smooth ride, like a mother's hand on her baby's cradle, and we have both had a number of very peaceful hours rocked to sleep as a result. It's bliss, how much better one feels riding level on top of the oceanic washing machine.

Just 532 miles to go to St Helena at around 130 miles per day; enjoy the maths.

We had been fortunate enough to see one white-chinned petrel, but we were concerned there was only one as they usually flock together in good numbers to fish. Sadly, they go to where there is longline fishing activity and die by the thousand, day and night.

23 March 2021. The wind has gone light but trustworthy today, so Henry is working with the Diva in a generally northerly direction at 3–4 knots; it's all progress and we are treasuring our last days of ocean sailing. It is a rare breed of people who love deep-sea sailing in short company or in solitude, and we are a part of that breed.

The companionway is open at night, now that we are in the tropics and night-times are as warm as daytimes are hot. So, we are having our meals out there if it is calm enough.

St Helena opens up

Usually when we approach a new destination there are at least two reasons to be happy. For one, the current voyage is nearing its successful end and our planning and tailoring of the journey has proved satisfactory; and second, there is the excitement of exploring a new place. But with St Helena in our sights from early morning on 28 March, we thought we would not be going ashore because of Covid, and that left us with a sad and empty feeling.

But, many people were dying of Covid, and we had survived it thus far, so we couldn't complain.

Light from the full moon outlined the island: a charcoal black modest-sized volcano without its eroded peak with a few lights twinkling near the shore.

As daylight spread its tentative fingers over us, so various shades of magenta materialised and then hints of green amidst the dark rusty rock and one big caldera and a number of smaller ones enclosed by sharp peaks with houses dotted around.

Would St Helena let us in?

We were in no hurry to arrive, to end this way of life. Too early into the North Atlantic and we might come across the remaining winter storms, and as we couldn't expect to explore the island, we'd just be waiting on *Zoonie* for the right time to leave.

So, we slowly motored around the east of the island to the little mooring field where Rob was already with our long-handled mooring device, whose cunning design uses a light heaving line attached to it to pass both sides of a metal loop or ring on the chosen mooring buoy. Then by clicking the closed part of the catch to the other side of the little horseshoe over the ring, Rob was able to retrieve said heaving line to which he had previously tied the mooring line. It's quicker and easier to do than to write about! Hey presto, we were attached.

We handed the device over to Janneke, standing amidships aboard *Anna Caroline*, who arrived a few hours behind us, and she used it to perfect effect. When Henk and Marjolein arrived on *Jori* they used another method by moving alongside their buoy until it was alongside them in the cockpit, where the freeboard is lower and the buoy easier to reach.

Soon after we got in, two gentlemen from Port Authority (one from Portsmouth and the other from Swindon) arrived with the best news. If we were going to stay around a few days then we could have a Covid test on 1 April, and provided the results were negative, we could go ashore, as they were opening their borders again from that date.

We had planned our departure from Cape Town with the hope this might happen, and we knew that they had taken delivery of enough vaccine for the entire population before we began the crossing. But we were still thrilled with the news.

We had four days to prepare *Zoonie* for our next and longest voyage of the entire circumnavigation – around 4,500 miles to the Azores, depending on our course, of course – before we were given the freedom of the island.

30 March 2021. Rob has scrubbed her hull, taking three days, and after he did the keel yesterday was rewarded with fresh baked scones topped with jam and cream for tea. Zoonie was using two litres of diesel per hour even at only 1500 rpm, so a clean bottom will help.

During the passage here, at one point I went up onto the foredeck in

Zoonie moored off Jamestown, St Helena

calm weather and laid down to gather some rays for a few minutes. Rob came up on deck and couldn't see me and had that dreaded, gut-wrenching moment until he spotted my foot idly swinging with Zoonie's roll.

Similarly, when he was scrubbing the hull wearing his snorkel for breathing, I tuned in to hearing him blow out the seawater from his mouthpiece every few seconds and counted how long he was underwater; roughly after 13 seconds down there scrubbing, I would hear him surface and blow out. Then I noticed I hadn't heard it for a while, 20 seconds (then 30, 40 – joking), so I dashed up on deck to see him lying face down and totally motionless in the water.

"ROB!" I yelled, and he rolled over, smiling, lifted his mask and said, "It's OK, hun, I was just looking at the next section."

We both know how it feels to think the other one could be in big trouble.

Will the news be good on April Fools' Day?

We listened to lots of whistles being blown as if youngsters were under the benevolent control of some footy maestro, but they turned out to be the cries of the beautifully elegant white tropicbirds with their long tail feathers. We were also in the company of booby birds, terns and noddies, and five other visiting boats who were also waiting to venture ashore.

1 April 2021. Things are looking good. The bread is rising well and Rob has just tuned in to the BBC World Service. The sun is out and the swell not too bad, at least not as keen as in Vanuatu and Woody Island, South Australia.

So, it is April Fools' Day, and we are sitting on Zoonie's coach roof as the medical team are rolled by the swell in their little wooden ferry boat alongside, and the nurse is offering up our nasal swabs on their little plastic sticks so we can do our own tests. Much better, I found, than wondering just how much further up my nose the lady in Richards Bay was going to push it before it started to affect my thinking. Not wishing to make a fool of myself I carefully and slowly inserted the stick, surprised by how far up it actually did go.

We will get our results this afternoon, but we cannot, in fact, go ashore for another four days, when the little ferry will be running from 4.00 am, mostly to taxi fishermen to their boats, until 7.00 pm and later by request, or so they say. Taking the dinghy ashore from here would not be a safe idea in this ocean mooring field.

Then from the start of next week we can call in to the hospital and get our first free Covid vaccination with a little vaccination passport to show to the authorities in the Azores and Falmouth.

Fingers crossed for our results in five hours!

Chapter 22

St Helena

Around Jamestown

After four days of being moored to the substantial yellow buoy and unable to go ashore, but relishing the ambience, and armed with negative test results, we were more than ready to start exploring our latest island.

3 April 2021. Our perambulations begin at the Jamestown harbour area. Walking across the bridge over the moat, and through the arched town gate, the castle on our left is now used as government accommodation and offices; a group of substantial buildings lie to our right including the two oldest buildings, which are still in use.

Nestling in the pretty Castle Gardens is Anne's Place: a bar/restaurant, immensely popular with yachties, especially, for many years, now run by Anne's daughter Jane. I can see we will patronise the bar many times, as the company and internet there are good.

Further up the hill on the same side and amongst numerous shops is The Consulate Hotel, where a huggable effigy of Napoleon stands on the balcony surveying the scene and looking decidedly peaky in the face. A remarkable place filled with memorabilia and where one could have a very comfortable stay.

Just beyond there the road splits and more shops, pretty painted homes, the bank and a couple more bars plus the market can be found. The town

Napoleon needed cheering up!

is well supplied with shops, but as the growing season is slowing for the very few horticulturalists on the island, fresh produce is only brought into town on a Thursday and distributed between the two supermarkets.

The fish are plentiful around here, as we saw while paddling our inflatable canoe along the cliff edge. A neighbouring sailor recently caught a massive tuna, much bigger than they could eat, so the skipper came around the moorings and gave each yacht a big chunk. We accepted because otherwise it would have gone to waste, and it lasted us nine days.

Six of us walked the long way up the hill to the hospital for our first Covid vaccinations. Shortly after arriving the senior health officer came out and tactfully suggested she would prefer to wait a few days so they could vaccinate everybody on the island first; I sympathised with her sentiments, but after the promise given by the medical team when we were tested, and the long, hot climb up the hill, she was out-voted by some amongst us and we got our jabs.

Immediately afterwards Rob and I walked on up the valley beyond Jamestown in search of the heart-shaped waterfall, which was beautiful. The water flows over an overhang, so it falls through the air as a gossamer mist, feeding the plants all around. We relaxed in the shade on a wooden lookout before making our way back downhill through the very young gumwood plantation – the island's attempt to replace some of the indigenous woodland.

On the way back we joined Henk and Marjolein from *Jori* on the balcony at the Consulate with Boney for lunch and a cool beer.

The ferry boats are interesting, we noticed on our trips ashore. Many of the craft in the small boat mooring field are very old and wooden, including the robust little ferry boats, thick with protective grey paint. The skipper pointed out to me the little craft, still in use, that was used to take Queen Elizabeth II and Prince Phillip ashore for their 1957 visit, and another craft that was over a hundred years old. It looked very much like the traditional Azorean whaling boats, seaworthy little skiffs with a mast and single sail, and it still had the rowlock holes for the oars.

Exile for French emperor Napoleon Bonaparte

There was a typical one-metre swell at the stone wharf, surging up, down and along, shining the rocks and swirling the green weed, as the British ship's sailing tender or pinnace from HMS *Northumberland* approached, containing a small contingent of officers, his secretary and personal servants, and he himself, distinguished prisoner and fallen emperor Napoleon Bonaparte. It was 17 October 1815.

Boney, as he was nicknamed, more from affection and admiration than disrespect, leapt across the watery gap onto the slippery steps as the shadows of the evening grew longer and darker around him.

His prison island awaited him. Since then, those steps have been encased in concrete forming a strong and durable wall, and a series of low concrete stages laid at different levels to try and ease the landing process, but the swell is unchanged in this corner of the bay, sheltered from the wind and tucked beneath the rocky cliff face, topped by James Fort (now The Castle).

7 April 2021. Two hundred and six years later, our little group of visitors arrives on a boat no bigger, and we use the hanging ropes suspended from a bar above the stage to swing across that watery gap.

As we sup the rich, aromatic and famous St Helena coffee at the little café by the dry moat with James, our unofficial guide, I wonder through which small gate Boney had entered the castle to spend his first night in a highly undesirable house for him, because it looked out over the street and folk could peer in through the windows to catch a glimpse of their new, significant visitor. The porch of the little gate can still be seen from Anne's Place looking across the Castle Gardens.

Would St Helena suit this reclusive man? Or, as with his confinement on Elba, did he yearn for his freedom more? How would he fill his time and cope with his isolation?

Boney rode a horse the next morning to inspect lofty Longwood, his future home atop the island, and on his way back down spotted the original green-roofed house of the Balcombe family (demolished in 1947) called The Briars and requested to remain there, in the garden in a folly cottage called the Pavilion, 20 metres from the main house, until Longwood was ready. It was very near the heart-shaped waterfall I mentioned, and for Boney to stroll the shaded banyan tree avenue listening to the birdsong and return to watch the four Balcombe children playing and squabbling in the grounds of the main house was music to his ears after his long campaigns and two gruelling months at sea. (A scene at the end of the film *Napoleon* recounts this agreeable part of his exile.)

The Pavilion is where he was happiest, with its secluded and luscious location amidst people who sympathised with him, and the building can be visited today.

We explore St Helena

Our first stop involved a lengthy climb, winding up narrow roads.

High Knoll Fort was built in 1798, and observers from its ramparts would have spotted ships in the offing 50 miles away. Beneath its robust walls is Donkey Plain, where the hard-working donkeys would rest and graze when they weren't turning the capstan that hauled up goods and equipment via the 699-step Jacob's Ladder from Jamestown.

In 1811 some of the soldiers on duty in the fort dared to mutiny because they wanted more alcohol, and six of the ringleaders were hanged as a result. Today the fort is home to a host of rabbits, six thirsty ghosts and odd human visitors who camp there, maybe on treks around the island. Life for the garrison soldiers on this remote island, so far from home, was often boring and bleak, up there in the clouds with little if any purpose to occupy them, and the suicide rate was high.

After a bracing few minutes soaking up the views, we head off to the governor's residence at Plantation House, in use for the same purpose since before Boney's time, having been built in 1792.

It's a fine Georgian mansion facing the sun's passage and overlooking a generous lawn, kept short and neat by Jonathan, a giant tortoise, who arrived in 1882 (sixty-one years after Boney died), the world's oldest reptile, aged 191, and his entourage of Frederik(a), who was once thought to be a female until she was examined by a vet who had the surprise of HIS long life, and two other reptilian lawn mowers. Beyond the lawn is a vast and carefully tended vegetable garden, and I cannot understand why, with the perfect climate and fertile soil, there aren't many more places for growing fresh vegetables, but at least we came across two on our day out.

Debbie shows us around the ground-floor rooms with great pride. Like Jonathan, she has seen the coming and goings of the governors, working out their four-year terms before moving on, including the first lady governor, Lisa Honan (née Phillips). She talks about the inspired local lad who went away to learn the art of furniture restoration and now has plenty of work in the house and around the island.

Our visit ends with a glass of chilled juice and homemade biscuits and mini samosas, which sets us up well for the drive south over the island to Sandy Bay, where James' parents, coincidentally another Debbie, and Neil, live in the late eighteenth-century mansion house they have restored on Wranghams Estate. Debbie was born and bred in a little house across the valley belonging to her grandmother, and in which relatives still live. Debbie married Neil from England, and they have lived around the world because of Neil's career postings. James was born in Africa and has been back on the island working on conservation projects, taking a day off to be our excellent guide. He will be off again soon, to England with his partner, Jesse, so she can have her baby in Portsmouth, her hometown.

The scenery here is green and abundant with steep hillsides covered in

Debbie's home-grown and -cooked luncheon

small pastures and woodland. Ridges on the hillsides tell of past grazing by sheep and cattle.

Debbie has taken just a few short years to transform the area around the house into a productive garden and even grows coffee beans on a small scale for home use. It tastes mellow and fruity. She is developing the house into a B&B with a separate self-contained unit under construction. (Now completed.)

We are fortunate enough to be invited to one of her special luncheons where the food is all home-grown and -cooked, and the spinach bread is delightfully different.

Coconut milk panna cotta with passionfruit rounds off the culinary experience. Being welcomed as complete strangers into her lovely home and fed with such carefully prepared food is an unexpected and very special experience.

Up amongst the plovers was our next stop, and we had to be very careful where we walked as we looked across the open heathland towards the airport runway. James' passion is wildlife, after Jesse, of course, and he couldn't wait to show us these dainty little birds, St Helena's only remaining endemic species.

They ran away from us, of course, challenging the skills of the best photographers, not including me, but I did manage to get a picture of one's nest with its two eggs, laid on shallow hollows on the open ground, hence having to be careful.

"She'll soon come back to her nest when we move away, and if the eggs are ready to hatch the only way you'll get her off is to lift her!" James explained.

Jesse, who had been driving the other vehicle in our tour, told me how scared she was on her first landing on the island, which is 47 square miles, roughly six by eight miles.

"We were just a few metres above sea level, it seemed, about to touch down, and we still couldn't see any land." The pilots are limited in the times they can circuit the island before landing, or they have to turn back to somewhere in Africa to refuel. The end of the runway drops off the cliff! I'm relieved we came in on *Zoonie*.

Next stop was for a brief look around Longwood atop the island as it was en route and was all we could manage since the house was closed because of Covid.

One can look across directly towards High Knoll Fort and to Diana's Peak (820-ish metres), both being kissed by cool clouds when we were there, and it was easy to see how bleak and exposed was Boney's 'prison', like the West Country moors on a grey day.

We meandered to the gate and a man near the house spotted us and came towards us with his friendly dog, both smiling. "We've just received our Covid test results, and we're all negative. So, if you'd care to come back tomorrow at 11.00 am, you'll be welcome to take a look around the house!"

Well, that was agreed then, and on we drove to our last stop, Boney's tomb in the Sane Valley.

Two of James' colleagues had been waiting in their vehicle to give him the gate key, and we walked a mile or so down a grassy track into the most beautiful valley of flowering plants, ferns and tall trees dripping with moisture.

Boney was entombed here in four coffins, one within the other, made of different materials. In 1840, nineteen years after his death, a distinguished group of Frenchmen arrived to exhume him and take him to his final resting place at Les Invalides on the banks of the Seine in Paris, amidst his beloved French compatriots.

As the final coffin was opened and the remnants of the white veil removed from his face, his near-perfect preservation caused his loyal rescuers to shed yet more tears. The books say his ashes were taken to Paris, but whether 'ashes' is a synonym for 'remains' I am not sure; if not, he must have been cremated on the island.

8 April 2021. For our final and dual-purpose visit to the island we had to do Tarzan and Jane leaps to the shore from the ferry boat clasping the knotted ropes, as the water not only surged between boat and harbour landing but also raced along pushing the two apart; there was no best time to make the leap. But we made it and went off to gather a bounty of food ready for our departure from the island. The produce had been brought fresh from the fertile uplands that morning by the market gardeners. Including butternut squash, big, tasty tomatoes, appropriately French beans, onions, potatoes, beautiful shiny aubergines, carrots and lettuce, all island-grown, but the eggs were as rare as, well, hen's teeth, and we found none. The minibus driver was perfectly happy to carry it on to his vehicle during our visit to Napoleon's exile home.

At last, to Longwood

Boney must have had mixed feelings when, on the morning of 10 December 1815, his small cart was loaded with personal effects and a few goods from his more privileged times: fine Sèvres porcelain, a small library of books and maps, some folding military camp beds and bed linen of the best French quality and, of course, his bathtub, and I am completely with him there. With his entourage of twenty officers, secretary and servants, he made his way from the Pavilion at The Briars, where he had spent a few pleasant months, to the house on the fog-capped hill.

We were politely asked to wander in the gardens for a few minutes until 11.00 am when the door would be opened into the, newly built for Boney, billiard room, effectively the reception room, facing the lawn and painted green outside.

The garden has been lovingly restored to how it was in Boney's time when he wandered along sunken grassy paths. He had them all lowered so the locals outside the walls would not be able to see him. Being a caged lion was enough; he didn't want to be a spectacle as well.

High Knoll Fort was in one direction atop the distant hill, but it was the view from his veranda with its green-painted trellis that provided his best entertainment. He could watch the activities of the various British battalions that were camped there, on the Deadwood Plain, over the years, and always had the best relations with the soldiers. As they came and went many of the soldiers were of the mind they would like to take Boney home with them and set him up in a pretty English country cottage; I think he would have liked that too.

Even more fun were the biannual horse races held on the Deadwood Plain that was once a 1,500-acre endemic gumwood forest before all

The extension to the left contained the billiard room and Napoleon's bedroom

the trees were cut down for firewood. The races were watched by most of the island's inhabitants and gave rise to many horsey stories. One Achille Archambault got himself into a state of inebriation and proceeded to gallop down the track in support of the two Longwood horses, Dolly and Regent. He was whipped soundly by a steward who was unaware he was employed by Boney!

At last, we were allowed into the sacred sanctum of the great man. We stopped at each numbered exhibit to listen to the account through our headphones. These mini talks were excellent, filled with information and given in a light way by various speakers.

Being an intelligent man who liked to make the most of his time, Boney set to writing up the histories of past military campaigns using his books, maps and the conveniently large surface of the billiard table in the first room one enters. His billiard table, two side tables and two big globes, one celestial and the other terrestrial, have recently been restored, and the globes were beautiful.

The next room, another oblong, was his plain bedroom with its small, canopied bed, still there and depicted in the museum photo as his death bed. The other rooms are directly linked from here with no external passage, so it seems he lived in a corridor, which must have felt uncomfortable.

After a testing six years and an attack of painful hiccups, he died in the evening on 5 May 1821 and was taken into the billiard room and laid on the table for the autopsy the next afternoon.

His father died of stomach cancer and so did Boney; maybe it was hereditary and/or lifestyle related. Understandably his consumption of French brandy was not modest, and he did have traces of arsenic in his hair, but then so did many of the French population, since it was used to create the blue colouring in wallpaper, commonly used in France at the time and probably in his system before he arrived on the island.

Our plans, which are always subject to change

We emerged from our fortnight on St Helena equipped with our first Covid vaccination and a negative test result letter: our modern armoury ready for entry to the Azores, around 4,500 miles north depending on our course and, as ever, the direction of the wind and weather. We didn't plan to stop at Ascension Island because the North Atlantic hurricane season started the next month, and we hoped to avoid a detour east to the Cape Verde islands should the wind be kind enough to let us sail a more direct course. This would be our longest passage yet, taking six weeks or so; I wondered what new adventures lay ahead of us!

Chapter 23

North to the Azores

13 April 2021. We are three days out en route to the Azores now, and the winds are light. The Diva is pulling us along with a gentle somnolent motion, and for once we are choosing our route as we go, across the ITCZ (Intertropical Convergence Zone), a band of low pressure near the equator, towards our outgoing track, from the Cape Verdes westwards in 2016.

Zoonie left St Helena in fine style, the island's rugged bijou outline falling quickly behind us into a fine weather mist. Our next waypoint is a watery one on the equator at 24° W, 1,357 miles away.

At night, under starry skies with just a fingernail moon, it is a joy to see the familiar Plough (part of the Ursa Major constellation) on our starboard, while in the same sky the Southern Cross reminds us that we are still in the South Atlantic, just, and getting very near that invisible 'lion' (as I used to picture it when I was a child having misheard the proper word 'line') running around the middle of the Earth.

Rob discovered one night that by shining a light onto the white water at *Zoonie's* midships not only was the luminescence obvious, although far from as bountiful as I have seen it in the past, but also, in the darkness beyond, specks of brilliantly lit creatures were leaping from the sea away from us. Were they krill or some other form of plankton?

We were now in the SE trade winds proper, and they were constant and trustworthy and proved to be so until we got to within 3 degrees of that puffing lion, the equator. This was the weather we had been promised from Cape Town but had eluded us because the summer was in its decline and La Niña was lurking around. So, enjoy it we did.

We spent afternoons sitting in the cockpit, looking to where we had just come from, chatting and reading until 4.00 pm, when the kettle goes on and we have tea and a small piece of cake. Then at 5.00 pm it's sundowners, as you know, and a glass of wine, music and more chat as the sun moves across in front of *Zoonie* and starts its routine descent. During one afternoon a shoal of salmon-sized fish escorted us for more than an hour. A definite blueness on their back suggested they were small tuna, but as they never surfaced, we couldn't be sure; we just felt privileged that they were interested in us.

16 April 2021. Today, on our seventh day at sea, we learned, via our satellite connection to our telecommunication service provider, of the arrival of our second granddaughter, Clara, a sister for her brother Milo, ten years and ten days after Ruby, our first granddaughter. In short, she is beautiful bouncing blonde baby Clara, BBBBC. Described by her lovely mum, Charly, as a gorgeous chunky monkey, she arrived screaming and weighed in at 9 lb 3 oz. Look out, Milo, here she comes! I still think the discovery of radio waves is amazing, and to learn this news via our constant satellite connection from our tiny home in the middle of the Atlantic Ocean is just incredible.

18 April 2021. These are such happy times, and we are heading home! The growing moon assists with our squall watch at night, and we hear terns squawking just outside the cockpit, "You in there? What're you up to?"

During the day there is the occasional mollymawk, sometimes in pairs and most likely to be the yellow-nosed albatross species as they are small, or possibly the black-browed albatross variety. Mean frigatebirds are pinching fish from the flock of terns hunting for their supper. Wilson's storm petrels come into view, and even a lone and lost red-billed tropicbird; "Thataway," I point, towards Ascension Island, the nearest of the remote mid-South Atlantic islands behind us.

It is getting warmer, of course, and we close the curtains against the sun which helps keep the cabin cool, and there is always a nice breeze in the cockpit from the following wind.

Zoonie **follows the Diva before disaster strikes**

Rob does a daily deck check of the rigging and has replaced two shackles that were shedding filings into the scuppers.

A diurnal weather pattern is becoming obvious to us: the wind rising in the morning to around midday and then dropping by late afternoon with a possible drum roll as the sun sets. At first, we would change rig to the poled-out genoa for the windy spells, but by careful experiment we found the Diva is comfortable up to 20 knots of wind, and the motion she provides is so much more comfortable than the more durable but confined genoa. Where the Diva leads, Zoonie willingly follows.

Headlong into disaster, and it's my fault!

19 April 2021. We had a nasty squall just before the ITCZ at just after midnight when I was on watch. It crept over us from ahead, while I had been checking the sky astern, so it caught me unawares. Suddenly the wind rose to 24 knots, and I dashed below to get Rob up so we could snuff the Diva.

As I made my way up the companionway steps again Zoonie went into a broach, heeling right over; I was walking up the inside edge of the companionway ladder! Her coaming, the raised surround of the central cockpit, now on its side, prevented water coming in, but even so this was a dose of what we have always dreaded.

Grasping rails as she spun back upright, we clambered forward. Rob hauled down the snuffer bag, which was at the top of the mast having previously been raised to let the sail fly. But it was too easy, because there was nothing in it, just the side tapes that the Diva's fabric had been sewn into. The Diva was no longer flying from the masthead; instead, her gorgeous blue gown was dragging alongside Zoonie's hull, and by now it was pouring with rain, making the shining material heavy, pushing it down into the sea. At least, as the sail fabric was still attached to the clew and tack, we weren't going to lose it.

Instinctively, neither of us went to turn on the engine because of the risk of trailing sheets getting around the prop, and by this time the wind had passed, and we just had the rain to soak and cool us while we dragged the masses of sailcloth safely onto the side-deck ready to bag it. For the rest of the night, we sloped along with the genoa poled out and I felt decidedly annoyed with myself, but I was relieved, in a sense, that it didn't happen on Rob's watch so he'd have had to deal with the emotions.

I was scrolling through one of the instruments a couple of days later and discovered that the daemon gust that blew out our Diva maxed out at 29.2 knots and was the only gust of that strength we'd had since leaving St Helena.

21 April 2021. Rob and I worked like a pair of Trojans along with the hand sewing machine; Rob used his hot knife to seal all the edges, and we were blessed with the calm of the Doldrums (who'd ever think I'd be praising them) for one and a half days to get the mammoth task done. Zoonie crossed the equator as the sewing machine whirred through the acres of the Diva's gown. I was not going to let that gust get in the way of the Diva's future career, and now she is back in her bag, all repaired and ready to go once more.

22 April 2021. We thought we'd try her out today, but now the NE trade winds are starting to set in so the wind direction will be all wrong for her.

We learned a few things from that experience:

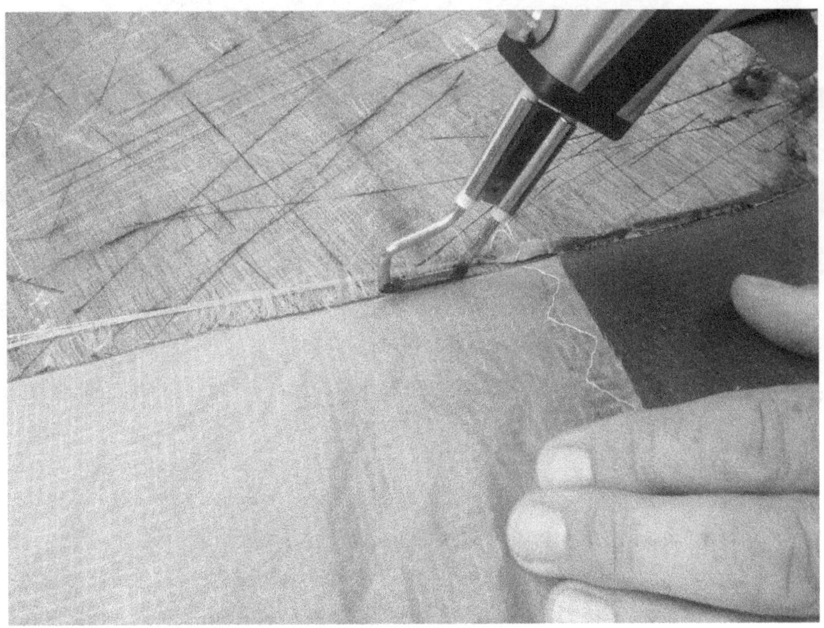

Rob heat seals the Diva's edges before taping and sewing

1   In a changing weather pattern: beware, as we found the squalls came at us from all directions. I don't need to tell you sailors that, do I!

2   Reset the max wind tolerance for the Diva to 19 knots, not because she might split again in higher winds but because she might not, and *Zoonie's* broach could be even worse.

3   The repairs were easy because the Diva's construction and fabric are very light and we were able to use the fabric left in her side tapes to repair the splits, rather like taking a skin graft from another part of the human body because it is the same type. Having a hand-operated sewing machine on board proved its worth yet again.

Approaching halfway

23 April 2021. Equator day was on 21 April, and to mark the occasion Zoonie did an involuntary turn under autopilot, due, perhaps, to the growing electrical activity to be encountered in this atmospherically volatile area. She has done two more since: veering and backing 70 degrees each way in an elegant serpentine manoeuvre when she just didn't know which way to turn. I know the feeling. Or maybe she was happy like us.

There has been plenty of thunder and some sheet lightning in the squalls, so retrieval of our devices for our use has been from the oven and microwave, our Faraday cages. To be honest, we were too busy on the day, heat sealing all the Diva's fraying edges, to think about having moved back into the northern hemisphere and North Atlantic for the first time since 25 March 2016; however, now we are approaching our outward passage from the Cape Verdes to Guadeloupe, at which point, in about eleven days' time, we definitely will celebrate.

24 April 2021. The ITCZ is like a box of chocolates: you never quite know what you are going to get. We have been crossing this area, known as the doldrums, either side of the equator and reaching from Africa to Brazil, now for four days and have had to motor most of the way because of lack of wind.

The area changes in width at different times of the year, and for us it will have been 300–400 miles wide.

The cloud formations in the ITCZ have been spectacular. Many clouds shapes, heights and colours all at one time and some developing into wet squalls.

The day before yesterday we grabbed the body wash and rushed to the foredeck for a wonderful rain shower in cool fresh water. It was bliss and lots of fun too.

Yesterday I was standing on the fourth step of the companionway, watching the rain and waiting for the bread dough to rise, not long in the 37°C cabin heat, when I thought we could have a second rainwater shower on the foredeck. So, we stripped off our singular items of clothing and, clasping the body wash, off we went again. All lathered up and ready for the rinse… guess what happened next. Well, nothing. It stopped raining! Two sudsy souls made their way back to the cockpit for a rinse off below.

We know we're in the North Atlantic because there is sargassum weed all around us and the Watt&Sea hydrogenerator cannot work because it clogs up.

In another four days we will be out of the path of nascent hurricanes, which can start forming from early May, so that will be a relief. Yesterday I asked Neptune for some sailing winds for our three yachts, and he has tentatively obliged; now we are creeping north at around 4 knots in the very start of the NE trades.

29 April 2021. Ship's log reads 'All good, 12° 20'31"N 30° 56'71"W @ 05.43 am = ½ WAY!' As if to celebrate with us, a delightful small black whale came alongside the cockpit in the evening, either a pigmy right or northern minke, so close I think he touched us as they sometimes do, and the odd tern and petrel come to see us. Luminescence at night sparkles in Zoonie's wash, and we cherish each lovely sailing day as they move seamlessly into our past.

Outrunning the sun

As we three yachts, *Jori* ahead and *Anna Caroline* behind, came through the ITCZ, I wondered if we had gone through a time warp: no ships, no planes, no vapour trails, no news, just almost daily chats with the other two yachts. Was the world still in lockdown? Or would we arrive in Horta, on the island of Faial, to see people on horseback and donkeys carrying burdens?

Later there was a ship bound eastwards for Gibraltar and another westwards, so that answers that question.

30 April 2021. Wietze on Anna Caroline alerted us to the cosmic fact we were chasing the sun, as it appears to move north for the northern hemisphere summer; in fact, the Earth is tilting south, which gives the same effect. The rate at which it does so is about 19.2 miles per day, from my astro tables, i.e. 0.8 miles per hour, one sixth of our speed, so we would at some point pass it, and that happened two nights ago at 8.02 pm. It was noticeable yesterday as we sat in the cockpit with the sun now clearly transiting behind us. It will be good for the solar panels, all mounted at the stern.

2 May 2021. So, we have already had cause to celebrate halfway with some nice mango, orange and lychee juice with a little addition, and tomorrow being Rob's birthday there will be more inventive ideas to 'push the boat out'. Then a few days on we will hopefully meet our two-thirds point, after which all attention will be on our destination.

Rob has requested a cream tea followed by veggie stroganoff for his birthday fayre, and I am onto baking bread and pizzas again today plus the scones.

We have finished all the salad veg and fresh fruit now, leaving just five bags of carrots (not quite sure what happened there), a white cabbage, sweet and white potatoes, onions and spring onions and a butternut squash.

Milestones and celebrations

As if that excitement was not enough, at 1.33 am this morning we crossed, under full sail, our outward track from the Cape Verdes to Guadeloupe on 4 January 2016 at 32° 55' 03" W and thus, by covering 35,584 miles, we have completed our oceanic circumnavigation in 391 days at sea. Of course, there will be another circumnavigation completed when we get back to English shores, but Guinness World Records purists would say we are not done until we reach Plymouth, our port of departure. However, a concluding pint of beer in the Chain Locker at Falmouth will do us fine.

After emerging from the ITCZ at around 3° N (180 miles, depending on the season), the sailing was all thanks to the NE trade winds that were blowing at 11–20 knots, constantly from the same trustworthy direction, which was, in fact, bending our course favourably towards the Azores. That's what Henry the Hydrovane does: he keeps us at a constant angle to the wind, so as the wind veers clockwise, so do we.

The autopilot had a rest as we sailed away from the equator, so the electricity produced by the Watt&Sea hydrogenator, the solar panels and the wind charger was sufficient to charge the batteries to 100% and keep the fridge and computer going, sargassum weed allowing and provided we were doing more than 5 knots' speed through the water. Carbon-free power! We only needed to run the engine to keep her on course while rig changing or to make water. In fact, apart from a one-and-a-half-hour water top up, we didn't used the engine for eight days.

Zoonie is sporting an off-the-shoulder look at the moment on a comfortable course 60–80 degrees from the wind. We haven't sailed this close to the wind for a long time, maybe years. Her full main and genoa pulling us along has felt like quite a novelty.

I read in my current notes of the recent gentle sailing and the warm winds; well, things are a little livelier and cooler at night now, and Zoonie is well reefed, bringing her more upright and, in fact, faster than when she is burdened with too much canvas and heeling on her ears, a state of affairs that is always short-lived.

I emerged into the cockpit pre-dawn the other morning looking astern to a coral/grey twilight sky on our left and a world lit by the banana yellow full moon on the right.

My morning routine

A mug of Milo always helped me get ready to write in the mornings; there's nothing like a nice cup of hot chocolate at that time of day.

I would start by going aft to collect the laptop from its safe home, tucked down beside all the 'goods' on the aft berth. Then I'd lock it to the saloon table with two clamps so it wouldn't take off when *Zoonie* did one of her long drops off a swell. I finished, with Rob's help, the definitions for the glossary (bow: 1 front or pointy end of vessel; 2 crew hair decoration) of my book about the first half of our circumnavigation, and then I'd be back on compiling and editing the blogs for my WordPress website so I could upload them, I hoped, in Horta.

Then there's writing and replying to emails and downloading three weather files, and by the time all that was done lunchtime would loom. Rob would see to that meal and sometimes breakfast too if my nose was to the grindstone.

I have just put in the fridge the night-time batch of vanilla yogurt. Last evening I didn't know if it would set with all this motion, so I sat it on the gimballed stove and that did the trick.

The Diva's triumphant return

The moon, like us, is a little tired as it rises later every morning, leaving the stars to fill the night sky with their silver light.

4 May 2021. Rob did have a good birthday, starting with a special on-board delivery card, followed by lots of emails from family and friends. He was excused from his washing up duties, as a special treat. In the afternoon, while we tucked in to our modest cream tea, we marvelled at the cloud formations: stacks of lenticular clouds like human rib cages, puffy summer day clouds and more threatening towering grey/white cumulus clouds all around the horizon. Every day is a birthday out here!

The weather was on the change again. We were moving towards the other side of the lovely constant NE trades, to where squalls warned of a change, along with worrying calms that necessitated hours of diesel-sapping engine time, which led to concern over whether the fuel would last. At least this was balanced by the knowledge we were covering the ocean miles in the right direction.

Then, when we had to use the autopilot, because the engine was on, it played up once more by taking us many degrees off course. We discovered that under the fixed bearing mode it was fine, only the 'go to waypoint' mode was affected.

At 11.00 am on 5 May we left the tropics at 23° N and a red-billed tropicbird came and flew around us as if to say "come back soon". We started to need more clothing and a blanket at night. Horta is on latitude 38°, so it was quite a way to go yet.

6 May 2021. At last, the wind is around 6 knots and coming from behind us, so we tentatively hoisted the Diva this afternoon, our caches of confidence needing a boosting, and she delivered in style. She might be a little saggy in places due to stretched fabric, I thought, as Rob hoisted her snuffer bag, but then so are we both and it doesn't make us any less lovable! Or useful, for that matter.

The only obvious sign of repair is the uneven line across the pale blue fabric just below the head. I can't tell you how elating it was to know she would yet give us many more relaxed and efficient miles of travel.

Now she is back in her bag, safe and sound, and we are determined to put her back up first thing tomorrow.

Later…

The weather is beautiful — blue skies and that wonderful mid-Atlantic blue ocean with the sun penetrating just the top few metres — but there is little life. Just the occasional bird and no fish or bigger creatures, instead lots and lots of sargassum weed. Rob has given up on picking it off the Watt&Sea prop because as soon as he stands to return to the cockpit,

Apart from the 'scar' at the top, the Diva is back on form

the next pom-pom of weed grabs hold.

We sit under the bimini, and like meerkats, we are watching all around for signs of animal life and doing the calculations on when, in engine hours, we should reach the southern limit of the SW trades (the same winds as the NE trades but on the other side of the circle.) The GRIB weather files, for a number of days, suggest from 30° N the trades should give us a straight run across them to Horta. We'll see.

By our calculations we knew we needed to turn off the engine before the gauge reached 3,442 engine hours to retain just a little fuel for entry into Horta. Our estimates were conservative, and we factored in the current that had been against us at a rate of 0.5–1 knots since the outset, reducing her speed to 4.6 miles, instead of 5 miles, for every 1.5 litres at 1500 revs. So, as you can imagine, this last quarter of the voyage did not have the same lack of stress as the first three quarters.

Ironically, *Anna Caroline* had been experiencing strong winds up to 30 knots where we had perfect trade winds, and *Jori* has sailed, for most of the time, a little further east than us.

Out of internet

9 May 2021. A couple of days ago I was trying to download the weather GRIBs and the third of three just would not come. When Rob checked our data supply, he found we had used all our valuable minutes. The length of the passage and downloading three weather files daily had taken its toll. We could neither receive nor send mail. This was a matter that needed to be resolved quickly before our family would be worried, and we could not keep an eye on the weather.

By way of distraction, I went and put the kettle on and set a load of towels washing in one of the big white buckets; after all, we had plenty of hot water and our motion through the water would soon dry them hanging beneath the bimini. Poking the towels around in the bubbly water, I realised we would need to call up a ship and ask if they would be kind enough to forward three emails. So, Rob and I sat down, and I wrote out three email addresses and two different messages: one to our providers, MailASail, and the other to Emily, and Henk and Marjolein on *Jori*. Next, we waited, watching the chart plotter screen to see who we could ask to be our sender.

Aha! The Federal Crimson — a cargo ship bound for Takoradi in Ghana, she'll do. She will pass closest to us in ten minutes, this being a half-hour after I first spotted her, and our VHF would easily reach that far out here with no obstructions.

Vince was on watch and firstly took our position and asked if we were in need of anything. I confirmed we didn't need to be rescued but asked if he could do us a favour. I explained what we needed, and he confirmed with the master that he could do this. Then a few minutes of fun ensued with me dragging the phonetic alphabet from my memory to help him write the emails his end. He read them all back, said he would send them straight away and would call us back when he was done.

Message to MailASail:

Run out of airtime on satphone. Please top up with usual amount and reinstate urgently.

Message to Emily and *Jori*:

We are fine on *Zoonie*. No internet, so may not be in touch until arrive in Horta 14/15 May. This being sent through a ship's internet.

We had turned the engine off for this procedure so I could hear and think, so when we were through it went back on again. A few minutes later Vince came back to confirm the messages had gone, and when I thanked him profusely, he just said, "Any time. Safe journey." The kindness of strangers!

That lifted our spirits and distracted us from the fuel issue for a while.

The next morning Rob checked the internet and Sue at MailASail had done her stuff, and we had another 600 minutes to use; so, I emailed Vince and let him know.

10 May 2021. That was yesterday morning, and at around 8.00 am a breeze came along, like a shy child brought before a maiden aunt, which we could use if only it would persist. It faded again, back through the doorway, maybe to build its confidence, and then a few minutes later it returned and stayed, so after 69 hours of motoring we were sailing again, albeit not directly on course. Hang in there, shy child.

Rob thinks we have enough fuel anyway, but I will not be happy until we have done 200 more miles under sail. As I type, we have done 54, so fingers crossed this wind continues. 587 miles to go.

How the trade winds spoil us

We found ourselves sailing directly towards Madeira, and Gibraltar, beyond, while we wanted to head north to Horta, so you can imagine our frustration, but we were moving north slowly in a lateral sort of way, and it was better than using the motor, so we persisted, like the squalls.

During the night of 10 May we tacked again and *Zoonie* headed much closer to Horta. What is more, we had done more than 100 of the 200 miles that was our comfort zone for the remaining fuel.

We learned that one of *Jori*'s jib seams had opened, so they were using their storm sail instead, which was slowing down their progress.

The weather was beautiful and still warm as we sat in the cockpit watching the long swells, 30 metres or so between them, pass southward, and *Zoonie* would rise high on one, maybe three metres up in the air, and we'd look down into the smooth watery valleys from our lofty viewpoint until we sank gracefully downwards. Looking out over the vast miles of water our minds wandered like the lonely Cory's shearwaters that had become our new companions.

Never before had we studied the engine hours slowly rising in relation to the increasing latitude quite so closely: 36° N before 3,443 hours, please?

In the meantime, I occupied myself chopping vegetables and allowing my mind to become absorbed in one of my writing projects: blogs ready for uploading, and the book which was then ready to go back to my editor, Rachel.

A sight for tired eyes was the Diva flying high and full of confidence, and true to the weather prediction, her morning performance ended at 3.55 pm and the poled-out genoa and reefed main set to work and got us our 200 miles just a few miles out from Horta; what a team.

Our harmonious marriage with the elements, away from all the influences of humankind, was coming to an end, and we were emotionally digging our heels in. We liked the ocean, our guide and leader, us its humble servants, and we were not at all sure we wanted the trials and trivialities of land life back again quite yet.

14 May 2021. Five-plus knots' speed and 87 miles to go, and we're enjoying our last sundowners at sea for a while. We're nearly there!

Azores, ahoy!

15 May 2021. My duty watch started at 5.00 am, and I wasn't surprised to not be able to see Ponta do Pico, the beautiful clean peak on the island of the same name, as it snuggled beneath its white quilt. Flocks of Cory's shearwaters were with us now, and a big pod of fishing dolphins, speeding across us, paying scant attention to the copper-painted whale in their path.

Just five miles off and a tiny slither of the slope either side of Pico peeped out from beneath its white cloud hat to say "hi", and the faint green hillsides of Faial, where we were heading, showed through the dismal grey.

As we turned into the harbour an orange RIB came along and waved us to an anchoring spot. After 4,107 miles and thirty-six days, we arrived. The wind and sails had worked their alchemy to get us in with 12 inches left in the fuel tank, around 120 litres, enough for another two and a half days' motoring. It was good to be back in this pretty harbour once more with its pastel buildings beneath their terracotta roofs, after the longest non-stop voyage of our entire circumnavigation.

Chapter 24

The Lovely Azores

After two days on board during strong winds and lots of rain, we were ready for a nice walk ashore. But first we had to tend to *Zoonie's* mooring. Our efforts to anchor had failed, so we had picked up a suspect buoy. Then, on a beautiful Sunday morning, we were both below on our tasks when a French voice called, "Allo, allo!" *Zoonie* was having a nice chat to a French yacht in close proximity.

Having held us superbly in all the tugging and pulling of the blow, the shackle pin decided to exit the shackle attaching the mooring line to the sinker on the seabed and release *Zoonie* to the whims of wind and tide.

I started the engine and took the wheel while Rob hauled in the slippery mass from the water and kept it on deck as we moved to one of the last two buoys in the harbour, which we hoped would hold us secure for our planned week-long stay.

The whalers' tale

Our legs loved the exercise through the charming town, and we wandered back along the beach for lunch at Peter Café Sport.

After lunch, we were shown around the world-famous scrimshaw museum above the bar by a charming young lady, who loved her job and missed the normally numerous visitors, vastly reduced during the Covid times.

The whalers used to be paid in whales' teeth and money from the whale oil, which would be divided amongst the boat crews when the payment arrived one year after catching the whale, the harpoon man getting the lion's share. This meant the whalers were always poor and waiting for what was owed.

First generation resident José Azevedo, who had a craft stall in the town centre, made it his business to keep the whalers in food and funds in the months they waited for their pay. He is remembered for posterity, depicted on the right-hand side of a whale tooth scrimshaw carving, wearing glasses, and his son, whose nature was equally hospitable, is to the left. Today's proprietor of the bar is another José Azevedo, the namesake of his great-grandfather.

Our José's father was Henrique Azevedo, and during WWII he served on the *Lusitania*. Because the commander of the ship thought he resembled his own son, Peter, he gave Henrique that name, and hence the name Peter Café Sport. The 'Sport' epithet coming from the fact Henrique loved sport.

The hospitality the generations of Azevedo men offered was extended to the crews of the early trading ships, the whalers, as mentioned, the crews of the telecommunications cable-laying ships and, of course, present days crews of pleasure sailing craft like us. A visit to Horta doesn't qualify until one pays a visit to Peter Café Sport!

Whaling finished in 1985, but since then hordes of whales' teeth have been found in the homes of whalers after they have died, and on clearing their homes, their families have donated them to the scrimshaw museum, ready for the contemporary artists' sharp scalpels.

The process of creating the engraved pictures is similar to enamelling. The bone is covered with ink (burnt whale oil in days of old) and then the picture is carved into the bone and revealed as white within the black. Ink is applied to fill the freshly carved scratches, then the original surface layer of ink is removed, leaving the black in the lines of the picture. A crude description for some beautifully fine work. The sculpting is done with great care to create objects ranging from miniature decanters and goblets to model ships and jewellery, to name just a few.

A fine Azorean whaling boat being put through its paces

I love immersing myself in the social history of places. I felt for the whalers, who were not able to prosper from their salary of teeth and instead lived lives filled with certain danger and insecure poverty. Their tough lives seemed to be in stark contrast to the beauty of the whaling boats they spent much of their time within.

On the eve of our much-anticipated day tour around the island, fine replica whaling boats were out racing each other in a brisk wind: a heartwarming tribute to the ancestors of the crews.

In 2005, I was in Horta on the *Stavros S Niarchos*, one of the Tall Ships Youth Trust training brigs, in my role as watch leader, and most of our trainee crew on that voyage were the local Sea Scouts. We were invited to compete against the other watches in rowing races on these same boats, and it was both a privilege and lots of fun to be the cox in one of the beautiful craft, steering our crew to a small victory. At the end of the voyage my watch gave me a beautiful wooden model of one such boat, complete with sails, oars and harpoon, and I treasure it to this day.

A day out with Leandro

The day of our excursion dawned amidst magnificent calm blue, one of the best days yet, and we met with Leandro, our guide, just before 9.00 am.

On the map, Horta is on the bottom right of the island, and we were driving in an anticlockwise direction for the day, except for the very first part that took us to a walk up the steep and pretty path to the top of Monte Queimado, with its array of colourful flowers, and down the other side, across the peninsular, where the first underwater telecommunications cable between Europe and the US was laid in 1893, and onto the lookout at volcanic Monte da Guia to view the beautiful double caldera, which we found is out of bounds to humans for the sanctity of the wildlife there. There were once vineyards here and some vines were still growing unattended within the walls of the lookout.

Then northwards we climbed, up to the Ponta da Espalamaca, to the high viewpoint beside one of the many windmills on the island, mostly now abandoned, and superseded by modern, towering wind turbines that produce 22% of the island's electricity.

We left tarmac roads for the red ochre colour of the dirt track upwards to the heart of the island: the Caldeira do Faial. The beautiful and quiet caldera, with its many hues of green and over 30% of the island's endemic flora, used to have much more water in it, but a small crack appeared during an earthquake and the water drained away. The caldera is 400,000 years old and has formed in active stages during that time. It is two kilometres in diameter and the highest point of the rim is 1,040 metres. Many people were happily walking the rim in the clear, warm weather; another time, maybe, for us.

After a few minutes admiring the silent majesty of this central basin, we descended the track once more, leaving above us the white clouds that had masked the peak of Pico on our way in, and headed for the viewpoint overlooking the fajã at Ribeira das Cabras, where the view to the north-east coast takes in the Capelinhos volcano. This flat (fajã) area, created by lava flows hissing and cooling on contact with the sea, is the youngest part of the island, formed in the last 10,000 years.

The Capelinhos volcanic eruption

Leandro drove us down the road to the viewpoint and lighthouse, past what was once the whalers' village; all that is left now after the 1957–58 eruption is the roof tops.

Down at the slipway there were three types of boats. Small rowing boats were in the foreground, behind which were long, elegant skiffs, the whalers' boats, with their oars and sails wrapped around the spars lying on the seats. Moored in the water were the longer motorised craft once used to tow the whales around to the whaling factory in Horta.

The first major seismic event on this island in modern times was back in the seventeenth century; then on 27 September 1957, when I was a fresh five-year-old with pigtails, the whalers set off towards the sight of some bubbles bursting on the sea surface they thought was a whale one kilometre offshore. As they approached, the heat and smell told them this was an eruption, so they turned about face and sped back to raise the alarm.

The undersea Surtseyan eruption lasted for seven and a half months, with sporadic massive explosions as the lava sped upwards through the water, detonating jets of black ash high into the sky and forming three islands, the first two of which were short-lived.

In May 1958 the eruption moved location and became a terrestrial eruption, maximising itself when pyroclastic clouds of ash, lapilli (rock fragments), bombs (shaped into rounds and ovals on contact with water), blocks and splatter projectiles shot high into the sky. This may well have been when the buildings to the north were buried. Imagine how terrifying that must have been, the noise, the stink and the likelihood of being consumed in the unimaginable heat.

A local hero emerged

The Capelinhos lighthouse keeper on duty at the time was the very talented Tomás Pacheco da Rosa, and he acted not only with great bravery but also with a sense of posterity. He grabbed a coin, pushed it into a slurp of molten lava and cooled it off in the sea, presumably using a shovel or something similar: a unique souvenir.

After the seismic activity settled down and nearly half the population had left for the USA, thanks to the help of senator John F. Kennedy and Rhode Island Representative John O. Pastore, Tomás was integral in the development of music on the island, the church choir and a philharmonic society, to encourage natives to stay and rebuild their culture.

I remember the lighthouse buildings being half buried in volcanic ash and only being allowed to walk around the outside of the buildings when I was here aboard the *Stavvy*. Today a visit to the museum, built since then, is a must because the concept of its design is extraordinary. The area in front of the buildings was excavated down to the level of the original floors, with subterranean display areas and corridors that emerge into the ground floor of the old living area. Then the ash was replaced so the buildings are once again buried, on the outside, to the original height, thus preserving the post-eruption impression of the place. Clever stuff.

Wandering around inside the living quarters of the lighthouse was fun, but when I asked if one could climb the tower these days,

Smiling Leandro and Rob on the ammonite staircase

Leandro's positive reply was a mini revelation. One hundred and forty-odd steps and lots of shiny stainless steel later, we emerged into the new glass cupola with panoramic views over the area.

I liked the way the spiral staircase looked like the inside of an ammonite shell.

Back in Horta and a gift for José Azevedo

It seemed appropriate to call into Peter Café Sport for a coffee so we could ask permission to add a posh, unused red ensign from *Zoonie* to the vast collection already pinned to the wall and ceiling.

"Are you José?" I asked as a familiar face leaned over a shelf behind the counter to retrieve something.

"I am indeed." And our conversation continued as he swapped our ensign for a flag showing the whale symbol and reef knot on blue, which is his café's flag and now adorns *Zoonie*'s mast in the saloon, as you can well imagine!

He has a son working full time with him, so the fourth-generation

With José in his Peter Café Sport

tradition of the business is ensured, and his other grown children help out when they can. I mentioned being a watch leader here on the tall ships with members of the Sea Scouts as my watch crew, and he told us how the organiser of the Sea Scouts, Luís Machado, was here only a couple of weeks ago having lunch with him.

Some of our crew referred affectionately to Luís, who was cruising on the brig with us back then, as 'Mr Click' as he was forever taking photos, more even than me! He is now organising the GPS locator side of hiking trails to make the hiking experience on the islands safer. José stamped our passports with the café stamp, and this was very special to us, to know that the history of the family Azevedo hospitality in Horta continues to all and sundry in these changing times.

As Rob went to pay, José said, "No need, it was my pleasure."

Our champagne moment

24 May 2021. Those aboard Jori, Anna Caroline and Zoonie, having travelled up the spine of the South and North Atlantic in close company, celebrated our joint arrival in Horta and our impending separate departures aboard Jori, with three bottles of bubbly, a bottle of wine and a bottle of gin; well, of course, Henk and Marjolein have to empty their booze cupboard as they are flying home soon, so we were helping them!

Chapter 25

Our Final Passage to Falmouth

Ships that pass in the night

9 June 2021. It is 5.20 am, the twelfth birthday of our oldest grandson, Henry, and it is a dismal grey day. For three days now we have been running towards Falmouth before the generous SW trade wind, an uneasy confluence of fast-moving air above the high, and, beneath, a powerful low moving eastward, to our north. Naturally, where the winds of a high and those of a low meet and run together there is a mixing of temperatures, resulting in… FOG – cloud at ground level.

In the fog the only evidence we had of the ships that were passing in both directions in front of and behind us, day and night, were the pale blue shapes creeping across the chart plotter screen revealing themselves by name through the AIS data. They were becoming more numerous as we moved towards the Channel, and one night we had a vessel that defied all my sailing experience.

It was a worryingly fast-moving craft travelling at 27 knots, due to pass less than two miles ahead of us, by calculation or coincidence we were not sure.

Flagged on the AIS as a pleasure craft, the name *Argo MOD70* would suggest otherwise (Ministry of Defence), but what had me foxed were her dimensions: 79-foot length, 79-foot beam and no entry for her draught. Was she a catamaran? Or was the 79 feet a measurement of diameter and we were dealing with a UFO using close proximity to the water surface for her passage-making, like a hurricane? How close would she come?

Google since has revealed *Argo* is an American-owned MOD 70 trimaran racing yacht, which has been winning races since 2012. But did she see us as she sped by on her foils? We will never know, and if she didn't, it could have been a catastrophic collision, the thought of which will haunt me always!

Journey's end approaches

The wind is a constant 15–22 knots, so too much for the Diva, who sits waiting in her yellow dressing room bag on the foredeck. The sea state is strangely benign, carrying us along with only the occasional roll. No more jellyfish, but we did see one whale spout in the distance yesterday when the fog lifted for a few hours. Also, a Wilson's petrel came to say "hello", and Rob identified a solitary laughing gull from our avian treasure book Seabirds of the World.

For a number of nights now the lack of any visible stars because of the fog has been more than made up for with the fabulous luminescence, such as we have not seen for a long time. Reaching as far from Zoonie as the limited visibility allows, ragged and random patches of sea appear to be lit to a brilliant white by underwater lighting.

By way of a distraction from thinking about the end of our circumnavigation, one afternoon we decided to try a game of Scrabble, but how to stop the letters slipping off the board as *Zoonie* rolled? Easy, a non-slip mat laid on top of the board did the trick. Importantly, we could still see the extra score squares through the holes in the mat. That's got to be worth a small reward on the 'sailors' initiative' page of *Practical Boat Owner*, hasn't it? 'Tested on the Azores High swell.'

We were on countdown to a land life again after six years and two days, if we arrived when we predicted. There is no next long passage to look forward to. Trans-ocean sailing was for us down to three more days after the 416 we had lived. We knew we would miss it, and the fabulous way of life it encapsulated, but then we are not selling *Zoonie*, and we enjoyed tentatively forming future plans for cruising

Scrabble on the Azores High swell

the coast of the UK the next summer. However, I can well understand the folk who go round again and the few who just keep going around; one British chap in St Helena in his green steel boat was on his seventeenth circumnavigation. Think I'd be a bit bored by then.

But worry not, if, indeed, you were at all worried; we would certainly do it again if we were much younger, but now it's time for home and grandchildren!

In our tunnel of fog

We could barely see 20 metres from *Zoonie* as we continued along our private little fog tunnel. Thank goodness for the radar and chart plotter for a visual on nearby and approaching ships. I called up a 958-foot *Maersk* leviathan at 12 miles distant, since she was going to pass us by a matter of metres – too close for my comfort. She altered course five miles away from us and left just over a mile between us, engines thumping and foghorn blaring as she sped onward towards Panama, totally invisible from the cockpit, lost in the fog.

On the ninth day of our short voyage from Horta we were closing the continental shelf and the 1,000-metre contour line, and within less than three hours the depth dropped to 500 metres and then 200 metres: positively shallow after the abyssal plains of the oceans, well over 6,000 metres down in places. Outside the colour of the shallow sea under the grey sky was a diesel wash. Rob moved the cursor of the chart plotter onto the Lizard waypoint 163 miles away.

The next day RV *Celtic Explorer*, a research vessel, appeared on the screen during my 5.00–8.00 am watch, and I thought, what an excellent title for a book, *Destination Explorer*.

As many as four ships were around us at any one time – cargo carriers, fishing boats, a research vessel, tankers, laden ships – and by bringing up their red direction lines on the plotter screen we could instantly see if we were on a collision course with them. It was still foggy and I listened to the distant fog horns from the dripping companionway looking into the gloom around us.

11 June 2021. It's mid-morning on our last full day at sea. The sky is starting to reveal its true colour in elusive patches, and the wind is dropping, so soon we must start the engine because we need to be able to move out of the way of ships approaching the separation lanes around Land's End: Journey's End.

Home, ahoy!

---

12 June 2021. The fog has cleared entirely and there ahead is the low-lying Lizard peninsula. But we cannot spend much time relishing our surroundings because we are busy pot-watching. The strongly ebbing tide sometimes pulls the red buoys under the water so they are hard to see, but the fact they are laid in lines helps us to predict where they might be. We mustn't be caught out by a local lobster pot at this late stage.

A warship passes and a handful of fellow sailors are out on the briny.

Then almost too soon Mark at Port Pendennis Marina took our lines, and with *Zoonie* safely moored, we were chatting to the locals and mingling with mindful visitors, supping tasty ale. Finally, back on *Zoonie*, the Red Arrows flew overhead to acknowledge our return, really part of the high-profile G7 summit celebrations, but we could pretend. A modest homecoming amongst all the hustle of the international political gathering nearby.

Our long journey was finally complete.

Epilogue

Zoonie started her transition from her marina berth to Freeman's Wharf Boatyard just before high water on 14 June under sunny skies and in the path of elves, baby eels, that we saw thriving in their little shoal in the marina.

Mark operated the swing bridge and waved as we passed through and negotiated the marina through to Falmouth harbour. Red and green buoys and little craft on their fore and aft moorings marked our route, and just a few minutes later, on this shortest of short passages for *Zoonie*, we scanned along the harbour wall to find the shed and yard we had explored the day before.

I chatted with Portuguese Manuel on the phone on our approach; both he and owner George and manager Cathie, with whom I had corresponded since we were in Cape Town about the mooring, were on hand to take lines as the route to our berth was quite tight.

Manuel, in his charming dialect, said to me, "You pass the first yard and continue towards the bridge. On your left you will see a gap in the pontoons between two yachts, *Unity* and *Chloe May*. Turn towards the harbour wall between them; you will see us ready for you, and your berth is around the pontoon to the right."

There were Cathie and Manuel standing on the harbour wall as Rob very slowly edged *Zoonie* directly towards the ancient stones. *Zoonie* crept with the stealth of a hunting big cat, so that her turning the corner to the right around a beautiful recently built traditional-style yacht was under perfect control and showed just how manoeuvrable she is at very slow speed. Well done, my man.

Warm greetings were exchanged, and a few hours later, to make sure *Zoonie* settled happily into the 14-foot depth of mud, of which

Zoonie around the bend in Freeman's Wharf Boatyard

she only needed six, we went to the office to complete the formalities at Freeman's Wharf Boatyard.

Zoonie has brought us safely and comfortably through our circumnavigation, covering 38,252 miles, taking 420 days at sea. What an adventure. I would recommend it to anyone who loves sailing and learning, by first-hand encounters, how other cultures work and how their history has shaped their present-day lives. The natural world has been a constant source of wonder and surprise. Despite the damage the natural world endures from man, it is, and I believe will continue to be, a beautiful world, well worth your exploration. And if you do garner the courage to pursue your dreams, whatever they are, you will for the rest of your life wear, like a warm winter coat, the pride and satisfaction of having achieved your goal.

Acknowledgements

In this, my second and concluding book about our circumnavigation in *Zoonie*, once again I must mention my great-grandfather who clearly carried the genes for a love of sailing, which he duly passed on to my mother and me.

Also, thanks must go to my late father who didn't so much teach me sailing as learned it with me.

I would like to extend my gratitude not only to Rachel Ramaekers (prev. Atkins), of Self Publishing House, who has again helped me along the path to publication, but also to her father, Jeremy Atkins, of Fernhurst Books, as he has played a valuable part in the lengthy process.

Allan Grey has worked his masterly skills once more on preparing the photos you have seen. Thank you, Allan.

It has been such fun seeking out people whom we met along the way and have subsequently appeared in my book. Jeannie and Merv, who were integral to the rescue team in preventing *Zoonie* from sinking to the bottom of the Whangarei River in New Zealand, are loving land life in their home country. Doroline is still welcoming people to her homely Melanesian guest house in Vanuatu. Tyronne Bell and his family in Canberra are busy serving their Aboriginal people. In Western Australia Malcolm and Christine are closely watching their five grandchildren growing up, and Mereh and John are thriving in their village community in Fiji, to name just a very few of the dear friends we made.

Finally, with his usual quiet attention to detail, hubby Rob has once again delved through my book to make sure all the details about our adventure are correct, and also ensured *Zoonie's* workings and systems were functioning as they should during the voyage. Thank you, Rob.

Glossary

aft	back/stern end of vessel
AIS	Automatic Identification System – an anti-collision aid which identifies nearby ships and allows one to call up another vessel by name
alongside tow	a working vessel ties to a vessel not under power, using breast and spring lines, so both vessels can be steered together
backed/backing	1 when the wind gets the wrong side of the sail 2 when the wind direction backs anticlockwise around the compass rose
bimini	open-fronted removeable awning for cockpit usually supported by metal frame
block	pulley(s) mounted within case(s) with flat cheeks on either side
boom	1 metal or wooden spar attached to bottom of vessel's fore and aft sails 2 noise of gas bottle explosion
bow	1 pointy/front end of vessel 2 crew hair decoration
bow thruster	small propeller mounted below waterline in tunnel at bow to aid manoeuvrability
brig	two-masted square-rigged sailing ship with some fore and aft sails
broach	sudden heeling and change in direction of vessel caused by a strong gust of wind hitting too large a sail area or an unstable sail
call up	contact another vessel/person using marine radio, VHF or SSB

chart	geographical map of oceans used for navigation at sea
chart plotter	device for showing electronic charts on a screen and vessel's position/progress using GPS
coach roof	raised portion of a boat's deck that forms the roof of the cabin/deckhouse/saloon, giving more headroom
coaming	raised border around the cockpit or hatch of vessel to keep water out
cockpit	seating area towards back of vessel where steering controls are housed and drinks are served
companionway	entrance leading from cockpit to inside vessel via a ladder or steps, slippery when wet
coral head	uprising of hard coral growth from seabed, not always visible and a potential danger to hull
course	**1** the direction of a vessel or river **2** the lowest square sail on a square-rigged ship
cruising chute	a loose-footed light-weight sail for downwind cruising and racing with wind coming from behind vessel
Diva (the)	alter ego of cruising chute on *Zoonie*
dinghy	small boat with motor and/or oars and sail, used for transit ashore from a larger vessel or for leisure and racing
downhaul	a line used to control or lower a sail or yard from below
draught	distance between the waterline and the lowest point of the keel, indicating how low a vessel sits in the water
engine hours	number of hours an engine has been running
ETD	estimated time of departure
ferry glide	moving a vessel forward into wind and/or current to create desired sideways movement
flight plan	document zont submitted to authorities by vessel's responsible person detailing intended journey
fo'c'sle	(also **forecastle**) cabin below deck at front of vessel, therefore tapering in towards bow, used for accommodation/storage
foils	wing-like appendages mounted under hull to lift vessel above water

fore   front/bow end of vessel

forecastle   see **fo'c'sle**

foredeck   front deck of vessel, above and forming the roof of the fo'c'sle

forestay   rope or wire connecting top of (fore)mast to deck, onto which foresail/jib/genoa is attached/furled

freeboard   distance from waterline to upper deck level measured from the lowest point where water can enter vessel

front   1 most forward part 2 see **frontal system**

frontal system   (also **front**) boundary between two different weather systems often leading to a change in weather

genoa   the large foresail, the foot or base of which reaches behind the mast

goose-winged   foresail polled out on opposite side to mainsail when wind coming from astern

GPS   Global Positioning System – a brilliant satellite navigation system

GRIB files   internet weather files sourced from US weather prediction models through various sites

gybe   changing the course of a sailing vessel by bringing sail and stern across the following wind

halyard   rope/wire used to hoist sails/flags/etc. up the mast, released to lower them

hank on/off   attach/release a sail's luff from the forestay using metal or plastic clips

headsail   sail at front of vessel attached to (fore)mast top and bowsprit/bow

headwind   wind 'bang on the nose' or bow, from directly ahead, preventing progress under sail

heaving line   light line with ball-shaped 'monkey's fist' knot at end to add weight, attached to a heavy mooring line and thrown to linesman to facilitate mooring

helm   1 act of steering vessel using tiller/wheel 2 person steering vessel

high pressure atmospheric pressure higher than in surrounding regions, leading to settled and clear weather conditions

hook variant of 'anchor'

hull shell and framework of vessel including deck, but not mast and rigging; essential!

Hydrovane wind power operated steering system with its own rudder, i.e. the helmsman that requires no pay or expenses

iron topsail engine when used instead of sail in light winds

ITCZ Intertropical Convergence Zone – belt of low pressure near the equator where the trade winds of the northern and southern hemispheres converge, leading to highly unstable weather and disaster for the Diva

jib triangular sail set in front of mast

keel in-built or bolted-on structure running beneath vessel to add stability, sometimes hollow and filled with heavy metal

latitude measurement of distance north/south of equator, expressed as an angle

lee shore shore onto which the wind is blowing, with a risk that a vessel might be blown onto it

leeward away from the wind; opposite to windward

line 1 rope/cord/wire with specific purpose 2 *pl. lines* evidence of ageing

longitude measurement of distance east/west from Greenwich meridian, expressed in degrees

low pressure atmospheric pressure lower than in surrounding regions, often leading to clouds and precipitation

main short for **mainsail**, sail attached behind tallest/principal mast

mainsail see **main**

panga big canoe suitable for numerous passengers/cargo, often powered by outboard motor

poop 1 deck at back of vessel 2 having a wave come on board over the stern 3 *past tense: pooped* tired crew

port   1 left-hand side of vessel when looking forward on board 2 vessel's harbour 3 fortified wine useful for recovering from being pooped

preventer   rope used to secure spar in relation to desired angle to wind to prevent wind taking control and gybing

prop shaft   metal rod attaching propeller to engine

propeller   spinning shaft with two or more blades attached to engine and used to propel vessel/aircraft

reach   sailing across the wind at an angle of between 60 and 160 degrees to it

reef   1 reduce sail area 2 hard rock/sand/coral growths/ridges to be avoided at all costs

sheet   rope used to adjust sail's angle

shipping lanes designated routes delineated with lines on paper/digital charts to provide safe passage for shipping in busy areas

spinnaker   large, colourful loose-footed sail flown in front of vessel's forestay while sailing downwind

squall   sudden violent gust of wind sometimes accompanied by rain or snow, can result in sail damage if reefing is too late

stanchions/bases vertical posts fixed through deck and around sides of vessel to support handrails

starboard   1 right-hand side of a vessel when looking forward on board 2 cry to establish right of way in race if wind on one's right side

steamer   useful means of stove-top cooking at sea

stem   principal upright structure at the front of vessel, could be wood/metal/concrete/GRP

stern   rear part of vessel, the equivalent upright structure being the sternpost

storm jib   small, tough and often orange sail, used in heavy weather instead of foresail

swell   the slow, usually long, upward and downward heave of the ocean that lifts and lowers vessels in waves that do not break

tack	**1** turn a vessel through the wind **2** lower, forward corner of the sail **3** rope attached to tack of sail
tender	see **dinghy**
tiller	horizontal bar fitted atop rudder and projecting into cockpit to facilitate steering
trade wind (trades)	regular winds circulating in oceans towards equator, trusted and used by mariners for eons
veering	change in wind direction clockwise in the northern hemisphere and anticlockwise in the southern hemisphere around face of compass
victualling	taking on food/provisions for a passage following an estimate of requirements calculated by persons x days at sea
waypoint	position marked on digital/paper chart towards which vessel travels
warship	vessel designed/built for demands of warfare
wash	disturbed white water created at bow by vessel's forward motion
wind generator	multi-bladed wind turbine of many sizes used to create electricity, common on modern sailing vessels/hillsides
windward	towards the wind; opposite to leeward
Zoonie	**1** fictitious character from the US children's TV Series *Fireball XL5* **2** name of Barbara White's heron dinghy (1962) and Oyster 406 (1989)

/pod-product-compliance